# INTERROGATING FR

# INTERROGATING FRANCOISM

## HISTORY AND DICTATORSHIP IN TWENTIETH-CENTURY SPAIN

*Edited by Helen Graham*

Bloomsbury Academic
An imprint of Bloomsbury Publishing Plc

BLOOMSBURY
LONDON · OXFORD · NEW YORK · NEW DELHI · SYDNEY

**Bloomsbury Academic**

An imprint of Bloomsbury Publishing Plc

50 Bedford Square
London
WC1B 3DP
UK

1385 Broadway
New York
NY 10018
USA

www.bloomsbury.com

**BLOOMSBURY and the Diana logo are trademarks of Bloomsbury Publishing Plc**

First published 2016

**British Library Cataloguing-in-Publication Data**

A catalogue record for this book is available from the British Library.

| ISBN: | HB: | 978-1-4725-7634-7 |
| | PB: | 978-1-4725-7633-0 |
| | ePDF: | 978-1-4725-7635-4 |
| | ePub: | 978-1-4725-7636-1 |

**Library of Congress Cataloging-in-Publication Data**

Names: Graham, Helen, 1959- editor.
Title: Interrogating Francoism: history and dictatorship in twentieth-century Spain / edited by Helen Graham.
Description: New York: Bloomsbury Academic, 2016. | Includes bibliographical references and index.
Identifiers: LCCN 2015047960 | ISBN 9781472576330 (paperback) | ISBN 9781472576347 (hardback)
Subjects: LCSH: Francoism—Historiography. | Spain—History—Civil War, 1936–1939—Historiography. | BISAC: HISTORY / Europe / Spain & Portugal. | HISTORY / Modern / 20th Century.
Classification: LCC DP269.A56 I58 2016 | DDC 946.082072—dc23 LC record available at http://lccn.loc.gov/2015047960

Cover design: Catherine Wood
Cover images: General Francisco Franco (Photo by Paul Popper/Popperfoto/Getty Images). Carabanchel Prison, Madrid (Photo by Miguel Palacios/Cover/Getty Images).

Typeset by RefineCatch Limited, Bungay, Suffolk
Printed and bound in India

*For Paul Preston*

# CONTENTS

Contents

# ACKNOWLEDGEMENTS

The editor would like to thank all colleagues and friends who generously offered help, advice and/or editorial assistance with various chapters or other aspects of the book's production – especially to Carl-Henrik Bjerstrom, Clive Burgess, Pedro Correa, Chris Ealham, Susana Grau, Becky Jinks, Rudolf Muhs, Richard Ryan, Sandra Souto, Gareth Stockey and Dan Stone.

Also to Carl-Henrik Bjerstrom, Alison Pinnington and Linda Palfreeman for their painstaking and punctilious translation work – and especially to Linda for stepping in at the eleventh-and-three-quarter hour.

The editor and publishers acknowledge the help of grants in-aid-of-publication from the Isobel Thornley Bequest to the University of London and from the Lincoln Record Society, which subsidized translation costs for two of the chapters.

For permission to quote from Louis MacNeice's *Autumn Journal* (1939) we thank the Louis MacNeice Estate.

To Penny Green, Renata Meirelles, and especially to Maria Thomas, Gareth Thomas and Yvonne Scholten, we owe thanks for their assistance with picture research for the cover. And the editor's thanks also go to Carl-Henrik Bjerstrom, Georgina Blakely, Rita Carvalho, Sebastiaan Faber, Casilda Güell, Richard Ryan, Josep María Solé i Sabaté and Sandra Souto for last-minute bibliographical assistance.

The editor is grateful to all the contributors for their work, and to Maria Thomas additionally for her efficient compiling of the bibliography of Paul Preston's major published work. In Rhodri Mogford and Emma Goode we have had efficient and humane editorial support from Bloomsbury Academic. As editor I would also especially like to thank Becky Jinks for all her editorial advice and for her calm, fast and efficient copyediting in preparing the manuscript for submission.

This book is dedicated by its authors and contributors to Paul Preston, in appreciation of his lifetime of scholarship in contemporary Spanish history, and especially for his intellectual generosity and support to us over many years as a teacher, colleague and friend.

# WRITING SPAIN'S TWENTIETH CENTURY IN(TO) EUROPE

*Helen Graham*

## The war in Spain

Even in today's Europe, where the twentieth century is in so many places proving 'unfinished' and unresolved, as ultranationalists seek to replace history with refurbished myths to serve as present-centred political weapons, Spain remains an acute and particular case for analysis, and one which focuses the anxieties and myths of the continent, just as it did in the 1930s. The memory and history wars inside Spain today revolve around the war of 1936–9 and around the record and legacy of Franco's dictatorship which was forged in that war, emerging victorious to rule the country for four decades. It is the impact of that war on Spain and the ensuing dictatorship which together form the core of this book's enquiry. But the war itself belongs not only to Spain but to Europe, because far more than a civil war, it was *the war* in Spain – the first round of a European contest fought to determine the future of society and politics across the continent. On the battlefields of Spain, the power of European states – including Britain[1] – was contested, as Hitler and Mussolini used the conflict to undermine Anglo-French hegemony and thus disrupt the European and imperial balance of power. Independently of this clash of states, but inevitably entangled with it, many groups of European nationals and citizens became, on their own account, involved in the war – whose impact they clearly understood as the continental game-changer, and in ways that went far beyond diplomacy and great power politics.[2]

The eruption onto the scene of aggressively expansionist Fascism and Nazism in the 1930s was itself a symptom of deeper conflicts inside not only Italy and Germany, but in many other polities and societies across continental Europe, and indeed in crucial qualitative regards in Britain too. The mass industrialized mobilization that had underwritten the Great War of 1914–18 – the fact of mass participation and of mass battlefield death – hugely reinforced already emergent perceptions of rights that had everywhere shaken to their core the old, exclusive order of the pre-1914 world, which was based on quite rigid social and political hierarchies and dependent on subaltern groups' sense of duty and of 'knowing their place'. But after 1918, even where there was no revolution (as in Russia) nor any form of radical reaction which sought to reconfigure society and politics without destroying the power of private capital (fascism), a sea-change inside society was still in train. The stakes were high, in that this was ultimately about power and how it would be distributed in the future inside European societies, in what kind of political systems and with what core values. How hierarchical would, or could society remain? How much hope was there that greater egalitarianism and social and political levelling could be achieved? Or, for those who feared it, how could the danger be avoided? Could hierarchies that offered comfort and convenience, or indeed which confirmed established power, be retooled or, failing that, re-imposed? For many of the continental European volunteers who fought for, or otherwise aided, the Spanish Republican war effort,[3] its cause was that of a young democracy assailed by the old-regime forces of army, church and landowning aristocracy, and thus clearly signed as one offering the wider possibility of open, transformative politics across the continent – and victory here could, most immediately, help roll back the tide of expanding fascism and authoritarianism. For British volunteers who fought with the International Brigades or served in the Republican medical services,[4] Spain offered a way of fighting back against an old order whose profound economic crisis (the post-1929 Wall Street crash) and the consequent unemployment it had inflicted on many of them, highlighted its decay and ripeness for extinction. But for British volunteers too, participation in Spain was often explicitly connected to their aspirations for the reform of social and political structures at home, and for making things fairer.[5] In this sense, then, Spain's battlefields of 1936–9 symbolized a broader European conflict, not only because of German and Italian (and later Soviet) military intervention, but because it was a transformative threshold, offering a *tableau vivant* of how the material and psychological legacy of the Great War had already changed European society and politics forever.

In an important sense too this realization also lay more than a little behind the unease of Britain's political establishment when it contemplated the Spanish Second Republic (established April 1931). In 1930s Britain, politics was still largely the preserve of a social elite; for the British government – which in July 1936, when the war in Spain erupted, was essentially a Conservative one – Spain's Republican experiment constituted the threat of a good example. In the same way, the official British preference for a rapid victory of the military insurgents reflected a desire to insulate British politics from change. And the fact that neither then nor even later during the war did the British cabinet consider a Franco and military-led Spain to be a risk to Britain's own imperial interests, removed any dilemma from the implementation and maintenance throughout the war of a Non-Intervention policy that handicapped and ultimately crushed the Republic. Appeasement as practised over Spain needs to be understood as something other than a strategy of imperial defence, and as a means of protecting a particular set of interests at home – i.e. the defence and stabilization of a preferred form of social and political hierarchy inside Britain.[6] For this same reason too Conservative leaders Baldwin and Chamberlain chose to adhere to the belief, in spite of all the evidence to the contrary, that the new German–Italian Axis represented old style European politics with whom they could do business, even if their titular heads (Führer and Duce) were leaders of 'new' origins. Hence British government and establishment complaisance over the initial military intervention of Hitler and Mussolini in Spain in July 1936 (to the consternation of the two fascist leaders themselves) because they saw them, and Hitler's regime especially, as a means of shoring up challenged European social and political hierarchies, whose shock waves, if uncontrolled, risked reaching the British polity. This rationale, as well as the reasons for its subsequent occlusion, are both neatly encapsulated in the proposed visit in 1939 of a Scotland Yard police chief to the concentration camp of Dachau on a fact-finding mission about modern methods of policing – a visit only cancelled when Germany invaded Poland in August.[7]

In Spain in the spring and summer of 1936, defending older forms of hierarchy was very much on the minds of the military conspirators and their civilian supporters, although they had no idea it would take an actual war to achieve it. What the insurgents had in mind when they launched the coup on 17 July from Spanish Morocco was simply to take control, and – as the chapter in this volume by Rúben Serém on post-coup Seville indicates – to do so by using overwhelming violence against incipient democratizing forces in order to disarticulate, and in considerable part physically to eliminate the threat of social change they posed. But the insurgents' garrison revolts across mainland Spain on 18 July met far more initial resistance than they had expected – especially in urban, populous Spain, so much so that the coup, left to its own devices, looked set to fail, leaving the Republican authorities to mop up its remaining redoubts. But it was at this point that the failing coup escalated into a full-scale, high-tech war courtesy of Nazi and Fascist military intervention, which gifted the insurgents an effective fighting force (by airlifting the colonial army of Africa to mainland Spain, where it began its 'reconquest'). Republican resistance, strengthened by later, if limited, military aid from the Soviet Union,[8] saw Nazi and Fascist support for the military rebels escalate hugely and become entrenched, thereby giving rise to the internationalized battlefield war which has ever since been enshrined in European and Western memory as 'the Spanish civil war'.

The fact of this supervening war would transform the insurgency (understood also to connote the social and political coalition aligned with the military rebels) just as much as it changed those who opposed them, in what gradually cohered as the Republican zone. The reality of a modern war created in both zones an accelerated process of political and ideological polarization far more intense and extreme than anything that had existed under the pre-war Republic and which the insurgents claimed had justified their coup in the first place. The war also produced in both zones a process of physical mobilization and forms of psychological conscription, which in insurgent territory, soon united under Franco's uncontested control (see the chapter by Angel Viñas), facilitated the official sculpting of a 'Francoist nation'. This was produced by means of the projection via the radio and press of myths, whose ensuing power derived from the fact that the authorities linked them integrally to a series of real social fears and, above all, to wartime losses. Crucial here were the elaborate, nationwide ceremonies to commemorate the insurgent dead which began very early in the war (see Julián Casanova's chapter). The first of these myths to be embedded in this way in real social landscapes of loss and grief drew on a long-standing one of Spain and Europe's extreme right, namely that of the Jewish-Masonic-Bolshevik conspiracy – which, as the Francoist media reported it, had supposedly taken concrete form in Spain in the spring of 1936, in the election to power of the reforming Popular Front coalition of centre-left parties. Those ultraconservative forces who were already plotting the coup fastened onto this occurrence – perfectly explicable in terms of electoral arithmetic and sociological change in Spain (expanding urban centres, worker migration from villages and the emergence of self-identified and politically aspirational urban middling classes, especially on Spain's eastern seaboard) – and claimed that it was all evidence of a directly Soviet-inspired revolutionary threat. From then on, and systematically in the wartime Francoist zone, the coup was publicly presented as a crusade to save the core of Christian civilization, epitomized by traditionalist Spanish values. For receptive constituencies (though these were far from making up the entirety of the population in Franco's zone) these values were received as now offering a solution to troublesome change, which was either disturbing their peace and sense of 'equilibrium' or their economic dominance or both. The military insurgents and their civilian base were thus united by their fears of levelling social change, and their preference for (and material and psychological investment in) an older order defined by church, but also by monarchy and army, the old alliance that had dominated late nineteenth- and early twentieth-century Spain (see the chapters by Thomas and Romero Salvadó) – which other constituencies among the Spanish population found an increasingly stifling state of affairs, and had therefore been contesting for some time. Now these fears and preferences were being recast as conspiratorial myth, and one, moreover, with an integral component of antisemitism. Except, in a country from which the Jewish population had been expelled hundreds of years earlier with causes and consequences endlessly debated since, this 'antisemitism without Jews' (see Isabelle Rohr's chapter) had more to do with social fears that had coalesced around the trope of the Jew, as the epitome of an anti-national force, wandering, refugee, heterogeneous, and supposedly 'disruptive'. For Spanish conservatives this label fitted very well what they saw as the perturbing influence of the new social constituencies formed through the recent and ongoing process of industrialization and urban expansion – especially the constituencies of organized labour, with their unions, parties, associations and 'alien' social presence on the streets.[9]

Thus it was too across 1930s Europe, in a continent witnessing accelerating social change and demographic shift that the evocative power of Franco's crusade found a receptive audience further afield among conservative sectors. Older notions of a defence of Christian civilization against change had become a means of expressing antisemitism even before this was codified by the early twentieth-century publication of the *Protocols of the Elders of Zion* (1903). After the Bolshevik revolution, Moscow was assimilated to the myth as 'Antichrist'.[10] The subsequent coming together in Spain in 1936 of a cause which combined a defence of established hierarchies with a much vaunted defence of Christianity (and whose legitimacy was reinforced far beyond core conservative constituencies by the widespread anticlerical killings of summer 1936 in wartime Republican territory) exerted an enormous attraction – doubly reinforced when conservatives across Europe saw those same constituencies among their own populations who were no longer content with or containable within the patrician structures of organized religion and village, also setting off as migrants and then fetching up to fight for the Republic in Spain.[11] It is, then, in this regard, as a war to defend familiar structures of power that we must understand the resonance of the Spanish war for conservatives across Europe. And it is thus that we need to understand the psychological appeal as well as the political power and strategic force of contemporary conservative imaginaries which were building around older ideas of social defence against cultural change.

Franco's crusade in Spain became the frontline of 'Christian Europe', and was configured mythologically as the once and future core and armour of this traditionalist/conservative defence.[12]

## Europe's myths, Spain's myths

After Franco's Nazi- and Fascist-backed victory in late March 1939 in the battlefield war, the dictator sealed his ideological alliance with the Axis, also in the expectation of acquiring in the wake of their Second World War victory, the gift of a new Spanish empire (i.e. France's) – something that had been the driving, not to say obsessive, goal of the entire conservative spectrum in Spain ever since the loss of the country's old empire in 1898. In the event, Axis military reverses from the end of 1942, as well as basic geopolitics, obliged Franco to make a pragmatic accommodation with the Western Allied powers, who in victory were prepared to bolster him in Spain as Cold War divisions hardened by 1948.[13] They were not deceived about Franco's ideological predilections, and nor did the dictator change much of the internal workings of his regime (see Viñas), but it suited Allied purposes to accept his new public projection as the anti-communist 'sentinel of the west'.[14] The relative ease with which this happened suggests, moreover, something that was already evident and which would prove enduring – the allure for conservative nationalists of Franco's proclaimed defence of older forms of social hierarchy. (And indeed within the West, the Cold War would have clear strategic political uses as an instrument to construct and preserve a certain model of socio-political order – anticommunism being deployed to this end in Western Europe as well as the US.) This narrative about Franco also allowed Western political establishments to elide the fact that they, as the democratic victors in the Second World War, were abandoning democratic forces in Spain, an awkward reality conveniently airbrushed behind another of the period's most serviceable and enduring myths: that the Spanish Republic which was militarily defeated in 1939 was essentially a 'communist enterprise'. This myth was almost as useful as the overarching one emerging after 1945 across Western Europe of entire populations as first-hour resisters, united in their *national* opposition to Nazi occupation, which may have served the purpose of 'vital lies' to encourage continental reconstruction, but which also ignored the reality of how a majority of people had actually behaved during the war – from passivity, through opportunism, to active and enthusiastic Nazi collaboration for both material and ideological reasons – and this latter category included considerable numbers of conservative nationalists across Europe.

A collateral effect at the time of this emergent postwar myth of mass European antifascist resistance, was that Franco's Spain – where many who had been among the first and most determined antifascist resisters were being shot and herded into the dictator's concentration camps and labour camps (see Jorge Marco's chapter) – was kept at the political margins of the new Christian- and Social-Democratic Western European order, its uneasy conscience kept at bay thereby on at least two counts. Inside Spain, the Cold War having given Franco a perfect – and magnified – opportunity, his regime set about vastly reinforcing its distorting version of the civil war in ultra Cold War mode. Now with all the full media and other state power at its disposal, it talked up the myths it had used, both to justify the military rising and to legitimize itself during the civil war – first, the myth of a Soviet-backed revolutionary plot (when the only plot on the horizon was the military conspirators' own); and second, their insurgent crusade to protect the Church and the established order (no matter that these defenders of order had to kill a large number of army officers who refused to support the July 1936 coup) and to protect the Catholic faith (but who had also killed and imprisoned many priests and lay Catholics who opposed the crusade).[15] The Franco regime had free rein to shape public discourse in Spain, entirely unchallenged from abroad and uncontested in the domestic public sphere: through terror, censorship and total control of education and the print and broadcast media the dictatorship confined other memories and the telling of other histories either to private subterranean spaces inside Spain, or to the confines of exile communities beyond. (Republican defeat saw some half a million leave in what has been probably the most intellectually powerful exile in modern history, if also one that has inevitably produced its own share of myths, albeit from, or indeed because of, its position of political powerlessness.) Meanwhile, to the Franco dictatorship's own more hoary myths was added the equally mythical 'resisting Hitler' to keep Spain out of the Second World War,[16] and then by the 1960s a pivotal new myth, that the regime's own particular expertise and policies were themselves instrumental in creating the 'economic miracle' – as if somehow Franco had engineered the European/Western economic boom of the 1960s, or indeed the sunny weather which together underpinned the country's success in the new era of mass tourism.

## The end of Franco?

In the end the dictatorship was undermined by the complicated effects of the economic developments that occurred during its incumbency, and through which Spain became fully integrated into the international economic system. As the Franco regime faced the crisis triggered by the oil shock of 1973 and by the supervening social unrest inside the country, it was to be influential sectors among the dictatorship's own political support base which crucially pushed for institutional change. They were motivated by a desire to curtail the potential for more radical forms of change that might have loomed onto the horizon if the now near forty-year-old dictatorship had hung on and then collapsed, having first allowed an explosive build-up of social anger and protest. Some inside the regime had their minds concentrated by other regional crises – notably the collapse of the Salazar dictatorship in neighbouring Portugal in April 1974 into a situation of apparent radical revolution. This also finally alerted international actors, notably the US, to the need to smooth the way for limited forms of democratizing change in southern Europe – where previously it had been quite happy to support dictatorial or quasi-dictatorial regimes (in Spain, Portugal and Greece).[17] Matters were hugely facilitated in Spain by the intervention of a biological imperative – i.e. the death of the octogenarian

Franco himself in November 1975. There then occurred an institutional transition from the structures of the dictatorship to those of a parliamentary democracy. But it was a process entirely supervised by a reformist Francoist elite and without any policy of lustration (the removal of a regime's political class and officials from power), thus ensuring a virtually total continuity of state and political personnel from the dictatorship to the new democratic system.

This was somewhat camouflaged at the time by the simultaneous influx to the political system of newly legalized democratic political parties – whether national (the social democratic PSOE (Partido Socialista Obrero Español) and communist PCE (Partido Comunista de España) or regional nationalist parties, as in Catalonia and the Basque Country. But even there in some cases (pre-eminently the PSOE's), a surge of new members, even some new leader cadres, who had Francoist backgrounds and/or were joining in search of political preferment, would soon dilute the 'new broom' effect. Moreover the greatest immediate limitation on any process of institutional or political renovation was given by the presence of an intensely pro-Franco army (i.e. officer corps) – both in itself a huge threat, but also an effective 'bogey' for the reformist Francoists leading the transition, which could be invoked against their democratic interlocutors pushing for greater change. So Spain's transition, seen from the inside, was a limited process of change which never really escaped the control of those reformist insiders driving it. This is true in spite of the fact that the transition was accompanied by mass political mobilizations on the streets of Spain's cities. Intensifying as a result of the 1970s economic crisis, they were also a continuation of earlier forms of popular protests stemming from the economic problems of the rapid urban development of the 1960s which was unmitigated by the dictatorship. (Michael Richards' chapter discusses the role in this grass-roots mobilization of social Catholic groups, neighbourhood associations and new trade unions which addressed the acute needs of the large, new migrant worker communities.) This neighbourhood and union mobilization ongoing into the 1970s certainly kept reformist Francoists on track during the transition, not least by serving as a reminder of what might happen if they back-pedalled on top-down political reform, but it also had weaknesses and structural limitations.

At the time it was not possible to discern what is clearer from today's vantage point – that the elite insider action towards institutional reform of the dictatorship was driven by a separate, freestanding policy, while the forms of 1970s mass mobilization, based on incipient practices of grass-roots democracy, were already beginning to wane. This loss of momentum came first because elite actors sought (successfully) to contain them politically, but more crucially because the very effects of the expanding economic crisis in the 1970s atomized them, as became most evident in declining trade union membership, assailed by the effects of economic recession and then also by the ensuing neo-liberal restructuring of the market and of workforce models and practices over the 1980s, which occurred in Spain as elsewhere in Europe. It was in the conservative logic of the limited transition, too, that the *memory* of the difficult recent past would also be closed down. During the 1980s the PSOE accepted this, for all that the social democratic party ostensibly represented the main axis of change inside Spanish politics at that point.[18] Nevertheless, it would take explicit coercion to head off and contain contemporary grass-roots attempts to open up that past – including between 1976 and 1981 some attempted local excavations of the mass graves of those extrajudicially executed by Francoist forces.[19] This coercion crystallized in the military coup attempt of February 1981, known as the 23-F, which, although it failed in explicit terms, injected such fear and shock into Spanish public life that in a sense it succeeded. In quite tangible terms too, the coup attempt ushered in what has since been an increasing stream of legal cases brought against journalists, filmmakers and historians who have sought to put the spotlight on Francoist atrocities committed in wartime or afterwards – and especially in cases which identified specific perpetrators.[20] So here, the continuity of judicial personnel, and even more the continuity from dictatorship to parliamentary democracy of certain beliefs and attitudes inside the judiciary, have resulted in a clear democratic deficit that endures in Spain into the present day.[21]

## Enduring Francoism: Spain from 1989 to the twenty-first century

In this climate of fear which significantly outlasted the transition proper – usually defined as from the promulgation of the new democratic constitution in 1978 up to 1982, when the PSOE won its historic absolute majority – it would take another ten years to unblock the situation even slightly. The 1980s saw new generations of historians inside Spain lay the impressive groundwork for recovering the empirical history of the Francoist repression (see Casanova), but what brought this into the mainstream and public gaze was the sea-change in international politics: the collapse of the Berlin Wall and the radical reform of the Soviet Union symbolized the formal end of the Cold War, and with it the rise of a new international discourse of human rights.

This ostensible post-Cold War thaw was the context which saw the rise of the historical memory movement in 1990s Spain, in that a changed international discourse to some extent opened up a broader audience inside Spain. The memory movement is composed of diverse civic associations, the most powerful of which, backed by the empirical evidence gathered by Spanish historians over the 1980s, sought to achieve the support and intervention of international bodies, such as the UN's High Commissioner for Human Rights, to oblige the Spanish authorities to recognize their democratic duty of care to the living relatives of the extrajudically killed by identifying and naming and accounting for them. But very soon this historical memory phenomenon provoked an angry backlash of outright denial or counter-claim. This was because it brought centre stage in Spain what was for other constituencies an encounter with an 'unseemly' side of Francoism which they had hitherto avoided and which clashed with their own, or their families' take on the past, with individual or family memories – and myths – and which they found deeply uncomfortable in that it unravelled their sense of their own 'rightness' (i.e. a claim to social superiority based on moral righteousness). This backlash has taken various forms – all of which we can describe as battles of memory conducted in the public sphere: from the 'war of commemorative death notices' in the national press ('la guerra de las esquelas'), through opposition to the removal of Francoist commemoration in public spaces – street names, plaques, statues and other war memorials, especially the long-running controversy over the future of the main Francoist site, the monument-mausoleum at the Valley of the Fallen (El Valle de los Caídos) just outside Madrid – through to acrimonious contributions to radio call-in programmes and heated panel discussions on popular television.

It is in such fora that the old Francoist myths have made a reappearance, albeit slightly reconfigured. First, the 'communist' threat posed by Republican democracy in the 1930s is rarely presented now as a Soviet threat, but instead as an indigenous one hinging on the allegedly totalitarian and 'exclusive' nature of the Second Republic's own reform project – with some commentators even denying that the Republic was a democracy at all, and many defining its pluralism as a pandering to 'separatist' nationalisms while risking Spanish unity. Second, the fact of thousands of anticlerical victims (priests and lay Catholics) killed in summer 1936 in Republican territory is held to prove that only Franco's 'crusade' represented a defence of Christianity. Many of these victims still receive Vatican beatification today, while the more awkward historical knowledge that Franco also killed and imprisoned priests remains marginalized and unassimilated.[22] Third, Franco is projected as a good, old-fashioned nationalist, shorn of his ideological alliance with Fascism and Nazism (his connection with the Third Reich dismissed as a purely territorial 'temptation' – Franco's desire for a new empire). Above all here, Franco the nationalist is seen as the undisputed architect of Spanish development and economic boom (this also tendentiously projected as having offered a life of plenty to all Spaniards, rather than to particular sectors of the population). Indeed it is remarkable, given how 'collective forgetting' was said to be the watchword of the transition, that these myths and reductive, facile narratives have re-emerged apparently unscathed, while it is only the more complicated 'knowledge' of the difficult past, hard won through the empirical investigation of the 1980s, which still remains largely outside the mainstream.

That said, in fact the 'embeddedness' of these myths across time is perhaps not the whole story here. There are, to be sure, still substantial sociologically Francoist strata in Spain – especially in the inland provincial centre-north, the area par excellence of *aquí no pasó nada* ('nothing happened here') – which respond to these Francoist myths when they are quite deliberately recirculated via politically conservative (including Church-run) media networks which have a presentist, ultranationalist political agenda (more on this below and also in the chapter by Casanova). But beyond such already-primed interlocutors, the old myths also reach other far less traditionalist sectors of the Spanish population, who perhaps have little or no historical knowledge about Spain's (or Europe's) recent past (which is also the legacy of the dictatorship and transition), but who now have a great many present anxieties and fears for the future, generated by the recent and ongoing economic recession. In such a context people are often avid for a simpler story than the one reality – or history – can deliver, preferring instead messages, often verging on conspiracy theories, which offer a distorted 'clarity', all the more especially appealing if it instructs them about who they can blame for aspects of their own present circumstances or uncertain future which they find threatening and troubling. In this way, neo-Francoist, ultranationalist lobbies can configure today in Spain a much larger potential audience *through fear*, of economic as well as social change – which is, in some ways, what happened in the 1930s too. Equally today there is a nostalgia for a past of apparent certainty and security – the Restoration monarchy, the boom of the 1960s; these are 'remembered' – by which we mean reconstituted or recreated, given memory is a dynamic process – with present goals in mind, made not only with the materials of the past but also driven by the imperatives of now.

## From memory wars to history wars: revisionism in the twenty-first-century Academy in Spain

Memory means, then, contrasting images of the past held publicly and privately in the present, by different sections of a population, in this case the Spanish one. Memory also in this case refers to how an international audience remembers the war in Spain and the ensuing dictatorship. Myth is present to some extent in both the public and the private spheres – myth understood here as a supercharged, emotionally and/or politically invested collective memory which, to a greater or lesser extent, has fictionalized the past. In dictatorships public memory is almost always made more of myth than of history; in the private spheres of dictatorial societies, memory can also have strong elements of myth, and among 'defeated' groups of counter-myth. Among the latter groups, memory too is often much more acutely fragmented (in some way counter-myths emerge from precisely such fragmentation),[23] but notwithstanding this, the private spheres of dissenting groups can also be the repository of real knowledge of what actually happened in the past but which has become politically awkward, so is repressed and cannot circulate in the public sphere because it is not convenient for those who rule (the 'victors', the powers that be, etc.). In democracies there is usually, by definition, a relatively greater possibility for the circulation in the public sphere not only of competing interpretations of the past (some could be based more on myth than on historical knowledge) but also of different kinds of real knowledge about the past – including awkward sorts – although in democracies too there often occurs a more subtle but recognizable process of the 'ignoring' of awkward truths, or of things that reflect badly upon those in power or on their political, social or institutional forebears.

While myth is not history, it does itself have a genealogy, as this introduction has already sought to show. So historians need to be interested in it, though not be taken in by it. But in Spain today that advice seems to have become increasingly sidelined as the memory wars of the 1990s have now turned into full-scale 'history wars'. This has occurred in two senses – in that these history wars have become a battle for access to and control of the sources of historical knowledge themselves (for example the present closure of the Foreign Ministry archives, or the aforementioned legal action taken against journalists and historians who seek to bring into the public domain 'off limit' historical material); and also because the battle has now entered the Academy to involve – and divide – professional historians.

As a result of this shift, this 'war' in Spain is not one of academic history against popularized history (a division evident in many countries), nor does it primarily set politicians or state interests against the accounts given by historians (although that division exists in Spain, as elsewhere): rather, it is increasingly evident as a division between professional historians of contemporary Spain inside Spain. As all historians have long known, a set of empirical facts is often open to more than one interpretation. Different historians might find one or other interpretation more or less compelling, but they will broadly agree on the specific range of empirical material adduced to sustain the varying and contrasting analyses. In other words, it is the facts themselves which set the limits on which interpretations are legitimate and which not.[24] But while interpretative truths can be plural, the line between history and myth is relatively easily identifiable. Myths may contain some reference to real historical fact, but in each case they have an overriding objective which requires the denial or occlusion of other empirically verifiable knowledge that clashes with the myth's assertions. So this is no longer about differing but nuanced historical evaluations, but about asserting an absolute view that denies clear evidence: for example, that the Restoration monarchy (1874–1931) was a paragon of social and political civility; that the Second Republic was not a democracy; that the Franco regime was not a dictatorship – this latter view became the core of a dispute over the entry in the recent Spanish Royal Academy of History's official dictionary of biography which omitted even the fact of dictatorship.[25]

How did things reach this point in Spain? The answer has both an international and a Spanish dimension, though these inevitably connect. Internationally, the post-1989 period saw the rise not only of the aforementioned human rights discourse, but also of an antithetical ultranationalist one which in Eastern Europe first, but also now in the West, has come to plant a right-wing populist banner in the space vacated by the demise of the post-Second World War myth of antifascist consensus. If the Cold War was indeed over, what exactly had emerged victorious? Was it democracy, or something rather more limited and specific in the shape of ultranationalism and right-wing populism? Certainly the 'foundational' myth of nations united in antifascist resistance during the Second World War has been shorn of its antifascist qualifier, leaving only the single 'good' of nationalism. And everywhere since the 1990s there has occurred a recycling of Cold War myths which has allowed the reinvention across Europe of fascist leaders as patriots and nationalists, purely on the basis of their anticommunism. This process has facilitated similar developments in Spain, with revisionist historians attempting disingenuously to distance the person of Franco from responsibility for the violent wartime repression carried out by Francoist forces,[26] and also the emergence of a vocal neo-Francoism – a reminder that a large portion of the mainstream right (clustered around the Popular Party (Partido Popular)) had always remained Francoist in terms of their political and cultural values. As the modern European historian Dan Stone has recently put it, there is being revealed everywhere a 'deep-seated resentment' of the normative social democratic values of 1945–89, 'when many, so it now seems, had to hold their tongues.'[27] The Spanish right is a prime example of the phenomenon Stone identifies: the long decades of Francoism meant the layer of conformist interface with the then more uniformly liberal democratic Western Europe was always quite thin. But now Spanish conservatism has 'lost its shame', as the rest of Europe comes to be more in its own image. Indeed, many Central and East European ultranationalists and extreme social conservatives explicitly lionize Franco as an anti-communist defender of Christian civilization virtually in the same breath as they 'explain' the good reasons behind interwar antisemitism.[28]

The consequences of this confluence of ultranationalism in Spain and Europe has been especially apparent in Spain's ignoring of UN calls to investigate the human rights abuses perpetrated by the Franco dictatorship – especially in regard of the extrajudicial dead. (Spain's judiciary has notoriously debarred the one judge, Baltasar Garzón, who had sought to put it on the political agenda nationally, and the Spanish government is still ignoring requests from an Argentinian judge to extradite two alleged Francoist perpetrators under the universal jurisdiction of human rights.) This stonewalling echoes something of the Franco regime's own attitude to international opposition (particularly over Gibraltar), including with the resort to a language of populist nationalism. Moreover, inside Spain there are, compared to elsewhere in Western Europe, relatively fewer forms of societal resistance to this, given the lack of general public awareness of these issues from the recent past, or about the lethal ends to which ultranationalist currents had previously led not just in Spain but also in interwar twentieth-century Europe more generally – and this lack has made the myths and distorting voices currently recirculating in Spain that much stronger.

This new context in Spain has also thrown into relief something else important about the limitations of the democratic transition which directly affected the sphere of academic history in Spanish universities. Looking back now, it is clear that from the transition onwards it was always a minority of university historians who were involved in the difficult work of excavating the Francoist repression or other equally thorny aspects of the dictatorship's history. A majority of the historians of contemporary Spain employed inside Spanish university faculties steered clear. Even though most were not ideologically pro-Francoist, they still saw the matter through the embedded and amorphous forms of Francoist conditioning: it was research which 'provoked unnecessary awkwardness' (*estorbaba*). While this may appear an 'apolitical' stance, it was (and is) a key Franco effect, and one that still resonates very widely in Spanish society – that uncovering the difficult past creates waves, and a resulting uneasiness, and thus is best avoided. At the very least – and this too is a dictatorial effect – the majority of historians of contemporary Spain working inside the Spanish university sector (and mostly Spanish-born) were reluctant to get involved in such research because they understood that it would not facilitate their professional careers.[29] Not that they had ever been explicitly warned off; that was not necessary, and it was rather an unspoken assumption of the transition that this was too 'risky' a subject – and nor did the PSOE offer any counter-message.[30] So in Spain in the 1980s it was a minority of university historians, reinforced by dozens of local citizen historians, who took on the task of interrogating Francoism.

But the converse issue manifesting itself today poses, if anything, a more thoroughgoing problem for history as an academic discipline in Spain. The appearance among contemporary historians, in new European times, of neoconservatives whose work does not focus on the Franco era directly but instead addresses other contemporary periods (predominantly the Restoration monarchy and the Second Republic of the 1930s) through a distinctly nationalist – and presentist – optic, thereby creating in an indirect way either an 'idealized', heritage past for today's conservative nationalism, or in the case of the Republic a supposed warning against extremism. In the process, these accounts from inside academia produce, if not more myth, then certainly binary or simplistic assessments which obstruct or paralyse historiographical innovation. This is most acute in the historiography of the Second Republic, an immensely crowded and complicated period where the emergence of neoconservative revisionism, and the increasing need to counter recrudescent myths and to recapitulate the history *we already know*, risks impeding the deepening of research. Ironically this war of words can also have the effect of preserving a set of counter-myths from the Republic's own *engagé* history. The resulting damage is sadly to the integrity of the pursuit of history *tout court*, and to the enrichment of historical knowledge and understanding.[31] The preoccupations of memory are inevitably and to a large degree presentist, even when they are not being politically predetermined. But today in Spain the situation is acute because neoconservative quarters of the historical profession seem themselves to overlap to an uneasy degree with the present-centred goals of neo-Francoist and ultranationalist propagandists.

At the centre of many of these history and media storms in Spain is the work of the British historian Paul Preston, the foremost historian of contemporary Spain in the world today, and in whose honour this current volume has been prepared. He is intrinsically part of these history wars precisely because his work is read so widely inside Spain as well as beyond. In Spain there has been little or no tradition of historical scholars addressing a large, popular audience, something which Preston has done for many years, both in English and Spanish, producing major new historical research in the form of essays and books for a broad readership.[32] Inside Spain he is also a major media presence – the appearance of a new book by Paul Preston is an event in itself. This has been especially the case with his biography of Franco, published in Spain in 1994, and with his *Spanish Holocaust*, published there in 2011.[33] But all his books without exception are received not just as themselves, but as part of the Preston *ouevre*, and he is also an immensely able communicator with a popular audience on TV and radio, as well as in print. It is this unique combination of factors – of a world-class scholar whose work also has a unique popular reach in Spain, which places him at the epicentre of the current polemic. Conservatives in Spain, just like Francoists before them,[34] have never been much exercised about elite or minority cultural products, since they circulate only among a small audience – indeed this may very well explain the lack of polemic when the major historical renovation of the 1980s first began to excavate the history of the Francoist repression. But Paul Preston's work has mass market appeal and he is a media star whose appearances include ones on peak-time daytime television. As a result, ultranationalists and revisionists target him in Spain's mainstream conservative media – digital, print and broadcast – in a way that makes his position unique for a European historian at this juncture, and which in turn redoubles the importance of this present assessment of his scholarly work and legacy.

## In defence of history: interrogating Francoism

This integrated volume of essays by specialists in their field will take stock of the current historiographical frontiers and future challenges in twentieth-century Spanish history – crucially of social history as well as the political variety. But in view of the current moment, it will do this stocktaking mindful of how the present historiographical debates (i.e. how we understand and interpret the past) are being shaped, and sometimes increasingly, by the enduring impact of Francoism, as Europe's most successful and adaptive dictatorial culture – which, as we have seen, has long outlasted its political host. As far as history is concerned, we see its effects in the present neo-Francoist and other conservative and nationalistic attempts to close down the complexity and hybridity of the past, of its multiple potentials for change, by collapsing history into a simplistic set of myths, old and new, which – while comforting for some (in that they confirm or justify their opposition to social change) – traduce the past, problematize the present and endanger the future by the intolerance and even bigotry which are frequently the by-products.

The structure chosen for this book (the endurance of the old regime; making dictatorship; making memory) is intended to elucidate two principal points: that the social battles for reform in 1930s Spain, including the ensuing war itself, all occurred on a political and cultural terrain still largely configured and dominated by the old – old power hierarchies, old values, old myths and obsessions; and that nevertheless the crucible of that war made of these old artefacts and ideas something new and extreme, which, militarily victorious, made not only itself (a long-lasting dictatorship) but also an even more enduring sociological memory and culture. This latter, because of the specificities and acute limitations of institutional change in late 1970s Spain, would long outlast the political Francoist state order which had generated it, and has today flowed into a new, post-1989 European confluence of revivified conservative nationalist paradigms, with which this sociological Francoism is perfectly at home.

This resurgent social and political fundamentalism is perhaps nowhere more evident today than in the redoubled efforts of the ecclesiastical hierarchy of Spain's Catholic Church – now far more socially and politically conservative than at the time of the transition – to encourage the Vatican in its beatification of the Catholic 'martyrs' of the Spanish civil war. It is with such a snapshot of present-day religious integrism that Maria Thomas opens the first of this volume's chapters on the institutional Church in twentieth-century Spain, its relationship to political power and the more varied forms of Catholicism as faith and social identity that were in existence throughout the century. Her chapter illustrates one of the central themes of this book, that a crucial Franco effect has been to sculpt the past, particularly of Catholicism in twentieth-century Spain, so that, retrospectively, it resembles the authoritarian image of that past which the dictatorship sought to create both for itself and also as a wider societal restraint on future change. In this Franco borrowed to some extent from a past model, the Restoration monarchy, and Thomas' chapter looks at the ways in which the monarchy co-opted institutional religion as a disciplinary instrument to preserve hierarchy and control subaltern groups in a time of accelerating change. As such the chapter needs to be read in close conjunction with Francisco Romero Salvadó's contribution on key political developments under the Restoration monarchy.

It has long been a historiographical commonplace that the monarchy restored in Spain in 1874 combined an advanced amalgam of formal constitutional rights with a real political system that in practice denied them for the vast majority of the population, and increasingly so. Alongside this there has always been a lively and complex historiographical debate on the possible potentials within the monarchist political system that might have produced internal democratizing reform, even if, in the event, they were not able to prosper in the social and political climate after the First World War. But alongside these long-standing and properly historiographical debates between historians who have assessed the evidence and weighed the factors in play in different ways, we are now also seeing enter the public sphere in Spain (increasingly since the 1990s) wildly cosmeticized and opportunistic descriptions of the Restoration monarchy by conservative nationalist politicians and media pundits who declare it to have been a democratic idyll in which social and political tranquillity reigned. This mythification is part of a search for a new usable past – and in particular something that can be alleged as a clear and unproblematic progenitor of the parliamentary democracy instituted after Franco in 1977–8. Attempts to present the later Franco dictatorship itself as the progenitor of post-1977 democracy have not ceased, but these have certainly been made more difficult by the emergence of a historiography revealing the extent of the Francoist repression. But the goal of such conservative commentators remains above all to avoid linking post-1977 constitutional democracy with the egalitarian potentials of the democratic Second Republic of the 1930s, an avoidance made all the more urgent since the historical memory movement has appeared. As the Italian philosopher Benedetto Croce once remarked, all history is contemporary history, and here we can see the multi-directional influence of Francoist culture, its barbed memory reaching back to reinterpret earlier periods, recoding the Restoration monarchy in spite of (or because of?) the fact that its democracy was a façade behind which there circulated institutionalized corruption.

Formal liberal freedoms, including the separation of powers, were constitutionally enshrined under the Restoration monarchy and from 1890 universal male suffrage was in place. But the formal separation of executive (government) powers from judicial ones was also nullified by the reality of government on the basis of institutionalized (electoral) fraud and systematic corruption.[35] A free press also existed and indeed formed the dynamic basis of a flourishing elite culture much analysed by literary scholars. But that free press existed alongside mass illiteracy which a deficient and highly segregated Church-run education system did little to diminish, if not actively to perpetuate. Organized religion was, for many sectors of the urban and rural poor, part and parcel of a seamless and repressive fabric woven by state and dominant social order, stifling their hopes and possibilities. Anticlerical actions and attitudes emerged from these perceptions, as an ingrained and angry popular response to this institutional and political whole. Freedom of association, though formally guaranteed too, was a dead letter for the urban and (rather less commonly) rural labourers. Moreover, their efforts to organize in defence of their working and living conditions was usually met by a blanket repressive response, via police action or sometimes military intervention.

As economic and social change accelerated in wake of the Great War, these aspirations to a political voice intensified, but the state response was to cultivate forms of institutional violence, for example the exponential increase across Spain of the use of a long-term police practice, the *ley de fugas* (protesting workers and strike organizers would be arrested then released and 'shot while trying to escape' in what was effectively a form of extrajudicial execution, whose deployment reached levels of an undeclared social war in Barcelona after 1917). The monarchy's response to socio-political turmoil came in the form of the regular, repeated declaration of martial law (in all or part of Spain), during which constitutional guarantees were suspended – as they would be *twenty-five times* between 1875 and 1923.[36]

All in all, then, there is a difficult trajectory to be traced within the Restoration monarchy – a long way from the images conjured by study of a vibrant free press and which indicates that, while constitutional forms may be a necessary precondition of democracy, they are not in themselves a sufficient guarantee of it. Nevertheless, as Romero Salvadó indicates in his chapter, there were other potentials in this period, and he argues that what set a strong course to an authoritarian outcome (the military dictatorship of Primo de Rivera in 1923) was not any inherent property of the monarchist political system itself, but rather a specific rapprochement of crown and military cupola determined to erect a wall against reform in times of pressure on the traditional model of Spain's economy, combined with pressure from below for democratization. This praetorian option saw the demise of the monarchist system – but not of the monarchy itself; indeed King Alfonso XIII himself was an active participant in this process which saw the traditional alliance of throne and altar, giving way to one of 'cross and sabre' mediated by the crown.[37] But acknowledging the role of the crown here in undermining constitutional rule between 1917 and 1923, or his personal support for Primo's coup, are topics which have always been much more 'difficult' for historians writing inside Spain since 1977, precisely because one of the unwritten rules of the democratic transition was that the institution of the monarchy was off-limits for criticism. In the same way, although much less clear-cut, is the relationship between the Spanish army's constraining role at the time of the democratic transition and especially after the military coup attempt of February 1981, and the relative marginalization, or at any rate (implicit) postponement of studies of colonial culture and atrocity in the army campaigns in Spanish Morocco during the 1920s. That said, we do now have the beginnings of historical accounts of how this 'came home' to the metropolis in the 1930s, both in terms of an ideological justification/imperial mindset and a practice of subduing 'rebellious' subaltern groups, such as the Franco forces practised during the civil war.[38]

Whatever else is historically disputable, this much is clear: the practices of political violence were deeply rooted in the Spanish state, polity and society long before the arrival of the Second Republic in 1931 which, many revisionists would have us believe, was the root of all disturbance and the *sui generis* generator of acute forms of social and political conflict. My own chapter on the reform projects of the 1930s locates the Republic's shortcomings, as a motor of reform, in deficient and sometimes contradictory *strategies* whose flaws were intensified both by structural factors (Spain's uneven development) and in some cases by the 'baggage' protagonists carried in terms of ingrained aspects of their own political culture. But I would reject the claim of much revisionist scholarship that the reforms were wrong-headed per se or indeed that they were 'extreme'. Indeed, revisionist arguments often seem to tell us less about the dynamic of what happened and why in 1930s Spain, than about just how far rightwards the 'political centre' has moved since the collapse after 1989 of the post-Second World War social democratic consensus.[39] Revisionist delegitimization of the Second Republic as undemocratic may no longer have recourse to the stock Cold War myths of Soviet control, but is still nevertheless indebted to Cold War political effects in its foreclosing of any discussion of the fact that some measure of economic democracy is the necessary precondition to enable and consolidate, indeed *to make*, political democracy. The 1930s in Spain, as across Europe, saw acute conflicts, later wars, of social and economic change. Even so, in Spain after 1931 other potential outcomes remained possible at least for a time. That it turned out differently was the consequence of a number of interacting factors, some to do with the aforementioned strategic shortcomings and downright errors of the political forces seeking to implement reform. But conservative mobilization was also a major actor shaping the course of events, not least in a dangerous strain of 'all or nothing' discourse deriving in part from the absolute refusal of patrician sectors to compromise their privileges, and in part from the potent blend of new colonial ideas plus social Darwinist currents circulating around Europe. This saw the Spanish right recode its own fears and anxieties, expressing them as a need for extensive social cleansing of the 'internal enemy' – a category that expanded rapidly to include not only workers (as an extension of African subaltern populations) but also to a racialization of the political (Republican) enemy which was recast as 'Jewish' because it disturbed social order, social peace and Spain's patriotic heritage (see the chapter by Isabelle Rohr).

It was the resulting social conflict as a symptom of change in train which the military coup of 17–18 July set out to erase – in no considerable part by physically eliminating at least some leading part of those social constituencies who sought democratizing change (see Rúben Serém's chapter). The war itself changed everything, however – including, in spite of themselves, the insurgents, who, under Franco's leadership, and the pressure of events, created new political forms and practices rather than achieving what they spoke of in their discourse as a return to the past or the enshrinement of social stasis. It is a truism that nevertheless bears repeating that Francoism was made in war, a war which also created a radicalized and mobilized civilian support base, and a war from which the ensuing Franco regime, as well as Franco personally, derived their greatest and most long-lasting legitimacy – not least from the fact of having remained militarily undefeated (unlike their defeated and discredited Axis allies). After the battlefield victory came Franco's institutionalization of the war, whose logic had been inherent in the original coup, but which was now made much more radical in its realization by dint of the experience of the intervening war, especially on Francoism's grass-roots supporters, who, in collaboration with the state authorities imposed a brutal subjugation (execution, imprisonment, surveillance, economic discrimination and general second-class status) on defeated sectors of the Spanish population (see the chapter by Jorge Marco).

But aside from the de facto power derived from mass killing and subordination, the emergent Franco regime keenly felt the need to bolster its formal authority, which it derived neither from the continuity of tradition (monarchy) nor from a conventional political mandate (constitutional democracy). This process of reinforcement we can see in the evolution of the figure of Franco himself (see the essays by Angel Viñas and Enrique Moradiellos) – from Generalísimo, or supreme war leader in both military and political matters, to the Caudillo of the 1940s. Franco was now head of state by dint of his status as warrior leader. Caudillo was a title which regime ideologues presented as symbolizing Franco's personification of power: he now embodied the charismatic force, based on the trial of war, which itself justified his permanent leadership and which implicitly legitimized everything that had been done in his name to reach that point.[40]

By unpacking further the notion of charismatic power, Angel Viñas considers Francoism in relation to other European fascisms. What fused the entire Franco coalition in a new and totalizing project – brutally hierarchizing and 'imperialist' – was precisely the common, transformative experience *and memory* of the war whose massive foundational violence was, through the person of the Caudillo, transmuted in the 1940s into an act of everlasting faith. Nor, argues Viñas, did these underlying values and memories really dissipate during the later dictatorship of the 1960s, for all the overlay of technocracy and economic growth. Francoism's ideological fundamentalism remained, as did its recourse to the memory of the state repression of the 1940s which performed a useful and ongoing disciplinary function exerting control over defeated and subaltern sectors of the population – what Paul Preston has famously referred to as Franco's 'bankable terror'.[41] The actual process of social and economic change in the 1960s was a far cry from its later mythologization as the 'economic miracle', and, as Michael Richards' chapter shows, for hundreds of thousands of (internal) migrants it was a process mediated by those same memories of terror. As Richards indicates, the history of the 1960s told from their point of view shows, close up, the texture and reach of those changes occurring deep inside society and economy,[42] but that process was a long way from that other myth of retrospective telling – Franco as the conscious architect of democracy.

It is precisely because Francoism's most enduring effect has been its ingraining of social fundamentalism among its supporting constituencies that the dictatorship's political ghost has proven so hard to exorcize; the persistent pattern of Francoist categories are still with us today, now forty years after the end of the dictatorship, as this volume seeks to elucidate. In this too Spain is once again intimately connected to ascending political currents in Europe more broadly, and once again, as in the 1930s, is a touchstone for contemporary continental anxieties – over migration, changing social and sexual values, the decline of 'tradition', the rise of Islam, changing geopolitical and macroeconomic systems and so on. Franco's sacred, nationalist dead now flow into a new populist nationalism in Europe, sharpened and intensified by economic crisis and by particular ideological agendas too. This burden of social fundamentalism is everywhere a legacy of the Cold War, but in Spain a particular burden of history means this reaches all the way back to the civil war of 1936–9 – a past which, in such present circumstances, inevitably remains the past that will not pass away, because the passage from myth to history has been temporarily blocked.

This current moment underscores the importance of the rigorous historical research carried out up to today. Historians have provided empirical evidence and conceptual tools to debunk many of the foundational myths Francoism elaborated about itself and about much else in twentieth-century Spanish history. But history stands today on a fault line in Spain as in Europe, and historians' defence of the complexity of the past over politically charged myths (and many people's strong desire to believe in them) becomes more of a challenge in these times in Spain of closed state archives and persistent legal challenges to any democratic reckoning with the violent past. Myth-busting thus remains a once and future challenge for historians. And while we can hope for more open times, in this age of entangled histories, jobbing, investigative historians in Spain as elsewhere learned some time ago that the historical record can also be excavated in crucial fragments and reassembled from a plethora of other public and private repositories as well as from (or in the absence of) the archives of the state in question.

## Notes

1.  The British policy of 'Non-Intervention', introduced as a result of the escalation from coup to full-scale war in August 1936, was itself a major form of intervention. See Gerald Howson, *Arms for Spain* (London: J. Murray, 1998); Enrique Moradiellos, *Neutralidad benévola: El gobierno británico y la insurrección militar española de 1936* (Oviedo: Pentalfa, 1990) and *La perfidia de Albión: El gobierno británico y la guerra civil española* (Madrid: Siglo XXI, 1996) and 'British Political Strategy in the Face of the Military Rising of 1936 in Spain', *Contemporary European History* 1:2 (1992), pp. 123–37. On the long-term impact on the Republic, see Helen Graham, *The Spanish Republic at War 1936–1939* (Cambridge: Cambridge University Press, 2002), pp. 316–23, 351–2, 356–9, 365, 373; and summarized in Helen Graham, *The Spanish Civil War: A Very Short Introduction* (Oxford: Oxford University Press, 2005), pp. 87–91.

2.  Although this is still occluded in the Anglo-American historiography, an example in Zara Steiner, *The Triumph of the Dark: European International History 1933–1939* (Oxford: Oxford University Press, 2013) pp. 181–251, esp. pp. 213–14 (which nevertheless seems oblivious to the continent-wide European social history of volunteer participation for the Republic, and in general provides a far too Soviet-centric explanation). A comment on this occlusion in Helen Graham, 'The Undefeated? Violence and the Afterlife of Francoism', in 'Review Forum. Paul Preston, *The Spanish Holocaust*', *Journal of Genocide Research* 16: 1 (2014), pp. 139–68: p. 152.

3.  A contextual summary in Helen Graham, *A Very Short Introduction*, pp. 42–9. See also Rémi Skoutelsky, *Novedad en el frente: Las Brigadas Internacionales en la guerra civil* (Madrid: Temas de Hoy, 2006), an archivally based overview.

4.  Richard Baxell, *British Volunteers in the Spanish Civil War: The British Battalion in the International Brigades 1936–1939* (London: Routledge, 2004), pp. 25–46 and *Unlikely Warriors: The British in the Spanish Civil War and the Struggle against Fascism* (London: Aurum, 2012), pp. 12–42. On the medical services see Linda Palfreeman, *¡Salud! British Medical Volunteers in the Republican Medical Services during the Spanish Civil War, 1936–1939*

(Eastbourne: Sussex Academic Press, 2012) and *Aristocrats, Adventurers and Ambulances: British Medical Units in the Spanish Civil War* (Eastbourne: Sussex Academic Press, 2014).

5. The testimony of International Brigade nurse, Patience Darton, indicates this very well, in Angela Jackson's biography *'For us it was Heaven'. The Passion, Grief and Fortitude of Patience Darton, from the Spanish Civil War to Mao's China* (Eastbourne: Sussex Academic Press, 2012), esp. pp. 18–25, 90. Other testimonies show how these egalitarian hopes were, among many things, also gendered: see the remarkable contemporary novel-memoir, *Savage Coast* by the American poet Muriel Rukeyser who was in Republican Spain in the first days of the war. Written between 1936 and 1939, it was only published in 2013 (New York: Feminist Press/CUNY) – see for example p. 12. Also, and impressionistically, Leila Berg's *Flickerbook* (London: Granta, 1997) and cf. Gustav's Regler's comment looking back from 1959 that 'Spain was where the light shone and the new geography began', *The Owl of Minerva* (London: Rupert Hart-Davies, 1959) p. 266.

6. Non-Intervention, it must be remembered, was a policy the British government favoured only when it became apparent that its preferred outcome to the 17–18 July 1936 military coup, a rapid insurgent victory, was *not* going to materialize. So whatever British policy makers' broader concerns about risks to the empire and to British trading links in 1936, this did not affect their pro-Franco stance. Indeed there is ample evidence of official British animosity to the Second Republic dating back to its emergence in April 1931. One would look in vain, of course, for a cabinet minute objecting to the Republic because it had allowed into political life far too broad a swathe of people. But disparaging and snobbish remarks from British civil servants, consular staff and advisors do exist to make the point amply: British National Archives, Foreign Office General Correspondence: Spain (TNA, FO371 W13853/29/41) includes a report referring to the wartime Republican Justice minister, the veteran union leader Ramón González Peña, as a tinker from Asturias. See also Maria Thomas, 'The Front Line of Albion's Perfidy. Inputs into the Making of British Policy towards Spain: The Racism and Snobbery of Norman King', *International Journal of Iberian Studies* 20: 2 (2007), pp. 103–23. It is remarkable that this particular connection between domestic and foreign policy in Britain seems largely unobserved within the British historiography even today. Yet the world it sprang from is perfectly well delineated in Kazuo Ishiguro's 1989 novel, *The Remains of the Day,* with its depiction of the British upper classes' attraction to Nazism for its potential to stabilize threatened hierarchies.

7. Mark Mazower, *Dark Continent: Europe's Twentieth Century* (London: Penguin, 1998), p. 100.

8. The definitive study of the international dimension's meshing with domestic politics is Angel Viñas' masterly trilogy, *La soledad de la República* (Barcelona: Crítica, 2006); *El escudo de la República* (Barcelona: Crítica, 2007); *El honor de la República* (Barcelona: Crítica, 2009).

9. On this process of constructing a new internal other in Spain, see 'Theorists of Extermination' in Paul Preston, *The Spanish Holocaust* (London: HarperCollins, 2012), pp. 34–51.

10. Cf. '. . . may Spain crush the Antichrist of Moscow and the Cross prevail over the hammer and sickle' in Joaquín Arrarás, *Franco*, 8th edn. (Valladolid: Librería Santarén, 1939), p. 314, cited in endnote 8 of Enrique Moradiellos' bibliographical essay in this volume.

11. Helen Graham, *The War and its Shadow: The Spanish Civil War in Europe's Long Twentieth Century* (Eastbourne: Sussex Academic Press, 2012), pp. 12–18, 75–95.

12. Judith Keene, *Fighting for Franco: International Volunteers in Nationalist Spain during the Spanish Civil War, 1936–1939* (London and New York: Leicester University Press, 2001) offers an analytical overview and discusses a range of memoirs.

13. Helen Graham and Alejandro Quiroga, 'After the Fear was Over? What came after Dictatorships in Spain, Greece and Portugal' in Dan Stone (ed.), *The Oxford Handbook of*

*Postwar European History* (Oxford: Oxford University Press, 2012), pp. 503–25: pp. 503–9; Boris Liedtke, 'Spain and the United States, 1945–1975' in Sebastian Balfour and Paul Preston (eds), *Spain and the Great Powers in the Twentieth Century* (London and New York: Routledge, 1999) pp. 8, 218–38.

14. Another piece of mythologizing that was later codified by Franco regime propagandists in the book, *Centinela del Occidente: Semblanza biográfica de Francisco Franco* by Luis de Galinsoga and Francisco Franco Salgado Araujo (Barcelona: Editorial AHR, 1956) and which is discussed in Enrique Moradiellos' bibliographical chapter in this volume.

15. Paul Preston's *Spanish Holocaust* details numerous examples of Francoist violence against priests and lay Catholics, for example, pp. 184–5, 213–4, 431–2. See also Julián Casanova, *La Iglesia de Franco* (Madrid: Temas de Hoy, 2001), pp. 138–46; Francisco Espinosa Maestre and José María García Márquez, *Por la religión y la patria* (Barcelona: Planeta, 2014), pp. 143–52 and Richard Ryan, 'A "gigantic struggle between believers and those without God"? Catholics in the Republic during the Spanish Civil War, 1936–9', University of London PhD Thesis, 2015. Many of the priests and lay Catholics targeted by Franco's forces consciously rejected the very idea of a 'crusade'. Here regional nationalism played an important role in the Basque Country and Catalonia, but the phenomenon of anti-crusade priests was a nationwide one. Although Basque priests became the focal point when in the 1940s photographs emerged of Franco's separate 'prison for priests' at Carmona (Seville), the gaol also held priests from a range of other areas in Spain. The photographs in the exile press, *Euzko Deya* (Buenos Aires), 10 May 1940, n.p. (my thanks to Richard Ryan for locating this photographic information).

16. Paul Preston, *Franco: A Biography* (London: HarperCollins, 1993), pp. 374–425; Paul Preston, 'Franco and Hitler: The Myth of Hendaye 1940', *Contemporary European History*, 1:1 (1992), pp. 1–16.

17. Helen Graham and Alejandro Quiroga, 'After the Fear was Over?', pp. 503–25: pp. 511, 514.

18. This extended to the Catalan Socialists. Ricard Conesa i Sánchez, 'Del duelo clandestino al recuerdo colectivo: el Fossar de la Pedrera del cementerio de Monjuïc', in Conxita Mir Curcó and Josp Gelonch Solé (eds), *Duelo y memoria: espacios para el recuerdo de las víctimas de la represión franquista en perspectiva comparada* (Lleida: Universitat de Lleida, 2013), pp. 171–98: pp. 173–4.

19. The case of Salvaleón (Badajoz) in 1980 in Francisco Espinosa Maestre, *La columna de la muerte: El avance del ejército franquista de Sevilla a Badajoz* (Barcelona: Crítica, 2003), pp. 249–50. The very first was in Granada in 1976, Francisco Espinosa Maestre, 'La memoria de la represión y la lucha por su reconocimiento: en torno a la creación de la comisión interministerial', Dossier: 'Generaciones y memoria de la represión franquista: un balance de los movimientos por la memoria', *Hispania Nova. Revista de Historia Contemporánea* 6 (2006) on Red Iris http://hispanianova.rediris.es/6/HISPANIANOVA-2006.pdf, p. 249 [accessed 3 August 2015].

20. Francisco Espinosa Maestre, *Shoot the Messenger, Spanish Democracy and the Crimes of Francoism* (Eastbourne, Sussex Academic Press, 2013), *passim*.

21. For a fuller discussion, Helen Graham, 'The Afterlife of Violence', in Helen Graham, *The War and its Shadow*, pp. 127–51.

22. Conversely, however, neoconservatives in Spain today still try to close off any discussion of Francoist state violence by referring to extrajudicial killings in the Republican zone during the war (and mostly immediately post-coup in 1936). They thus entirely miss the point (or not?) of the asymmetricality of the situation, given that the Republican killings have already been investigated twice over – first by the Republican authorities themselves during the war, and thereafter by the Franco regime itself, in the form both of the nationwide military

tribunals and also the *Causa General*, the postwar nationwide investigation of crimes committed in the wartime Republican zone. Although the pivot of the Franco state's legitimating propaganda drive, and judicially unsafe, being based largely on hearsay and uncorroborated denunciation, both were, nevertheless, also forms of large-scale investigation. On the military tribunals, Peter Anderson, *The Francoist Military Trials: Terror and Complicity, 1939–1945* (New York and Abingdon: Routledge, 2010) and also Anderson's two articles, 'Singling Out Victims: Denunciation and Collusion in the Post-Civil War Francoist Repression in Spain, 1939–1945', *European History Quarterly* 39:1 (2009), pp. 7–26, and 'In the Interests of Justice? Grassroots Prosecution and Collaboration in the Francoist Military Trials, 1939–1945', *Contemporary European History* 18:1 (2009), pp. 25–44, which also looks at the period 1936–9. On the *Causa General*, Isidro Sánchez Sánchez, Manuel Ortiz Heras and David Ruiz, *España franquista: causa general y actitudes sociales ante la dictadura* (Albacete: Universidad de Castilla-La Mancha, 1993) and a summary, plus analysis of its long-term cultural impact, in Graham, *The War and its Shadow*, pp. 141–2, 172 (n. 44). On Republican wartime investigations, Preston, *Spanish Holocaust*, p. 379, and Oriol Dueñas and Queralt Solé, *El jutge dels cementiris clandestins: Josep M. Bertran de Quintana 1884–1960* (Maçanet de la Selva, Girona: Gregal, 2012), pp. 71–123; and for the reconstruction of Republican state and judicial authority, Helen Graham, *Spanish Republic at War*, esp. pp. 338–9, 350.

23. Cf. the extraordinarily subtle and suggestive treatment of counter-myth in many of the novels of Juan Marsé, one of Spain's greatest writers, and unique in his capacity to convey the complex and enduring impact of the civil war on defeated constituencies. *The Fallen* (transl. London: Quartet Books, 1994), and originally published in Mexico in 1973, is usually cited as his greatest work. But *Un día volveré* ('One day I will return'), sadly still unavailable in English translation, is arguably as extraordinary in content, if not as innovative in form.

24. A similar sentiment expressed by Richard Evans, *In Defence of History* (London: Granta, 1997), p. 106.

25. The scandal also sparked leading senior Spanish historian and former diplomat, Angel Viñas, to publish an edited volume, *En el combate por la historia: La República, la Guerra Civil, el franquismo* (Barcelona: Pasado y Presente, 2012) (*The Fight for History: The Republic, Civil War, Francoism*) which he delivered as an explicit 'counter-dictionary'; see also Angel Viñas (ed.), *Los mitos del 18 de julio* (Barcelona: Crítica, 2013).

26. Stanley G. Payne and Jesús Palacios, *Franco: A Personal and Political Biography* (Madison: University of Wisconsin Press, 2014), p. 203.

27. Dan Stone, *Goodbye to All That? The Story of Europe since 1945* (Oxford: Oxford University Press, 2014), p. ix.

28. For example, Poland's Law and Justice Party, whose leader created a controversy in 2001 by opposing a national apology for the Jedwabne pogrom when he implicitly denied the responsibility of 'ordinary Poles' for the massacre of their Jewish neighbours in July 1941. In late August 2011 the local memorial at Jedwabne was vandalized. There are also numerous ongoing attempts in Poland to erase the public memory of Polish International Brigaders, declaring them to be 'anti-patriots' and adducing 'reasons' which amount to a recycling of Francoist and Cold War myth, see Helen Graham, *The War and its Shadow*, pp. 144, 211–12.

29. See the account by one of the pre-eminent researchers on the Francoist repression, the Seville-based historian, Francisco Espinosa Maestre. In 1978 his university supervisor rejected his research proposal to work on an aspect of the Francoist repression in Seville (and also refused to do anything to help him gain access to the necessary sources), but then many years later, the fruits of this project, which Espinosa had subsequently undertaken as an independent researcher, would be published (in 1990) in a volume edited by the very same professor. Francisco Espinosa Maestre, *Shoot the Messenger?*, p. 9.

30. It was a further Franco effect that the entirety of the mainstream post-transition political class shared an underlying distrust of civil society, or at least wanted to keep it in its place, which was not to concern itself with politics.

31. Alejandro Quiroga, 'La trampa de la equidistancia: Sobre la historiografía neoconservadora en España', in Carlos Forcadell, Ignacio Peiró and Mercedes Yusta (eds), *El pasado en construcción: Revisionismos históricos en la historiografía contemporánea* (Zaragoza: Institución Fernando El Católico, 2015), pp. 339–62.

32. See the cumulative bibliography of Paul Preston's work included in this volume.

33. Paul Preston, *Franco, Caudillo de España* (Barcelona: Grijalbo, 1994) which went very rapidly through numerous reprints); Paul Preston, *El holocausto español: Odio y exterminio en la guerra civil y después* (Barcelona: Editorial Debate, 2011) – this Spanish version is 164 pages longer than the 700-page English edition.

34. Hence by the 1960s in Spain's years of economic boom, it was possible to acquire deluxe editions of, for example, works by Marx and Engels, but as soon as a number of publishers tried to issue cheap mass market paperbacks of socially critical material – whether fiction or non-fiction – then the Franco state moved to block them. See Jo Labanyi's essays, 'Censorship or the Fear of Mass Culture' and 'Literary Experiment and Cultural Cannibalization' in Helen Graham and Jo Labanyi (eds), *Spanish Cultural Studies* (Oxford: Oxford University Press, 1995), respectively pp. 207–14: pp. 211, 213–14 and pp. 295–9: pp. 295–6.

35. The term most frequently used to describe these practices was *caciquismo* (cronyism or 'bossism') and referred to the monarchist system of government whereby the two rotating political parties of the (largely landowning) economic and social elites controlled power and politics in the localities of Spain through a nationwide system of political agents or *caciques* (the latter's power base locally usually being based in some other form of pre-existing coercive power, for example, they controlled employment, finance or the law). Joaquín Costa entitled his classic contemporary critique of the system's stagnation and corruption *Oligarquía y caciquismo como la forma actual de gobierno en España: Urgencia y modo de cambiarla* ('Oligarchy and *caciquismo* as the present form of government in Spain: the urgency and means of changing it') (Madrid: Establecimiento Tipográfico de Fortanet, 1901). Slightly later on, insider critics would also refer to the monarchist system's disbursal of bribes and other 'largesse' as '*el grifo*' ('the tap').

36. Manuel Ballbé, *Orden público y militarismo en la España constitucional, 1812–1983* (Madrid: Alianza, 1985), pp. 247–50; Joaquim Lleixá, *Cien años de militarismo en España* (Madrid: Anagrama, 1986), pp. 60–1; for more on this see the chapter by Francisco Romero Salvadó in this volume.

37. Julián Casanova, 'Rebelión y Revolución: "Abajo la Iglesia, que caiga el poder". La violencia desde abajo', in Santos Juliá (ed.), *Víctimas de la Guerra Civil* (Madrid: Temas de Hoy, 1999), pp. 117–158: p. 153.

38. Cf. Paul Preston, *Spanish Holocaust*, pp. 20–3 for a description by high-ranking Spanish military of Spanish workers as akin to African tribes – and for the addition of antisemitism to the mix, pp. 46–8; see also Gustau Nerín, *La guerra que vino de Africa* (Barcelona: Crítica, 2005) for an anthropological analysis of the origins, development and consequences (during the civil war) of the culture of the colonial officer corps (*Africanistas*), which constituted a 'cultivation of hatred' familiar in the post-1918 European world.

39. For an overt expression of the linkage between this collapse and the ascendancy of revisionism in Spain, see Stanley Payne, 'Mitos y topicos de la Guerra Civil', *Revista de Libros* 79–80 (2003), pp. 3–5. Consider too the comment in 2011 of another of the leading revisionists, Manuel Alvarez Tardío: 'arguments emphasizing structural factors which stress

[…] the extremes of wealth and poverty […] are effectively justifying the radical political project of left republicans and socialists, their political intransigence and even the violence emanating from political and union organizations representing the "disinherited"'. Manuel Alvarez Tardío, '¿Para cuando un debate histórico sin prejuicios? A propósito de la reseña de Samuel Pierce sobre *El Precio de la Exclusión: La política durante la Segunda República*', *Bulletin for Spanish and Portuguese Historical Studies* 36:1 (2011), pp. 153–7: p. 154. Again Tardío assumes something that is not at all clear in comparative European terms – that the political project of progressive republicans and social democratic forces in 1931–33 in Spain was in fact 'radical', notwithstanding the fact that many on the Spanish right, unaccustomed to any serious challenge to traditional authority/power, may have perceived it as such.

40. With its martial overtones, 'Caudillo' linked Franco to the warrior chiefs of medieval times in Spain, and also to their nineteenth-century equivalents – the Spanish army officers who made the palace coups through which changes of government were then settled (although, in those days there was obviously a much reduced 'political nation' inside which there circulated political clienteles served by rival Caudillos). Indeed even as impeccable an integrist as Cardinal Segura, the former Primate of Spain and, at the time, Archbishop of Seville, got into trouble immediately after the war, when in an implicit anti-Falange political spat, he drew attention in one of his sermons to the alleged origins of the word 'caudillo' in 'king of thieves' ('*capitán de ladrones*'). The source is Ramón Serrano Súñer, cited (for example) in José Manuel Sabín, *La dictadura franquista (1936–1975)* (Madrid: Ediciones Akal, 1997), p. 295.

41. Preston, *Franco*, p. 783; see also Preston, *Spanish Holocaust*, pp. 469–517.

42. For a full analysis of the role of civil war memory in postwar economic and social development, see Michael Richards, *After the Civil War: Making Memory and Re-Making Spain since 1936* (Cambridge: Cambridge University Press, 2013) *passim*; see also Antonio Cazorla Sánchez, *Fear and Progress: Ordinary Lives in Franco's Spain 1939–1975* (Chichester: Wiley-Blackwell, 2010) and Pamela Beth Radcliff, *Making Democratic Citizens in Spain: Civil Society and the Popular Origins of the Transition, 1960–78* (Basingstoke: Palgrave, 2011).

# PART I
## THE ENDURANCE OF THE OLD REGIME: STRUCTURES, MENTALITIES AND EVERYDAY LIFE

# CHAPTER 1
## TWENTIETH-CENTURY CATHOLICISMS: RELIGION AS PRISON, AS HAVEN, AS 'CLAMP'
*Maria Thomas*

> ... With shadows of the poor, /The begging cripples and the children begging.
> The churches full of saints /Tortured on racks of marble---/The old complaints/ Covered with gold or dimly lit with candles./With powerful or banal/Monuments of riches or repression ...
>
> Louis MacNeice, *Autumn Journal*, 1939[1]

In August 2011, Pope Benedict XVI visited Madrid to preside over World Youth Day (Jornada Mundial de la Juventud – JMJ), an international meeting of around 1.5 million young Catholics. Cardinal Antonio Rouco Varela, head of the Spanish Episcopal Conference and a vocal critic of the then ruling social democratic (PSOE) government's social policies, especially those enacting a clearer separation of Church and State, inaugurated the six-day celebration with a huge open-air mass in central Madrid.[2] The JMJ, overseen by a Pope who has repeatedly identified Spain as the key twenty-first-century battleground between Catholic faith and 'aggressive laicism', provoked strong reactions among its population.[3] On 17 August, as the city's public spaces filled with Catholic pilgrims, music and symbols, thousands of protesters – many of them linked to secularist groups, including feminist and LGBT organizations, but also to various grass-roots Christian groups – took to the streets to demonstrate against the economic cost of the JMJ and in favour of a complete separation of Church from State. That afternoon, demonstrators and pilgrims coincided in the central Puerta del Sol. As hymns and chants of 'Benedict!' did battle with slogans denouncing the 'ostentation' of the publicly funded event and the 'ignorance' of the pilgrims, the atmosphere became increasingly heated. The confrontation ended with the violent dispersal of the secular demonstrators by the police and the arrests of six people.[4]

These polarized reactions to the papal visit demonstrate that in today's Spain, perhaps more so than in any other country, the Catholic Church's social and political role and its relationship with the State remain extremely polemical issues. This polemic not only sets Catholics against secular humanists, but – as the presence of grass-roots Catholic protesters in the JMJ demonstrations displays – also entails a division between different sectors of the Catholic population. For large numbers of Spaniards, the acceptance or rejection of religion, as well as arguments over its public role, still form key elements of identity in ways that reach far beyond matters of personal faith or agnosticism.

The reasons for this are deeply rooted in Spanish history. Crucially, attitudes towards the Church continue to be informed by memories and perceptions of Catholic experiences and actions during the Second Republic, the civil war and the Franco dictatorship – memories and perceptions which have themselves been inflected, intensified, interpellated and even in some cases remade by the ideology of Francoism, especially by the legitimating narratives powerfully spun by the dictatorship across its four decades. On one side of the spectrum are many whose otherwise varying republican, left-wing, secular or atheist identities have been reinforced by knowledge of the institutional Church's legitimation of the Francoist war effort, and its material complicity in repression during the civil war and the dictatorship. At the other end are conservative Catholics who, still influenced by the enduring dictatorial narrative, but also for other more contemporary reasons, collapse all the social conflicts of the 1930s in which the Church was involved, including the violent anticlericalism of the beginning of the war, into a seamless story of an 'innocent and persecuted' Church. While the historical picture was necessarily more complicated, it is currently this conservative, Catholic discourse which more readily filters into mainstream politics and the media in Spain.[5]

The existence of conflicting attitudes towards the Church in Spain, as well as social conflicts implicating it, long predate the civil war and Francoism. By the late-nineteenth and early-twentieth centuries, Catholicism was already a divisive force capable of generating strong passions. These passions generally crystallized around the issue of the Church's unshakeable alliance with the in-practice undemocratic and repressive Restoration monarchy (1874–1931). While the ecclesiastical hierarchy and many Catholics felt that the Church needed urgent protection from what they saw as the dangers of modernization, liberalism, secularization and workers' political movements, rejection of the throne–altar union among workers and intellectuals alike ensured that anticlericalism became a key component of the new collective identities of emergent republican and worker movements.[6]

But these divisions were far from being binary or clear-cut ones. In the early years of the twentieth century, the Catholic world was a complex one inhabited by diverse groups and actors, from the highly conservative ecclesiastical hierarchy, to liberal exponents of social Catholicism, even to self-proclaimed anticlerical workers themselves. For some, religion represented a 'haven', a protection from the erosion of tradition by unfamiliar and threatening modernizing forces. For others, Catholicism lay at the heart of new possibilities for reformist political and social activism. For many, the Church's use of religion as a mechanism of social control – for example in religious educational centres and penal institutions – provoked more outright negative reactions and, at times, violent rejection.

However, subsequent events – and the recording and representation of these events – have functioned to obscure the multiple meanings which 'Catholicism' contained in Spain during the first third of the twentieth century. After the July 1936 military coup, the institutional Church became the key legitimating force behind the Francoist 'crusade' and emerging dictatorship; alongside the State it played a crucial part in rewriting the history of the civil war as a battle between the Catholic, patriotic saviours of the fatherland and the immoral anti-Spanish Republicans who had attacked them. According to this Manichean and monolithic narrative, there were – and had always been – 'two Spains': one Catholic and one anti-Catholic, which had eventually confronted one another on the battlefield.[7]

Through the construction and embellishment of this narrative, the Franco regime and the Church would achieve a crucial piece of 'spin', thus rewriting – from the period of the civil war's eruption onwards – not only the whole history of social conflict and war in the 1930s but the history of twentieth-century Catholicism itself. In the all-consuming rhetoric of good versus evil, religious faith was portrayed as synonymous with centralizing ultranationalism and support for the dictatorship and as absolutely incompatible with reformist or pluralist tendencies of any kind, especially with Republican political identity, whether of the centre or left.

As Helen Graham observes in her opening essay to this volume, the emphasis on 'collective forgetting' and the other strong institutional continuities which underlay Spain's post-1975 transition to parliamentary democracy have allowed many of the mythic binary narratives constructed by the dictatorship to survive into the present day. This Francoist ideological projection ensures that significant numbers of Catholics who in the 1930s did not side with or believe in the Francoist 'crusade' idea have been removed from the mainstream narrative of the civil war. The Franco regime, then, effectively 'captured' Catholicism as being no more than a homogeneous form of ultraconservatism, thereby also occluding a religious landscape which was varied and nuanced at the turn of the century, and remained so throughout the twentieth century. In this context, the present chapter will examine – indeed excavate – the different faces and functions of Catholicism in twentieth-century Spain. In doing this, it will show how religion came to be mobilized as part of larger pivotal social and political conflicts which were later played out in the civil war. But the resulting shape of official Catholicism was a contingent product of this particular complicated history, rather than innate to Spain's Catholic values or 'self', as we will see from the real historical complexity investing twentieth-century Catholicisms in Spain.

## The Restoration monarchy: roles, uses and meanings of Catholicism

At the beginning of the twentieth century, Spain's doctrinally and politically ultraconservative institutional Catholic Church was enjoying a period of buoyancy and expansion. Having survived the destabilizing liberal reforms of the nineteenth century, its alliance with the Restoration monarchy regime afforded it institutional protection and financial assistance.[8] The settlement between Church and State was reciprocally beneficial. While the Church relied on the regime to defend and augment its economic, social and cultural power, the inefficient and under-resourced State looked to the Church to direct and staff Spain's educational, penal and welfare institutions and to reinforce its own restrictive old-regime notions of social hierarchy.[9] This role gave the ecclesiastical authorities a vast capacity to transmit to the population a religious and ideological message favouring rigid hierarchy and natural inequality, and in particular to target this at politically mobilizing workers, the sector viewed as most threatening by the regime and the rural and industrial elites who still constituted its core support. The Church and its personnel thus became agents of social control and guarantors of a rigidly hierarchical social and cultural order.[10] The writer and broadcaster Arturo Barea, who was educated at a Madrid Catholic secondary school in the 1910s, gained first-hand experience of this rigid control. Barea discovered that workers' children who had won scholarships were forbidden from mixing socially with the school's richer students. He also recalls being warned of the perils of non-Catholic faith by a teacher who informed his class that a nearby Protestant school was full of violent, bomb-throwing anarchists.[11]

The multiplication of Catholic schools like the one Barea attended was one of the most visible results of the 'Restoration settlement', which allowed for the expansion of ecclesiastical personnel, and particularly the religious orders.[12] As restrictions on the establishment of congregations were lifted in the late 1870s, new convents, monasteries and schools were founded with the assistance of Catholic benefactors.[13] Members of the religious orders inhabited an enclosed world underpinned by the ideological and theological assumptions which dominated the 'mind of the Church'.[14] In the face of the rapid, Europe-wide social change and worker mobilization underway during the first third of the twentieth century, Catholic teachings staunchly rejected any challenges posed to religious authority by a de facto increasing ideological and religious pluralism, instead advocating a static view of society based on obedience to authority and acceptance of a divinely ordained inequality. In their institutions, members of the religious orders for the most part absorbed and reproduced a dominant, integrist vision of Catholicism grounded in hierarchy, defensive xenophobia, imperial nostalgia, nationalism and categorical condemnation of non-Catholic identities.[15]

Outside the walls of these institutions, the national distribution of parish priests was very uneven. The most favourable ratios of priests to parishioners were found in northern Spain, while the lowest ratios existed in the south and in urban workers' districts.[16] This geographical imbalance reflected patterns of faith, religious observance and attitudes towards the Church. In an overwhelmingly rural country, many of central and northern Spain's fervently Catholic and socially conservative peasant smallholders and tenant farmers were firmly bound to the Church. In villages and nearby provincial towns, religious ritual lay at the heart of communities and marked the tempo of daily life, providing a constant, reassuring presence perceived as a form of protection against new and encroaching social and cultural influences.[17] Catholicism was reinforced in these areas by the intimate connections between the clergy and the community. In rural Santander, the parish priests were 'local boys without a great deal of education. They often kept cows themselves and sometimes wore regular work clothes'.[18]

By the beginning of the twentieth century, this rural and provincial Catholic world was itself becoming increasingly mobilized. In the rural north, small farmers were drawn to Catholic agrarian unions which provided them with financial assistance while shaping and reinforcing their collective identities and worldviews. Others gravitated towards the ultraconservative, confessional Carlist movement.[19] Simultaneously, the Church authorities called upon Catholics to join a burgeoning network of lay associations, women's organizations and student groups.[20] Many of these associations sprung up around the resurgence of devotions, particularly the Marian cults. Devotions were encouraged by an ecclesiastical hierarchy which felt extremely threatened by secular challenges to its own authority from the population and (some more liberal) politicians at home and from changes abroad.[21] For ordinary rural and provincial Catholics, joining associations devoted to cults was a means of reaffirming their collective religious identities (in some ways this too was impelled, even if not always consciously, by an awareness of looming change).[22] For state and church authorities, the devotions were a way of underlining the adamantine linkage between Church and State, and of constructing a concept of Spanishness anchored in the absolute inseparability of Catholicism and the Spanish nation. This was illustrated dramatically in 1919, when King Alfonso XIII unilaterally consecrated Spain to the Sacred Heart of Jesus, a cult strongly associated with the highly conservative Jesuit order and with Catholic political activism.[23]

From the first decade of the twentieth century, these mobilized Catholics were engaged in protest in defence of 'Catholic interests', using a politicized version of the Church's 'traditional' repertoire of pilgrimages, processions and masses.[24] They found themselves competing for control of Spain's public spaces with newly emergent politically active workers who professed a radically different collective view of the Church. The political cultures of republican, anarchist and socialist movements – which were becoming a mass social force during this period – were all underpinned by an anticlericalism grounded in repudiation of the institutional Church and the conduct of the clergy.[25] Although traditional anticlericalism had existed in Spain since at least the Middle Ages, it now took on an increasingly vehement and politicized character as industrialization, rural-to-urban migration and urbanization changed the faces of Spain's cities, creating new worker experiences and consciousness, and also to some extent, therefore, the beginnings of power too.[26]

In contrast to the high concentration of priests in the rural centre-north, the Church had failed to penetrate the growing, insalubrious districts inhabited by urban migrant workers.[27] Against this backdrop, many urban workers' experiences of the Church – which occurred within penal, charitable and educational institutions and Catholic schools rather than in an environment of community or worship as in the north – were resoundingly negative and often psychologically harmful in what was already a harsh and unforgiving environment. Although formal constitutional freedoms such as trial by jury and universal suffrage existed under the Restoration monarchy, these were perpetually circumvented by the recurrent suspension of constitutional norms, state police violence and economic coercion (including institutionalized corruption (*caciquismo*)). The endemic lack of protection which Spain's poor urban and rural populations endured, and the explicit violence to which they were frequently subjected at the hands of the state security forces led many workers to view a Church with such close links to the regime as an intrinsic component of its 'architecture of repression'.[28]

Contact with religious personnel in prisons and reformatories; the draconian disciplinary regimes imposed in religious schools for poor children; the involvement of Catholic unions in strikebreaking; the recurrent presence of the security forces in religious processions; the seemingly limitless power of the Church over individual rites of passage and public space; religious personnel's use of charity and welfare as disciplinary mechanisms to ensure religious and ideological uniformity (and above all passivity): all of these fragments of shared experience underlined the entanglement between religion and the established authorities, causing many of the urban poor to identify the Church as part of a 'vast repressive coalition that structured everyday life against them'.[29]

Anticlericalism was not solely an urban phenomenon. Spain's rural south, which was dominated by great estates (*latifundios*) rather than smallholdings, was another area with an extremely low ratio of religious personnel – and correspondingly low levels of religious observance.[30] As in urban Spain, many of the landless day labourers (*jornaleros*) who suffered unregulated working conditions, extremely long working days and starvation wages while labouring on the *latifundios* possessed an unremittingly negative view of the clergy. Many *jornaleros* firmly identified the priest as an ally of their employers and of the militarized rural police force, the Civil Guard, which kept order in the deeply unequal and stratified society of the rural south. Abandoned and 'betrayed' by a Church which had, as they saw it, abandoned the poor in order to align itself with the powerful, southern day labourers joined the anticlerical, utopian anarchist movement in huge numbers from the 1860s.

The moral criticism that the Church had 'betrayed' the humble was not confined to anarchist activists. While most self-professed politically active anticlericals would have denied vigorously that they belonged to the 'Catholic world', the discourses and frameworks of their organizations, as well as their own subliminal mental categories, were inflected by the very religious principles they consciously rejected. Socialists, republicans and anarchists alike were inevitably conditioned by the Catholic-generated dominant cultural discourse of the era. Many newly politicized workers had experienced Catholic educational and family environments which had infused them with a belief in Christian moral precepts.[31] In an unevenly developed country like Spain, in the throes of industrialization and urbanization, 'traditional' religious and 'new' secular modes of thought intermingled in activists' mental landscapes. Accordingly, they accused churchmen of betraying the values of the Gospel, praised activists' austerity and self-discipline, peppered their speeches and writings with biblical references, discussed sainthood, redemption, salvation and martyrdom, and constructed eschatological portraits of an evil, immoral past and a utopian future.[32]

This overlap between the moral universes and mental landscapes of anticlerical workers and Catholics was also evident in the social and political activism of a significant number of Catholic priests and laypeople who challenged the ecclesiastical hierarchy's dominant definition of what 'being Catholic' meant. Many of these Catholic activists were, from quite early in the twentieth century, motivated by their experiences of living alongside workers and witnessing their living and working conditions. This fuelled their desire to respond to the 'social question' posed by Pope Leo XIII's 1891 encyclical *Rerum Novarum*, which had called for new approaches to dealing with the effects of industrialization and urbanization.[33] Maximiliano Arboleya, for example, an Asturian priest who was appointed a Canon of Oviedo Cathedral in 1923, strived from the first decade of the twentieth century onwards to form worker-only unions free of employer influence with the mineworkers of Asturias. Arboleya, whose initiatives earned him the enmity of mine owners and prominent ecclesiastics alike, remarked in 1901 that: 'My ideas made me much more dangerous than Pablo Iglesias himself since he did not have to wear a habit to justify his socialism.'[34]

Luis López-Dóriga, a canon of Granada Cathedral, also worked during the 1910s and 1920s to create workers' organizations grounded in 'justice instead of charity' in rural Andalusia, a goal which repeatedly brought him into confrontation with the ecclesiastical authorities.[35] Local priest Basilio Álvarez possessed a similar empathy with agricultural workers in north-west Galicia. As one of the leaders of the regional agrarian movement in the 1910s and 1920s, Álvarez argued that workers' conditions could only be improved through an end to institutionalized corruption and local bossism (*caciquismo*) and changes to the debilitating conditions imposed by tenant farmers' contracts (*foros*). His political activism, collaboration with socialist and republican groups and fierce criticism of government and Church authorities led to his being suspended from priestly duties in 1914, allegedly for the 'scandal' of his personal life.[36]

These priests' commitment to a social Catholicism deemed inconvenient by their superiors was shared by numerous other religious figures, both in Spain and throughout Europe. In 1922, as the Restoration monarchy system became ever more deeply immersed in political crisis, many strands of Spain's Catholic world came together in the Partido Social Popular (PSP). The PSP encompassed a wide spectrum of Catholic opinion, from traditionalists to democrats and advocates of social change. Its founders – like their Christian Democratic political counterparts in Italy and other European countries – shared a commitment to implementing the social teachings of *Rerum Novarum*.[37] Its brief life was cut short by the coming of Primo de Rivera's military dictatorship in 1923 – an event welcomed enthusiastically by the ecclesiastical hierarchy. Nevertheless, the fact of the PSP's establishment indicates the existence of a reformist and democratic Catholic potential in early twentieth-century Spain.[38]

## The 1930s: secularization and Catholic mobilization

The component strands of this Restoration-era Catholic world would react in different ways to the collapse of Primo's dictatorship and the coming of the Second Republic in April 1931. Its first real government was a Republican-Socialist coalition intent upon redistributing social and economic power through agrarian, labour and secularizing reform, and equally set on restricting the social and cultural power of the Church to a purely religious sphere. This democratizing and reformist intent was greeted with dread by most Spanish bishops.[39] From spring and summer 1931, the bishops exhorted Catholics to mobilize against the secularizing measures and in defence of the Church's 'sacrosanct and inalienable rights'.[40] Suffering an acute case of historical amnesia, they used a language which portrayed the Church as an entirely passive victim of Republican persecution.[41]

As the government put into place its secularizing legislation, beginning with the formal separation of Church and State and the declaration of religious liberty, Catholic lay and ecclesiastical unease increased. However, the swathes of rural and provincial Catholics who ended up answering the bishops' calls to mobilize against the Republic were not alienated chiefly by these superstructural changes. Instead, what moved them to action were the many measures which threatened the traditional religious practices – celebrations of local saints' days, pilgrimages and processions – which were an integral part of daily community life and interaction.[42] Most of the Catholics who joined associations and political groupings during the early Republican period would eventually invest their hopes and votes in the mass Catholic coalition party, the CEDA.[43] CEDA propaganda continually reasserted that Spanish identity, which was synonymous with Catholicism, was being attacked by a menacing, atheistic Republican 'anti-Spain'. One Salesian novice, writing from his seminary in Guadalajara to his parents in Salamanca in 1933, expressed what was a common view of the CEDA's leader, José María Gil Robles, among conservative Catholic constituencies: 'Yesterday I heard Gil Robles on the radio and I was very excited. He is the saviour of Spain.'[44]

Catholic collective action, as during the Restoration monarchy, saw many faithful read what Church authorities still claimed was a purely religious repertoire of processions and masses as being saturated with politics. So the above-described Catholic mass mobilization was met during the 1930s by an equally dramatic surge in anticlerical collective action, generally orchestrated by worker constituencies who perceived their hopes for secularizing change frustrated by a combination of Catholic obstruction, and Republican caution and lack of resources. These workers also employed a mixture of 'traditional' anticlerical action – such as church burning – and a repertoire of newer, more discernibly 'modern' kinds of political protest. The simultaneous grass-roots mobilization of these two blocs, and the conflictive, reciprocally exacerbating dynamic into which they entered between 1931 and 1936, generated an ever more intense struggle to determine the meanings of Spain's public spaces, which underpinned the making of mass democracy.[45] This was a moment of rapid and profound social and cultural change, captured in a powerfully impressionistic way by Irish poet Louis MacNeice in *Autumn Journal*, which appears in this chapter's epigraph. MacNeice's first-hand portrait of Spain in spring 1936 depicts an old, decaying, authoritarian religious culture being shaken and thrown into disarray as it confronted new social perceptions and modes of thought.

While many members of the clergy and laity opposed these new modes of thought completely, some sectors of the Catholic world did see Catholic identity and culture as naturally compatible with republican, socialist and anarchist political options. Liberal Catholic intellectual currents, which had been present during the Restoration monarchy and which continued well into the 1930s, continued to challenge dominant integrist narratives. One group of Catholic laity which welcomed dialogue and cooperation with non-Catholic thinkers formed around the experimental journal *Cruz y Raya*, founded in 1933 and directed by the poet José Bergamín. Aimed at incorporating multiple literary and philosophical approaches, its contributors ranged from liberal philosophers to orthodox Catholics.[46]

Less orthodox views were also to be found among those priests who had been collaborating with workers' and progressive political groups since the 1920s, a number of whom now involved themselves fully in progressive Republican politics. Among them was Basilio Álvarez, who was once again practising as a priest after the lifting of his suspension. Álvarez embraced the chance to participate in the new political system: he was elected to the *Cortes* as the politically centrist Republican Radical Party's candidate for Orense.[47] Luis López-Dóriga was also elected to Parliament as an independent candidate, going on to join the (also centrist in spite of its name) Radical Socialist Republican Party in 1932. López-Dóriga's decision to vote in favour of both the separation of Church and State and the 1932 divorce law earned him his excommunication.[48]

As their public statements demonstrate, many of the clerics and lay Catholics who found common ground with workers' movements and progressive Republican groups did so because they saw a genuine convergence between the values of the Gospel and the discourse and ethics of these new political forces. Many of these priests had been involved in Catholic grass-roots social activism since at least the 1920s, and their collective beliefs and views of society were embedded in a tradition of Catholic social reform which had existed in Spain and across Europe since the beginning of the twentieth century.[49] The Madrid-based priest and publicist Juan García Morales, for example, a member of the pro-Republic intellectual grouping Agrupación al Servicio de la República praised the Belgian theorist of social Catholicism Walter Van Tricht as 'a disciple of a working men's God' and opined that 'communist, socialist and anarchist ideas' should be 'left to follow their natural course'.[50] In many ways, these actors were a Catholic mirror image of anticlerical activists whose activism was also imbued with Christian elements and denunciations of the Church's betrayal of the humble. Through direct contact with workers in their parishes, these churchmen identified the obvious convergence between the values of the 'Gospel of the poor' and the needs and principles of parishioners affiliated to egalitarian, utopian and millenarian movements.[51]

## Religion and civil war

These alternative Catholic voices, which came to be powerfully outnumbered between 1931 and 1936, would effectively be smothered by the national-Catholic 'crusade' rhetoric which evolved following the military coup of 17–18 July 1936. The coup, orchestrated by a group of army officers in the wake of the victory of the progressive Popular Front coalition in the February 1936 elections, aimed to reverse the social levelling encouraged by the Republic and to restore the hierarchical and authoritarian pre-Republic order. While the institutional Church was not directly involved in the uprising, after July it became quickly and totally implicated in the rebel war effort.

The ecclesiastical hierarchy's almost unanimous support for the rebels was apparent from the summer of 1936. The Spanish bishops' public statements and writings began to generate a discourse which, gathering force as it amalgamated with contributions from Franco's emerging state authorities and other parts of his social support base, functioned to justify *a posteriori* the illegal military coup, by transforming it into a 'holy crusade' against evil.[52] This discourse, as historian Michael Richards argues, created, within the crucible of war, a new notion of the 'sacred nation', by eliding religion and nationalism, and then identifying both exclusively with Franco's ultraconservative, centralized brand.[53] The coup was welcomed – although by no means unanimously – by many priests and lay Catholics, who saw it as a means of restoring order and ensuring protection for religion.[54] Those who were already mobilized behind conservative or authoritarian political organizations – from the Carlists, to the CEDA, to the fascist Falange – were united by an understanding that the order they aspired to establish would be underpinned both by Catholicism and by the violent rejection of Republican and political cultures.[55]

The 'persecuted Church' was thereafter the central feature of the discourse being constructed by both the Church and the evolving Franco regime. This image had been developed between 1931 and 1936 as the ecclesiastical authorities, some members of the clergy and political groups like the CEDA denounced the Republic's 'attacks' on religion. Although the image was rejected by significant numbers of the Catholic laity and clergy with links to workers' and republican organizations, it quickly became ubiquitous in the insurgent zone media and discourse. Moreover, the anticlerical violence which erupted in Republican territory following the rebellion – the direct result of the virtual collapse of the State caused by the coup – enabled the Church to intensify the victimist rhetoric. In territory which remained under Republican authority the coup paralysed the security forces, leaving power in the hands of groups of armed workers. These workers often used their fragmented, suddenly acquired power to carry out a spontaneous revolution aimed at eliminating those perceived to be the coup's 'natural supporters'.

In terms of workers' treatment of the clergy, the July rebellion was the spark which ignited an ever-growing tinderbox of collective popular anticlerical resentment, accumulated social hurt and frustration regarding the Republic's failed secularizing initiatives. Religious personnel – almost 7,000 in total – were detained and murdered almost everywhere across Republican Spain.[56] The majority were killed during the first six months of the conflict, before the Republican government – which categorically condemned all forms of grass-roots violence in the Republican zone[57] – regained control of the state apparatus.

This anticlerical violence emboldened the ecclesiastical hierarchy in its explicit support for the rebels. The 'martyrs' of the 'persecuted Church' were now placed at the heart of the mythicized narrative of the civil war's meaning constructed both by the Church and the Franco regime. This narrative, which ignored the fact that many priests had actually been saved from anticlerical violence in the Republican zone due to their specific welfare activities within the community or lack of pro-insurgent political allegiances,[58] recast the entire civil war as a 'crusade' against an alien, irreligious 'anti-Spain'. This crusade, as the ferocious anticlerical assault endured by the Church demonstrated, was necessary to save Spain and to impose order, religion and hierarchy.[59] This narrative conflated the secularization attempts of the pre-war Second Republic and the post-coup anticlerical murder to produce the decontextualized impression that the entire Republican experience of 1931–9 was nothing more than a violent, atheistic bloodbath. The Republican government and its supporters, capable of such atrocious, anti-Christian crimes, were presented as bestial, barbarous and inhuman.[60]

In binary opposition to these 'barbarians' were the Church's 'martyrs', constructed as blameless, heroic individuals who had suffered to save Spain. They were celebrated in the martyrological literature published by religious personnel and lay Catholics – and consumed in great quantities. The martyrologies were filled with atrocity stories, exaggerations of victim numbers and dehumanizing descriptions of 'savage cruelties' committed by perpetrators 'drunk with satanic hatred'.[61] This image was being constructed simultaneously by state as well as religious authorities. Indeed, thematically identical to the martyrologies were Franco's wartime speeches, the news summaries published by the Francoist authorities and the deluge of journalistic and state-sponsored paperback books and leaflets depicting 'lurid details of ghastly killings' which appeared in Franco's zone from 1937 onwards.[62]

The glorification of the martyrs and the repetition of a dichotomy of 'good' against 'evil' was a key discursive component in the forging of the embryonic Francoist nation. 'Martyr', which theologically speaking described only non-combatant victims, became a catch-all term to refer to all of the Francoist dead. Imagery of martyrdom and redemptive suffering – already embedded in the political cultures of the Carlists, the Falange and the CEDA – served to unite the different groups which comprised the insurgent coalition, providing a common language with which to honour their dead.[63] Martyrdom was also a unifying, mobilizing force within the wider community, as civilians who commemorated 'the fallen' assimilated and reproduced a discourse which lent consolatory meaning to their relatives' deaths.[64] Conversely, the dehumanization of the regime's enemies which ran through the 'martyrs and barbarians' discourse legitimized the extermination of those sectors which did not belong in Franco's brutal national community-under-construction, both during the battlefield war of 1936–9 and after, in the period of institutionalized state violence through which the Franco regime embedded and consolidated itself.[65] This extirpative violence which this discourse fuelled also tied the perpetrators of repression together with bonds of blood, uniting and strengthening the Francoist coalition.

The Francoist interpretation of the civil war and the Republic allowed very little room for nuances or ambiguities. However, during the war the ecclesiastical authorities found it impossible in practice to silence completely the pro-Republican Catholic minority which had developed before 1936. Individuals like Juan García Morales, Madrid-based parish priest Leocadio Lobo, Catalan priest Joan Vilar i Costa and Cordobese Canon José Manuel Gallegos Rocafull put themselves at the service of the Republican war effort, producing domestic and international propaganda.[66] They were united in their condemnation of a coup which had attacked the legally constituted government and argued that the massive anticlerical violence in the Republican zone, reprehensible as it was, had been the immediate consequence of the coup itself, and a long-term result of the Church's political protagonism and failure to promote genuine, Christian equality.

This understanding of the connection between oppressive politics and anticlerical violence, a result of the fact that many of these priests had inhabited and experienced the same world as their working-class parishioners, was shared by significant numbers of Basque clergy and by Catholic Republican politicians, diplomats and intellectuals such as Ángel Ossorio, Manual Irujo Olla and José Bergamín.[67] Alongside these more prominent figures, the Republican zone also contained large numbers of ordinary Catholics who had no history of political activism and whose support for the military rebels was by no means a foregone conclusion at the outset of the conflict. Their positions evolved and changed over the course of the war as a reaction to conditions in the Republican zone, the restricted options available to them and their attempts to make sense of their own circumstances in the complex maelstrom of civil war-torn Spain. In this process, personal experiences mixed with macro events – such as the bombing of the Basque Country in spring 1937 – and with Catholics' growing practical relationship with the Republican state in the form of conscription and social service provision, to create a complex and nuanced spectrum of Catholic wartime attitudes.[68]

As during the pre-war Republic, many pro-Republic Catholics explained their kinship with the Republic and its supporters as being grounded in the true Christian values and teachings which had been abandoned by the institutional Church. In an appearance on Communist Party radio in September 1936, Leocadio Lobo asserted: 'The masses are rebelling against an absurd and brutal economic system. Know that I am on their side, because the Church has been on their side for a long time, even if our selfishness has made us forget the teachings of the popes.'[69] Gallegos Rocafull, in the 1937 leaflet 'Crusade or Class War?' underlined this convergence even more firmly, remarking that: 'Among those who call themselves Marxists there is a high spiritual life which is shown courageously in their moral elevation, in their sacrifice to the ideal, their magnificent solidarity, their Christian disregard for worldly goods.'[70]

The Church dealt with these critical clerics by suspending them from their duties and branding them 'proponents of false ideas' and 'the dross of the Spanish clergy', effectively denying their identities as Spaniards and as Catholics.[71] Punishment of dissenting Catholics was not only verbal. Across Franco's Spain priests, ex-priests and lay Catholics were executed for questioning the constructed narrative of the 'crusade'. This included the execution in October 1936 of sixteen Basque priests who were killed due to their perceived support for the Republic and the goals of Basque nationalism.[72] These killings functioned to shape and nuance Catholic opinion regarding the Francoist 'crusade' elsewhere in Republican Spain.

## The Franco dictatorship: continuity and change

Once Franco had achieved military victory in 1939, religious personnel executed by the Francoists, along with all of those Catholics who had sympathized with the Republican programme before or during the war, were removed from a state-driven narrative based on the binary opposition between good and evil. Not only did this narrative depict the entire Republican period of 1931–9 as a deluge of anticlerical carnage; it also denied the existence of the multifaceted voices which had constituted the Catholic world at the beginning of the twentieth century, and well into the 1930s. The Francoist version of history was propagated by the dictatorship not only during the battlefield war and the extremely repressive immediate postwar period, but well into the 1960s. The Church hierarchy, whose institution gained an extremely privileged public and private role within the new Francoist order, remained allied to the dictatorship for its entire duration.

By the late 1960s, however, serious changes were under way within the Spanish Church. The process of change was driven from below, by individual priests and grass-roots Catholic organizations. In terms of their political and social thought, these actors can be linked clearly to the progressive Catholic options which had existed during the 1920s and 1930s and which were then closed down by the Franco dictatorship. But subsequent rural-to-urban migration, accelerating over the 1960s and sparking tremendous demographic and social change, was one of the main driving forces behind the (re-)emergence of progressive social and political agendas among many Catholics.

In large cities like Madrid, Bilbao and Barcelona, members of the clergy saw it as their duty to tackle the severe difficulties faced by the recently arrived migrants inhabiting the ever-expanding urban shanty town communities. This situation led to the emergence of *curas obreros* (worker priests), members of the secular clergy who – like the socially committed priests of the 1920s and 1930s – inhabited and understood the communities of their worker parishioners. They maintained that in order to identify with these workers, they should earn a living through manual work.[73] While many *curas obreros* limited their field of action to workers' spiritual and practical welfare, some also became actively involved in politics. One such figure was José María de Llanos, the Jesuit priest, former Falangist and clandestine Communist Party affiliate who committed himself to addressing misery and extreme inequality and poverty in his rapidly expanding parish in Vallecas (Madrid).[74] These priests worked closely with grass-roots lay workers' organizations like the HOAC (Hermandad Obrera de Acción Católica) and the JOC (Juventud Obrera Católica), whose activists had been denouncing human rights abuses and the absence of social justice in Spain since the early 1950s.[75] These groups' repeated public challenges to the Francoist authorities and the Church hierarchy itself – acts such as the organization of petitions denouncing the violence of the Francoist security forces – crucially functioned to change the parameters of acceptable debate within the institutional Church.

By the early 1970s, some members of the ecclesiastical hierarchy – spurred on by these grass-roots currents – were slowly beginning to engage with pluralistic and democratic principles. This evolution was also influenced hugely by the impact of the Second Vatican Council's teachings on democracy and human rights. As the Franco regime found itself increasingly besieged by political and social protest, the ecclesiastical authorities worked to distance themselves from the decaying dictatorship. In September 1971, the declarations of a Joint Assembly of Priests and Bishops appeared to communicate a new, democratic and reflexive direction. As well as announcements calling for an end to the mutual dependence of the Church and the Francoist State, delegates proposed a resolution which would effectively apologize for the Church's spiritual legitimation of the Francoist war effort.[76] Although their statement was never officially ratified, it was clearly indicative of a religious institution which was reflecting upon its role in fomenting decades of violence, division and exclusion. Similar conciliatory sentiments would be common – yet by no means unanimously supported – at all levels within the Church following the death of Franco in 1975 and during the transitional period which saw the restoration of democratic institutions to Spain.

## Myths, martyrs and memory: democracy and the present

The period before and during the transition, as outlined above, was marked by the increased visibility of democratic, reformist tendencies within the Church, coupled with a readiness on the part of the ecclesiastical hierarchy to reflect upon the Church's divisive role during the civil war and the dictatorship. However, although many lay Catholics and priests in Spain have maintained a commitment to democracy, pluralism and self-reflection, the ecclesiastical hierarchy's liberal direction during the 1960s and 1970s has proved to be little more than a parenthesis. The progressive Catholic spirit of the transition, fragile at the best of times, has subsequently been undermined by both national and international developments, such as the triumph of Vatican conservatism embodied in the papacy of Pope John Paul II and the Spanish ecclesiastical authorities' own growing awareness during the 1980s that the Church had survived a potentially traumatic move from dictatorship to parliamentary democracy largely unscathed.

By the mid-1980s, with the ecclesiastical authorities on the defensive after the election of a social democratic (PSOE) government, it soon became clear that key and formative Francoist narratives had never really been reassessed or questioned within the upper echelons of the Church. This is demonstrated not least by the Church's ongoing quest to beatify the 'martyred' victims of anticlerical violence. The beatifications began in the late 1980s against a backdrop which saw the crumbling of the Soviet bloc in Eastern Europe, and the accompanying collapse of the social democratic consensus in place in Western Europe since the post-Second World War period. They continue into the present, reproducing an image of the Church as a blameless victim with no political or social agency which was attacked in the 1930s simply because its Republican assailants hated religion. These views were on clear display during the JMJ event discussed at the beginning of the chapter. The official guidebook distributed to participants described the 1930s as the era of 'the bloodiest persecution known in the history of Christianity, with over 7,000 martyrs'.[77]

This fossilized discourse, which is reproduced across Spain today by the Church's extensive media network, Catholic lay associations and in numerous new martyrological texts written by religious personnel and laypeople, denies the Church's complicity in Francoist violence. It is accompanied by opposition to the activities of civic memory associations working to locate and commemorate the victims of Francoist repression. The official ecclesiastical position regarding these activities, and the 2007 Historical Memory Law which established structures to fund them, is that they are 'reopening old wounds' and threatening 'peaceful coexistence'.[78] This stance, which is identical to that of Spain's governing conservative Popular Party, is deemed both disingenuous and offensive by many of the relatives of the victims of Francoist violence. In this context, Spain's historical memory associations used the Pope's 2011 visit to call upon the Church to condemn officially the Franco dictatorship and to apologize for its role in repression.[79] Predictably, their appeals were ignored by an ecclesiastical hierarchy which still maintains that: 'The Church, in the Civil War, was not an active participant; in other words, it was a victim.'[80]

The persistence of these Francoist myths, which in the late twentieth and twenty-first century are still a recurrent feature of the discourse of conservative, Catholic sectors, is partially a result of the nature of Spain's transition to democracy. As Helen Graham's opening essay makes clear, the post-1975 democratic transitional process was underpinned by intense fear, especially of a pro-Franco army. This tended to reinforce general acceptance of the exhortations of political leaders (and not only former Francoist ones) to 'forget' the recent, violent past. But it was a process which favoured continuity rather than a decisive effort to break with the dictatorship, leaving many Francoist myths unchallenged and Francoism's 'frame of meaning' largely intact.[81]

The ultraconservative mentality of Spain's present-day ecclesiastical hierarchy has also manifested itself in the Church's vigorous mobilization of its followers against social legislation considered to be contrary to Catholic morality. During the PSOE legislature of 2004–11 mass Catholic demonstrations were staged against the legalization of same-sex marriage and express divorce, thus indicating the extent to which the institutional Church in Spain has staked its contemporary function and appeal as a bulwark against social pluralism.[82] In 2014, the Church backed the Popular Party's bid to make abortion illegal except in the case of rape or grave risk to the mother's life.[83] This stance has been encouraged by – and, in turn, encouraged – the high profile ultra-Catholic populist conservatism of sectors of the Popular Party, Spain's philo-confessional conservative right. The ascendency and political and social discourse of the Popular Party form part of a wider post-1989 European context which has seen the steady, continent-wide rise of aggressive arch-conservative popular nationalist movements.

The Popular Party's stance on the historical memory movement and a variety of other social issues reveals a thinly veiled sociological or 'nostalgic' Francoism. This sociological Francoism is also evident today in emerging broader representations of the Restoration monarchy, which brings us full circle in this chapter. The former Popular Party Prime Minister José María Aznar has on several occasions praised Spain's period of Restoration monarchy as a 'long period of institutional stability, peaceful coexistence and respect for freedoms' which was the precursor to Spain's current democracy.[84] This convenient myth (because it allows the excision of the Second Republic) is propagated today by numerous other conservative politicians and historians.[85] In 1997, on the centenary of the death of Antonio Cánovas del Castillo, the architect of the Restoration political system, the Popular Party's then-Secretary-General Francisco Álvarez Cascos described him as 'a reference point for our present and our future' and a champion of 'democratic coexistence'. The idea of Spain's post-1975 democracy as a 'second Restoration' first appeared during the transition itself, advanced by Francoist politicians like Manuel Fraga, who used it as a tool to carve out an explicitly conservative space within the new democratic apparatus.[86] This glorification of the Restoration allows the political right to preserve what is essentially the Francoist representation of the Second Republic as an undemocratic, chaotic bloodbath. Aznar made this point clearly in 2007 at an event organized by the Popular Party social policy think-tank FAES. For Aznar, the Restoration had been a period of 'parenthesis in a tumultuous century'. In contrast, the Second Republic was 'the failed political experiment of a revolutionary political system' which 'ended in a dramatic civil confrontation'.[87]

This highly idealized vision of the Restoration, by focusing purely on the existence of formal constitutional liberties, obscures the ways in which these were consistently circumvented by the constant brutality which lay just under the system's liberal façade – not to mention the many times constitutional guarantees were themselves suspended during the various 'states of alarm' or 'states of war' to which Restoration governments regularly had recourse.[88] In overlooking the experiences of those at the bottom of the Restoration system's rigid, Church-enforced social hierarchy, this idyllic vision of a harmonious society free of exploitation and inequality functions to delegitimize both the critical, politicized anticlericalism of vast numbers of workers, and the positions of those Catholics who advocated reform and some redistribution of economic and social power during both the Restoration years and the Republic. Moreover, the tendency among cultural studies scholars in recent decades to analyse the output of the Restoration's elite sectors rather than the experiences of popular – and frequently illiterate – constituencies has, albeit unintentionally, added to this highly distorted image of the Restoration as a liberal, democratic system characterized by press freedom and uncensored cultural production.

## Conclusions

This chapter has examined the long-lasting and corrosive impact of a number of divisive Francoist myths which have separated Spaniards into rigid categories of 'good' and 'evil', as 'martyrs' and 'barbarians'; 'Catholics' and 'unbelievers'. It has also problematized these categories through the exploration of a far less binary historical reality – that is, the forms and practices of a more complex, heterogeneous Catholic world which has also existed across the twentieth century, if with less powerful political and state support. These Francoist myths, which are still present to this day in the discourse of the Church and the political right, as well as exerting a more extensive passive influence in Spanish society, have excluded the stories of huge swathes of Catholics from the official twentieth-century history of the Church and indeed from mainstream perceptions of twentieth-century Spain more broadly. Simultaneously, the way in which conservative forces in Spain today hold up the period of the Restoration monarchy as Spain's only successful pre-1977 'democracy' functions to reinforce the Francoist idea of the Second Republic as a bloody, atheistic, revolutionary regime responsible for persecuting the Church and unleashing civil war.

The refusal of today's ecclesiastical hierarchy to confront its own role in manufacturing these Francoist myths, and its censure of those attempting to locate and commemorate the victims of the violence which it endorsed and legitimated, ensures that large numbers of Spaniards – and particularly those linked to the historical memory movement – still associate the Church with the physical and moral repression of the Francoist past. Furthermore, the Church's present-day mobilization on social issues, and attempt to impose integrist Catholic moral norms upon a pluralistic society means that many, particularly those connected to the centre-left politically or to the new social movements, see the institution as still formed in an image of its past, as an aggressive saboteur of social change. Against this backdrop, anticlerical attitudes like those witnessed during the JMJ in 2011 remain widespread and passionate. Continuing internal and external migratory processes, and the evolution of an ever more diverse and cosmopolitan society, means the contemporary Catholic world in Spain is even more hybrid than it was during the twentieth century. However, in a pattern which has defined the modern history of the institutional Church, the ecclesiastical hierarchy still appears intent on imposing a single, homogeneous way of 'being Catholic' upon the rapidly evolving population of Spain.

## Notes

1. Louis MacNeice, *Autumn Journal* (London: Faber and Faber, 1939), p. 26.

2. *ABC*, 16 August 2011.

3. *Público*, 14 August 2011; *El País*, 6 November 2010.

4. *El País*, 17 August 2011.

5. *El País*, 22 November 2010.

6. Julio de la Cueva Merino, 'Movilización popular e identidad anticlerical 1898–1910', *Ayer* 27 (1997), pp. 101–26: pp. 120–1.

7. *Causa general: la dominación roja en España: avance de la información instruida por el Ministerio Público en 1943* (Astorga: Akrón, 2008), *passim*; Paul Preston, *The Spanish Holocaust: Inquisition and Extermination in Twentieth-Century Spain* (London: Harper Press, 2012), p. 51.

8. William Callahan, *The Catholic Church in Spain, 1875–1998* (Washington: Catholic University of America Press, 2000), pp. 20–37; Adrian Shubert, *A Social History of Modern Spain* (New York: Routledge, 1996), p. 147.

9. Chris Ealham, *Class, Culture and Conflict in Barcelona, 1898–1937* (London and New York: Routledge/Cañada Blanch, 2005), p. 39.

10. Helen Graham, *The War and its Shadow: Spain's Civil War in Europe's Long Twentieth Century* (Eastbourne: Sussex Academic Press, 2012), pp. 38–9. Maria Thomas, *The Faith and the Fury: Popular Anticlerical Violence and Iconoclasm in Spain, 1931–1936* (Brighton: Sussex Academic Press, 2012), p. 23.

11. Arturo Barea, *La forja de un rebelde: La forja* (Barcelona: Random House, 2006), pp. 130–53.

12. Frances Lannon, *Privilege, Persecution, and Prophecy: The Catholic Church in Spain 1875–1975* (Oxford: Clarendon Press, 1987), p. 3.

13. Callahan, *Catholic Church*, pp. 189–93, 217; Shubert, *Social History*, pp. 148–9; Mary Vincent, *Spain 1833–2002: People and State* (Oxford: Oxford University Press, 2007), pp. 26, 62–3.

14. Shubert, *Social History*, p. 154; Frances Lannon, 'The Socio-Political Role of the Spanish Catholic Church: A Case Study', *Journal of Contemporary History* 14:2 (1979), pp. 193–210: p. 208.

15. Lannon, 'Socio-Political Role', pp. 199–201; Shubert, *Social History*, pp. 154–8.

16. Shubert, *Social History*, p. 150: Callahan, *Catholic Church*, pp. 193–5; Lannon, *Privilege*, pp. 3–4, 10–15.

17. Helen Graham, *The Spanish Republic at War* (Cambridge: Cambridge University Press, 2002), p. 5; Paul Preston, *The Coming of the Spanish Civil War: Reform, Reaction and Revolution in the Second Spanish Republic 1931–1936* (London: Routledge, 1994), pp. 42–6; William Christian, *Visionaries: The Spanish Republic and the Reign of Christ* (Berkeley: University of California Press, 1996), p. 18.

18. William Christian, *Person and God in a Spanish Valley* (New York: Seminar Press, 1972), p. 180–1.

19. Shubert, *Social History*, p. 159.

20. María Pilar Salomón Chéliz, 'El anticlericalismo en la calle. Republicanismo, populismo, radicalismo y protesta popular (1898–1913)', in Julio de la Cueva and Feliciano Montero (eds), *La secularización conflictiva: España 1898–1931* (Madrid: Biblioteca Nueva, 2007), pp. 126–33.

21. Rafael Cruz, *En el nombre del pueblo* (Madrid: Siglo XXI, 2006), p. 29.

22. William Christian, *Moving Crucifixes in Modern Spain* (Princeton: Princeton University Press, 1992), p. 4.

23. Luis Cano, *Reinaré en España: la mentalidad católica a la llegada de la Segunda República* (Madrid: Encuentro, 2009), pp. 86–94.

24. Julio de la Cueva Merino, 'Clericalismo y movilización católica en la España de la Restauración', in Julio de la Cueva Merino and Ángel López Villaverde (eds), *Clericalismo y asociacionismo católico de la restauración a la transición* (Castilla la Mancha: Universidad de Castilla la Mancha, 2005), pp. 31–50.

25. Thomas, *Faith and the Fury*, pp. 34–9.

26. Manuel Pérez Ledesma, 'Studies on Anticlericalism in Contemporary Spain', *International Review of Social History* 46 (2001), pp. 227–55.

27. Mary Vincent, *Catholicism and the Second Republic: Religion and Politics in Salamanca 1930–1936* (Oxford: Oxford University Press, 1996), pp. 12–13; Lannon, *Privilege*, p. 18.

28. Quote from Chris Ealham, 'The Myth of the Maddened Crowd: Class, Culture and Space in the Revolutionary Urbanist Project in Barcelona, 1936–1937', in Chris Ealham and Michael Richards (eds), *The Splintering of Spain: Cultural History and the Spanish Civil War, 1936–1939* (Cambridge: Cambridge University Press, 2005), p. 26. See also Manuel Ballbé, *Orden público y militarismo en la España constitucional, 1812–1983* (Madrid: Alianza, 1985), pp. 247–8.

29. Ealham, *Class*, p. 39; Thomas, *Faith and the Fury*, pp. 24–44.

30. Shubert, *Social History*, pp. 160–1.

31. Ronald Fraser, *The Pueblo: A Mountain Village on the Costa del Sol* (London: Allen Lane, 1973); Diego Abad de Santillán, *Memorias 1897–1936* (Barcelona: Planeta, 1977), p. 29.

32. Santos Juliá, 'Fieles y mártires: raíces religiosas de algunas prácticas sindicales de la España de los años treinta', *Revista de Occidente* 23 (1983), pp. 61–75; José Álvarez Junco, 'El anticlericalismo en el movimiento obrero', in Gabriel Jackson (ed.), *Octubre 1934: Cincuenta años para la reflexión* (Madrid: Siglo XXI, 1985), pp. 290–5; Gerald Brenan, *The Spanish Labyrinth: An Account of the Social and Political Background of the Spanish Civil War* (Cambridge: Cambridge University Press, 1960), pp. 139–66.

33. Callahan, *Catholic Church*, p. 107.

34. Shubert, *Social History*, p. 158. On Arboleya, Shubert, 'El fracaso del sindicalismo católico en Asturias', in Jackson, *Octubre*, pp. 246–8.

35. Marisa Tezanos Gandarillas, 'Luis López Dóriga (1885–1962): del catolicismo social al republicanismo de izquierdas', in Feliciano Montero et al. (eds), *Otra iglesia: clero disidente durante la Segunda República y la guerra civil* (Gijón: Trea, 2013), pp. 31–40 and 'El clero ante la República.

Los clérigos candidatos en las elecciones constituyentes', in Julio de la Cueva and Feliciano Montero (eds), *Laicismo y catolicismo. El conflicto político-religioso en la Segunda República* (Alcalá de Henares: Servicio de publicaciones de la Universidad de Alcalá, 2009), pp. 276–8.

36. Daniel Arasa, *Católicos del bando rojo* (Barcelona: Styria, 2009), pp. 47–8.

37. Lannon, *Privilege*, pp. 143–5.

38. Frances Lannon, 'The Church's Crusade against the Republic', in Paul Preston (ed.), *Revolution and War in Spain* (London: Methuen, 1984), p. 37 and *Privilege*, p. 170.

39. Vincent, *Catholicism*, pp. 172–3; Juan de Iturralde, *El catolicismo y la cruzada de Franco*, vol. 1 (Vienne-Toulouse: Egi-Indarra, 1958), pp. 338–9.

40. Quotes from Boletín Oficial del Obispado de Madrid-Alcalá, Tomo XLIV, 01/06/1931, Núm. 1,537, *Declaración Colectiva*, p. 221; 15/06/1931, *Declaración de los Metropolitanos*, p. 260; 01/08/1932 and Núm. 1,588, 'Horas Graves', p. 273. See also 'Carta pastoral de Bernardo Martínez Noval (obispo de Almería), 23/10/1931' in Manuel Pérez Montoya, *Las derechas almerienses durante la II República: el primer bienio 1931–1933* (Almería: Instituto de Estudios Almerienses, 1991), p. 135.

41. Boletín Oficial del Obispado de Madrid-Alcalá (Madrid: Asilo del S.C de Jesús), Tomo XLIV, 01/06/1931, Núm. 1,537, p. 221.

42. Helen Graham, *The Spanish Civil War: A Very Short Introduction* (Oxford: Oxford University Press, 2005), pp. 10–11; Vincent, *Catholicism*, pp. 187–9; Lannon, *Privilege*, pp. 181–6.

43. Julián Casanova, *La Iglesia de Franco* (Barcelona: Crítica, 2005), pp. 36–7.

44. Archivo Diocesano de Madrid, Caja 7: Tomo II, 12/211, Don Justo Juanes Santos, Carta a sus padres desde Mohernando, 19/11/1933.

45. Cruz, *Pueblo*, pp. 50–62; Thomas, *Faith and the Fury*, pp. 46–7; Ángel Luis López Villaverde, 'El conflicto católico-republicano "desde abajo", 1931–1936', in de la Cueva and Montero (eds), *Laicismo y catolicismo*, pp. 400–19.

46. Lannon, *Privilege*, pp. 36–7, 43.

47. Marisa Tezanos Gandarillas, 'Basilio Álvarez: "Una sotana casi rebelde"', *Espacio, Tiempo y Forma* V,H, t. 10 (1997), pp. 156–74; Arasa, *Católicos del bando rojo*, pp. 45–52.

48. Tezanos Gandarillas, 'Luis López Dóriga', pp. 31–40 and 'El clero ante la República', pp. 276–8.

49. Julián Sanz Hoya, *De la resistencia a la reacción: las derechas frente a la Segunda República* (Santander: Universidad de Cantabria, 2006), pp. 65–6; Julio de la Cueva Merino, *Clericales y anticlericales: el conflicto entre confesionalidad y secularización en Cantabria, 1875–1923* (Santander: Universidad de Cantabria, 1991), pp. 41–2.

50. *Heraldo de Madrid*, 24 November 1931; *El Progreso*, 17 January 1934 in Antonio César Moreno Cantano, 'Juan García Morales: Anticlericalismo y denuncia social', in Montero, *Otra iglesia*, pp. 111–15.

51. For an elaboration of these ideas, and of the heterogeneous nature of the Catholic world during the 1930s, see Richard Ryan's University of London doctoral thesis, '"A gigantic struggle between believers and those without God"? Catholics and the Republic in the Spanish Civil War, 1936–1939' (Royal Holloway University of London, 2015). I would like to thank Richard for his generous help with information and bibliographical suggestions.

52. Lannon, *Privilege*, pp. 199–205; Sid Lowe, *Catholicism, War and the Foundation of Francoism* (Brighton: Sussex Academic Press, 2010), pp. 190–4; Javier Rodrigo, 'Santa guerra civil: Identidad relato y (para) historiografía de la cruzada', in Ferrán Gallego and Francisco Morente (eds), *Rebeldes y reaccionarios: Intelectuales, fascismo y derecha radical en Europa* (Mataró: El Viejo Topo, 2011), pp. 190–2.

53. Michael Richards, 'Civil War, Mass Murder and the Nation State in Spain: Review of Paul Preston, The Spanish Holocaust: Inquisition and Extermination in Twentieth-Century Spain', *Journal of Genocide Research* 16:1 (2014), pp. 148–9.

54. Juan de Iturralde, *El catolicismo y la cruzada de Franco*, vol. 2 (Vienne-Toulouse: Editorial Egi-Indarra, 1960), pp. 56–7; Hilari Raguer, *Gunpowder and Incense: The Catholic Church and the Spanish Civil War* (London: Routledge/Cañada Blanch, 2007), pp. 50–1.

55. Lannon, *Privilege*, pp. 199–201.

56. Antonio Montero Moreno, *Historia de la persecución religiosa* (Madrid: BAC, 1961), p. 762.

57. See, for example, the speech by Socialist politician Indalecio Prieto published in *La Prensa de Gijón* in August 1936. Prieto called on Republicans to: 'meet their [the enemies'] cruelty with your pity, meet their savagery with your mercy, and meet the excesses of the enemy with your generous benevolence'.

58. Thomas, *Faith and the Fury*, pp. 154–7, 164–5.

59. Alfonso Álvarez Bolado, *Para ganar la guerra, para ganar la paz: Iglesia y Guerra Civil, 1936–1939* (Madrid: Universidad Pontifica de Comillas, 1995), pp. 36–7; Casanova, *Iglesia de Franco*, pp. 57–62.

60. Guiliana di Febo, 'De la victoria incondicional a la no reconciliación. El discurso de la propaganda (1937–1939)', in F.J. Lorenzo Pinar (ed.), *Tolerancia y Fundamentalismos en la Historia* (Salamanca: Universidad de Salamanca, 2007), p. 253.

61. Joan Estelrich, *La persecución religiosa en España* (Buenos Aires: Difusión, 1937); Luis Carreras, *Grandeza cristiana de España. Notas sobre la persecución religiosa* (Tolouse: Les Frères Douladoure, 1938). Quotes from Antonio Pérez de Olaguer, *El terror rojo en Cataluña* (Burgos: Ediciones Antisectarias, 1937), pp. 13–16, 63 and *El terror rojo en Andalucía* (Burgos: Ediciones Antisectarias, 1938), pp. 25, 31.

62. Peter Anderson, *The Francoist Military Trials: Terror and Complicity, 1939–1945* (New York and Oxon: Cañada Blanch, 2010), p. 35. See also Rodrigo, 'Santa guerra civil', pp. 192–3.

63. Mary Vincent, 'The Martyrs and the Saints: Masculinity and the Construction of the Francoist Crusade', *History Workshop Journal* 47 (1999), pp. 91–4; Lowe, *Catholicism*, pp. 41–3, 89–90.

64. Gutmaro Gómez Bravo and Jorge Marco, *La obra del miedo: Violencia y sociedad en la España franquista, 1936–1950* (Barcelona: Península, 2011), pp. 70–6.

65. Rodrigo, 'Santa guerra civil', pp. 195–203.

66. Moreno Cantano, 'Juan García Morales', pp. 119–23; José Luis González Gullón, 'Leocadio Lobo, un sacerdote republicano', *Hispania Sacra* LXII 125 (2010), pp. 280–98; Enrique Orsi Portalo, 'Joan Vilar i Costa (1889–1962): catalanista y republicano', in Montero (ed.), *Otra iglesia*, pp. 183–9; Lannon, *Privilege*, p. 102.

67. Leocadio Lobo, 'Open Letter to the Editor of The Times' (June 1938) and 'Primate and Priest' (Press Department of the Spanish Embassy in London); José Manuel Gallegos Rocafull, *Crusade or Class War?: The Spanish Military Revolt* (London: Press Department of the Spanish Embassy, 1937), LSE Archives, COLL MISC 0091/38 and 0091/13; Arasa, *Católicos*, pp. 123–9, 207–12, 273–82.

68. On the evolution of these attitudes see Ryan, 'A gigantic struggle'.

69. González Gullón, 'Leocadio Lobo', p. 280.

70. Gallegos Rocafull, *Crusade or Class War?*

71. Constantino Bayle (1937) and 'Centro de Información Católica Internacional' (1938), as cited in Miguel Ángel Dionisio Vivas, 'Disidencias clericales: hacia un replanteamiento de la imagen

del cura en la segunda república', Seminario de Historia UNED/UCM/Fundación José Ortega y Gasset-Gregorio Marañón, 16 May 2013, p. 16.

72. Juan de Iturralde, *La Guerra de Franco, los Vascos y la Iglesia, Tomo II: Cómo pudo seguir y triunfar la guerra* (San Sebastián: Usúrbil, Gráf. Izarra, 1978), pp. 331–41; Casanova, *Iglesia de Franco*, pp. 161–70.

73. Xavier Corrales Ortega, *De la misa al tajo: la experiencia de los curas obreros* (Universidad de Valencia: Servicio de Publicaciones Universitat de València, 2008), pp. 22–36; Gregorio Alonso, 'Children of a Lesser God: The Political and Pastoral Action of the Spanish Catholic Church', in Gregorio Alonso and Diego Muro (eds), *Politics and Memory of Democratic Transition: The Spanish Model* (London: Routledge, 2010), p. 115; Lannon, *Privilege*, p. 238; Michael Richards, *After the Civil War: Making Memory and Re-Making Spain since 1936* (Cambridge: Cambridge University Press, 2013), p. 251.

74. Richards, *After the Civil War*, pp. 234–5.

75. Mary Vincent, 'Spain', in Tom Buchanan and Martin Conway, *Political Catholicism in Europe, 1918–1965* (Oxford: Clarendon Press, 1996), pp. 126–7.

76. Paul Preston, *The Triumph of Democracy in Spain* (London: Methuen, 1986), p. 30; Audrey Brassloff, *Religion and Politics in Spain* (Basingstoke: Macmillan, 1998), pp. 44–5; Richards, *After the Civil War*, pp. 246–73; Alonso, 'Children of a Lesser God', pp. 120–1.

77. *Público*, 16 August 2011, 25 August 2011.

78. Asamblea Plenaria de la Conferencia Episcopal, 'Orientaciones morales ante la situación actual de España', 23 October 2006.

79. *ABC de Sevilla*, 11 October 2013.

80. *El País*, 8 April 2000.

81. Graham, *War and its Shadow*, p. 126.

82. *ABC*, 22 July 2004 and 28 December 2008; *El País*, 2 May 2007.

83. *The Guardian*, 12 February 2014; *El Mundo*, 30 March 3014; *El País*, 15 August 2014.

84. *Público*, 15 November 2008; *ABC*, 8 August 1997.

85. Stanley Payne, *The Collapse of the Spanish Republic, 1933–1936* (New Haven: Yale University Press, 2006), p. 7; Manuel Álvarez Tardío, *El camino a la democracia en España, 1931–1978* (Madrid: Gota, 2005), p. 35.

86. José Antonio Piqueras, *Cánovas y la derecha española: del magnicidio a los neocon* (Barcelona: Península, 2008), pp. 454–73.

87. *El País*, 8 February 2007 in Gareth Stockey, 'Spain's First Democracy: The 1931 Constitution and its Detractors', in Adam Sharman and Stephen G. H. Roberts (eds), *1812 Echoes: The Cadiz Constitution in Hispanic History, Culture and Politics* (Cambridge: Cambridge Scholars Press, 2013), pp. 314–66.

88. Manuel Ballbé, *Orden público y militarismo en la España constitucional (1812–1983)* (Madrid: Alianza, 1984), pp. 247–303, esp. pp. 247–8; for a conceptual discussion, see Eduardo González Calleja, *El máuser y el sufragio. Orden público, subversión y violencia política en la crisis de la Restauración (1917–1931)* (Madrid: CSIC, 1999), pp. 11–18.

## Further reading

Callahan, W., *The Catholic Church in Spain, 1875–1998*, Washington, DC: Catholic University Press of America, 2000.

Christian, W., *Visionaries: The Spanish Republic and the Reign of Christ*, Berkeley: University of California Press, 1996.

Graham, H., *The War and its Shadow: Spain's Civil War in Europe's Long Twentieth-Century*, Brighton: Sussex Academic Press, 2012.

Lannon, F., *Privilege, Persecution, and Prophecy: The Catholic Church in Spain 1875–1975*, Oxford: Clarendon Press, 1987.

Raguer, H., *Gunpowder and Incense: The Catholic Church and the Spanish Civil War*, London: Routledge/Cañada Blanch, 2007.

Richards, M., *After the Civil War: Making Memory and Re-Making Spain since 1936*, Cambridge: Cambridge University Press, 2013.

Shubert, A., *A Social History of Modern Spain*, New York: Routledge, 2013.

Thomas, M., *The Faith and the Fury: Popular Anticlerical Violence and Iconoclasm in Spain, 1931–1936*, Brighton: Sussex Academic Press, 2012.

Vincent, M., *Spain 1833–2002: People and State*, Oxford: Oxford University Press, 2007.

# CHAPTER 2
## BUILDING ALLIANCES AGAINST THE NEW? MONARCHY AND THE MILITARY IN INDUSTRIALIZING SPAIN
*Francisco J. Romero Salvadó*

### Historiographical perspectives

It is only relatively recently that historians have begun to undertake thorough historical analyses of the Restoration monarchy (1874–1923). For most of the twentieth century, the definition of the Restoration's political system coined by the nineteenth-century essayist Joaquín Costa as 'oligarchy and *caciquismo*' (corruption and clientelism) remained the accepted paradigm. Whether for progressive reformers such as the anticlerical intellectuals of the Second Republic (1931–9) or for propagandists of the Franco dictatorship (1939–75), it was merely a period of economic backwardness and political corruption. For the Francoists, the military coup of 1923 (as much as that of 1936) was an attempt to save a fatherland endangered by an inefficient and even immoral civilian political class. The army was thus on both occasions the instrument of national regeneration, and its respective leaders, Miguel Primo de Rivera and then Franco himself, were Costa's 'iron surgeons', the providential figures supposed to heal the country's perennial ills. In the first years of the democratic transition, in the late 1970s and 1980s, contemporary historians focused primarily on the immediate origins, course and legacy of the civil war, but since the 1990s the Restoration has received increasing scholarly attention.

In recent years, a number of historians, not necessarily conservative-leaning, have stressed the need to re-examine the Restoration period, and to avoid overly deterministic readings, especially binary notions of it as an incorrigibly corrupt system or simply the tool of a narrow elite. These scholars have stressed its proto-democratic potential – the existence of formal constitutional guarantees, a limited degree of representation and a capacity to absorb some persons or interest groups from outside the ruling order. This scholarly shift has to some extent also played into the hands of a distinct group of revisionists, some of whom are historians, many more politicians or pundits, but all with a strongly conservative and present-centred agenda – to draw a direct descent from the Restoration system to Spain's post-1977 constitutional democracy. By doing this they can excise the history and memory of the democratic Second Republic of the 1930s which they view as too egalitarian to be a 'safe' model for the present. Some among this latter group of revisionists go further, declaring the Republic to have been 'illegitimate', or, 'not even a democracy at all'. These conservatives include neo-Francoist authors such as Pío Moa and Cesar Vidal, whose object is to justify outright the military coup of July 1936, but also others who view the turbulence of the 1930s as somehow itself delegitimizing the Republic. This is an odd position given the not inconsiderable turbulence of much of their 'paragon' Restoration, as we will see in this chapter. Ironically too, they ignore how social and political turbulence – whether under monarchy or Republic – and notwithstanding Spain's idiosyncrasies (all countries have them), constituted a broadly similar 'crisis of modernity' to others in Europe at that time, as Spain's polity and society faced accelerating social change in a period of significant urban and economic transformation.[1] Taking this comparative perspective as our point of departure, we can now analyse the key role played by both crown and army in obstructing democratizing political reform in Restoration Spain.

Right from the start, elite military ('praetorian') intervention was key: it had been decisive in creating the Restoration political system, just as in the end it would play a crucial role in destroying it. On 29 December 1874, a palace coup (*pronunciamiento*) restored the Bourbon dynasty to the throne in the person of King Alfonso XII (1875–85). Far from being a democracy, Restoration Spain was the national variant of an 'oligarchic', 'liberal' order still common across Europe. It was known as 'liberal' since it was based on formal constitutional practices and significant civil liberties, such as separation of executive and judicial powers or freedom of association. However, these remained in practice non-existent, for in Spain, as in much of Europe, strong elements of the Old Regime persisted, meaning that real power continued to be monopolized by a small ruling elite or 'oligarchy'.[2] Two dynastic parties – Conservatives and Liberals – succeeded systematically in office, in the so-called *turno pacífico* (peaceful rotation) which allowed key agrarian interests and their clienteles a regular turn in power. Both parties consisted of political notables whose hegemony rested on widespread clientelism, popular apathy (or at least passivity) and – importantly – endemic electoral falsification organized by the local *caciques* (political bosses or bigwigs). This two-party system was eventually toppled by a coup headed by General Miguel Primo de Rivera in September 1923, although the monarchy itself would remain in place until 1931.

Throughout its existence the Restoration system faced a mounting challenge from growing literacy and accelerating (if uneven) industrialization and urbanization, and a crucial question concerned the regime's potential for being reformed from within, to become more genuinely representative of a wider proportion of the population, until one day it could become a democracy. As one of Britain's leading historians of Spain, Raymond Carr, expressed it some thirty years ago: while Primo de Rivera claimed he was finishing off 'a diseased body', he was in fact strangling a 'new birth', since the Restoration system had itself been capable of changing.[3] Carr's view triggered a wide-ranging historiographical debate that continues to this day, not least because it is inseparable from another key question: that of Spain's troubled transition from elite to mass politics. The contributors' essays in a recent study on the crisis of Restoration Spain indicate there is still no consensus over Carr's dictum.[4] One contributor noted the near-impossibility of convergence between the negative and positive assessments of the regime, given the number of variables involved in historical analysis of this complex period.[5] In order to promote further research, this present chapter takes a middle position, if one slightly closer to the negative view. While I have previously argued against Carr's conclusion,[6] it is nevertheless important to stress that even after the Restoration managed to thwart both reformist and revolutionary challenges in 1917, still nothing was predetermined. However, the system's survival that year was dependent on support from crown and army, which rapidly faded as Spain became caught in the cycle of revolutionary tumult spreading across most of Europe in the aftermath of the Great War of 1914–18.

As in other *fin-de-siécle* European regimes, so too in Spain economic modernization (increasing industrialization and urbanization) saw growing worker protest, the spread of labour organizations and a rise in awareness among both rural and urban workers and also more middling urban sectors that they were excluded from any political voice and thus from any real citizenship. This growing protest and dissatisfaction eroded the foundations on which Restoration Spain rested. Still, except for in Russia, the challenge of change – whether revolutionary or democratic – was defeated across Europe by the triumphal march of reinvigorated political reaction. Within these parameters, this chapter will focus on the central role played by the crown and the armed forces in shaping the course and ultimate demise of Spain's constitutional monarchy.

## Praetorian politics in Restoration Spain

Precisely because the consequences of a militarized, non-democratic polity lasted so very long in Spain – until the end of the four decades of the Franco dictatorship in 1975 – it was only then, after the dismantling of the Francoist propaganda apparatus, that elite military interventionism was finally able to become a subject of independent academic study. This began with scholars such as Carlos Seco Serrano who suggested that the colonial disaster of 1898 – with the loss of the overseas empire (Cuba, the Philippines, Puerto Rico) in a war against the United States – marked the 'return of the sabres' to mainland Spain.[7] In other words, colonial defeat put an end to one of the greatest achievements of the Restoration's political settlement: the supremacy of civilian sovereignty. After 1898, an embittered officer corps turned its anger against the domestic political system. A glaring example was the ransacking of the offices of a satirical Catalan journal (*Cu-Cut*) in November 1905, by officers incensed by its publication of an anti-militarist cartoon. Caught between the need to punish the perpetrators and military solidarity, one Liberal cabinet collapsed to be replaced by another more willing to placate the military by passing the Law of Jurisdictions in March 1906. Under this, any offence against the army, the monarchy or the fatherland would be tried by military courts, thus eroding the Constitution.[8]

After 1898, the army grew ever more sensitive to criticism and the division widened between it and the civilian governing class, who the army officers felt had let them down. However, this still did not mark the start of praetorian intervention. Between the 1830s and 1870s, the army had protected the liberal state against both insurrection from below and absolutist reaction. *Pronunciamientos* had been a regular mechanism of political change.[9] While the Restoration system ended this, conditions still ensured that the army would be called on as an instrument to protect the ruling order in an age of mounting protest, and especially given the weakness of the small and under-resourced urban police (in contrast to rural Spain's effective paramilitary constabulary, the Civil Guard).[10] Under the Restoration monarchy then, public order became militarized. Both dynastic parties responded, not only after 1898 but throughout the entire period, to socio-political turmoil with the regular, repeated declaration of martial law, during which constitutional guarantees were suspended – as they would be twenty-five times (in all or part of Spain) between 1875 and 1923.[11] The army was thus allotted the role of the regime's supreme line of political defence and, as such, was never subordinated to civilian sovereignty or the Constitution. For the same reason, governments abstained from tackling military inefficiency, symbolized above all by the bloated officer corps, payment of whose salaries left little for new equipment.[12]

The military also focused popular discontent as Spain began a new colonial adventure in North Africa. In 1906 the international Conference of Algeciras gave Spain control over a strip of land surrounding its possessions of Ceuta and Melilla (Morocco). Then in the summer of 1909 an indigenous revolt led to the call-up of Spanish reservists, mainly composed of poorer constituencies, as middle-class youngsters could afford the 1,500 pesetas required to gain exemption from conscription. This unfairness, combined with the dreadful memories of the malaria-ridden walking wounded of the Cuban wars and then the carnage of 1898, triggered widespread popular unrest. In Barcelona, events exploded into the 'Tragic Week', which saw riots and church-burning, followed by a brutal military repression.[13] But nor was the colonial campaign in Morocco a cause which united Spain's military lobby: in fact it was a source of internal tensions. For a restless officer minority who were fighting in Morocco – the *Africanistas* – the new colonial quest offered the opportunity to prove their bravery and bypass state bureaucracy, thus allowing rapid promotion by war merits. However, peninsular army officers, who were the majority, soon voiced their dissatisfaction. In January 1910, several hundred gathered outside the offices of the military journal *La Correspondencia Militar* to back its campaign to end the easy rewards being handed out in Morocco and a return to adherence to the closed scale of promotions (i.e. based on strict seniority). Although the protest led to some officer punishments and dismissals, including senior ones, the discontent in the peninsular officer corps simmered on.[14]

## Alfonso XIII: King of Swords

As with Europe's other *fin-de-siécle* regimes, Restoration Spain's formal constitutionalism also concealed potential autocracy. The monarch was both the army's commander-in-chief and head of state. He could dissolve parliament, appoint governments (which needed his approval to introduce legislation), sign international treaties and declare war. He also retained vast powers of patronage, conferring titles, granting pardons and appointing dignitaries to Spain's upper chamber.[15]

There is an abundant historical literature which sees Alfonso XIII's exercise of this power in a broadly favourable light.[16] He was certainly a charming man whose outstanding personal courage was proven during the numerous attempts on his life. For instance, on his wedding day to the English Princess Victoria Eugenie of Battenberg (31 May 1906), both miraculously survived the carnage caused by a bomb thrown at the royal carriage, after which the young king attended the wounded, dismissing the incident as 'an occupational hazard'.[17] He also took on an active international role during the Great War of 1914–18 through his founding and funding in July 1915 of a very successful prisoner information service, the Oficina Pro-Cautivos (Bureau for Prisoners) which worked on behalf of prisoners of war and missing civilians of the belligerent countries, as well as organizing humanitarian work such as prisoner exchanges, repatriations and the concession of pardons.[18]

But Alfonso also sought a prominent new role for himself within Spain, in the political decision-making of the state – which contrasted sharply with his father's reign. Born the posthumous son of King Alfonso XII and of the Austrian Archduchess Maria Christina Habsburg-Lorraine (who assumed the role of regent), the young Alfonso had been a sickly boy brought up by military and clerical preceptors and cut off from the real world. Crowned aged 16, in 1902, he ascended the throne under the shadow of the colonial disaster of 1898 and in an age of economic modernization, yet without realizing the significance of either for the monarchy's future. He shocked his ministers during his first meeting with them by reminding them of the extensive prerogatives the Constitution allowed him.[19] Historians who have defended his interventionism present it as a sign of a reformist spirit and see his role as that of a privileged interpreter of the national will, above petty party interests.[20] However, there is a different view.

In Spain foreign policy had traditionally been the preserve of a clique.[21] But under Alfonso XIII, it became even more a specifically royal preserve, as shown by his enthusiastic pursuit of the Moroccan adventure (earning him the sobriquet of 'Alfonso el Africano'); similarly his involvement in Portugal, after the overthrow of the Braganza dynasty in 1910, was a bid to secure some control over the neighbouring country. Alfonso's imperial ambitions and concerns about the safety of his throne brought him close to sectors of the officer corps. An example was his pro-army stance after the Cu-Cut incident in November 1905.[22] Alfonso was also the first Spanish monarch since the sixteenth century to wear military regalia in official ceremonies: he saw himself as a Soldier-King (a recent biography even bears the title Rey de Espadas (King of Swords)).[23]

Spain's constitutional framework, by affirming that national sovereignty was shared by king and parliament, in fact facilitated Alfonso's interference in politics. Indeed, he abused his already extensive prerogatives to appoint and dismiss cabinets – political crises even becoming known as 'orientales', because they were manufactured at the royal palace, the Palacio de Oriente, in order to achieve Alfonso's preferred results.[24] His meddling in governmental affairs undermined civilian sovereignty, causing political instability and obstructing long-term projects. In this regard, the king also exerted a fateful influence on the careers of the two key political leaders of Spain's dynastic political system after 1898: the Conservative leader, Antonio Maura, and the Liberal Party's José Canalejas.

The most influential and controversial statesman of this period, Maura warned in parliament in 1901 that unless a revolution was carried out from above, Spain's monarchy would face a formidable challenge from below.[25] His ultimate objective was to strengthen the monarchy through pertinent administrative and political reforms which would permit the so-called *masas neutras* (the passive masses) to participate actively in public life and rally around the existing social order. During Maura's long period in office (January 1907 to October 1909), he embarked upon an unprecedented cycle of parliamentary activity intended to reform electoral law, the justice system and, above all, local administration, the stronghold of the *caciques*. This reform programme has been described by the leading scholar on Maura as the Restoration's only global project.[26] However, for all his democratizing rhetoric, Maura's approach to politics was intrinsically autocratic: he believed himself infallible and reacted witheringly to anyone he saw as opposing him or even disagreeing. While winning a legion of admirers who regarded him almost as a deity, Maura also aroused unprecedented levels of hostility not only amongst the regime's traditional enemies who saw him as the epitome of tyranny, but also within a dynastic political class wary of any change to the status quo and from a monarch who loathed being relegated from the spotlight.[27] Unlike the Conservatives who could aspire to becoming a modern mass party based on the Catholic middle classes, for the Liberals such a transformation would be harder, for how to attract either the urban middling classes or worker constituencies away from the established republican parties or the organized labour movement? For their own tactical reasons then, the Liberals were even prepared to break the dynastic consensus, joining forces with republicans in a broad bloc to stop the 'clerical and reactionary' Maura.[28] The result was the collapse of most of his proposals. Frustratingly too, the only part salvaged actually exacerbated the system's own flaws, such as the approval of Article 29 (the automatic election of unopposed electoral candidates), which reinforced the power of the local *caciques*.[29]

Maura's downfall came from an unexpected quarter – Morocco. An indigenous revolt there led to the call-up of fresh troops, but this triggered widespread mass protests and riots in Barcelona. After these were savagely repressed by the army, in the aforementioned Tragic Week, a massive international campaign was echoed inside Spain by a vast domestic mobilization (which included the Liberal Party) under the slogan ¡Maura No!. The Conservative government was safe with a large majority, but the king stepped in and 'accepted' a resignation which Maura had not in fact submitted.[30] The historian Joaquín Romero Maura noted: 'By supporting the Liberal veto, King Alfonso bought civil peace and halted political modernization'.[31] A few months later, he exacerbated the factionalism inside the Liberal Party by refusing the decree of dissolution of parliament to the sitting prime minister, instead entrusting power to another leading Liberal, José Canalejas.[32]

A charismatic and congenial leader, Canalejas was regarded at the time, as he also is by some historians today, as the Liberal response to Maura's brand of Conservative reform from above. But Canalejas' programme would be cut short by his assassination by a lone anarchist in November 1912. This frequency of political assassination under the Restoration (its architect, Conservative Party leader Antonio Cánovas del Castillo, had suffered the same fate in August 1897) indicates the structural violence and political exclusion perpetuated by the dynastic system itself.

Canalejas aimed at broadening support for the regime through state intervention in the social sphere. New legislation included the regulation of working conditions, provision of national insurance and the reduction of excise duties on staple products, thus reducing indirect taxation which fell most heavily on the poorest in society. Other measures comprised military reforms such as ending the possibility of buying exemption from conscription, and religious reforms designed to reduce the power of the Catholic Church, including by allowing confessional freedom in public and by restricting the growth of religious orders (via the 'Padlock Law').[33] Unlike Maura, however, Canalejas sought to govern in close collaboration with the king. He thus incensed the anti-dynastic opposition by endorsing the Monarch's interventionist plans in Portugal and his increasing involvement in Morocco (established as a protectorate in 1912). Faced by increasing labour protest, Canalejas' government, for all its vaunted reforms, reverted to the standard repressive measures, including calling out the army and suspending constitutional guarantees. Ironically, while Conservative Maura lectured Congress on the right to strike, the Liberal Canalejas conscripted workers to break the massive rail strike of 1912.[34]

By 1913, the hope of reform from above had vanished. One year after Canalejas' death, and with the Liberals as faction-riddled as ever, the austere, reform-minded Maura too was being sidelined by the monarch, in favour of more 'worldly', complaisant and deferential Conservatives – these epitomized by Eduardo Dato, who formed a government with majority Conservative support in October 1913.[35] The historian Melchor Fernández Almagro wrote: 'Walking on tiptoe, Dato was going far; Maura walking firmly was on his way to [political] exile.'[36] In fact, Maura's defenestration gave way to an unprecedented grass-root mobilization as young conservative middle-class students and some white-collar workers rallied around the vilified leader and even adopted his name: *Mauristas*.[37] But it was symptomatic of the dynastic system that it remained inert before these potentials for relatively less threatening modes of change. After the Great War, Maura would fulfil a different role, as 'the regime's fireman', the leader of monarchist coalitions in difficult times.[38]

## Spain's 1917

The Great War acted everywhere as a catalyst for popular awakening and mass politics, and Spain was no exception. Although spared from the human slaughter, non-belligerent countries were still not immune to its dramatic impact. As the dominant forms of elitist rule broke down, Europe's old regimes were confronted with the unwelcome prospect of more genuine democracy, as popular pressure for reform increased, including in the form of socialism, which was threatening in their eyes.[39]

Thus, as this author has previously observed, 'Spain did not enter the war but the war entered Spain'.[40] Basking in its neutral status, the country enjoyed an unprecedented boom based on the growing industrial and food requirements of the belligerents.

However, the economic upsurge also exacerbated social distress and class conflict inside Spain. While a minority of profiteers and industrial and financial barons enjoyed a golden era of fabulous profits, ordinary people saw their living standards plummet due to shortages of staple goods and soaring prices caused by the export boom, the limits of domestic production and the hoarding of basic goods. Feelings of social injustice and growing distress helped the formation of class consciousness and triggered popular unrest in the form of food riots, fist-fights in markets and strike action.[41] The gathering storm exploded in 1917. In the course and outcome of events, crown and army were both leading protagonists and also the substantial winners.

In April 1917, the unabated campaign of illegal German activities on Spanish soil (sabotage operations, submarine attacks, espionage) spurred on the Liberal Prime Minister Count Romanones, whose Allied sympathies had always been evident,[42] to break diplomatic relations with Germany (as the United States had recently done). But the king promptly blocked this, forcing the resignation of the Romanones government, and, in a typical *oriental* crisis, appointed a rival Liberal cabinet led by the Marquis of Alhucemas. In fact, by 1917, King Alfonso's initial good relations with the Western democracies – cultivated in order to expand Spain's influence in North Africa and neighbouring Portugal – had faded away. The Spanish king was shocked by Allied 'pragmatism' in recognizing the new Provisional Government in Russia which emerged from the revolution and which had ousted his cousin, Tsar Nicholas II. Alfonso believed, almost until the end of the war, that it would end in a stalemate which would place him, through his work with the Bureau for Prisoners, in a privileged position to be the arbitrator in peace negotiations.[43]

One month later, in August 1917, a new royal initiative triggered Spain's turbulent situation alight: its epicentre was located in the Juntas Militares de Defensa. Set up in late 1916, they were quasi-army trade unions, intended to protect the professional interests of officers up to the rank of colonel, that is, those most affected by the war's economic hardship. Although they used the language of reform (ridding the army and Spain's ruling order of corruption), their main concern was to protect their corporate interests (better conditions, pay increases and promotion strictly according to seniority).[44] However, the appearance of Spain's military juntas against the backdrop of the February revolution in Russia led a terrified Alfonso to draw erroneous parallels with the Russian officers who had just advised the Tsar to abdicate: accordingly the Spanish king instructed his government to disband the juntas.[45] Their leaders in Barcelona refused and were arrested. On 1 June, the officers struck back with an ultimatum – either the government accepted their demands or they would withdraw their support. Dumbfounded, Alhucemas' Liberal cabinet resigned.[46] His pro-Allied coreligionary, Romanones, noted that the army was the virtual owner of the country.[47] Nevertheless, the Juntas' was predominantly a corporate triumph, without any real appetite or motive to push for thoroughgoing reform of Spain's dynastic system.

To general disbelief, the monarch called to power the other dynastic party, the Conservatives (led by Dato), as if everything was normal. But as army officers launched an onslaught of praetorian criticism from *La Correspondencia Militar*, against a 'repulsive' regime accused of ruining Spain morally and economically,[48] so this galvanized the opponents of the dynastic system who saw the fall of Tsarism as their signal to act. Although the regime responded with censorship, a suspension of constitutional guarantees and closure of parliament, the Catalan Lliga Regionalista (Lliga) seized the initiative. A socially conservative party with reformist and (Catalan) nationalist objectives, the Lliga did not seek to storm the Bastille but rather to make a peaceful political revolution, precisely to forestall the thoroughgoing social one it believed inevitable if the Restoration regime was not reformed.[49] It summoned an assembly of parliamentarians to gather in Barcelona (19 July 1917) to initiate a process of constitutional reform, including the concession of home rule to Catalonia. Supported by republicans and socialists, who hoped it would be the start of a democratizing political period, the Assembly raised expectations enormously at the time. But it was killed stone dead by Maura himself when he refused to endorse it, despite being urged to by some leading *Mauristas* (including his own sons Gabriel and Miguel), who viewed it as the longed-for 'revolution from above'. Without Maura, the army was unlikely to side with any reform initiative emanating from Catalan nationalists or the left.[50]

Moreover, Maura's stance played into government hands, allowing Prime Minister Dato to regain the initiative, at least in the short term. In August 1917, the Socialists, believing Spain's monarchy, like Russia's, was at its moment of eclipse, led the labour movement into a revolutionary strike in support of the Assembly. But they acted prematurely. Unlike Petrograd, there were no scenes of fraternization between soldiers and strikers. In Spain the dynastic system (which had suffered no process of delegitimation comparable to wartime Tsarism) granted immediate economic concessions to the military juntas and officer corps. This, together with rumours spread by the government itself that Allied gold, bent on pulling Spain into the European war, was behind the general strike, guaranteed the government the army's support. It was unleashed on the strikers, drowning the Spanish revolution in blood.[51]

However, Dato's own victory was short-lived. The officers saw him as a prevaricator who sought to have the army take the political blame for a repression orchestrated and required by the entire dynastic system. On 26 October they therefore petitioned the king to change the government. In return, they guaranteed the dissolution (by force, if necessary) of any future parliamentary assembly that might represent a democratizing challenge to the dynasty. The king, having quickly reversed his earlier criticism of the Juntas, now reassured them of his total support, and promptly complied.[52]

## Towards a praetorian monarchy

The army's repression of parliamentary and labour protest indicates the military's key function as the final guarantor of establishment order, keeping at bay demands for democratization. Even more crucial was the ensuing military petition direct to the king: for historians who argue against the dynastic system's own capacity for self-renewal, this signalled the looming end for the forty-year-old system, even if Liberal-Conservative fearful and faction-ridden governments ground on for a few more years. Historians who take this view see it as sealed by the military disaster in Morocco in summer 1921 when some 9,000 troops perished in the retreat from Annual.[53]

Alternatively, historians taking a more open view of the next few years interpret the Moroccan debacle as an opportunity to rally public opinion behind a patriotic enterprise to avenge national honour. Whether under the immediately ensuing national government headed by Maura, or subsequent dynastic cabinets, these historians see signs of the dynastic parliament genuinely becoming a sounding board for issues of national concern, such as its wide-ranging debates on the responsibilities for Morocco.[54] Moreover, in December 1922, a government formed by all the Liberal factions under Alhucemas was expanded to include moderate republicans of the Reformist Party. Its ambitious programme (constitutional revision, greater religious toleration, reforming the upper house, the installation of a civilian protectorate in Morocco, greater investment in public works) raised expectations that, finally, Spain was embarking upon genuine democratization. According to these historians, the military coup of Primo de Rivera, nine months later, halted this process of modernizing public life just as it also gagged the parliamentary committee enquiring into responsibilities for Annual, whose pending report it was widely supposed would also have personally implicated Alfonso, the Soldier-King.[55]

Both the positive and negative interpretations make valid points but both also display flaws of reasoning. Against the positive school, it can be argued that it was highly improbable that seasoned politicians of the dynastic system such as Romanones or Alhucemas would concede power willingly at a stroke – which is what 'becoming democrats' would have meant. Indeed most of the historiography on the last Restoration government concurs that it was faction-ridden and failed to deliver.[56] A fear of democracy was deeply rooted in the Liberal Party, lacking as it did any sizeable electoral constituency. One of its leaders, Natalio Rivas, commented in his diaries that a clean ballot meant a straight road to political oblivion.[57] Accordingly, the Liberal Party continued to engage as blatantly as ever in vote rigging and corruption during the elections of April 1923. Outside of the big cities where it was no longer possible to manufacture the results (in Madrid, for example, the Socialists obtained five out of the total seven seats), the old ways held, producing a record number of MPs (146) returned uncontested, under Article 29; while more than a third of MPs (144) had family ties to dynastic politicians. Both Alhucemas and Romanones had nine relatives each in parliament. Rivas, a veteran of electoral corruption, had predicted months earlier the final landslide Liberal victory (220 out of 407 MPs), adding that even Alhucemas' wife was involved in the process of ballot-rigging.[58]

By the same token, we should not over-determine the historical outcome as do some historians who tend towards a negative assessment of the dynastic system's internal capacity for change. After the 1917 crisis, the dynastic regime, even though compromised, lasted for six more years and proved remarkably adept at staving off alternatives.[59] Moreover, even though the two dynastic parties were factionalized and, with the exception of *Maurismo*, devoid of any popular base, the anti-dynastic opposition was in a far worse state. Republicans were small urban-based parties with scant followers; leading Socialists, though backed by a substantial labour movement, were traumatized by the memory that after the revolutionary general strike of 1917 the state could have confiscated all their organizational resources (funds, newspapers, buildings, equipment). They thus returned to their traditionally cautious stance and were soon absorbed elsewhere in a bitter debate over whether or not to join the new Third (Communist) International. The other major labour organization, the anarcho-syndicalist Confederación Nacional del Trabajo (CNT) at first capitalized on the tumult following the Russian revolution, in the process expanding rapidly from 15,000 members in 1915 to 700,000 by 1919. But even though it was a formidable mass protest movement, the CNT never represented a *political* threat to the dynastic regime: its actions remained extra-parliamentary, all channelled into direct action (mainly strikes) in the labour and economic sphere, which could be repressed by army and police action. Similarly the CNT's lack of a central or controlling leadership (true to anarchist beliefs, it remained a conglomerate of regional federations) neutralized it as a political opponent to the regime.

After 1917, the dynastic regime did broaden its base by integrating some forces which hitherto had been outsiders – such as the Lliga (1917–18 and 1921–2) and the Reformist Party (1922–3).[60] The discarded *turno* gave way to new formulas which ranged from national governments to faction-based administrations. It was not a lack of willingness but rather an inability to respond successfully to the hugely changed conditions both domestically and internationally that constrained further reform. This is the heart of the matter: the failure in Spain properly to reform the dynastic system was another example of the general crisis that engulfed most of Europe after the 1914–18 war. At this dawning of mass politics, European governments which had represented very limited franchises or a cosmetic constitutionalism, were everywhere eroded by the actions of sectors of the traditional ruling elites who saw them as weak in the face of social unrest and who thus turned to support authoritarian – and military – alternatives.

In Spain, as elsewhere, reports of revolutionary agitation abroad ran parallel with growing labour protest at home. Recent scholarship bears out Lliga leader Francesc Cambó's assessment that the climate in Spain's main industrial capital, Barcelona, paved the way to military dictatorship. But unlike Cambó, it locates the causes of the dynastic regime's demise not only in trade union activism, but also in the attitudes of the Lliga itself, as well as in intransigent employers but, above all, in the army.[61]

Barcelona contained a lethal combination of components: a large radicalized labour force, many middling constituencies imbued with Catalan nationalism, an unyielding employer class and a restless officer corps. All also shared a mistrust of a distant Madrid administration. This explosive situation was ignited by the effects of the Great War (the huge disparity between fast-acquired opulence and an adjacent worker misery – due to inflation of food prices and rents plus an influx of poor peasants lured by the industrial boom). It was events following the Armistice which triggered the destruction of Spain's dynastic regime.

In November 1918, following US President Wilson's declaration in favour of small nations' right of self-determination, the now semi-political insider Lliga launched its campaign for Catalan home rule. In early February 1919, this polarizing issue was compounded by the outbreak of an industrial dispute which lasted 44 days in Barcelona's Traction, Light and Power Company, the Anglo-Canadian main electricity supplier of the city (known as *La Canadiense*).

Both the Catalanist and labour conflicts opened a chasm between the government and Barcelona's local garrison. In office since December 1918, Romanones showed a willingness to find conciliatory formulas to address both challenges. He kept channels open with the Lliga's leaders, appointed by royal decree an extra-parliamentary commission to produce a draft statute of autonomy and instructed the authorities to avoid repressive measures.[62] The government also finally opted for negotiation in the *Canadiense*. A new civil governor and chief of police together with the cabinet undersecretary were sent to Barcelona. Under the final settlement, the company had to recognize the CNT as the official workers' collective representative and satisfy the bulk of its employees' demands. In turn, the government promised to release all those imprisoned during the strike and introduced an eight-hour day in the construction sector, the first in Europe to do so.[63] By contrast, army officers, incensed by what they perceived as separatist insults to the sacrosanct unity of the fatherland, joined the newly emerged Patriotic League and, often in civilian dress, joined violent street brawls. They counted on the sympathy of their senior commanders including Captain General Joaquín Milans del Bosch.[64]

The *Canadiense*'s outcome was for them the final straw. For the first time, calls were made in the right-wing press for a dictatorship to save Spain.[65] Bordering on military sedition, Milans refused to comply on the sensitive question of the jailed militants in order to sabotage the social truce.[66] The CNT fell into the trap and declared a general strike on 24 March 1919. Without consulting Madrid, the Captain General decreed martial law. A bewildered government suspended constitutional guarantees across the country. The deployment in the streets of one particular entity, the Somatén, indicates the close collaboration between the military and the reorganized employers' federation of Barcelona (Patronal). The Somatén, once a rural constabulary designed to combat petty theft, was now functioning, in Barcelona, and soon in other Spanish cities, as the local variant of the continent-wide counter-revolutionary militias that emerged from the First World War.[67] Its ranks included humble shopkeepers but organizational command was held by aristocrats and rich industrialists and ultimately by the captains general.

Apart from inflicting a lethal blow to the labour movement, the behaviour of the Barcelona garrison suggests that it intended to subvert the constitutional order. During the general strike, the government itself sought a conciliatory formula (legislation for a compulsory scheme of workers' pensions and it agreed to extend the eight-hour working day to all industrial sectors from 1 October). But the army's response was swingeing. On 14 April, the civil governor and the chief of police were 'invited' to catch the train to Madrid, which in turn provoked the cabinet's resignation.[68] This outcome seems in retrospect a dress rehearsal for the coup of 1923, and an early example of the increasingly violent forms of reaction appearing across Europe after the First World War when state authority came to be implicitly invested in ad hoc paramilitary forces tasked with the defence of the established political order. Indeed in 1921 the Italian Marxist leader, Antonio Gramsci, one of the twentieth century's greatest political thinkers, even discerned in Spain the precursor of fascism.[69]

The Lliga, fearful of losing its conservative support, put its autonomist demands on the back burner and identified with the praetorian-led offensive.[70] The next three years saw the intensification of an authoritarian climate in Catalonia. Governments lived under the threat of a parallel power in the shadows. For instance, in late 1919 when the new Conservative administration attempted to restore social harmony by establishing a state-sponsored Joint Employer and Labour Arbitration Commission, this was sabotaged by the Patronal which declared a lock-out (3 November 1919 to 26 January 1920) which had the support of both the Captain General and the king.[71] Intended to starve the workers into abandoning the CNT, it left a quarter of a million people jobless. The subsequent vicious circle of bloodshed, into which all of Spain, but particularly Catalonia, began to sink, provided the justification to persuade the Dato administration in November 1920 to appoint as the new civil governor of Barcelona, General Severiano Martínez Anido, who then during his nearly two years in office, imposed an unprecedented reign of terror.[72]

What brought about the military coup of September 1923 in Spain was a confluence of particular national and international factors. Whether the Conservative cabinet headed by José Sánchez Guerra, in power since March 1922, and the Liberal coalition which succeeded him in December, really intended to initiate a process of genuine democratic reform is debatable, but they did constitute a bid to normalize public life and reinstate the rule of law after nearly three years of constitutional suspension. With regard to Morocco, the government moved to establish a civilian form of protectorate and, much to the fury of the king, appointed a cross-party select committee to investigate the question of responsibilities for the Moroccan defeat.[73] Constitutional guarantees once again functioned and the system of terror was dismantled. This meant that from October 1922 the state was neutral in social disputes, trade unions were free to organize, and hardliners such as Martínez Anido and his henchman, Barcelona's chief of police, General Miguel Arlegui, were removed from office. But the political tide abroad continued running in the opposite direction: when Mussolini took power, in October 1922, backed by Italy's social and political elites, the move was hailed by Spain's right-wing press which called upon a Spanish Mussolini to arise.[74]

The Italian Fascist example as well as the resurgence of the CNT inside Spain brought a return to the backlash of 1919 against the dynastic political system. Only this time the 'praetorian option' no longer aimed at a temporary solution (toppling specific cabinets) but rather sought to overthrow the Restoration regime entirely. Willing to take this step was the Captain General of Barcelona, Miguel Primo de Rivera, an aristocrat from one of Spain's leading landowning families. Previously, as Captain General of Valencia (another centre of class conflict), Primo had concluded that the existing system was not robust enough to combat social turmoil.[75] Upon his transfer to Barcelona in 1922, he became the hero of the political establishment when he bypassed the local authorities in order to break a massive transport strike which between May and July 1923 had brought back memories of the *Canadiense*'s. Then, on the night of 12 September 1923, he staged his coup.

But Primo's claim that the ruling order's debility justified his actions was disingenuous: the coup was no mercy killing, for it had been the military's own prior actions over a number of years which had actually subverted and eroded the stability of the Restoration system and which was thus in large measure responsible for the political debility to which Primo referred. 1923 was also a precedent for the civil-war-provoking military conspiracy of July 1936 when it too claimed to be 'saving' Spain from the twin threats of social unrest and civilian politicians' mismanagement. Thus Primo and his backers formed part of the wave of radicalized conservatism which engulfed Europe in the wake of the First World War. In Spain, as sometimes elsewhere, the military provided the lynchpin of a broader counter-revolutionary coalition. In 1923, Primo's coup was wholeheartedly endorsed by Catalonia's economic elites. At the sharp end of confronting strikes and social unrest in the city, they knew that new structures were needed to stabilize labour relations and to achieve closer cooperation between government and business, and for many the safest route to this was via the enforced integration of labour into a corporatist bargaining system supervised by a strong state (*sindicalización forzosa*) which would manage economic modernization from above.[76]

Some scholars have argued that Alfonso XIII was ignorant of the military conspiracy, and that given the discrediting of his political class, he simply went along with a coup which nobody was prepared to oppose.[77] But key contemporary witnesses of the events considered it implausible that the monarch could have been taken so completely by surprise.[78] Even those scholars who forego judgement on whether the king was involved in the coup mostly agree that he was ultimately responsible for its outcome.[79] To make a contrasting case, in February 1981, his grandson King Juan Carlos faced an even bleaker coup situation when his entire parliament was held hostage. In 1981 as in 1923, most senior commanding army officers adopted a stance of 'negative *pronunciamiento*' (neither actively with the coup nor predisposed to fight it). Juan Carlos's public opposition saw the 1981 coup fall apart. By contrast, his grandfather's silence signalled acquiescence, thus ensuring the triumph of Primo's coup in 1923. Alfonso, increasingly critical of the two-party Restoration political system, had already confided his readiness to act to the British ambassador in August 1923.[80] That month too, Antonio Maura was spurred to action when informed by his son Gabriel that the king was toying with the idea of a personal dictatorship. In an attempt to dissuade him, he advised Alfonso to let 'those who do not let others govern assume the responsibility of government themselves'.[81] That is what the king did when the coup caught him on vacation in San Sebastián. Instead of expressing support for constitutional legality, Alfonso left it to the chief of his royal household, the well-known hardliner General Milans del Bosch, to sound out opinion amongst the different garrisons. Once their loyalty to the crown regardless of its position was confirmed, the king travelled to Madrid the next day, dismissed his government and called Primo to form a military cabinet. Rather than troubled, pictures showed the king with a broad smile.[82] Faced with the threat of mass politics in an age of rapid modernization, Alfonso bet on an authoritarian formula of social control to be implemented via the safe hands of the army. Little did he know then that he was signing not only the death warrant of the dynastic political system but also of his own throne.

## Notes

1. For an introductory analysis in English of recent scholarship vis-à-vis the old reductionist paradigm see Javier Moreno Luzón, *Modernizing the Nation* (Brighton: Sussex Academic Press, 2012), pp. 1–6. See also Mercedes Cabrera and Fernando del Rey, 'De la Oligarquía y el caciquismo a la política de intereses. Por una relectura de la Restauración', in Manuel Suárez Cortina (ed.), *Las máscaras de la libertad* (Madrid: Marcial Pons, 2003), pp. 289–325; Manuel Suárez Cortina, 'La Restauración y el fin del imperio colonial. Un balance biográfico', in Suárez Cortina (ed.), *La Restauración, entre el liberalismo y la democracia* (Madrid: Alianza, 1997), pp. 31–107; and works by Ángeles Barrio Alonso, *La modernización de España, 1917–1939* (Madrid: Síntesis, 2004), pp. 211–42 and 'Introducción: La crisis del régimen liberal en España, 1917–1923', *Ayer* 63:3 (2006), pp. 11–21.

2. Cf. Arno Mayer, *The Persistence of the Old Regime* (London: Croom Helm, 1981). It covers Great Britain, Russia, France, Austria-Hungary and Italy.

3. Raymond Carr, *Spain, 1808–1975*, 2nd ed. (Oxford: Oxford University Press, 1982), p. 523.

4. Francisco J. Romero Salvadó and Angel Smith, 'The Agony of Spanish Liberalism and the Origins of Dictatorship', in Romero Salvadó and Smith (eds), *The Agony of Spanish Liberalism* (Basingstoke: Palgrave/Macmillan, 2010), p. 10.

5. Javier Moreno Luzón, 'Los políticos liberales y la crisis del liberalismo', in Suárez Cortina, *Las máscaras*, pp. 360–1 and 'The Government, Parties and the King, 1913–1923', in Romero Salvadó and Smith, *The Agony*, pp. 32–61: p. 56.

6. Francisco J. Romero Salvadó, *Foundations of Civil War* (London: Routledge, 2008), p. ix.

7. Carlos Seco Serrano, *Militarismo y civilismo en la España contemporánea* (Madrid: IEC, 1984), pp. 232–3.

8. Ibid., pp. 238–44.

9. Carr, *Spain*, p. 215.

10. *El Debate* (7 August 1920) placed the figure at 7,000 police agents at the time, while London alone then had 25,000. Fernando del Rey Reguillo, *Propietarios y patronos: la política de las organizaciones económicas en la España de la Restauración, 1914–23* (Madrid: Ministerio del Trabajo y Seguridad Social, 1992), pp. 452–5.

11. Manuel Ballbé, *Orden público y militarismo en la España constitucional, 1812–1983* (Madrid: Alianza, 1985), pp. 247–50; Joaquim Lleixá, *Cien años de militarismo en España* (Madrid: Anagrama, 1986), pp. 60–1. Fundación Antonio Maura, *Antonio Maura's Papers* (AAM), 273/4.

12. In 1900, there were 499 generals, 578 colonels and over 23,000 officers for some 80,000 troops (six times more officers than in France which had a standing army of 180,000 soldiers). Figures in Seco Serrano, *Militarismo*, p. 233.

13. The best study remains Joan Connelly Ullman, *The Tragic Week. Anticlericalism in Spain, 1875–1912* (Cambridge, MA: Harvard University Press, 1968). Voluminous documentation can be found in Archivo del Palacio Real (AGPR), *Alfonso XIII's Reign*, 15418/8.

14. Biblioteca de la Real Academia de la Historia (BRAH), *Natalio Rivas' Papers* (ANR), 11/8896 (10–12 January 1910) and 11/8897 (14–15 January 1910). For army tensions see Stanley Payne, *Los militares y la política en la España contemporánea* (Madrid: Ruedo Ibérico, 1968), pp. 107–8; Carolyn P. Boyd, *Praetorian Politics in Liberal Spain* (Chapel Hill: The University of North Carolina Press, 1979), p. 41; Sebastian Balfour, *Deadly Embrace: Morocco and the Road to the Civil War* (Oxford: Oxford University Press, 2002), p. 158.

15. Pedro Carasa, 'La Restauración Monárquica (1875–1902)', in Ángel Bahamonde (ed.), *Historia de España. Siglo XX, 1875–1939* (Madrid: Cátedra, 2000), pp. 45–7.

16. For example, Pilar de Baviera and Derek Chapman-Huston, *Alfonso XIII* (Barcelona: Juventud, 1945); Julián Cortés Cavanillas, *Alfonso XIII* (Barcelona: Juventud, 1966); Victor Espinos Moltó, *Alfonso XIII, espejo de neutrales* (Madrid: Revista de archivos, 1977); Javier Tusell and Genoveva Queipo de Llano, *Alfonso XIII* (Madrid: Taurus, 2001); Juan Pando, *Un rey para la esperanza* (Madrid: Temas de Hoy, 2002); and Carlos Seco Serrano, *Alfonso XIII y la crisis de la Restauración* (Barcelona: Ariel, 1969) and *La España de Alfonso XIII* (Madrid: Espasa Calpe, 2002).

17. Cortés Cavanillas, *Alfonso XIII*, p. 125.

18. Vast records of the *Oficina Pro-Cautivos* are in AGPR, 12,106/1, 12,788/1, 15,624/7, 16,232/4 and 16,240/3. For a summary see Pando, *Un Rey*, pp. 479–81.

19. Conde De Romanones, *Notas de una vida* (Madrid: Marcial Pons, 1999), pp. 160–1.

20. Seco Serrano, *Alfonso XIII*, pp. 52–3.

21. Fernando García Sanz, *España en la Gran Guerra: Espías, diplomáticos y traficantes* (Barcelona: Galaxia Gutenberg, 2014), p. 23.

22. Romanones, *Notas*, p. 209.

23. Gabriel Cardona, *Alfonso XIII, el rey de espadas* (Barcelona: Planeta, 2010). See also Carolyn P. Boyd, 'El Rey-Soldado', in Javier Moreno Luzón (ed.), *Alfonso XIII* (Madrid: Marcial Pons, 2003), pp. 216–18.

24. Cardona, *Alfonso XIII*, p. 64.

25. Gabriel Maura and Melchor Fernández Almagro, *Por qué cayó Alfonso XIII* (Madrid: Ambos Mundos, 1948), p. 40.

26. María Jesús González Hernández, *El universo conservador de Antonio Maura* (Madrid: Biblioteca Nueva, 1997).

27. María Jesús González Hernández, '"Neither God nor Monster": Antonio Maura and the Failure of Conservative Reformism in Restoration Spain, 1893–1923', *European History Quarterly* 32:3 (2002), pp. 307–34: p. 309.

28. Appendix by Joaquín Romero Maura, in Raymond Carr, *España, 1808–1975* (Barcelona: Ariel, 1983), pp. 468–74.

29. Teresa Carnero, 'Élite gobernante dinástica e igualdad política en España', *Historia Contemporánea* 8 (1992), pp. 59–64.

30. Maura and Fernández Almagro, *Por qué,* p. 155.

31. Romero Maura, in Carr, *España,* p. 474.

32. ANR, 11/8898 (9 February 1910).

33. Moreno Luzón, *Modernizing*, pp. 61–3; Salvador Forner Muñoz, 'La crisis del liberalismo en España y en Europa: Canalejas en la encrucijada de la Restauración', in Suárez Cortina, *La Restauración*, pp. 199–228: pp. 199, 216–18.

34. Francisco J. Romero Salvadó, 'Antonio Maura: From Messiah to Fireman', in Alejandro Quiroga and Miguel Ángel del Arco Blanco (eds), *Right-Wing Spain in the Civil War Era* (London: Continuum, 2012), pp. 1–26: p. 8. On royal imperialist designs see Hilario de la Torre, *El imperio y el rey* (Mérida: Junta de Extremadura, 2002), pp. 79–87. See also ANR, 11/8899–8902 (January–November 1911). For the Socialists' harsh criticism of Canalejas see correspondence from Pablo Iglesias to Isidoro Acevedo (November 1910–October 1912), Fundación Pablo Iglesias.

35. Tellingly, days before, Dato had signed a letter to Maura with '*tu súbdito*' (your servant): AAM, 34 (19 October 1913). For Maura's attitude see BRAH, *Eduardo Dato's Papers* (AED), Maura to Dato (23 October 1913). The crucial role played by the king in Maura's downfall is in ANR, 11/8893 (10 and 30 June 1913). See also Maura and Fernández Almagro, *Por qué*, pp. 258–64.

36. Melchor Fernández Almagro, *Historia del Reinado de Alfonso XIII* (Barcelona: Montaner, 1977), p. 191.

37. Ángel Ossorio, *Mis Memorias* (Buenos Aires: Losada, 1948), pp. 103–4.

38. Maura's close collaborator, Cesar Silió, coined the term 'Fireman'. Romero Salvadó, 'Antonio Maura', pp. 12–19.

39. Martin Blinkhorn, 'Introduction: Allies, Rivals or Antagonists? Fascists and Conservatives in Modern Europe', in Martin Blinkhorn (ed.), *Fascists and Conservatives* (London: Unwyn Hyman, 1990), pp. 1–13: p. 3.

40. Francisco J. Romero Salvadó, *Spain 1914–18* (London: Routledge, 1999), p. ix.

41. Instituto de Reformas Sociales, *Movimientos de precios al por menor en España durante la guerra y la posguerra* (Madrid: Sobrinos de la Sociedad de M. Minuesa, 1923), pp. 10–11. See also Benjamin Martin, *The Agony of Modernization* (Ithaca, NY: Cornell University Press, 1990), pp. 177–9. A draft of the note including a list of German subversive deeds in Spain is in BRAH, *Count Romanones' Papers* (ACR), 63/46 (April 1917).

42. On 19 August 1914, Romanones published an editorial titled 'Neutralidades que matan' (Fatal Neutrality) in his mouthpiece, *El Diario Universal*, where he advocated closer alignment with the Allies.

43. For the crisis of April 1917 see Romanones, *Notas*, pp. 384–6; Romero Salvadó, *Spain 1914–1918*, pp. 77–84; Ron M. Carden, *German Policy Toward Neutral Spain, 1914–18* (New York: Garland, 1987), pp. 172–8. A good analysis of the crown's changing stance is in National Archives, *Foreign Office Papers* (FO), FO 371-3033/96,857, report by Military Attaché Jocelyn Grant (5 May 1917).

44. Benito Márquez and José M. Capó, *Las juntas militares de defensa* (La Habana: Porvenir, 1923), pp. 23–5; Boyd, *Praetorian*, pp. 50–8.

45. Romanones, *Notas*, pp. 413–16.

46. Juan Antonio Lacomba, *La crisis española de 1917* (Málaga: Ciencia Nueva, 1970), pp. 124–37. A letter of the artillery captain Salvador Furiol explaining plans for a coup if the government resisted is in AAM, 402/22 (5 June 1917).

47. Romanones, *Notas*, p. 416.

48. *La Correspondencia Militar* (6–10 June 1917).

49. Lacomba, *La crisis*, p. 201.

50. Despite his scathing criticism of the regime in general, and of the Dato administration in particular, Maura's old-fashioned legalism prevented him from backing any alternative which could imperil the throne. See Romero Salvadó, *Foundations*, pp. 78–80.

51. A narrative of the August events is in Fernando Soldevilla, *El año político de 1917* (Madrid: Julio Cosano, 1918), pp. 370–98. On slanderous claims about foreign gold see FO 185-1346/433 and 371-3034/175,803, Hardinge to Balfour (24 and 31 August 1917). See also Eduardo González Calleja and Paul Aubert, *España, Francia y la Primera Guerra Mundial, 1914–1919* (Madrid: Alianza, 2014). For socialist optimism see Andrés Saborit, *La huelga de agosto de 1917* (México City: Pablo Iglesias, 1967), pp. 68–9.

52. Francisco J. Romero Salvadó, 'Spain's Revolutionary Crisis of 1917: A Reckless Gamble', in Romero Salvadó and Smith, *The Agony*, pp. 62–91. The army's message in Márquez and Capó, *Las Juntas*, pp. 216–23.

53. For the deadly blow embodied by the crisis of 1917 see Lacomba, *La crisis*, p. 287; Maura and Fernández Almagro, *Por qué*, p. 308. The shattering blow of Annual noted in Charles J. Esdaile, *Spain in the Liberal Age* (London: Blackwell, 2000), p. 252; and Seco Serrano, *Militarismo*, pp. 292–3.

54. Pablo La Porte, 'The Moroccan Quagmire and the Crisis of Spanish Liberalism, 1917–23', in Romero Salvadó and Smith, *The Agony*, pp. 230–54: pp. 236–7.

55. Shlomo Ben-Ami, *Fascism from Above* (Oxford: Oxford University Press, 1983), pp. 19–24; Boyd, *Praetorian*, pp. 238–9.

56. As recognized by its labour minister, Joaquín Chapaprieta, *La paz fue posible* (Barcelona: Ariel, 1971), p. 130. See, for instance, María Teresa González Calbet, 'La destrucción del sistema político de la Restauración: el golpe de Septiembre de 1923', in José Luis García Delgado (ed.), *La crisis de la Restauración: España entre la Primera Guerra Mundial y la II República* (Madrid: Siglo XXI, 1986), pp. 101–20; José María Marín Arce, *Santiago Alba y la crisis de la Restauración* (Madrid: UNED, 1990), p. 251; José Luis Gómez Navarro, *El régimen de Primo de Rivera* (Madrid: Cátedra, 1991), pp. 490–1; Javier Tusell, *Radiografía de un golpe de estado: El ascenso al poder del General Primo de Rivera* (Madrid: Alianza, 1987), pp. 266–7; Thomas G. Trice, *Spanish Liberalism in Crisis* (London: Garland, 1991), pp. 283, 295–8.

57. ANR, 11/8904 (29 October 1917).

58. ANR, 11/8909 (January 1923); Archivo Histórico Nacional, *Serie A Gobernación* (AHN), 29A/3-7 (January–April 1923).

59. Quintin Hoare and Geoffrey Nowell Smith (eds), *Selection from the Prison Notebooks of Antonio Gramsci* (London: Lawrence and Wishart, 1986), p. 276.

60. Created in 1912, the Reformist Party initially had support from intellectuals and progressive sectors of the middle classes. But its greater commitment to democratic possibilism than to republicanism saw this support gradually fade when the party joined a monarchist administration in 1923.

61. Jesús Pabón, *Cambó, 1876–1947* (Barcelona: Alpha, 1999), p. 921; Soledad Bengoechea, '1919: La Barcelona colpista; L'aliança de patrons i militars contra el sistema liberal', *Afers* 23/24 (1996), pp. 309–327: p. 311; Romero Salvadó, *Foundations*, p. 192; Angel Smith, 'The Catalan Counter-revolutionary Coalition and the Primo de Rivera Coup, 1917–1923', *European History Quarterly* 37:1 (2007), pp. 7–34: pp. 28–9.

62. ACR, 10/6, Romanones' notes (December 1918) and 12/31, exchanges with Civil Governor Carlos González Rothwos (December 1918–January 1919) 19/20. Francesc Cambó, *Memorias* (Barcelona: Alianza, 1987), pp. 295–7. Javier Moreno Luzón, *Romanones* (Madrid: Alianza, 1998), p. 363.

63. Albert Balcells, *El Sindicalisme a Barcelona, 1916–23* (Barcelona: Nova Terra, 1965), pp. 67–76; and Joaquim Ferrer, *Simó Piera* (Barcelona: Portic, 1975), pp. 78 96. See also FO 371-4120/35476, Hardinge's report (18 March 1919).

64. ACR, 20/18 (December 1918–January 1919); AAM, 67/43, Milans to Maura (15 January 1919).

65. *El Debate* (12 and 19 March 1919); *La Acción* (8 March 1919); *La Correspondencia Militar* (10 and 17 March 1919).

66. Romanones, *Notas*, p. 434.

67. Eduardo González Calleja and Fernando del Rey, *La defensa armada contra la revolución* (Madrid: CSIC, 1995), pp. 74–96. AHN, 59/9, Somatenes (1919–1923).

68. Milans' seditious stance can be seen in AED, 83 (April 1919) and ACR, 20/5 and 96/60 (April 1919). See also Romanones, *Notas*, pp. 436–45. The collaboration between the army and the employers can be seen in AHN, 57A.

69. Antonio Gramsci, 'On Fascism, 1921', in David Beetham (ed.), *Marxists in the Face of Fascism* (Manchester: Manchester University Press, 1983), pp. 82–7: pp. 82–3.

70. Angel Smith, 'The Lliga Regionalista, the Catalan Right and the Making of the Dictatorship of Primo de Rivera, 1916–23', in Romero Salvadó and Smith, *The Agony*, pp. 145–74: pp. 155–7.

71. AHN, 45A/13, *Federación Patronal* (October–December 1919). Soledad Bengoechea, *El Locaut de Barcelona* (Barcelona: Curial, 1998).

72. Maria Amàlia Pradas Baena, *L'anarquisme i les lluites socials a Barcelona 1918–1923* (Barcelona: l'Abadia de Montserrat, 2003), pp. 157–202.

73. According to Romanones (*Notas*, p. 465), the king described it as 'temerity'.

74. *El Correo Catalán* (31 October 1922); *El Debate* (26 November 1922); *La Acción* (30 October 1922).

75. AED, Primo de Rivera to Dato (22 and 26 January 1921).

76. Angel Smith, 'The Catalan Counter-revolutionary', pp. 15–16; Fernando del Rey Reguillo, 'El Capitalismo Catalán y Primo de Rivera: En torno a un golpe de estado', *Hispania* XLVIII: 168 (1988), pp. 294–307; Soledad Bengoechea, *Organització Patronal i conflictivitat social a Catalunya* (Barcelona: l'Abadia de Montserrat, 1994), pp. 279–83.

77. Seco Serrano is the Monarch's strongest advocate. See for instance his *Militarismo* (pp. 308–9) and *Alfonso XIII* (pp. 158–62). See also Tusell, *Radiografía*, pp. 268–9; Marín, *Santiago Alba*, p. 244.

78. Romanones, *Notas*, pp. 473–4; Gabriel Maura, *Bosquejo histórico de la dictadura* (Madrid: Tipografía de archivos, 1930), pp. 27–8.

79. See, amongst others, Boyd, 'El Rey-Soldado', pp. 235–7; Romero Salvadó, *Foundations*, pp. 292–4; Cardona, *Alfonso XIII*, pp. 206–12; Gómez Navarro, *El régimen*, pp. 107–121; María Teresa González Calbet, *La Dictadura de Primo de Rivera* (Madrid: El Arquero, 1987), pp. 111–16; Moreno Luzón, *Modernizing*, pp. 140–3.

80. FO 371/9490-27 (2 August 1923).

81. AAM, 259/7-8 (August 1923).

82. The picture of a smiling king can be seen in Moreno Luzón, *Alfonso XIII*, p. 338.

## Further reading

Balfour, S., *Deadly Embrace: Morocco and the Road to the Civil War*, Oxford: Oxford University Press, 2002.

Ben-Ami, S., *Fascism from Above: The Dictatorship of Primo de Rivera in Spain, 1923–1930*, Oxford: Oxford University Press, 1983.

Blinkhorn, M., 'Introduction: Allies, Rivals or Antagonists? Fascists and Conservatives in Modern Europe', in M. Blinkhorn (ed.), *Fascists and Conservatives*, London: Unwyn Hyman, 1990, pp. 1–13.

Boyd, C.P., *Praetorian Politics in Liberal Spain*, Chapel Hill: The University of North Carolina Press, 1979.

Carden, R.M., *German Policy Toward Neutral Spain, 1914–18*, New York: Garland, 1987.

Carr, R., *Spain, 1808–1975*, Oxford: Oxford University Press, 1982.

Connelly Ullman, J., *The Tragic Week. Anticlericalism in Spain, 1875–1912*, Cambridge, MA: Harvard University Press, 1968.

Esdaile, C.J., *Spain in the Liberal Age: From Constitution to Civil War, 1808–1939*, Oxford: Blackwell, 2000.

González Hernández, M.J., '"Neither God nor Monster": Antonio Maura and the Failure of Conservative Reformism in Restoration Spain, 1893–1923', *European History Quarterly* 32:3 (2002), pp. 307–34.

Martin, B., *The Agony of Modernization. Labor and Industrialization in Spain*, Ithaca, NY: Cornell University Press, 1990.

Mayer, A., *The Persistence of the Old Regime,* London: Croom Helm, 1981.

Moreno Luzón, J., *Modernizing the Nation. Spain during the Reign of Alfonso XIII, 1902–1931*, Brighton: Sussex Academic Press, 2012.

Romero Salvadó, F.J., *Spain 1914–18: Between War and Revolution*, London: Routledge, 1999.

Romero Salvadó, F.J., *Foundations of Civil War. Revolution, Social Conflict and Reaction in Liberal Spain, 1916–1923*, London: Routledge, 2008.

Romero Salvadó, F.J., 'Antonio Maura: From Messiah to Fireman', in A. Quiroga and M.A. del Arco Blanco (eds), *Right-Wing Spain in the Civil War Era*, Continuum: London, 2012, pp. 1–26.

Romero Salvadó, F.J and A. Smith (eds), *The Agony of Spanish Liberalism*, Basingstoke: Palgrave Macmillan, 2010.

Smith, A., 'The Catalan Counter-revolutionary Coalition and the Primo de Rivera Coup, 1917–1923', *European History Quarterly* 37:1 (2007), pp. 7–34.

Trice, T.G., *Spanish Liberalism in Crisis: A Study of the Liberal Party during Spain's Parliamentary Collapse, 1913–1923*, London: Garland, 1991.

# CHAPTER 3
# REFORM AS PROMISE AND THREAT: POLITICAL PROGRESSIVES AND BLUEPRINTS FOR CHANGE IN SPAIN, 1931–6

*Helen Graham*

Spain's Second Republic was born in April 1931 at a moment of gathering crisis across Europe, with the rise since 1918 of political authoritarianism and fascism, and since 1929 of an intensifying economic depression. In Spain too there was a crisis-in-waiting, but first came a political opportunity for sectors of society who aspired to progressive forms of change. The Republic enshrined a powerful will to domestic structural change, sustained by different (and sometimes contradictory) progressive political forces who would clash – fiercely – both with each other and also with those political sectors, new as well as old, who opposed democratizing, socially levelling change (although not all for the same reasons). These latter groups clung to a dream of stasis, and to this purpose sought to reinforce social and political hierarchy in ways that resonated with other contemporary conflicts right across Europe, in what were also battles to decide the shape of the social and political future, just as they were in Spain. This chapter will look at the crowded Republican period from 1931, but will concentrate particularly on the struggles for reform during the coalition government of 1931–3, what type of reforms were tabled, and how these were to be achieved. It will also look at the significance of forms of counter-mobilization, which emerged concurrently and then became interlocked with the movements for reform, the two shaping each other quite considerably during the period 1933–6. This chapter does not consider what later happened to the projects for reform and counter-reform after the anti-reform military coup of 17–18 July 1936, when the subsequent escalation to full-scale war, enabled by Nazi and Fascist support, would transform Spain's domestic environment. Moreover, this internationalization of the war also mostly removed control over outcomes from all Republican actors, as the locus of control shifted to external European players – including, crucially, Britain (on this see my essay introducing this volume).

The historiography of the Republican period, 1931–6, would come of age fully in the post-Franco era of archival thaw inside Spain during the 1980s, although it has taken rather longer to open up a dialogue with the comparative historiography of the interwar European period more broadly, in order to allow the scholarship on Spain an important extra avenue of conceptual and theoretical enrichment. In itself the historiography on Republican Spain has been throughout – and remains still – a hugely contested and polemical one.[1] In part this is because of the political charge it still carries, a result of its later discursive entanglement with Francoism and the Cold War, which is to say, the ways in which the Franco regime itself subsequently spun the history of Spain's 1930s for its own political purposes (again see my essay introducing this volume). These same, Cold War-related factors may also partly explain why the history of the Second Republic still remains distant from the comfort zone of other jobbing Europeanists, although this may also be an issue of language, as relatively little of this specialist historiography on 1930s Spain is available in English (or French). In some part too, the strength and durability of the disagreements between historians of the Second Republic is also due to the sheer complexity of the 1931–6 period itself: a polemical historiography, then, for a period which, in Spain as in many places across Europe, the tectonic plates had shifted as a result of the 1914–18 war, producing accelerating clashes over different ways of organizing polity and society.

But it is also true that since the turn of the twenty-first century some of the arguments, and presentational styles, of the historical revisionists in Spain – many of whom focus on the period of 1931–6 – seem to have become more and more caught up with concerns of the political present or future, in what is their implicit (more occasionally explicit) refusal to countenance social democratic policies and goals as legitimate ones per se. Revisionists tend to focus their explicit criticism on the social turbulence such reforms produced in 1930s Spain, particularly from 1934, although they seem peculiarly oblivious to similar eruptions of violence when provoked by the (usually anti-reform) policies or interventions of Spain's earlier monarchical system.[2] Nevertheless, the authorial implication on the 1930s is usually clear: that the symptoms should be seen as a disqualifier of social reform in itself.[3] Linked to this too, there is a tendency among revisionists towards an ever more reductive interpretation of democracy which eschews any notion of creating democratic *content* (whereby all members of the population become citizens with a voice and stake in the system), so that democracy seems now only to mean playing by the parliamentary-political rules of the game. And here again ahistorical assumptions creep in – disingenuously or otherwise – given that the rules of the game and democratic norms revisionists apply belong to a late twentieth-century Western world which was far removed from anything ever experienced by reform-minded forces in Spain, who, if they had learned the 'rules of the game' from anywhere, had done so from the realpolitik and repression of the same Restoration monarchy which revisionists now represent – and here certainly disingenuously – as the acme of political tolerance.

Historical controversy can sometimes be useful in that it stimulates all the participants to substantiate their own empirical cases further and to refine their arguments in order to propel the debate forward to a greater nuance and depth of historical understanding. But if the polemic becomes too severe, as it has now in Spain's history wars, then it can also lead to an entrenching of positions which, as in any 'war', produces quite the opposite – a tendency to reductionism and Manichaeism (which in this particular case is also another 'Franco effect') and also increasingly to a 'stand-off' where participants simply do not engage with each other.[4]

Another ingrained methodological problem which also negatively affects this polemic is that quite a lot of the new historiography of the 1980s onwards – especially, but not exclusively, produced inside Spain – still presents the dynamic of the years 1931–6 as springing from the abstract ideological will of different leaders or leadership groups, without computing sufficiently the impact of structural factors (economic circumstances, ingrained political or institutional cultures, or other social and cultural factors shaping collective mindsets and behaviour) on both the leaders themselves and on their constituencies of supporters. Given this approach of a predominantly top-down political focus, the ensuing intensification of conflict in Spain, especially from 1934 onwards ('polarization', as it is usually termed) is also seen as a consequence largely of leaders' volition. Indeed in its most simplistic rendering, this is also seen as being 'imposed' on pliant and impressionable followers.[5] A more social-historical approach can open up this far too restrictive framework, and it is this approach which the present essay seeks to recommend. For the 1930s were times of intense mass social and political mobilization, even well before the onset of the civil war itself, and this mobilizing process, driven in great part from the bottom up, was about the emergence of new collective social and cultural identities and imaginaries, particularly perhaps among younger cohorts. And even though these occurred within specific new organizational forms (people joined political parties, trade unions, youth associations and so on), what that membership meant was much bigger in social and existential terms than the circumscribed aims of this party or that union,[6] and still less was it about the following of leaders' orders by a robotic mass or 'chorus'. Rather, violence was committed by members of political parties and/or trade unions in response to a gamut of motivations that could be professional or social pressures as well as factors of a personal or local nature. Ordinary people of different levels of affluence translated a range of their needs and desires into political action, and in pressured and/or confrontational circumstances this action could become violent (as indeed it had pre-Republic too).[7] To ignore all this, and resort instead to almost-conspiracy theories, makes for bad history in that they have little capacity to offer a convincing, three-dimensional explanation that does justice to the complexity of any modern social fabric and indeed of human motivations themselves. But leadership-heavy explications seem to remain overly present in the interpretative schema of events in Spain between 1931 and 1936, and have recently made a major and unhelpful return in some strands of post-1990s revisionism.[8]

More usefully, revisionist scholars remind us that the Republican period from 1931–6 needs to be analysed on its own terms, rather than – ahistorically – as the mere antechamber of the military coup of July 1936.[9] Even though the coup was in itself unquestionably the result of a conspiracy, we should nevertheless be wary of seeing an unbroken causal link right back to the hard core of patrician civilian and military opposition to the Republic in 1931–2. That itself was, to be sure, intransigently and absolutely opposed to Republican reform, had no intention of playing by the new 'rules of the game', and was thus conspiratorial from the start. But, notwithstanding its great social and economic force, its viability and success would still be dependent on many other things which had not yet happened, most especially, the crystallization of a substantial civilian base of mass mobilized populist conservatism which helped to legitimize the July 1936 coup. (On the evidence of General Franco's *discurso del alzamiento* of 17 July – the broadcast he made from Spanish North Africa announcing the military rising – even the insurgents, for all that they would have wished to reverse the political consequences of the French revolution of 1789, still grasped the paramount strategic need to justify their coup 'in the name of the people'.)[10] In the same way too, and for all that military intervention in politics already cast a long shadow in Spain, attributing everything to a conspiratorial coup does not get to the bottom of why during 1931–6 no effective *political* impediment to such a coup emerged, nor any confluence of a new 'natural' social majority to delegitimize it a priori.

Historians will doubtless continue to debate the relative weight and importance of the factors in play from spring 1931 to spring 1936: the obstruction of Republican reform and the ensuing radicalization of some grass-roots sectors desperate and disillusioned by this; the emergence of a new counter-mobilization of the mass Catholic right (also desperate and radicalized in its own way); the debilitating internal dispute in the 'broad church' that was Spain's socialist movement; the marginalization and fragmentation of pro-reform republican constituencies from 1933. But it was the complex interaction of these emergent and competing mobilizations which 'made' history in Spain between 1931 and 1936. History is, after all, a dynamic process, so these years cannot simply be reduced to a 'pre-history' hurtling down the track to a coup 'pre-destined' always to be successful.

Far less credible in terms of recent revisionist argument is the simplistic claim that the Second Republic was itself to 'blame' for triggering or decreeing change, as if this was conjured by sheer force of will out of a historical vacuum. What gets lost here in the heat of the historiographical polemic is the fact that the arrival of the Republic was itself already a symptom of the substantial social and structural change that had been occurring in Spain for several decades, and which was much accelerated from the end of the Great War and throughout the international (and Spanish) boom years of the 1920s too. In geographical terms these changes were most evident in the larger cities, especially Barcelona and to some extent Madrid, but also most especially on the north-eastern and eastern seaboard of Spain where urban and industrial development had also been accelerating in a number of medium-sized cities and their hinterlands (throughout Catalonia and also in what was then called the Levante (Valencia and Alicante) and continuing down to Murcia and Almería). The result, both in terms of demographic shift and the consolidation of urban middling constituencies in this part of Spain – also long associated with federal and relatively more progressive political currents – intensified a long-standing difficulty in Spain, that of uneven development.[11] With the birth of the Second Republic and the combination of mass aspirations to change, plus, for a time, a top-down reforming impetus, these internal fault lines became clearly delineated in political form, as the contrasts and tensions became evident between the above-described areas of greater urban social shifts, and those more comprehensively (though never totally) conservative areas[12] (especially in the heartlands of Castile and León in the centre-north and north-west).

An indication of these accelerating processes of social change lay in the very circumstances of the Second Republic's origins, in the overwhelmingly anti-monarchist vote returned in the municipal elections of April 1931. Even so, the fact that the Republic was then able to emerge peacefully and without any ostensible opposition had much to do with the political disarray of the monarchist political establishment – resulting from the preceding years of military dictatorship under Primo de Rivera from 1923. (With his coup, the monarchist political class had been unceremoniously jettisoned by King Alfonso XIII in favour of his dictator, a situation which continued until a number of thorny political problems combined with the world economic recession convinced the king to do the same to Primo (whom he had once described as 'My Mussolini').) The monarch had hopes of being able to reinstitute the old political system of the rotation of dynastic parties which guaranteed a small political nation, effectively excluding large parts of the population from citizenship – middling as well as industrial and agrarian worker constituencies.

But urban Spain had been pulling in a different direction for some time, that distance opening up significantly across the 1920s, such that the 1931 urban vote was precisely a vote against a return to exclusion and reflected, above all, the consolidation and social advances of middling constituencies who now saw themselves as such – and thus increasingly in cultural contradistinction to that old system and the social order it protected.[13] In many other areas of inland provincial and rural Spain it remained business as usual in April 1931 – including in the agrarian 'deep south' which would still remain largely socially and politically controlled by the old landed elites – Second Republic notwithstanding. They exerted vast social and economic influence over large dependent populations of landless labourers, even if some modest inroads against this would be made by post-April 1931 labour and land reforms. But the really significant social shift signalled by the April 1931 vote was not among the most economically disadvantaged or socially excluded constituencies, such as the southern rural poor, but among the aforementioned urban middling class constituencies in towns and cities, especially on the north-eastern and eastern seaboard, who had been steadily republicanized across the 1920s precisely because the Primo dictatorship had blocked their route to any form of genuine political representation. These trends, coupled with monarchist disarray, allowed Spain in April 1931 to buck the larger European trend to greater authoritarianism, and sometimes outright fascism. (The still lower levels and more spatially circumscribed nature of labour mobilization in Spain (which had not been a belligerent in the First World War) made the political emergence of its urban middling classes a less fear-marked process than elsewhere in continental Europe.)[14]

Thus was the new Republic born, trailing these signs of supervening change. But it was also born into a national and international context of economic crisis and saddled to boot with huge debts from the previous dictatorship. Added to which, from the beginning it also had ranged against it considerable establishment hostility inside Spain. First the Republic immediately faced a flight of capital, which exacerbated the economic problems soon to be faced by social democratic treasury minister, Indalecio Prieto, during his brief incumbency (April–December 1931).[15] Second, it also faced political opposition in the shape of patrician sectors of mostly reactionary monarchist elites who almost from the start began organizing to resist the Republic root and branch, while also simultaneously drawing closer to disaffected sectors in the military whose plans to crush the Republic by force began immediately, and who were for this reason together termed the 'catastrophist' right.[16]

But these sorts of opposition were, if formidable, only to be expected. The Republic's chances of succeeding as a vehicle of social reform would therefore depend on how strategically skilled were its advocates – now holding national office for the first time ever in twentieth-century Spain – in making new social coalitions and alliances in order to withstand this gathering opposition from some of the most powerful socio-economic forces in Spain.

By late June 1931 a coalition government was in place, led by progressive republicans representing largely urban professional sectors, and incorporating three ministers from Spain's broad socialist movement (party and union) – in Labour; Education; and with Prieto himself now in Public Works – and on whose parliamentary votes the new coalition rested. This combination of republican progressives and the socialist movement seemed a feasible one because by the 1930s there was a large area of overlap between the two, created by the substantial presence in the socialist movement (mainly in the party, PSOE) of a social democratic wing of similar progressive urban middle-class sectors. These had joined, increasingly from the post-First World War period, because they saw the PSOE as a more reliable vehicle for political reform than any of the small and fragmented republican groupings.[17] The latter already seemed to many outdated and last century, and or in some regards implicated in the machine-clientelist politics of the 'old system' (state power as access to spoils system) which the reformers wanted to eradicate.[18]

This perception (and the ensuing fragmentation) was intensified after 1931 by the fact that many erstwhile monarchists rapidly joined republican formations (or created new ones) as a means of doing politics in the new circumstances, but with an at least questionable commitment to structural reform. These included establishment figures such as the later Republic's first prime minister and later president, Niceto Alcalá Zamora, and its first home office minister, Miguel Maura. The middle class and reform-minded who preferred to join the PSOE, however, frequently also represented very affluent middling groups, not the threadbare or fearfully downwardly mobile – indeed in some cases they represented even very wealthy sectors (an example being Juan Negrín, the later Republican wartime premier himself):[19] what moved them was a sense, often in very practical terms (skills, education), and often as a result of a knowledge of the broader European context, of the need for economic reform and cultural opening (*aggiornamento*) in Spain. This is probably something that is becoming increasingly lost from sight in the twenty-first-century world – that neither in the 1930s, nor earlier, was it only the poor or culturally marginalized who were social democratic in their political outlook.

## The republican-socialist coalition government of 1931–3

The strong social democratic bolster underpinning the new government by providing the essential parliamentary 'muscle' (i.e. votes), was made infinitely easier too by the strong personal friendship of its two leading exponents, the leading progressive republican intellectual and former minister of war, now prime minister, Manuel Azaña, and Prieto himself, as the most influential social democratic politician in Spain.[20] In a sense this factor was reminiscent in its form of an older politics of nineteenth-century notables. But of course the Second Republic was not that, but a new mass political system: and the socialist votes sustaining the reforming coalition also represented other distinct and numerically larger sectors of the movement to Prieto's, in particular those associated with its trade union, the UGT (Unión General de Trabajadores), whose general secretary and most important leader, Francisco Largo Caballero, was labour minister in the 1931–3 coalition, and who had other and distinct policy priorities.

The UGT's leaders sought to institute social and welfare reforms to benefit their own existing members, but also working constituencies in Spain more broadly, and which Spain's socialist trade union leadership viewed very much as a 'rightful' preserve to be assimilated to its own organizations. Thus a form of clientelism also informed trade union culture in Spain, and increasingly from 1931 brought the UGT into even greater conflict with the other labour giant, the anarcho-syndicalist CNT, which in many places organized less qualified, unskilled, occupational sectors, such as textile workers, street cleaners and building labourers – those with little bargaining power in the market place who had little use for the UGT's preferred model of arbitration-based unionism. Many of the CNT's cadres, constituents and supporters were already suspicious of, or outright hostile to, the Republic's reforming claims, but very particularly of the UGT's role therein, because of their memories of how its leaders had sought to use their collaboration with the Primo dictatorship, when the UGT had staffed the official state labour arbitration boards in urban Spain in the 1920s, to marginalize the CNT and eradicate it as an organization.[21] But after 1931 the UGT's union leaders, for all their renewed connection with the highest echelons of state power, were themselves also under increasing pressure as demands grew from their own expanding base. Spain's socialist movement, like Europe's generally, had since its late nineteenth-century origins, always been an urban-focused movement, but with PSOE-UGT's accession to government in 1931 it had to cope with a massive influx of the rural landless of the south demanding something be done for them – and immediately – to realize the 'promise' of land and labour reform.[22] These were expectations which, in the minds of the landless, were strengthened precisely by the memory of the UGT's collaboration with Primo, and which thus placed a huge political strain on the UGT's leadership and its credibility in the 1930s. This sharpened the organizational conflict with the CNT which, on the outside of power, had a critical credibility that grew as did the financial and other obstacles to the realizing of reform across 1931–3.

For their part, the progressive republicans in coalition with the socialist movement were most concerned with top-down reforms. Their political vision was one of reforming the state, which they saw as the key to enshrining and consolidating a new republican order. They thus chose – in line with their model of the French Third Republic – to concentrate on structural reform of education and the army, the goals of both being to ensure civilian control and republicanization of the state. Education, their overriding concern, was to be uncoupled from the highly conservative institutional Catholic Church.[23] In particular they were concerned to achieve full state primary education provision, in order to ensure that new generations could be inculcated with republican values, and perhaps even more importantly (though they often saw it as the same thing) that an open attitude to scientific and other knowledge could be fostered in the new (and for those times controversial) co-educational environment – for the Second Republic introduced the first model of education ever in Spain where boys and girls were taught together.

The same nation-building goal informed the republicans' ideas for economic reform: they wanted a land reform also on the French model, so it was intended to be individualist in order to create a nation of republican smallholders. But they were not themselves technicians, lacked trained personnel to initiate the detail of agrarian reform, and anyway the smallholder model was not well suited to Spanish agricultural conditions in many areas, especially not in the deep south where landlessness constituted the biggest – indeed a truly immense – social and economic problem. Although agrarian reform would be instituted in 1932, it was hugely compromised by technical and financial constraints. As the Spanish republicans were not socialists in the sense of being anti-capitalist (this was another Francoist myth), nor indeed were they really even Jacobins (except perhaps in their rhetoric), they would not countenance any revolutionary solution by means of expropriating land in the south. The republicans' weddedness also to balancing the budget meant that they refused, even in this time of recession, to take out loans to facilitate any of the UGT's desired labour and welfare reforms. (The only loans they would countenance were those for the exclusive purpose of their cherished educational reforms of 1931–3.)

Stringent financial orthodoxy combined with the inevitably increasing mass aspiration to land and welfare reform, stimulated further by the birth of the new regime, produced a highly problematic situation. But it became alarmingly problematic in political terms precisely because of the republicans' other fixation: the maintenance of public order, which they understood in remarkably traditional, rigid and unimaginative terms. For theirs was a view of politics that looked decidedly backwards to the nineteenth century: at the very most they saw the proper place of politics as within the walls of parliament, not, as now beckoned, on the streets of Spain's towns and cities, as aspirant and mobilizing mass constituencies pressured for demands, for a voice, for political inclusion – as had already been augured in the many thousands of people who had thronged the public spaces of the capital and of Spain's bigger cities to greet the regime change in April 1931.

Nor was this limited understanding of politics confined to republicans among the progressives; it was also the view of more than a few parliamentary socialists, including notably of their pre-eminent representative, the public works minister, Prieto. For him the Republic was its parliament and elected representatives: the 'people' were nowhere in the picture, other than as a discursive trope. For the republicans this chimed perfectly with their state-oriented philosophy of reform. But for both, and especially the progressive republicans, it flags up a big political flaw – the inability to comprehend the new age of mass politics which 'the Republic' was and had ushered in, and of which they themselves were an integral part, and which urgently required a strategy, and the ability to grasp some means of acquiring and servicing a social base of support to sustain a viable electoral majority. There was in Spain no experience of this of course – except as an entirely clientelist rather than democratic practice – so it was inevitable that progressive forces would lack experience. But what was much more damaging was the continuing failure even to perceive that this was the *sine qua non* of achievable reform. That it was an abiding failure of strategy and of understanding is clearly indicated by that fact that Prieto himself could still comment, as late as February 1936, in the days after the election victory of the centre-left coalition of the Popular Front, that the presence in the streets of its supporters was an 'entelechy' – i.e. something that no longer had any reason to exist.[24]

Neither parliamentary socialist nor progressive republican leadership seemed to grasp that in order to make reform under the new system they needed to construct and maintain a social base outside parliament in order to support their legislative project within it. Prieto's comment in 1936 points up the lost opportunity of 1931–3 to capitalize on the potential of the 1920s 'republicanization' of urban middling constituencies whose political imaginaries lay fragmented, unattended and largely ignored by the increasingly stagnant and unimaginative 'progressive' republican parties who, looking backwards to a politics of notables, were unaware that that nineteenth-century political world had already departed. They remained oblivious even though by that point, in spring–summer 1936, the Republic's pro-reform forces were already facing the full and highly negative material consequences of their own strategic failure across 1931–3 to consolidate a viable or cohesive support base. Indeed, those who had been much more successful in mobilization terms, especially since 1933, were precisely those opposing any measure of redistributive socio-economic reform at all, and who by 1936 had shown themselves adept at using, in the new conditions of political engagement, both their old advantages (of social power and wealth) but also the newly apparent shortcomings and strategic errors of the republican-socialist coalition itself, in order to mobilize a formidable mass base on a platform of strident counter-reform.

So now we must turn to explore the combination of factors, already briefly alluded to, which led to the internal disintegration of this coalition government across 1931 to 1933 – and also to the severe internal fragmentation of each of its component parts. These resulted from the wrecking combination of internal and external pressures (including, but not only, the intensifying dynamic of a mass counter-reform movement), all of which inevitably fed off each other. This period of 1931–3 is the key to understanding how the Republic was unmade as a viable instrument of reform. The result by September 1933 would be not only the formal end of the republican-socialist coalition, but in the general election of November would mean its components entered the hustings separately – which was suicidal, given the explicit terms of the electoral law they themselves had been involved in implementing in 1931 – an outcome which is itself the clearest indication of how erosive the 27-month period of tenure in government had been.

## Reform in Spain 1931–3: a clash of projects and mentalities

The two reform projects – on one side, republican reform of the 'state heights', and, on the other, the social democratic settlement sought by the socialist movement, in particular its union wing – constituted formidable challenges, the latter especially given the acute lack of financial resources facing the coalition government. The impossibility of squaring this circle would generate severe tensions within it, particularly around the issue of public order – tensions which were then hugely exacerbated by the sheer lack of funds for welfare relief. Added to this was the further erosive impact of political opponents' own tactics, whether the filibuster (obstruction) of reform in parliament or the blocking of its implementation in the localities (as happened across 1931 to 1933 with legislation promulgated to try to guarantee both the right to work and a minimum wage, especially in areas of large numbers of landless labourers where often employers declared a virtual lock-out in 1931). There were regular flare-ups exacerbated also in urban areas, especially Barcelona and its surrounding industrial belt, by the slenderness or indeed sometimes the virtual lack of a social welfare budget where the needs were also great and increasing.[25] Hopes and aspirations raised at grass roots amongst impoverished rural workers too quickly flared into anger, especially when goaded by local elites (landowners and estate bailiffs, whose power remained largely intact at local level, let us remember), including in the famous taunt to the still-hungry that they should '¡comed República!' ('eat the Republic', or, less literally 'let the Republic feed you'). To all of this, the response of the progressive republicans added a further turn of the screw with a string of swingeing public order measures in 1931, 1932 and 1933,[26] which while at least in part aimed, including discursively, at the radical (and conspiratorial) right, had the most immediate, long-standing and greatest negative effects precisely on the impoverished urban and rural constituencies who had expected so much of the Republic.[27]

## Enabling democracy?

These popular expectations were often unreasonable and illogical, especially in terms of the instantaneity with which many of the 'believers' expected emancipation, or indeed 'deliverance'.[28] But they raise a crucial question that is now a properly historical one, just as it needed realistically then to have been a political one, but was never posited as such by progressive republicans, nor, really, by parliamentary socialists either: how would it be possible to make the basis of a functioning democracy in Spain if policies could *not* be implemented to make enough of the previously excluded sectors of the population feel they had a real and meaningful stake in the new political system? The new Republic was not, as we have seen, socialist in the sense of being committed to the expropriation of capital (for this very reason its social and economic enemies remained powerful, for all that the Republic had won a strong mandate in the ballot box). Notwithstanding this fact, in some ways all sections of the socialist movement assumed that the new Republican democracy needed to be some form of social democracy, and especially for the union wing (and irrespective of how they chose to term it) more directly to embrace a measure of economic democracy, via redistributive reform. But coalition treasury policy was controlled by republicans committed to financial orthodoxy, which also effectively ruled out the financing of major welfare reform via the raising of extra loans (in the style of Primo). The overall result was the weakening of the coalition overall by dint of the acute internal tensions this produced inside the socialist movement, and also between it and other significant urban and rural worker constituencies outside the PSOE-UGT's own organizations.

## The erosion of the left, 1931–3

When the socialist movement's ministers entered the coalition government in June 1931, the parliamentary socialists (Prieto and Fernando de los Ríos as Education Minister) were mainly concerned to bolster the republicans in their project of state reform. On the other hand, Largo Caballero as Minister of Labour came with a particular agenda of social and labour reform intended not least to bolster the kudos of the UGT, to increase its membership and to expand its influence beyond the socialist organizations, in order to achieve the 'historic' mission of Spain's socialist movement – both to encadre all of Spain's workers and to direct the state[29] (though they were, and really always remained, hazy on what exactly such a 'revolution' constituted beyond the fact of UGT presence in power and its control of labour policy). Certainly theirs was never a coherent, still less a Leninist blueprint for revolution.[30] Confronted as Largo then was almost immediately in 1931 by an acute lack of funds and also soon by the no-holds-barred (and highly personal) campaign against him by Spain's confederation of industry (employers' federation),[31] not only did these cherished goals recede, but the danger also loomed of the UGT becoming discredited in the eyes of its own members and prospective ones precisely because it could not deliver on its promises of material reform, a risk made all the more acute given that unemployment was rising across the early 1930s – especially in urban areas (in the rural south mass unemployment was a structural constant).

One of the consequences of this pressure was to intensify the UGT's already pronounced belief that it had a right, indeed a duty, to monopolize labour organization in Spain. In practical terms on the ground this translated from a UGT labour minister to UGT control of labour machinery, markets and exchanges across the country which in many places froze out and alienated non-UGT aligned workers as well as those specifically affiliated with other labour organizations.[32] In a national context of what had been the long-standing political culture of clientelism under the prior monarchist system in Spain (1874–1931), it should scarcely surprise us that the organizations of the left were also embedded in such a culture,[33] nor that the UGT should seek to reactivate this kind of control as it had in the 1920s under Primo, and all the more especially faced with the acute employment crisis of the 1930s in which their other options (such as unemployment relief disbursement) were so limited by republican fiscal controls.

In particular the UGT was worried about loss of members, but also of 'organizational face', to its historic rival the CNT with whom relations in most areas of Spain had long been conflictual, under monarchy as well as Republic. But the ascendancy too of a number of broadly communist formations, in the main in Spain's northern and north-eastern industrial centres (but also in the southern city of Seville), posed what the PSOE-UGT leadership saw as multiple threats to socialist pre-eminence on the left nationally.[34] Again it was economic constraints which intensified these internal organizational conflicts on the left across the country. For example, in the industrial centres of Catalonia (which achieved a measure of self-governing powers under the autonomy statute of September 1932) a similar conflict played out between its own left coalition government, which was cash strapped and public-order fixated, and popular constituencies, who were organized or semi-organized by communists and anarcho-syndicalists, and eking out a living, often on the urban margins, and desperate for all-too-scarce work and welfare relief.[35] It was a scenario replicated if to a lesser extent in many regions of Spain, even if in Catalonia there was an additional ethnic-outsider charge to the conflict in that the CNT, while having Catalan members and leaders, operated in Spanish and above all represented and was identified with the large number of (often unskilled) labour migrants from other regions of Spain of whom there had been a steady influx since the industrial expansion of the nineteenth century, and much accelerated since the First World War.[36]

The anarchist movement nationally in Spain had its own grave internal political schisms and conflicts which had also been intensified by the coming of the Republic, precisely because the emergence for the first time of genuinely democratic political channels, however imperfect still, had opened up an internal debate in what was an immensely regionally varied organization (the product of the aforementioned uneven development). At stake was the possibility and wisdom of the CNT engaging in parliamentary politics – something it had hitherto proclaimed to be against its fundamental anti-statist principles.[37] For the CNT especially, then, the Republic was a particular amalgam of 'promise and threat' combined, since its very political promise (of a political emancipation that might now be possible through the state) threatened to dislocate the movement internally, as possibilists (often powerful in certain of the CNT's trade union federations, particularly in the industrial north-east and east) clashed with anarchist purists – who saw Republican democracy as a dangerous chimera – in an organizational duel that would run on and into the civil war itself.[38] Such internal fractures might in other circumstances have defused at least somewhat the political threat the CNT posed to the socialists of the UGT in power. But it was precisely the swingeing approach of republicans to the public order question that effectively maintained the CNT as a major threat to the UGT. The erosion of its political credibility among many of the worker and labour constituencies it considered its 'natural' supporters in reality or in potential, and even with many sectors of its own union base, was the inevitable result of the constant targeting by police of the unemployed and also those engaged on the margins or in the black economy. Also detained and imprisoned under the terms of the republicans' draconian public order legislation were the union officials – usually CNT or sometimes communist – who organized and aided the unemployed and against whom the police regularly intervened to hamper their activities. Prieto's parliamentary socialist wing of the movement was more prepared to accept the resulting erosion of support as a political price to be paid, and indeed was much closer anyway in temperament and philosophy to the republicans.[39] But Largo's union base was far less sanguine, and along with the industrialists' campaign against Largo personally as labour minister, public order policy constituted a significant factor in their alienation from the parliamentary socialists (who had drafted some of it and also shaped policing policy),[40] from the government coalition and in their disillusion at the diminishing prospects of a parliamentary route to reform. In turn this explains Largo's own lack of enthusiasm for and preparedness to abandon the coalition in 1933.

### The 'logic' of progressive republicanism: anticlericalism as strategic error?

Given the republicans' commitment to fiscal orthodoxy, combined with their conservative stance on public order, it is hard not to conclude that they had effectively ruled out for themselves from the start any viable popular social base on the left such as the UGT's leaders would be able to endorse for long (at least from inside government). But the necessity of finding a social base remained if they hoped to succeed in achieving a programme – any programme – of state reform via parliamentary legislation. The republicans could potentially have configured an alternative social base for their project because there were lower middling constituencies available, as a number of different historical studies have shown. These were both urban and rural bases – tenant farmers and middling sorts, in some areas of the north-east, east and even south, who, if not quite the targets of the wholesale political exclusion during 1931–3 that some revisionists have claimed, were nevertheless *unrepresented* by the PSOE-UGT because these groups often disagreed with the socialists' labour-focused policies.[41]

But logically such a reconfiguration would also have demanded a strategic rethinking of some of their immediate goals, in particular their approach to Church–State relations and their programme of secularizing reforms – this in order to ensure as little dissipation of political support as possible at the political centre, away from themselves, and also to damp down the danger of counter-mobilization amongst more conservative rural and provincial middling sectors especially in the north-central heartlands of Castile. This is not to suggest that the progressive republicans could or should have abandoned their Church reform altogether, simply for fear of opposition – indeed it is hard to conceive of how else the republicans could have generated a social environment in Spain propitious to sustain themselves and their modernizing reform of the 'commanding heights' of the state without instituting a nationwide system of secular primary education and separating Church and State – the latter not least to recoup state subsidy to the Church and thus save treasury resources to help fund the educational reform. Both measures would have provoked opposition from Spain's integrist ecclesiastical hierarchy, but it would have had to have learned to live with the separation – as the Church in France had after 1905, and especially if they had been unable to 'call on' the agitated base of ordinary Catholics which had appeared by 1933. The intensity of this mass base was in substantial part enabled by the progressive republicans themselves, by dint of their strident anticlerical rhetoric and – as is well known – their interference in the grass-roots cultural worlds of the Catholic laity, for example via the plethora of petty measures which restricted or prohibited Catholic ceremonies and local religious festivals.[42]

The whole issue of Church reform was of course an unavoidably contentious one. There is no way the republicans could have avoided controversy or indeed some degree of Catholic counter-mobilization, and especially around the socially fraught (though not, for all that, 'extreme') proposal of installing secular schoolrooms across town and village Spain. In particular, the *co-educated* Republican nation in prospect was a considerable psychological shock delivered to the Spanish right's ingrained social fundamentalism, and as such it had to be faced.[43] But Azaña and his colleagues seemed unable to think tactically, to weigh up which battles of Church reform to fight and which not – and with the additional municipal wars against everyday Catholic rites and custom, they helped arm a cultural counter-revolution at a nuclear level and in a way that education reform undertaken in isolation might not have done to such an extent – especially if we think of how in some regions strong *local cultural* identities (of *patria chica*) were very much bound up with village religious festivals, over and above their relationship to a specifically religious identity. Thinking through these implications is, of course, a counterfactual activity, and thus as historians we cannot pursue it too far, but the important point to grasp is the generic, and not at all counterfactual, failure of progressive republicans to think through their own policies strategically at the time. Moreover, if they had set the tone more clearly against local anticlerical campaigns, then something else also would also have been much more readily visible: that very often, especially in rural Spain, the root of local tensions was economic in nature, over land or control of other local resources, even when these became enmeshed with and strongly coloured by anticlerical expression.[44] (This was something that would also subsequently facilitate the Franco dictatorship's 'explaining' and 'remembering' of such conflicts post hoc as *entirely* generated by the Republic's anticlerical permissiveness, a 'memory' whose cultural power is still alive today.)

The republicans' weddedness in the 1930s to a vehement intellectual anticlericalism was, at root, yet another nineteenth-century mark of identity – we might even describe it as an 'article of faith'. But it was an immense mistake, producing politically devastating effects in the new mass parliamentary system whose consequences the republicans seemed literally oblivious of. And not only were theirs qualitative errors around policy choices, they were also doubly damaging failures of implementation: for example, the attempt to place a legal ban on Church personnel working as teachers created a storm of opposition – popular as well as patrician – and, via this, a Catholic counter-mobilization which neither republicans nor the (significantly less anticlerical) socialist leaderships had any strategy for defusing or circumventing. Indeed those who actually did the circumventing were Catholic activists and religious personnel themselves, such that there was very probably never any single period during the Republican years, 1931–6, when religious personnel were unable to continue teaching.[45] Thus the interdiction failed, serving only to help arm a dangerous and politically experienced patrician adversary which was then, in turn able, via the new parliamentary-political dispositions, and by deploying the organizational networks of the Catholic Church along with extensive private funding, to accelerate from 1933 the grass-roots crusade against Republican laicization into a mass movement of counter-reform – effectively generating a political party – called the CEDA (Confederation of Spanish Right-Wing Groups).[46]

This clerical conservative mobilization was doubly unaffordable in view of the other key republican structural reform in prospect – of the army, or more specifically of Spain's over-large officer corps inherited from the colonial wars of the nineteenth century and a major and growing political problem in Spain's post-colonial twentieth century. But as with the Church, so with the army, the republicans' tactical clumsiness intensified the already substantial political and economic challenge of military reform. There was the noisy goading of the officer corps via the arguably ill-advised campaign-enquiry of 1931 into political and military 'responsibilities', including for the defeat at Annual in Spanish Morocco in 1921 and also for collaboration with the Primo dictatorship.[47] The allegation of wrongdoing incensed the military, at once confirming powerful and already politically hostile sectors of the officer corps in the route of intransigent opposition and anti-republican conspiracy which would first erupt in August 1932 with the failed Sanjurjo plot. As with their anticlerical rhetoric, the republicans lacked tactical deftness – in both cases the rhetoric was noisy but ineffective, they 'armed' (in this case literally) a more powerful political enemy when they had nothing with which to control or counteract it. And whatever their cherished marks of identity, the progressive republicans could not, logically, afford to take on the Church and the elite clerical lobby head on, when their fiscal orthodoxy meant they had no alternative social base to the middling ground. This all the more especially when their chances of addressing even minimally the dream of Republican economic relief harboured by the impoverished evaporated, as the effects of the international recession hit home harder in Spain from 1933 and unemployment rose.

In the course of 1933 the republican-socialist coalition finally internally dissolved under the weight of its numerous internal stresses, especially the ones affecting the by now seriously internally fractured socialist movement.[48] For Largo Caballero and the trade union wing, the patronal assault on him as minister, and even more what seemed like the unremitting targeting of violent and repressive police action against worker constituencies, proved too much. At the same time, however, the republicans were by this point also largely unwilling partners in the coalition.[49] (Azaña and Prieto were both swimming against the tide of their own supporters in seeking still to hold the coalition together.) So Largo's veto on its continuation came as a useful point of deflection to disguise the republicans' own underlying unwillingness. In short, they were able to leave without taking visible responsibility for the decision or any of its consequences, not the least of which was the initiation soon afterwards of a period of big and effective counter-reform mobilization at the same time as the forces for change became increasingly fragmented and ineffective.

## Counter-reform 1934–6: the counter-revolution mobilized, the coalition for change atomized

In most of the extant historiography the years 1934–6 in Spain are seen as the core period when events spiralled 'out of control', with left and right offering mirror images of mass radicalization and popular mobilization in the streets of Spain's cities. Between them they are seen to have made the polarized social conditions propelling the descent into armed conflict and confrontation, which then in turn became the distorted 'justification' for the catastrophist-inspired military coup, launched with the support of civilian elites, and backed by mass mobilized integrism via the CEDA, its fascistized youth wing, JAP, and other regional entities such as the Navarrese militia, the Requeté.[50] (The escalation from coup to full-scale civil war itself was something else again, of course, and only made possible by Nazi and Fascist intervention with their injection of aircraft and modern armaments.) But it is the contention of this chapter that much of what happened between 1934 and spring 1936 was far less 'symmetrical' than the standard account suggests, and that the asymmetry was precisely the result of the earlier failure during 1931–3 to identify and consolidate a viable social base among progressive forces to support a programme of reform. So instead of an equally politically 'strong' mobilization on left and right ('polarization'), what actually occurred across 1934–6 was the consolidation of a coherent, well organized and powerful mass movement of counter-reform, while, on the other, progressive forces were increasingly fragmented and powerless, lacking as they did any operative or coherent political strategy.

The fact that this asymmetry was for a long time hidden behind the strident revolutionary rhetoric of Largo Caballero's 'left wing' of the socialist movement, should not be confused with his supporters having a coherent plan – still less a revolutionary one. That the socialist left was not at any point able to translate rhetoric into strategy was long ago elegantly and fully elucidated in the seminal work of Santos Juliá, one of Spain's leading historians of the contemporary period.[51] He rightly located the crux of Largo's dilemma in his desire, after the loss of government power in autumn 1933, and in a context of paralysed reform at home and ascendant fascism and quasi-fascism across Europe, to keep the forces of counter-reform at bay inside Spain while not risking the organizational fabric, or 'patrimony' of the socialist movement in any sudden or direct action. Largo thus alighted on a radical language as a way of supposedly squaring this circle, and also keeping angry and disillusioned grass-roots sectors of the UGT from 'straying' towards the CNT. It was thus a paradox that a strident revolutionary discourse was in fact an expression of political weakness not strength, and a strategy whose logic was rooted in the underlying political culture of the socialist movement in Spain that its *organization* had to be protected at all costs. Santos Juliá's analysis was of course corroborated by the events of the early civil war period when Largo and the UGT leadership not only played no role in the grass-roots revolutionary initiatives triggered by the military coup itself, but also spent the rest of 1936 desperately seeking to bring the popular revolution under Republican government control. Since then, many other historians have elaborated detailed analyses exploring the complex, competing and fundamentally contradictory strands within the social left[52] – contradictions which in the end played a considerable part in shattering the Spanish socialist movement as it came under the immense pressures of sustaining the Republican war effort between 1936 and 1939.

In view of all this work, it seems wilfully obtuse that more recent revisionist historical accounts seem to be doing little more than revisiting the old Francoist canards of the 'revolutionary' socialist left – and once again confusing and conflating words with realities in a category error and without adding much at all to the historical argument either empirically or conceptually. There is also an unhelpfully Manichean tendency among some revisionists to apportion 'blame' to some players while exonerating others, as if they were somehow bystanders or 'wronged parties'.[53] But, historically speaking, everyone was a player – from Largo and his supporters with their strategically ill-conceived rhetoric which further armed the counter-revolution, via the mass mobilized grass roots of UGT and CNT, through to the institutional Church with its clear political alignment with counter-reform and own intemperate public discourse, on to the ordinary citizens of inland provincial towns and villages who, in rallying to the CEDA, constituted Spain's equivalent of the post-1918 European gentry pact with *ancien regime* forces seeking together to block the emergence of a 'new world'. All were players, all participants, so the lexicon of blame and innocence makes no real sense in a historical analysis. The historical difference, of course, was that some players were more powerful in real terms than others. While the left had a large street presence, it was – again, paradoxically – weaker and weaker, bitterly divided by political strategies, and by experience, by the ensuing failure of 1931–3. It was divided too, in the end, by the structural consequences of uneven economic development in Spain which produced such vastly conflicting experiences, ideologies and strategies among the grass roots of progressive parties and organizations themselves, but which we can nevertheless define as a single and recognizable 'something' in itself – which is to say, all those who had a substantial investment in promoting political and economic change away from the old order.

By 1934 the movement for counter-reform had all the advantages: having coalesced around the patrician conservative nucleus of 1931, it had funds; being composed of conservative middling urban and provincial middling constituencies with conservative Catholic identities, it had the cementing force of tradition, with all the solidity of what existed and could be conceived of; it was both coherent and numerous; and most of all it had the supreme organizational advantage of being able to rely on the pre-existing organizational networks of the Catholic Church, a terrain which gave this new mass conservative politics its biggest advantage of all. Nor is it really surprising that this anti-reform coalition should have been more effective, given its leaders were, or else had close links with, former power elites secular as well as religious who had recourse to much that the reform lobby did not in terms of insider political knowledge and experience derived from decades of real political power and access to the state. This is not to say that the mass base they mobilized were mere foils or pawns of the old power. For this was also a *sui generis* grass-roots anti-modernization 'crusade', of a different set of subaltern constituencies who were fearful of how Republican reform would affect them (whether secularizing or, in some cases, land reform)[54] and thus informed by local and personal agendas, hopes and fears. These were then further intensified via the act of mass political mobilization itself, and also in the wake of the continuing and increased protests of worker constituencies – this in part because of the intensification of the effects of the international recession inside Spain from 1933.

In this context of parallel mass mobilizations for and against reform, the induction of fear was also reciprocal. The revolutionary general strike of October 1934 and the workers' rising in the recession-hit northern coalmining region of Asturias was fuelled by fear that the recent inclusion in government of the CEDA into the highly sensitive ministerial portfolios of labour, justice and agriculture signified the triumph by legal means (as in Germany and so very recently in Austria) of a domestic fascism that would erode and destroy Republican democracy from within. But the fact of October frightened Spain's counter-reform masses whose fearful imaginaries were made more stark by the circulation of the right's black propaganda myths, increasingly disseminated in the conservative press across 1934–6,[55] which in turn facilitated the linking of the counter-reform movement to the growing military conspiracy which was then, in its turn, able to legitimize itself by reference to a popular voice.

In the historical account which emerges from recent revisionism, the October 1934 revolution is taken to signal the end of the democratic Republic.[56] But there is a large problem here in its underlying assumption, which equates all the different groups of political opposition with one another – elite catastrophists with the radicals of the CNT, as if each was possessed of an equal amount of destabilizing capacity vis-à-vis the Republic. This is analogous to the Weimar fallacy of seeing the outsider KPD as being as much of a threat to German democracy as was the NSDAP (Nazis), with their imperial and old regime connections. In Spain, anarchist and even most socialist constituencies remained on the outside of the political system after 1931, while the catastrophists included social and economic elites and members of the officer class who were still supremely the establishment insiders, and ones with a direct line to the superior coercive force of the army. What the army's repression of October 1934 in Asturias showed (using colonial Moroccan troops and taking over 40,000 prisoners), was that progressive forces could only win as a united reforming coalition, such as 1931–3 was intended to be. For Spain's parliamentary socialist leaders especially, the attempt to restore that long-lost chance of reform and to prevent further political erosion among progressive, pro-change forces, was the main objective behind the formation of the republican-socialist Popular Front electoral coalition to fight the general elections of February 1936.

## Spring 1936: the continuing fragmentation of reform, the unity of counter-reform

It was the late-joining and relatively peripheral presence of the Spanish Communist Party (PCE) in the Popular Front electoral alliance which boosted the Spanish right's propagandizing around the myth of an imminent Soviet-backed coup.[57] The period after the Popular Front's electoral triumph did see increased social turbulence and protest, but, as before, this was never at a level that came even close to challenging the power of the state or established police forces (and as before most of the victims/fatalities were the protesters themselves);[58] nor was it evidence of any coordinated revolutionary plot. In the spring of 1936 in Spain the only conspiracy in town was the counter-revolution – and one that the all-republican government issuing from the February elections was ill-equipped to face down. It is doubly ironic then that the abiding image of the new prime minister (soon to be Republican President), Azaña, remains the one of him recoiling from the 'revolutionary masses' in the famous open-air electoral meetings which he had addressed prior to the February polls,[59] while the real subterranean threat of military subversion remained 'hidden', including in some of the most fashionable drawing rooms of elite society.

While many of today's revisionists replicate the contemporary Spanish right's critique of the danger posed to 'democracy' by political progressives, the real opponents were already lodged deep inside a Spanish establishment far older than the Second Republic and entirely undisplaced by its electoral mandate for reform. They were planning a coup invested with the power of Spain's patrician civilian and military elites – including those of the colonial army of Africa. Its implementation on 17–18 July 1936 was the continuation of politics by other means, in which was fused the ideology of corporate military privilege and European eugenicism, as well as a hoped-for return to patrician-controlled politics to vanquish the threat of mass democracy. The strategic goal of the military coup was not to launch a war, but certainly to impose overwhelming force – that violence was part of the plan is crystal clear from the secret instructions issued by the coup's director, General Emilio Mola.[60] This was deemed necessary precisely because change inside an emergent democratizing society had gone so far that it could only now be eradicated by exemplary violence. But this counter-reforming response was not, in spite of appearances, the catastrophism of 1931 unchanged: it was something else, not least because it was backed by a mass civilian coalition of the fearful, whose hatreds the coup was about to unleash. What they and the coup would become was different from what Mola envisaged, and precisely because of the war's massive escalation thereafter. While he had always intended his forces to inflict a great deal of 'exemplary' killing, the radical mobilized project that emerged from the war – fascism, or some new hybrid created in Spain?[61] – would become something that not even the coup-makers or their civilian supporters could have conceived or imagined a priori.

## Conclusion: the chances of reform

In those areas of Spain where the military coup and its civilian supporters were able to be resisted and defeated after 18 July 1936, this territory was gradually brought together as the Republican zone. It was a unification process which involved the containment in some areas – predominantly Catalonia and the Republican (i.e. eastern) parts of Aragón – of a popular grass-roots revolution whose hallmarks were the collectivization of land and/or of factories and municipal services. Through this revolutionary containment the wartime Republic sought not only to achieve the Herculean requirements of a modern industrial war effort under what were effectively conditions of international embargo, but also to recreate the Popular Front alliance, which for all the recent revisionist obfuscation, meant in essence the original reform programme of 1931–3. This was intended to consolidate a broad social base for the war effort, to integrate multiple sectors of Republican society and also to serve as a stimulus to improve the morale of a war-beleaguered population. For some it was an incentive, at least for a time, though not of course for everyone in the Republican zone, including not for those sectors who had invested themselves politically and emotionally in the radical new world glimpsed during the 1936 revolution. But for most of the population the war itself, under the conditions in which the Republic had to fight, was the greatest eroder of hope and belief in a positive future – and far more than any form of any ideological disillusion. Crucially too, as a strategy the wartime Popular Front had come too late, for by 1937–8 the locus of power controlling the outcome in the Spanish war lay outside the country, in the cabinets and chancelleries of a transformed Europe.

In this sense then, and although the Republic fought hard for its life between 1936 and 1939, the real opportunity of reform was long behind – in 1931–3, when a crucial window had existed to build up a viable coalition for reform, even if not necessarily one that would satisfy the visionary goals of any of its component parts, indeed which could not have done without raising a too powerful group of political opponents. But the opportunity itself had evaporated – the progressive republicans lacking any strategic political understanding, and wedded to a loud and inefficient anticlericalism which locked them in a backward-looking world that evoked a nineteenth-century politics of notables, and themselves also alarmed by the advent of the new mass politics. Spain's social democratic movement could potentially have fulfilled the 'missing' role, given the sociological configuration of its parliamentary wing, but this was in practice neutralized in the crossfire of its own intensifying conflict with its trade union wing. The parliamentary socialists were too weak on their own, and had no strong progressive republican sector to fall back on or make common cause with. Indeed the latter's financial orthodoxy and even more their law and order fixation only exacerbated the internal conflict in the socialist movement. Truth be told, the Spanish socialist leaders were all also wary of the ascendant era of mass politics. This would also have more than a little to do with the movement's wartime eclipse by a strongly republicanized Spanish Communist Party – a set of events which even today rarely get the structural analysis they require empirically and historiographically, and are instead scripted according to the mythic narrative of Cold War and conspiracy theory that was also a legacy of Republican defeat in the civil war.

## Notes

I would like to thank my colleague Chris Ealham for his inestimable assistance with aspects of the chapter (as some of the following endnotes attest), and for sharing with me his draft article,

'Social History, Revisionism and Mapping the 1930s Spanish Left', even though there are arguments and assessments here which he will not agree with.

1.  One of the foundational polemics set the work of Paul Preston, *The Coming of the Spanish Civil War: Reform, Reaction and Revolution in the Second Spanish Republic 1931–1936* (London: Macmillan, 1978; revised 2nd edition, London: Routledge, 1994 is cited henceforward as *CSCW*) against that of Richard H. Robinson, *The Origins of Franco's Spain: The Right, the Republic and Revolution, 1931–1936* (Newton Abbot: David & Charles, 1970) over the causes of the reform versus counter-reform confrontation of 1931–6. The 1980s saw a massive new expansion of historiographical production inside Spain, but from the end of the 1990s the revisionist production referred to later in this chapter has returned historians to this earlier, polarized debate, and often not in an empirically productive way.

2.  For example, Stanley Payne's comment on the Restoration monarchy as 'Spain's only liberal regime of tolerance', in his *Collapse of the Spanish Republic, 1933–1936: Origins of the Civil War* (Yale: Yale University Press, 2006), p. 7; also Manuel Alvarez Tardío and Fernando del Rey, commenting on the Restoration monarchy's renunciation of violence in the Introduction to their edited book, *El laberinto republicano, La democracia espanola y sus enemigos* (Barcelona: RBA, 2012), pp. 15, 18–19. As Chris Ealham points out in 'Social History, Revisionism and Mapping the 1930s Spanish Left', this idealization of what went before the Republic also allows revisionists to give the impression that socio-political conflict *began* in 1931 in Spain – so here they are doubly ahistorical.

3.  Cf. 'Structural approaches [to the history of the Second Republic] by emphasizing social and economic inequality only provide an alibi for the Socialists' reform project [...] and even justify the violence emanating from the political and labour organizations representing the so-called "disinherited"', Manuel Alvarez Tardío, '¿Para cuando un debate histórico sin prejuicios? A propósito de la reseña de Samuel Pierce sobre *El Precio de la Exclusión: La política durante la Segunda República*', *Bulletin for Spanish and Portuguese Historical Studies* 36:1 (2011), pp. 153–7: p. 154, and also cited in Ricardo Robledo, 'El giro ideológico en la historia contemporánea española', in Carlos Forcadell, Ignacio Peiró and Mercedes Yusta (eds), *El pasado en construcción: Revisiones de la historia y revisionismos históricos en la historiografía contemporánea* (Zaragoza: Institución Fernando el Católico, 2015), pp. 303–38: p. 303. A more positive interpretation of the Republican constitutional settlement and the quality of its democracy in Gareth Stockey, 'Spain's First Democracy: The 1931 Constitution and its Detractors', in Adam Sharman and Stephen G.H. Roberts (eds), *1812 Echoes: The Cadiz Constitution in Hispanic History, Culture and Politics* (Newcastle: Cambridge Scholars Press, 2013), pp. 314–36.

4.  For the revisionist debate today in Spain, see Carlos Forcadell, Ignacio Peiró and Mercedes Yusta (eds), *El pasado en construcción: Revisionismos históricos en la historiografía contemporánea* (Zaragoza: Institución Fernando El Católico, 2015); also Chris Ealham, 'The Emperor's New Clothes: "Objectivity" and Revisionism in Spanish History', *Journal of Contemporary History* 48:1 (2013), pp. 191–202.

5.  A clear example of this in Stanley G. Payne, *Spain's First Democracy: The Second Republic, 1931–1936* (Madison: University of Wisconsin Press, 1993) which presents the anarchist grass roots especially as an irrational mass, 'inveigled' by ideologues. But the tendency goes back to earlier historians such as the above-cited Richard H. Robinson, and continues with some of today's neoconservative revisionists in Spain, discussed later in this chapter, and also in the opening essay to this volume.

6.  A discussion of this, including regarding youth constituencies, in Helen Graham, *The Spanish Republic at War 1936–1939* (Cambridge: Cambridge University Press, 2002), pp. 181–2 and in Sandra Souto Kustrín, *'Y ¿Madrid? ¿Qué hace Madrid?' Movimiento revolucionario y acción*

*colectiva (1933–1936)* (Madrid: Siglo Veintiuno, 2004), pp. xix–xxviii, 37–41, 405–22 and *Paso a la Juventud: Movilización democrática, estalinismo y revolución en la República Española* (Valencia: PUV, 2013), *passim*, but especially evident in the section on young women's mobilization, pp. 254–72. In terms of conservative mobilization too it is a broader thesis running through Peter Anderson's work on grass-roots pre-civil war mobilization fuelling later denunciations within the Francoist military trial system, see *The Francoist Military Trials. Terror and Complicity, 1939–1945* (New York and Abingdon: Routledge, 2010), p. 68 for an encapsulation.

7. On the varied nature of earlier internecine violence between organizations of the left, see Chris Ealham, *Anarchism and the City: Revolution and Counter-Revolution in Barcelona, 1898–1937* (Oakland, CA: AK Press, 2010), pp. 130–48.

8. For example in Manuel Álvarez Tardío, 'The Impact of Political Violence During the Spanish General Election of 1936', *Journal of Contemporary History* 48:3 (2013), pp. 463–85: pp. 471, 484.

9. Manuel Álvarez Tardío and Roberto Villa García, *El precio de la exclusión: La política durante la Segunda República* (Madrid: Encuentro, 2010), p. 6.

10. Helen Graham, *The Spanish Civil War: A Very Short Introduction* (Oxford: Oxford University Press, 2005), p. 19. On the emergence during 1931–6 of competing concepts of 'the people', Rafael Cruz, *En el nombre del pueblo: República, rebelión y guerra en la España de 1936* (Madrid: Siglo XXI, 2006), *passim*, but especially pp. 25–67.

11. Graham, *The Spanish Republic at War*, pp. 1–21; in this uneven development are also to be found the sociological specificity of forms of repression on the wartime Republic's home front too, for example the participation in this (as perpetrators) of lower middling groups of professionals and artisans never before encadred in politics and public life, see José Luis Ledesma, *Los días de llamas de la revolución: Violencia y poítica en la retaguardia republicana de Zaragoza durante la guerra civil* (Institución Fernando el Católico, 2003), pp. 240–2.

12. For the heterogeneity of the nominally conservative interior townscapes and the effects in such areas of the military coup, see the story of the Barayón family in Chapter 4 of Helen Graham, *The War and its Shadow: Spain's Civil War in Europe's Long Twentieth Century* (Eastbourne: Sussex Academic Press, 2012), especially pp. 54–5, 57–8, 60–2.

13. Enrique Montero, 'The Forging of the Second Spanish Republic: New Liberalism, the Republican Movement and the Quest for Modernization, 1868–1931', University of London PhD thesis (1989) and also 'Reform Idealized: the Intellectual and Ideological Origins of the Second Republic', in Helen Graham and Jo Labanyi (eds), *Spanish Cultural Studies: The Struggle for Modernity* (Oxford: Oxford University, 1995), pp. 124–33. This process was also consolidated by the failure of Primo's own policies, as Alejandro Quiroga argues in *Making Spaniards: Primo de Rivera and the Nationalization of the Masses, 1923–30* (Basingstoke: Palgrave-Macmillan, 2007), pp. 5, 183–9.

14. This is the converse of Luebbert's well-known argument that fascism in interwar continental Europe was the product of the *simultaneous* political mobilization of middling groups *and* of labour unions/left political organizations, Gregory M. Luebbert, *Liberalism, Fascism or Social Democracy* (New York: Oxford University Press, 1991). Luebbert's arguments could of course also be deployed to corroborate later developments in 1930s Spain with other distinct constituencies of a middling type.

15. Mercedes Cabrera, *La patronal ante la II República* (Madrid: Siglo Veintiuno, 1983), pp. 15–17; Paul Preston, 'A Life Adrift: Indalecio Prieto', in Paul Preston, *Comrades: Portraits from the Spanish Civil War* (London: HarperCollins, 1999), pp. 234–75: 248–9.

16. Paul Preston, 'Alfonsist Monarchism and the Coming of the Spanish Civil War', *Journal of Contemporary History* 7:3–4 (1972), pp. 89–114; and the ambiguous turn of some elite

monarchist components to a legalist position in Preston, *CSCW*, pp. 38–73 and in his 'The "Moderate" Right and the Undermining of the Second Republic in Spain 1931–1933', *European Studies Review* 3:2 (1973), pp. 369–94.

17. On the fragmentation of republicanism, continuing through the 1931–6 period, an overview in Gabriel Jackson, *The Spanish Republic and the Civil War, 1931–39* (Princeton: Princeton University Press, 1965), pp. 41–2, 81–2, 103–4, 519–20 (and for 1934–6, see pp. 184–5) and Santos Juliá, 'La Experiencia del Poder: La Izquierda Republicana, 1931–1933', in Nigel Townson (ed.), *El Republicanismo en España (1830–1977)* (Madrid: Alianza Universidad, 1994), pp. 165–92.

18. This old, and often corrupt, politics was epitomized in Alejandro Lerroux's Radical Republican Party, Nigel Townson, *The Crisis of Democracy in Spain: Centrist Politics under the Second Republic 1931–1936* (Brighton and Portland, OR: Sussex Academic Press, 2000), *passim*, and 'Una República para todos los Españoles: el Partido Radical en el Poder 1933–1935', in Nigel Townson (ed.), *El Republicanismo en España (1830–1977)*, pp. 193–222. Although by the 1930s in some places (e.g. Valencia) the Radical Party did have transitional potential in terms of emerging as a modern mass party of the centre-right.

19. Helen Graham, 'War, Modernity and Reform: the Premiership of Juan Negrín, 1937–1939', in Paul Preston and Ann L. Mackenzie (eds), *The Republic Besieged: Civil War in Spain 1936–1939* (Edinburgh: Edinburgh University Press, 1996), pp. 163–96: pp. 163–6.

20. Santos Juliá, 'Manuel Azaña: la razón, la palabra y el poder', in Vicente Alberto Serrano and José María San Luciano (eds), *Azaña* (Madrid: Edascal, 1980), pp. 297–310 which remains a classic and incisive set of insights, and into the political predicament of progressive republicanism; also Santos Juliá, *Manuel Azaña: Una biografía política* (Madrid: Alianza, 1990); Paul Preston, 'The Prisoner in the Gilded Cage: Manuel Azaña', *Comrades*, pp. 194–233 and on Prieto, ibid., pp. 234–75.

21. For many this was happening again under the Republic. CNT strike action in summer 1931 was an attempt to claw back the wage erosion that had affected the poorest and most unskilled workers during the final, recession-hit years of the Primo dictatorship. But as early as October 1931, one Barcelona CNT activist complained that union activity was 'useless' since the authorities 'don't allow us to act'. Minutes of the Plenum of the Barcelona CNT Local Federation, 24 October 1931 (Centro Documental de la Memoria Histórica, Salamanca). My thanks to Chris Ealham for providing this reference.

22. They joined the UGT's landworkers' federation, FNTT, whose membership increased exponentially across 1931–6. With nearly 400,000 members even by 1932, it became the UGT's largest section: Manuel Redero San Román, *Estudios de historia de la UGT* (Salamanca: Ediciones Universidad de Salamanca, 1992), pp. 112–3; Preston, *CSCW*, p. 78; Helen Graham, *Socialism and War: The Spanish Socialist Party in Power and Crisis 1936–1939* (Cambridge: Cambridge University Press, 1991), pp. 219–20.

23. The Republic's liberal intellectual origins lay, as is well known, in the nineteenth-century Institución Libre de Enseñanza (Institute of Independent Education, i.e. not conforming to religious dogma or controlled by the Church) and it was frequently referred to as the 'Republic of teachers' because of the direct lineage to the ILE of many of its leading figures. On the ILE legacy in the 1930s, Christopher Cobb's analysis, 'The Republican State and Mass Educational-Cultural Initiatives 1931–1936', in Helen Graham and Jo Labanyi (eds), *Spanish Cultural Studies*, pp. 133–8; also Sandie Holguín, *Creating Spaniards: Culture and National Identity in Republican Spain* (Madison: University of Wisconsin Press, 2002), *passim*.

24. J.S. Vidarte, *Todos fuimos culpables*, Vol. I (2 Vols. Barcelona: Grijalbo, 1978), p. 99. On liberal republican anxieties and obsession with 'the neutrality of the street', Juliá, *Manuel Azaña: Una*

*biografía política*, pp. 459–69. Both the central Republican government under Negrín and its Catalan opposite under the Esquerra's Lluís Companys would be similarly focused during the war period.

25. Ealham, *Anarchism and the City*, especially pp. 72–84, 90–101, 130–40; Graham, *Spanish Republic at War*, pp. 35–41. The most well-known rural examples of 1931–3 are also included in Gabriel Jackson's useful chronology to *The Spanish Republic and the Civil War, 1931–39* (Princeton: Princeton University Press, 1965), pp. 502–3.

26. Respectively the Law for the Defence of the Republic (October 1931); Public Order Law (July 1932); the Vagrancy Law of August 1933 (*Ley de Vagos y Maleantes*) which the jurist and leading parliamentary socialist, Luis Jiménez de Asúa, helped draft and which would remain on the statute books of the Franco dictatorship until 1970. Chris Ealham, *Anarchism and the City*, pp. 77–80. From October 1931 until the end of the coalition in September 1933, the home office minister was Azaña's friend and colleague, Santiago Casares Quiroga, who would be prime minister in the all-republican cabinet in spring 1936 (after Azaña became Republican president) and when Casares' refusal to act against the open secret of military conspiracy became notorious.

27. Most of those who died at the hands of the Republican security forces were protesting workers, unionists or the unemployed, Eduardo González Calleja, *En nombre de la autoridad: La defensa del orden publico durante la Segunda Republica espanola (1931–1936)* (Granada: Comares, 2014), pp. 321–26. Revisionist authors entirely ignore this, Álvarez Tardío and Villa García, *El precio de la exclusión*, pp. 155–202.

28. Graham, *Very Short Introduction*, p. 14 and cf. *Spanish Republic at War*, p. 416.

29. Cf. Julio Aróstegui, *Francisco Largo Caballero, el tesón y la quimera* (Madrid: Editorial Debate, 2013), p. 260; Graham, *Spanish Republic at War*, p. 45.

30. See the discussion of this later in the chapter, in relation to the classic and revisionist debates over the nature of the political position of Largo Caballero and his supporters, 1934–6.

31. Santos Juliá, 'La Experiencia del Poder: La Izquierda Republicana, 1931–1933', pp. 181–3; the general context in Mercedes Cabrera, *La patronal ante la República*, pp. 15, 202–15.

32. Fernando del Rey Reguillo, *Paisanos en lucha: Exclusión política y violencia en la Segunda República española* (Madrid: Biblioteca Nueva, 2008), *passim*, especially pp. 147–57, 162. See also the review by Nigel Townson in *English Historical Review* CXXV: 517, pp. 1573–5. In that del Rey accepts that the PSOE-UGT did tackle rising unemployment, his later criticism of them as practising a policy of exclusion seems oddly formulated – all the more especially in the context of socialist participation in what was the first government ever to take seriously the social rights of those previously the most politically excluded – i.e. the new mass constituencies of urban and rural workers. But Fernando del Rey's point about other economically modest, middling groups feeling alienated from the new political process at local level is very well made – moreover this would destabilize the new democracy.

33. For the persistence of clientelist practices on the left during the civil war, especially in the PCE, as a result of which the Socialists were to some extent the losers in the organizational competition, see Graham, *Socialism and War*, especially pp. 118–19 and *Spanish Republic at War*, pp. 182, 293, and esp. 328–9.

34. The appearance/appeal of communist parties (whether the official PCE or others in Catalonia) in the 1920s had had more to do with local economic (and trade union) conditions than Bolshevik revolutionary kudos – note that the main centres of their strength in the industrial north and north-east were precisely where the forms and practices of UGT unionism did not 'fit' or deliver in local conditions. Still later, by 1935–6, Spain's and Catalonia's communist parties would, in evolving political circumstances, attract a popular

base from among urban middling and professional constituencies, a gift made by the continuing disinterest of progressive republican groupings in the cultivation of any social base, Graham, *Spanish Republic at War,* pp. 61–78, esp. 74–5, 77.

35. The trilogy of severely repressed local CNT risings occurred in January 1932 (Llobregat (Barcelona)); January 1933 (Casas Viejas (Cádiz, Andalusia)) and December 1933 (Hospitalet (Barcelona)). Ealham, *Anarchism and the City*, pp. 30–40. On Hospitalet see also Chapter 3 of Chris Ealham, *Living Anarchism: José Peirats and the Spanish Anarcho-syndicalist Movement* (Oakland, CA and London: AK Press, 2015). On the particular relationship between socially and economically marginalized urban populations, grass-roots protest and the CNT grass roots, see also Helen Graham, 'Against the State: A Genealogy of the Barcelona May Days, 1937', *European History Quarterly* 29:1 (1999), pp. 485–542: pp. 489–94; 513–4, 518.

36. The scarcely veiled xenophobia of the centre-left Esquerra did not only affect progressive Catalan republicans but spilled over into various 'eugenicist' comments made by Catalan socialists, deriding the CNT base as 'down-and-outs', even 'sub-human' and 'degenerate', *Justicia Social,* 1 August 1931, 29 April, 22 July, 11 November 1933; *Cataluña Obrera*, 26 May, 9 June 1933. My thanks to Chris Ealham for these references. See also Ealham, *Anarchism and the City*, pp. 66–9, 82.

37. As Chris Ealham has noted, 'the period 1931–3 was a time of schism, witch hunts, trials of moderates and a debilitating split that led to the haemorrhaging of *cenetistas* and the diminishing importance of the CNT […] hundreds of thousands of workers never returned to its ranks', unpublished article, '"History Wars" and the Anatomy of the Left during the Second Republic'; also Juan Pablo Calero Delso, 'Vísperas de la revolución: El congreso del la CNT (1936)', *Germinal: revista de estudios libertarios* 7 (2009), pp. 97–132.

38. Julián Casanova, *Anarchism, the Republic and the Civil War in Spain, 1931–1939* (Abingdon and New York: Routledge, 2004), pp. 47–63, 116–57.

39. Prieto famously referred to the need for the PSOE to behave as republicans, interview in *Le Populaire* (Paris), 17 January 1931, cited in Graham, *Socialism and War*, p. 258, n. 5; cf. also Prieto's speech in the Cine Pardiñas, *El Socialista*, 6 February 1934, cited in Indalecio Prieto, *Discursos fundamentales*, pp. 181–203: p. 185.

40. Ealham, *Anarchism and the City*, pp. 72–4, 77–80, 83–4. (Ángel Galarza, the PSOE Chief of State Security, shaped the *Guardia de Asalto* (Assault Guards), a new paramilitary police force created under the Republic and recruited predominantly from republicans and socialists.)

41. For example, Francisco Cobo Romero discusses local labour conflicts between municipal authorities, small proprietors and agricultural labourers in some areas of the south over the implementation and workings of the social and labour legislation of 1931–3, in *Revolución campesina y contrarrevolución franquista en Andalucía: Conflictividad social, violencia política y represión franquista en el mundo rural andaluz, 1931–1950* (Granada: University of Granada, 2004), pp. 66–99, esp. 77–8.

42. A useful short analysis of Republican policy and strategic shortcomings in Frances Lannon, 'The Political Debate within Catholicism', in Helen Graham and Jo Labanyi (eds), *Spanish Cultural Studies*, pp. 139–44.

43. Many of the young women trained up as Republican *maestras* (primary teachers) and sent out to village Spain to run the new local schoolrooms endured the blast of this ingrained conservatism, as explored in the award-winning documentary film, *Las Maestras de la República* (Spain (FETE-UGT), 2013). It also serves as a reminder that the primordial cultural frontline in 1930s Spain (in contrast to that frontline *in memory*), was between rural and urban worlds rather than between the religious and the anticlerical per se, which in urban

environments managed perfectly well to coexist at the level of everyday life (often within families) and in spite of the polarization of 1934–6, only being totally cashiered as a form of functioning *convivencia* by the July 1936 military coup itself. For an indication/imaginative recreation of this complex social reality, see Juan Sales' important autobiographical novel *Incerta glòria* (1971) – now available in English translation, *Uncertain Glory* (London: MacLehose Press, 2014).

44. Francisco Espinosa Maestre, *Contra la República: Los 'sucesos de Almonte' de 1932. Laicismo, integrismo católico y reforma agraria* (Seville: Diputación de Huelva, 2012), *passim*.

45. Graham, *Very Short Introduction*, p. 12, and the chronology in Gabriel Jackson, *The Spanish Republic and the Civil War*, pp. 502–3.

46. On the CEDA, José Ramón Montero, *La CEDA: el catolicismo social y político en la II República*, 2 vols (Madrid: Ediciones de la Revista de Trabajo, 1977); Richard H. Robinson, *The Origins of Franco's Spain*; Preston, *CSCW*; Manuel Alvarez Tardio, 'The CEDA: Threat or Opportunity?', in Manuel Alvarez Tardío and Fernando del Rey Reguillo (eds), *The Spanish Second Republic Revisited: From Democratic Hopes to the Civil War (1931–1936)* (Brighton: Sussex Academic Press, 2011), pp. 58–79; and on the rapidly fascistizing CEDA youth wing, JAP, Sid Lowe, *Catholicism, War and the Foundation of Francoism: The Juventud de Acción Popular in Spain, 1931–1939* (Brighton: Sussex Academic Press, 2010).

47. Carolyn P. Boyd, '"Responsibilities" and the Second Spanish Republic 1931–1936', *European History Quarterly* 14:2 (1984), pp. 151–82; Preston, *CSCW*, p. 50.

48. Preston, *CSCW*, especially pp. 74–119, 211–38; also Marta Bizcarrondo, 'Democracia y revolución en la estrategia socialista de la Segunda República', *Estudios de Historia Social* 16–17 (1981), pp. 227–459. The classic study of the internal breakdown of the socialist left (Largo Caballero's wing) is Santos Juliá, *La izquierda del PSOE (1935–1936)* (Madrid: Siglo Veintiuno, 1977).

49. Townson, *The Crisis of Democracy in Spain*, pp. 170–1; José Manuel Macarro Vera, 'Causas de la radicalización socialista en la II República', *Revista de Historia Contemporánea* 1 (1982), pp. 178–224: pp. 214–16, 218–19.

50. Javier Ugarte Tellería, *La nueva Covadonga insurgente: Orígenes sociales y culturales de la sublevación de 1936 en Navarra y el País Vasco* (Madrid: Biblioteca Nueva, 1998); Lowe, *Catholicism, War and the Foundation of Francoism: the Juventud de Acción Popular in Spain, 1931–1939*.

51. Santos Juliá, *La izquierda del PSOE (1935–1936)*.

52. For example, Graham, *Socialism and War*; Souto, *Paso a la Juventud*.

53. For example, the title of the 2011 collective volume, *Palabras como puños: La intransigencia política en la Segunda República española* ('Words like Fists: Political Intransigence in the Second Spanish Republic') (Madrid: Tecnos, 2011), edited by Fernando del Rey Reguillo, and some of whose essays imply that the political left was the principal, indeed sole, cause of escalating violence, and can somehow be viewed in isolation from the broader historical dynamic of 1931–6 as 'responsible' for the entire political breakdown. For a survey of the dynamic of political violence 1931–6, and the evolution of the historiographical debate on the role played therein by the political left/reform-minded constituencies across 1931–6, and which also points up some of the empirical flaws in revisionist arguments, see Eduardo González Calleja, 'La historiografía sobre la violencia política en la Segunda República española: una reconsideración', *Hispania Nova: Revista de historia contemporánea* 11 (2013), http://hispanianova.rediris.es/11/dossier/11d004.pdf [accessed 30 August 2015], p. 15, n. 33. See also, González Calleja, 'The Symbolism of Violence during the Second Republic in Spain, 1931–1936', in Chris Ealham and Michael Richards (eds), *The Splintering of Spain: Cultural*

*History and the Spanish Civil War, 1936–1939* (Cambridge: Cambridge University Press, 2005), pp. 23–44, 227–30.

54. CEDA propaganda (and that of many of its constituent parts prior to 1933) implicitly linked the two, thus inducing fear through misinformation in Castilian smallholders and tenant farmers, who then worried that the Republic intended to seize their small amounts of land, Preston, *CSCW*, p. 55; cf. also pp. 45–6.

55. A number of historians, including Paul Preston, have noted from their own detailed reading of the 1930s press, how conservative newspapers magnified isolated acts of everyday violence and exaggerated any breakdown of public order in a bid generally to discredit the Republic. Moral panics also played their part in this, Ealham, *Anarchism and the City*, pp. 149–55. Ealham has also more recently observed the similarity between this approach and that of some of the neoconservative revisionist historians writing today (unpublished article, 'Social History, Revisionism and Mapping the 1930s Spanish Left').

56. As Chris Ealham remarks in 'Social History, Revisionism and Mapping the 1930s Spanish Left', revisionism often appears to see the Second Republic as *never* really having been a proper democracy. (This is the sub-text of several of the contributions to Álvarez Tardío and del Rey Reguillo (eds), *The Spanish Second Republic Revisited*.)

57. The PCE was a small, marginal party until the civil war period. In 1931 it had fewer than 5,000 members and even by spring 1936 it is unlikely to have had more than approximately 14,000, Rafael Cruz, *El Partido Comunista de España en la Segunda República* (Madrid: Alianza, 1987), p. 57. After the July 1936 military coup the PCE grew in what were the vastly changed circumstances of the wartime Republican zone, and recruiting from often socially conservative middling constituencies and from among professional army officers, Graham, *The Spanish Republic at War*, pp. 181–4, 324–5. See also Fernando Hernández Sánchez, *Guerra o Revolución: El Partido Comunista de España en la guerra civil* (Barcelona: Crítica, 2010). But the PCE's own exaggerated pronouncements of its pre-war strength have since helped fuel Francoist and revisionist myth, Fernando Hernández Sánchez, 'El PCE en la Guerra civil', PhD thesis, UNED, 2010, pp. 79, 352.

58. And equally as before, a majority of the fatalities were inflicted by the Republican state's security forces themselves, Eduardo González Calleja, 'La necro-lógica de la Violencia sociopolítica en la primavera de 1936', *Mélanges de la Casa de Velázquez* 41:1 (2011), pp. 37–60: p. 51. This is ignored by the revisionists, cf. Manuel Álvarez Tardío, 'The Impact of Political Violence During the Spanish General Election of 1936', *Journal of Contemporary History* 48:3 (2013), pp. 463–85. Even direct clashes in spring 1936 between reform and counter-reform activists led to a greater number of fatalities among the former, González Calleja, 'La necro-lógica', p. 47.

59. Paul Preston, 'The Prisoner in the Gilded Cage: Manuel Azaña', p. 219. A witness at the Madrid meeting on the Campo de Comillas (Carabanchel) was the journalist Henry Buckley, *The Life and Death of the Spanish Republic* (London and New York: I.B. Tauris, 2013 – first published by Hamish Hamilton in 1940), pp. 182–5 whose commentary has an arresting freshness and shocking incisiveness even today.

60. A relevant extract from these cited in translation in Paul Preston, *The Spanish Holocaust: Inquisition and Extermination in Twentieth-Century Spain* (London: HarperPress, 2012), p. 119.

61. An original approach stressing imperialism as the unifying strand between the self-proclaimed fascist Falange and other components of the Spanish right, in the classic chapter by Herbert R. Southworth, 'The Falange: An Analysis of Spain's Fascist Heritage', in Paul Preston (ed.), *Spain in Crisis: Evolution and Decline of the Franco Regime* (Hassocks, Sussex:

Harvester Press, 1976); Paul Preston, 'Populism and Parasitism: The Falange and the Spanish Establishment, 1939–1975', in Martin Blinkhorn (ed.), *Fascists and Conservatives: The Radical Right and the Establishment in Twentieth-Century Europe* (London: Unwin Hyman, 1990), pp. 138–56; Paul Preston, *The Politics of Revenge: Fascism and the Military in Twentieth-Century Spain* (first published 1990, 2nd edn, London: Routledge, 1995); Ismael Saz, 'El franquismo. ¿régimen autoritario o dictadura fascista?', in Javier Tusell (ed.), *El régimen de Franco, 1936–1975: política y relaciones exteriores*, Vol. I (Madrid: UNED, 1993) and *Fascismo y Franquismo* (Valencia: Universitat de València, 2004). See also the chapter by Angel Viñas in this volume.

## Further reading

Álvarez Tardío, M. and Rey Reguillo, F. de (eds), *The Spanish Second Republic Revisited: From Democratic Hopes to the Civil War (1931–1936)*, Brighton: Sussex Academic Press, 2011 (translation of a revisionist work).

Casanova, J., *Anarchism, the Republic and Civil War in Spain: 1931–1939*, London: Routledge, 2004.

Casanova, J., *The Spanish Republic and Civil War*, Cambridge: Cambridge University Press, 2010.

Ealham, C., *Anarchism and the City: Revolution and Counter-Revolution in Barcelona, 1898–1937*, Oakland, CA: AK Press, 2010.

Ealham, C., 'The Emperor's New Clothes: "Objectivity" and Revisionism in Spanish History', *Journal of Contemporary History* 48:1 (2013), pp. 191–202.

Ealham, C. and Richards, M. (eds), *The Splintering of Spain: New Historical Perspectives on the Spanish Civil War*, Cambridge: Cambridge University Press, 2005.

Graham, H., *The Spanish Republic at War 1936–1939*, Cambridge: Cambridge University Press, 2002 (also has a chapter on 1931–6).

Graham, H., *The Spanish Civil War: A Very Short Introduction*, Oxford: Oxford University Press, 2005.

Graham, H., *The War and its Shadow: Spain's Civil War in Europe's Long Twentieth Century*, Eastbourne: Sussex Academic Press, 2012.

Moradiellos, E., *1936. Los mitos de la guerra civil*, Barcelona: Península, 2004.

Payne, S., *Spain's First Democracy: The Second Republic, 1931–1936*, Madison, WI: University of Wisconsin Press, 1993.

Preston, P., *The Coming of the Spanish Civil War: Reform, Reaction and Revolution in the Second Spanish Republic 1931–1936*, London: Macmillan, 1978 (revised 2nd edition: Routledge, London, 1994).

Preston, P., 'Agrarian War in the South', in Paul Preston (ed.), *Revolution and War in Spain, 1931–1939*, 2nd edn. London: Routledge, 1993, pp. 159–81.

Preston, P., *The Spanish Civil War: Reaction, Revolution and Revenge*, London: Harper Perennial, 2006.

Stockey, G., 'Spain's First Democracy: The 1931 Constitution and its Detractors', in Adam Sharman and Stephen G.H. Roberts (eds), *1812 Echoes: The Cadiz Constitution in Hispanic History, Culture and Politics*, Newcastle: Cambridge Scholars Press, 2013, pp. 314–36.

Thomas, M., *The Faith and the Fury: Popular Anticlerical Violence and Iconoclasm in Spain, 1931–1936*, Brighton: Sussex Academic Press, 2012.

Viñas, A., *Los mitos del 18 de julio*, Barcelona: Crítica, 2013.

# PART II
## MAKING DICTATORSHIP: DISCOURSE, POLICY AND PRACTICE

# CHAPTER 4
## 'PRODUCTIVE HATREDS': RADICAL SEGREGATIONIST DISCOURSES AND THE MAKING OF FRANCOISM
*Isabelle Rohr*

The last decade has witnessed a growing interest in the question of the Franco regime's antisemitism.[1] Discussions of the dictatorship's antisemitism and Spain's Jewish policy during the Second World War have not only built on the larger trend that examines the role of neutral countries during the Holocaust, but have also placed them in the context of the historiographical debates on the nature and shape of Francoism. Apologists for the Franco regime have claimed that the fact that Spain did not promulgate antisemitic legislation and allowed a number of Jews to pass through its territories distinguished the dictatorship from fascism and Nazism. But, while the regime did not systematically persecute Jewish refugees who were in Spain at the time, it used antisemitism to demonize and dehumanize imaginary Jews: the Republicans whom it had defeated in the battlefield war of 1936–9 and whom it would subsequently configure as a marginalized 'enemy' community or 'anti-nation'.[2] Francoist antisemitic rhetoric blended modern racial antisemitism with traditional anti-Judaic notions and incessantly invoked the fifteenth-century Catholic Kings' anti-Jewish policies and the need to purify Spain. This rhetoric paved the way for the use of repressive practices which again fused modern and traditional: among the modern methods were many observed via Nazi Germany with whom the Franco regime had a close relationship, while older techniques, turned to new ends by Franco, included those dating back to the era of the Inquisition.

On 31 March 1492, the Catholic Kings Isabella and Ferdinand issued the Edict of Expulsion, giving Jews four months either to accept baptism or to leave the Kingdoms of Castile and Aragon. While some went into exile to neighbouring Christian lands, mainly to Italy and Portugal, a great many Jews chose to convert. Anti-Jewish sentiments in Spain did not disappear after Jews were expelled. For centuries to come the many Jews who had chosen to convert (*judeoconversos*) were considered to be different from the rest of the population and were stigmatized. They were called opprobrious names such as *Marranos* (pigs) and were the subject of popular satire. Between the fifteenth and seventeenth centuries, the *Estatutos de Limpieza de Sangre* (the 'Blood Purity Statutes') were introduced, denying the new converts and their descendants entrance into universities, religious orders and governments.[3] From this religious doctrine arose the concept of Spanish *casticismo* (casticism), which gave a higher social status to the families that did not count Jews or Muslims among their ancestors. Prejudices against descendants of converts persisted even after the Inquisition was revoked in 1834, and in the conflict which opposed conservatives – who wanted to defend the privileges of the Church – to anticlerical liberals, the former often accused the latter of being *judeoconversos*.[4] Even though Jews were largely absent from Spain after 1492, they survived as a phantasmagorical construction against which a Spanish Catholic identity was built.

At the end of the nineteenth century this anti-Judaic rhetoric took on a new dimension as the work of French antisemites, such as Edouard Drumont, was propagated in Spain in the wake of the Dreyfus Affair of 1894. Traditionalist thinkers in Spain came to equate the Jews with liberalism and Freemasonry. In 1891, the Catalan translator Peregrín Casabó y Pagés produced a Spanish equivalent to Drumont's *La France Juive,* entitled *La España Judia* in which he denounced the economic dominance of Jews in modern Spain.[5] As Hazel Gold has pointed out, the figure of the 'Jew' became omnipresent in the philosophical, theological and political discourses of Spanish society even though there was no Jewish community.[6]

The First World War and the success of the Bolshevik revolution produced new myths about the Jews, which also found enthusiastic propagators in Spain. Like their counterparts in other European countries, Spanish ultraconservative thinkers claimed that there existed an age-old Jewish plot for world dominance. To achieve that goal, Jews used their alleged control of world finance to cause economic and political upheaval. The *Protocols of the Elders of Zion*, a forgery first published in Russia in 1903 by the Tsarist secret police, and which purported to be transcripts of Jewish conspirators plotting to dominate the world, first appeared in 1930 in Spain. The book became the bible of Spanish antisemites, who took its central argument to heart and used it in their struggle against progressive forces. They depicted freemasonry, liberalism and socialism as the tools of a Jewish plot that sought to annihilate Catholic Spain.

The myth of the Judeo-Masonic conspiracy was supplemented by another myth: that of the *Reconquista*. According to traditionalist thinkers, there existed an eternal Catholic-Spanish essence, *Hispanidad*, born in the Visigothic age between the fifth and eighth centuries and resurrected during the centuries-long fight to recapture Spain from the Moors, the *Reconquista*. In this version of history, the fall of the last Moorish kingdom of Granada in 1492 and the ensuing Decree of Expulsion of the Jews from Spain ushered in the Golden Age during which the Spanish kings stood as the world's standard bearers of Catholicism. Ultraconservative intellectuals asserted that Spain's declining fortunes since the loss of its last substantial colonies in 1898 was the result of the reformism of the Bourbon monarchs and the Napoleonic invasion, which introduced non-Spanish liberal ideas to the Peninsula.[7]

Borrowing heavily from the Europe-wide contemporary scientific discourse of Jews as a race, some thinkers took the argument one step further, claiming that Spain's 'decline' or 'decay' was due to the racial mixing between Jews and Spaniards. Hence, in 1916 the Catalan writer, César Peiró Menéndez, declared that 'the ulcer that corrodes Spain, the gangrene that rots it and the cancer that kills it is Jewish'.[8] He asserted that descendants of converted Jews, 'the Jews by blood', suffered from 'racial bastardization' and had caused the degeneration of Spain. He listed the physiological characteristics that distinguished them from other Spaniards, including an oval face, a large forehead, ears that stick out, and thick nostrils. According to him, they were the bearers of all kinds of diseases, ranging from hysteria and neurasthenia to syphilis and leprosy.[9] Their exclusion from politics and public administration was a prerequisite for the regeneration of Spain.

In the 1930s, the abolition of the monarchy in Spain, the establishment of the Second Republic, the ensuing declaration of religious freedom and the bid to restrict the privileges of the institutional Catholic Church also inflamed the hostility of conservatives towards the Jews. Anti-Jewish themes were already conspicuous in their political lexicon during the municipal elections of April 1931, which saw the birth of the Republic. While campaigning against the Republican-Socialist electoral alliance, the monarchists predicted that in the new regime 'Bolshevik Jews will dominate Spain, spreading terror and misery, corrupting and ultimately destroying our traditional home life.'[10] After the Republican centre-left won the elections, the argument that Jews controlled the newly established Second Republic became further entrenched among social and political conservatives and was especially frequent in radical right-wing circles. Accordingly, in June 1931, the Carlist newspaper, *El Siglo Futuro*, accused three of the new government ministers of being Jewish: the Prime Minister Niceto Acalá Zamora, the Minister of the Interior Miguel Maura (both former monarchists turned republicans) and also the Minister of Education and Fine Arts, the parliamentary socialist and law professor, Fernando de los Ríos.[11]

The greatest promoter of the Judeo-Masonic-Bolshevik conspiracy and the *Reconquista* myths during the Second Republic was probably the Catalan priest Juan Tusquets. Tusquets belonged to a Jesuit secret society, linked to the International Anti-Masonic League, an organization whose aim was to unveil Masonic plots to seize power.[12] He wrote an exhaustive series *La biblioteca de las sectas* (the library of the sects), whose principal targets were Jews and Freemasons. The first book of the series, *Origenes de la revolución española* (Origins of the Spanish Revolution), was published in 1932. That book, according to historian José Luis Rodriguez Jiménez, had the distinction of being the first one to use the *Protocols* to account for the course of Spanish history.[13] According to Tusquets, Jewish machinations against Catholic Spain predated the forming of the Judeo-Masonic coalition, indeed that it was the treachery of the Jews which had brought about the Inquisition. He explained how during the fifteenth-century *Reconquista*, the Jews had loaned money to both sides at 'usurious rates of interest', always helping the weaker side in order to prolong the war. Tusquets praised the decision of the Catholic Kings Isabella and Ferdinand to promulgate the Edict of Expulsion. Using the pathological language so in vogue at the time, he wrote that after the *Reconquista*, Spain had 'felt sufficiently strong to cast out the microbes that were poisoning it'.[14] Tusquets' work was very influential: his bulletin on Freemasonry was distributed to senior army officers, and later Franco's brother-in-law, Ramón Serrano Súñer, a key figure in his regime, praised Tusquets for contributing to 'the creation of the atmosphere which led to the National uprising', by which he meant the military coup of 17–18 July 1936.[15]

Others on the extreme right also invoked the twin myths of the *Reconquista* and the Judeo-Masonic-Bolshevik conspiracy to explain some of the key events under the Republic, such as the incident in December 1931 in the village of Castilblanco, located in

Spain's impoverished deep south, in which four Civil Guards were lynched after opening fire on protesting villagers. In a review of the *Protocols of the Elders of Zion* in the monarchist journal *Accion Española*, the Marqués de la Eliseda claimed that by bringing 'liberal and democratic venom' to the Peninsula, the Jews were responsible for the exacerbation of class hatred in Southern Spain.[16] In the same vein, after the events in Asturias in October 1934, during which some twenty to thirty thousand miners rebelled against the new right-wing government which stood poised to rescind key social reforms enacted earlier, the Bishop of Oviedo wrote in a pastoral letter in November that: '[t]he revolutionary and criminal strike has been organized by the Jews and Freemasons'.[17] In the face of this perceived Jewish danger, the radical right believed that a re-enactment of the *Reconquista* was necessary. Indeed, Gil Robles, the leader of the mass Catholic party CEDA (Confederación Española de Derechas Autonómas), had already called in 1933 for the 'reconquest' of Spain and the 'purging' of 'Judaizing freemasons' from the fatherland.[18]

These themes were repeated again and again across the near three years of battlefield war, triggered by the military coup of July 1936 against the Republic. In one of his radio broadcasts, the leading insurgent general, Queipo de Llano, declared from his Seville HQ, that the fight was 'not a Spanish Civil War but a war of western civilization against world Jewry'.[19] The propagation of antisemitic ideas was such that the philosopher Hannah Arendt noted at the time that 'even Franco, in a country where there are neither Jews nor a Jewish question is battling the troops of the Spanish Republic while mounting antisemitic slogans.'[20] There were indeed only about 6,000 Jews in Spain in 1936, mostly composed of Moroccan Jews who had immigrated in the late nineteenth century, but describing the war as a crusade against the 'Jewish hordes', the Spanish generals who rose against the Republic and their allies were able to use a myth to avoid dealing with the myriad real social and economic issues that had provoked the conflict.[21] The Judeo-Masonic-Bolshevik conspiracy theory provided a straightforward, and to many a satisfying 'explanation' of a complicated situation. As historian Javier Domínguez Arribas has pointed out, it explained the incomprehensible, including aspects as diverse as the criticism against the insurgents levelled by some Catholics during the civil war, as well as the black market and the extreme scarcity of staple goods in the postwar period.[22] The Judeo-Masonic-Bolshevik conspiracy theory also fulfilled another function during the war years and afterwards: by enabling the various conservative groups which supported the Francoist coalition to focus their attention on a group of imaginary enemies it boosted their sense of unity.[23] Given the coalition and its supporters were composed of heterogeneous groups, they certainly needed a binding agent. The coalition ranged from Alfonsine monarchists (who strove for a restoration of Alfonso XIII), ultra-traditionalist Carlists who supported an alternative candidate for the throne, the members of the former mass Catholic party CEDA (effectively disbanded on the eve of the civil war), who had come in their majority to favour a Catholic corporatist state, and the fascist Falange, whose purist sectors sought the establishment of a modern, national socialist state in which the privilege of hereditary wealth would be abolished. Nevertheless, a shared intense hatred of Republicans, Freemasons and Jews helped these different rightist forces overcome their not inconsiderable formal political divisions. Thus, in times of internecine conflict between the Falangists and the military, the regime's propagandists could call for unity against the common enemy.[24] Finally, antisemitism was also used to recruit Moroccan mercenaries, many of whom came from rural areas where there was little awareness of communism or freemasonry but where there was a history of pillaging local Jews.[25] The insurgents disseminated pamphlets in Morocco, in which Jews were accused of being the 'representatives of Red Spain'. Muslims were warned that if the Republicans triumphed, the mosques would be burned, the harems would be violated, properties would be destroyed and the Jews along with the Communists would be in command and would treat the Muslims like animals.[26]

From the outset of the war, the insurgents and their allies described the conflict as a crusade against the 'Jewish-Masonic-Bolshevik' conspiracy to conquer Spain. The insurgents' press repeated tirelessly that the Soviet Union, which provided military assistance to the Spanish Republicans, was in the hands of Jews. It also emphasized that a large proportion of Jews were fighting on the side of the Republic in the International Brigades.[27] In October 1938 the newspaper *ABC* (Seville) noted that 'thousands of Jews from all corners of the world have flocked to the defense of the Reds'.[28] But the principal targets of the Francoist antisemitic rhetoric were the Republicans themselves. In the insurgents' version of the war, the Republicans were cast as descendants of the Jews who had converted formally to Christianity but continued to practise Judaism. The Republicans were accused of being 'judaizers', 'illegitimate children of Israel' or 'camouflaged Jews' who hated Spain for the forced conversion of their ancestors and plotted against it with their co-religionists abroad. Juan Pujol, Franco's Press Chief, who received subsidies from the Nazis, revealed that while some Republican leaders, such as the Minister of National Defence, Indalecio Prieto, did not know that they were Jewish, others tried to conceal their true name and religion.[29] Chief among the latter was the former cabinet minister, Fernando de los Ríos, the Republic's wartime Ambassador in Washington, whom the insurgents called the 'Rabbi of Spain'. According to the San Sebastian-based weekly *Domingo*, which had been set up by Pujol, de los Ríos was a *marrano* who had been ordained rabbi in Amsterdam in 1926 and had then taken the name of Solomon. His family, which had been forced to convert to Catholicism during the Inquisition, had long wanted 'to take revenge on traditional Spain'.[30]

Catalan nationalists were also denounced as Jews. Pujol revealed that the success of separatism in Catalonia was largely due to the fact that 'an enormous portion of the population' there was 'of Jewish origin'.[31] Some of these Jews 'had been there since the Inquisition'. These were 'converted Jews, scattered among the rest of the inhabitants' who 'lived in urban centres' and 'ended up concealing the real Catalan population of rural origin'. According to Pujol the Jews formed the 'nucleus' of the middle-class Catalanist movement, the *Lliga Regionalista*. Even though the leaders of this 'wicked organization' did not really profess Judaism, they were 'of Jewish race'. Pujol asserted that Lluís Companys, the leader of the Catalan autonomous government of the 1930s, the *Generalitat*, was another camouflaged Jew: 'Companys', he wrote in *ABC* (Seville) in December 1936, 'is Jewish, the descendent of converted Jews. One does not need to explore his genealogical tree to realize it, one look at his face is enough'.[32] Basque nationalists were also accused of being Jewish. After the bombing of the Basque market town of Guernica by the German Condor Legion on 26 April 1937, a massacre that caused an international outcry, the Francoist journalist Víctor de la Serna declared that the Basques themselves had destroyed the city. Using the word 'Jew' as a synonym for Basque nationalist, he asserted that Guernica had 'perished on the Basque altar in the hands of the Jews'.[33]

Antisemitism was also used against another group hated by the insurgents: emancipated women, whose liberated lifestyle was perceived as a threat to traditional gender norms. Hostile to the relative permissiveness of the Second Republic, which had granted women the right to vote and legalized divorce and civil marriage, conservative Catholics also expressed their sexual anxiety in antisemitic terms. Drawing on the traditional Catholic notion that Judaism was a religion of no morality and that Jewish sexuality, beginning with the ritual circumcision, was deviant, the insurgents claimed that Jews manipulated 'the inexperienced minds of women' through their 'poisonous' cinema, thus giving clear voice to the now crucial and articulating anti-modernist and anti-city dimension of their antisemitism. They urged women living in Spain's largest cities to cease following 'tastes decreed by the disgusting but guilded Parisian Jews' and to adopt styles in line with 'Holy Nationalism', which meant dressing modestly, covering their legs with stockings and refraining from the use of make-up.[34] Attacks against Margarita Nelken, the intellectual, writer, social reformer and Socialist MP whose family was of German Jewish origin, reflected this fusion between antisemitism and antifeminism. Her free sexual life – she was the single mother of two children – clashed with the prejudices of conservative sectors, which the Francoists espoused as part of their credo. Nelken was characterized as a witch, a temptress who led a scandalous private life and had frightening sexual power. In *El Poema de la Bestia y del Ángel* ('Poem of the Beast and the Angel'), the journalist, writer and Francoist ideologue, José María Péman who furnished some of the most forceful expressions of these ideas, wrote the following about her:

> Oh, cursed, cursed
> You, the Hebrew
> You, unmarried mother: Margarita!
> Name of a flower and spirit of a hyena![35]

Intolerable to the Francoists was Nelken's spirited defence of the rights of the impoverished landless labourers of Spain's large southern estates, when she was MP for the south-western province of Badajoz (Extremadura) during the Second Republic. Thus, the journalist Manuel Sánchez del Arco wrote that 'the Jewish Amazon Señora Nelken' 'has spread poison among the men of Extremadura, who are in rebellion today because of her Marxist preachings'.[36] Similarly in *Domingo* Juan Pujol contrasted Nelken, a 'Red Jewess', 'cursed from birth', 'dressed in expensive clothes' to the virginal Spanish Catholic women, whose place was at home. He claimed that she hated them 'for their virtue, their moral qualities and their faith'.[37] According to Pujol, Nelken's disturbing sexual nature made her the antithesis of god-fearing Catholic women. She was 'a snake with skirts', who had 'induced her rural followers' and 'used her sexuality to arouse the virile crowds of Extremadura'. The idea that Jews used their sexual depravity to delude Christians was also a recurring theme in insurgent propaganda. Hence, in September 1936, Queipo de Llano declared that 'pornographic literature' was 'one of the most powerful weapons' used by 'the Freemasons, the Jews and the Marxists'.[38]

While the insurgents denounced the Republicans as Jews or converted Jews, they portrayed themselves as the heirs of the Catholic Kings Ferdinand and Isabella, and discursively fashioned the war of 1936–9 as a re-enactment of the *Reconquista*. In an attempt to graft modern antisemitic ideas to the ancient trunk of the Catholic Kings' anti-Jewish policies, they argued that a 'cleansing operation' was needed to eradicate the 'Jewish-Masonic-Bolshevik' threat and called for the expulsion of the Jews and a revival of the Inquisition. In 1938, the *Correo Español* pledged that Francoist Spain would keep its territories free of Jews.[39] Ernesto Giménez Caballero, the principal ideologue of Spanish fascism, advocated the re-establishment of traditional forms of religious persecution, such as the 'auto-da-fe', to 'purify' Spain from the Jews who had 'infiltrated' the country.[40] In the same vein, Antonio Vallejo-Nágera, head of psychiatric services in Franco's armies, also believed that the Inquisition had to be reintroduced to Spain, justifying it in terms of the new biological imperatives of the age:

The blood of the inquisitors flows in our veins and inquisitorial chromosomes are in our paternal and maternal genes [. . .]. Those who wish can label us reactionaries or obscurantists; nothing will halt our impulse to resurrect the Tribunal of the Holy Inquisition. It would be a modernized Inquisition and would have new orientations, aims, means and organization; but it would be strict, austere, wise and sensible.[41]

Nor was this a mere rhetorical flourish: some inquisitorial forms of persecution were indeed revived to deal with these imaginary Jews and to 'purify' Spain. Indeed in many ways the insurgents' treatment of all those they considered the 'anti-Spain' – liberals, Freemasons, those on the left, Basque and Catalan nationalists, women who did not conform to authoritarian Catholic prescriptions of womanhood – echoed the Catholic Kings' policies against the Jewish population. Those deemed enemies of Franco's new regime were forced either to 'convert' to the National-Catholic credo – which fused fascist corporatism with traditional Catholic values – or to leave Spain or be eliminated. About half a million Republicans fled the country, including the bulk of Spain's liberal intelligentsia and cultural elite, which constituted a brain drain in some ways reminiscent of that caused by the Inquisition which had led to the departure of Jewish scholars, mathematicians and doctors.[42] Those who went to France were detained in overcrowded and insalubrious internment camps, some of which were outright punishment or concentration camps. After the Nazi occupation of France, many Spanish prisoners were deported to German concentration camps, when the Franco regime effectively removed their Spanish nationality.

Those who remained inside Spain suffered the swingeing Francoist repression in which the death toll during the period from the military coup of July 1936 through to the end of the institutional repression of the 1940s was not fewer than 150,000.[43] The Franco regime also retained use of the garrotte (*garrote vil*) to execute some of the Republican prisoners. This was a form of execution, common during the Inquisition, in which the executioner tightened an iron collar around a person's neck until strangulation occurred, and whose use in Francoist Spain did not end entirely until 1974.

Also echoing the rituals of the Inquisition were the wartime public executions, which were followed by the exhibition of corpses in the streets and the burnings of bodies.[44] Just as in medieval times, these forms of punishment had much to do with theatre and propaganda.[45] In Valladolid, where 1,300 men and women were tried between July and December 1936, most of whom faced the death penalty, crowds of well-to-do and pious supporters of the insurgents, including small children, came to see the executions, and stalls selling coffee and churros were set up so that they could eat and drink while they watched.[46] The underlying aim was to provoke 'an effect of terror through the spectacle of power wreaking havoc on the culprit'.[47]

The physical punishments imposed on the Republicans, such as the forced ingestion of castor oil, a powerful laxative, were not simply arbitrary. They were motivated by the Francoists' fear and yearning to purify Spain, to purge the Republicans of their Judeo-Masonic-Bolshevik beliefs, thus controlling and disciplining them. Also to be read in this context is the shaving of the heads of thousands of Republicans, particularly women – there also introducing the powerful element of shaming. Michael Richards has noted that the shaving ritual replaced the penitents' caps worn during the Inquisition.[48]

Book burnings, another common practice during the Inquisition, were also encouraged by the Francoist authorities. However the complex amalgam of motives driving these went far beyond the Inquisition's range, and to understand them fully we need to compare Francoist practices to those of other roughly contemporaneous regimes and movements which engaged in similar activities, most notoriously those in Nazi Germany in 1933. On 1 August 1936, *Arriba España*, the newspaper of the Falange, the fascist party, exhorted its readers to destroy and burn the periodicals and books of Jews, Freemasons and Marxists.[49] The call was heard and many private libraries were burned during the civil war, while public libraries were closed for 'purification'.[50] Particular targets were books written in Catalan and Euskera, a reflection of Falangist (and Francoist) visceral opposition to competing peripheral nationalisms. In Barcelona, the Francoists burned 72 tons of books from public and private libraries, as well as from bookstores and publishing houses. The library of the founding father of the Catalan language in Spain, Pompeu Fabra, was burned in the street. In 1939, the Falangist student organization Sindicato Español Universitario (SEU) celebrated the *Dia del Libro* (Day of the Book) with a public burning of books in Madrid's Central University. Among the targeted authors were the founder of the Basque Nationalist Party, Sabino Arana, as well as Rousseau, Voltaire, Marx and Freud. Literary scholars Raquel Sánchez García and Ana Martínez Rus have suggested that these inquisitorial practices were more akin to those of the Holy Office than those of a twentieth-century government, but this assessment tends to confuse form with function.[51]

These forms of control and authority, inherited from the pre-modern era, were now being deployed to new effect – an indication of which is that they existed and were used alongside some of the most modern manifestations of state discipline and segregation, including the new use of prison and the emergence of concentration camps, both used for the preventive political detention of whole categories of people. Some of Spain's ultra-rightists had been aware of the existence of the German camps from the time the very first ones were established in 1933 to incarcerate the Reich's political enemies – Jewish or non-Jewish alike. The antisemitic propagandist Juan Tusquets, who visited Dachau in 1933 under the auspices of the International Anti-Masonic Association, declared that 'they did it to show what we had to do in Spain', thus also underscoring the way in which Spain's radical right had developed a discourse, rapidly assumed by Francoism, which defined their ideological opponents as also racially degenerate.[52] It did not take long before the Francoist authorities took the next step in developing their own segregationist initiatives – indeed the Spanish dictatorship created one of the largest and longest operating networks of concentration camps and prisons in Europe. As elsewhere too, the distinction between prisons and camps was often blurred. There was a massive expansion of the postwar prison population: in 1940 even the official figure, a likely underestimation, was 233,373 – which represented nearly an eight-fold increase on the pre-civil war Spanish prison population, the vast majority of whom were now political detainees.[53] In total, the dictatorship also opened 188 concentration camps across Spain between 1936 and 1947, but there were also additionally army-run penal detachments and work brigades of various kinds in which forms of forced labour long outlasted this period.[54] While there was no systematic policy of extermination in Spanish prisons or concentration camps, the extreme precarity of daily life in both was in many ways similar to those of Nazi Germany. Prisoners were frequently transported to detention in cattle wagons, they were exposed in the camps to extreme weather conditions, and in both camps and prisons to thirst and hunger, as well as to torture and arbitrary abuse and mistreatment by guards which in some cases caused the deaths of prisoners. Epidemic disease also took its toll, including malaria and tuberculosis.[55]

The function of prison and camp was not only to deprive the prisoners of their autonomy but also to re-educate them so completely that they ceased to be themselves. Based on the research of Franco's military psychiatrist-in-chief, Vallejo-Nágera, the victorious coalition established 'de-Marxization' programmes on the grounds that separation and re-education could cure 'political democratic-Marxist fanaticism'.[56] The main component of this re-education agenda was the imposition of very specific forms of authoritarian-Catholicism. Priests were omnipresent in the camps, and prisoners were required to attend mass regularly. They also had to attend religious lectures, given twice a day by priests and chaplains, in order to be 'detoxified' from the 'satanic atheist-Marxist propaganda' that had poisoned them.[57] This missionary campaign was also in some ways reminiscent of that carried out by Dominican and Franciscan friars in the medieval period, compelling Jews to listen to sermons. The Francoist mission of re-Catholicization was reflected in the regime's decision to use religious buildings, such as monasteries, seminaries and convents – although of course there was also a powerful practical reason for this deployment, given that the existing prison infrastructure could not have coped with the vast increase in the prison population occurring during the early 1940s. As Alfredo González-Ruibal has pointed out, these religious buildings offered the requisite setting to make the prisoners internalize the punishment of God.[58]

Francoist propaganda and repression during and after the battlefield war of 1936–9 borrowed both from Spain's own inquisitorial past and more modern disciplinary models, including notably Nazi Germany with whom Franco's Spain had a close 'tutorial' relationship in matters of the control and surveillance of state enemies. Calls by Francoists for the revival of the Inquisition and 'cleansing actions' against imaginary Jews – Republicans, Catalan and Basque nationalists, emancipated women – were, as we have seen, far from mere rhetoric, and were followed through in practice, as public executions, book burnings and the establishment of a network of state surveillance and control via concentration camps and a massively expanded prison system in which the regime sought to purge and re-sculpt its 'enemies'. The ultimate goal was the construction of a homogeneous and re-hierarchized Spain, organized according to authoritarian Catholic principles – but principles which now demanded not demobilization, but the full-scale discursive and actual *mobilization* of the subject population, in a process which had been begun by the war itself. The similar nature of the antisemitic propaganda and the chosen instruments of repression is not that surprising since many of the regime's propagandists took an active part in the repression. Hence Tusquets managed both the dictatorship's propaganda vehicle, the influential publishing house, Ediciones AntiSectarias, and the anti-Masonic section of Franco's military intelligence.[59] Under the pall of crusade and inquisition, the vanquished Republicans were cast as *judeoconversos*, who thus had no choice but to leave Spain or convert to the new National-Catholic credo. Just like their alleged ancestors, those who remained suffered discrimination in all walks of life and spheres of society.

This discrimination would last, in mutating forms, as long as did the brutal order of the dictatorship itself. As is well known, Francoism long survived its Nazi ally, having been initially saved from political ostracism, even from potential Western Allied military overthrow, by the incipient Cold War already emerging from the military settlement of the Second World War. Franco was able to whitewash his regime, cosmetically distancing it from its Nazi affinities by playing up its anticommunism. Franco himself was portrayed by the regime as a cunning statesman who had managed to keep Spain out of the world war, while also saving thousands of Jews from extermination – either by allowing them safe transit through the country or through the actions of his diplomats abroad.[60] Inside Franco's Spain there was never any public recognition either of the Nazi extermination of European Jews (the Third Reich continued to be lionized as an anti-communist bulwark),[61] nor of Spanish Republican experience and suffering during the civil war. While war memorials were erected for the Francoist dead, Republicans could not be publicly mourned and Republican memory was confined to the private sphere.[62]

This exclusion of Republican memory from Spain's public sphere would continue long after the death of the dictator in November 1975. The particular constraints on Spain's transition from dictatorship to parliamentary democracy (especially the watchfulness of a pro-Franco army) and the extent of institutional and personnel continuities, would mean that only towards the end of the century, in the 1990s, did Republican memory emerge into the public eye inside Spain via the activities of civil pressure groups such as the Association for the Recuperation of Historical Memory (ARMH), with its excavations across Spain of the mass graves in which extrajudicially murdered Republicans had lain since the war of 1936–9.[63] In an interesting historical twist, Alejandro Baer has pointed out how the only recent emergence of Holocaust commemoration in Spain has also led to public recognition of the plight of Spanish Republicans deported to Nazi concentration camps, which has in turn played a part in highlighting occluded Republican histories.[64] At the same time, however, the historical memory movement has been targeted by a backlash from social and political conservatives in Spain, some of whom have come to the defence of Franco by reiterating the old myth of Spain's benevolent attitude towards the Jews during the Second World War[65] – whose spurious credibility has been prolonged precisely because of a lack of knowledge and understanding of the longer history and ideology of antisemitism in modern Spain.

## Notes

1.  For a selection of recent bibliography, see the further reading suggestions at the end of this chapter. In this article the word antisemitism is spelled without a hyphen. The hyphen was put into the English translation of the original German and French terms but grammatically it was incorrect, implying that there is such a thing as 'semitism' which it is against, or that it is equally applied to all Semites, neither of which is the case.

2.  See Gonzalo Álvarez Chillida, *El antisemitismo en España: La imagen del judío (1812–2002)* (Madrid: Marcial Pons, Ediciones de Historia, 2002); Paul Preston, *The Spanish Holocaust: Inquisition and Extermination in Twentieth-Century Spain* (London, New York: W.W. Norton, 2012); Isabelle Rohr, *The Spanish Right and the Jews: Antisemitism and Opportunism 1898–1945* (Brighton: Sussex University Press, 2007).

3.  Joseph Kaplan, 'Jews and Judaism in the Social and Political Thought of Spain in the Sixteenth and Seventeenth Century', in Shmuel Almog (ed.), *Antisemitism through the Ages* (Oxford: Pergamon Press, 1988), pp. 153–61.

4.  Maite Ojeda Mata, 'Thinking about "The Jew" in Modern Spain: Historiography, Nationalism and Anti-semitism', *Jewish Culture and History* 8:2 (2006), pp. 53–72: p. 56.

5.  Peregín Casabó y Pagés, *La España Judia* (Barcelona: F. Bertrán, 1891), pp. 100–7.

6.  Hazel Gold, 'Illustrated Histories: The National Subject and "The Jew" in Nineteenth-Century Spanish Art', *Journal of Spanish Cultural Studies* 10:1 (2009), pp. 89–109.

7.  José Alvarez Junco, 'The Nation-building Process in Nineteenth-Century Spain', in Clare Mar-Molinero and Angel Smith (eds), *Nationalism and the Nation in the Iberian Peninsula: Competing and Conflicting Identities* (Oxford/Washington, DC: Berg, 1996), pp. 89–107: pp. 100–1.

8. César Peiró Menéndez, *Arte de conocer a nuestros judíos* (Barcelona: Imp 'La Catalana', 1916), p. 16.

9. Ibid., pp. 9, 14 and 51.

10. Quoted in Schlomo Ben-Ami, *The Origins of the Second Republic in Spain* (Oxford: Oxford University Press, 1978), p. 224.

11. *El Siglo Futuro*, 8 June 1931 and 10 June 1931.

12. Álvarez Chillida, *El antisemitismo en España*, p. 316.

13. José Luis Rodríguez Jiménez, 'Los Protocolos de los Sabios de Sión en España', *Raíces* 38 (1999), pp. 27–40.

14. Juan Tusquets, *Orígenes de la revolución española* (Barcelona: Editorial Valamala, 1932), p. 132.

15. Quoted in Preston, *The Spanish Holocaust*, p. 37.

16. *Accion Española* II:10 (1932).

17. Quoted in Julio Rodríguez-Puértolas, *Literatura fascista española: volumen i historia* (Madrid: Akal, 1987), p. 70.

18. *El Debate*, 17 October 1933 quoted in Paul Preston, *The Coming of the Spanish Civil War*: *Reform, Reaction and Revolution in the Second Spanish Republic 1931–1936* (London: Routledge, 1994), p. 71.

19. Caesar Aronsfeld, *The Ghosts of 1492: Jewish Aspects of the Struggle for Religious Freedom in Spain* (New York: Columbia University Press, 1979), p. 44. For more on Queipo's views and role, see the chapter by Rúben Serém in this volume.

20. Quoted in Soledad Fox, 'Violence and Silence: The Repressed History of the Franco Regime', in Carlos Jerez-Farrán and Samuel Almago (eds), *Unearthing Franco's Legacy: Mass Graves and the Recovery of Historical Memory in Spain* (Notre Dame: University of Notre Dame Press, 2010), pp. 30–41: p. 31, quoting Hannah Arendt, *The Jewish Writings* (New York: Shocken Books, 2007), p. 43.

21. On the construction of the 'anti-Spain' as a means of avoiding a class analysis of the conflict see Michael Richards, *A Time of Silence: Civil War and the Culture of Repression in Franco's Spain 1936–1945* (Cambridge: Cambridge University Press, 1998), p. 27.

22. Javier Domínguez Arribas, 'The Judeo-Masonic Enemy in Francoist Propaganda (1936–1945)', in Charles Asher Small (ed.), *Global Antisemitism: A Crisis of Modernity, Volume III Global Antisemitism Past and Present* (New York: Institute for the Study of Global Antisemitism and Policy, 2013), pp. 63–70: p. 69.

23. Regarding the social psychological functions of conspiracy theories see Carl F. Graumann and Serge Moscovici, *Changing Conceptions of Conspiracy* (New York: Springer-Verlag, 1987).

24. Domínguez Arribas, 'The Judeo-Masonic Enemy', p. 69.

25. Michael Seidman, *The Victorious Counterrevolution: The Nationalist Effort in the Spanish Civil War* (Madison, WI: University of Wisconsin Press, 2011), p. 38.

26. *Depêche de Toulouse*, 11 August 1937.

27. Albert Prago estimates the number of Jewish Brigaders between 7,000 and 10,000 in 'Jews in the International Brigades', in Alvah Bessie and Albert Prago (eds), *Our Fight: Writings by Veterans of the Abraham Lincoln Brigade, Spain 1936–1939* (New York: Monthly Review Press, 1987), pp. 94–103, while Arno Lustiger regards 6,000 as a more likely figure in 'The Jews and the Spanish War', in Ricardo Izquierdo Benito, Uriel Macías Kapón and Yolanda Moreno Koch (eds), *Los judíos en la España contemporánea: historia y visiones 1898–1998, VIII curso*

*de cultura Hispanojudía y Sefardí de la Universidad de Castilla-La Mancha* (Castilla la Mancha, Spain: Ediciones de la Universidad de Castilla-La Mancha, 2000), pp. 173–89: p. 179.

28. *ABC* (Seville), 14 October 1938. During the civil war there were two editions of *ABC* – one produced by the insurgents in Seville and the other produced in Madrid, the Republican-held capital.

29. *ABC* (Seville), 20 December 1936.

30. *Domingo*, 3 October 1937 and 22 May 1938.

31. *Domingo*, 4 April 1937.

32. *ABC* (Seville), 20 December 1936.

33. *ABC* (Seville), 19 April 1937.

34. Michael Seidman, *The Victorious Counterrevolution*, p. 38.

35. Quoted in Julio Rodríguez Puértolas, *Historia de la literatura fascista española I* (Madrid: Ediciones Akal, 2008), p. 270.

36. Manuel Sánchez del Arco, *El sur de España en la reconquista de Madrid: diario de operaciones glosado pour un testigo*, 2nd ed. (Seville: Editorial Sevillana, 1937), pp. 78–80, quoted in Paul Preston, *Doves of War: Four Women of Spain* (London: Harper Collins, 2002), p. 356.

37. *ABC* (Seville), 19 February 1939.

38. Quoted in Carlos Fernández, *Antología de cuarenta años 1936–1975* (La Coruña: Ediciós do Castro, 1983), p. 19.

39. Cesar Aronsfeld, *The Ghosts of 1492: Jewish Aspects of the Struggle for Religious Freedom in Spain 1848–1979* (New York: Columbia University Press, 1979), p. 44. Aronsfeld quotes a paraphrased report of the *Correo Español* from *The Jewish Chronicle,* 24 June 1938, pp. 34–5. Antisemitic statements were frequently found in the Francoist press both during the civil war and the Second World War. These identified Jews as the 'enemy' and the 'anti-nation', but the deployment of any closely 'argued' biologically racist case (as opposed to vaguer metaphorical references concerning race) was much rarer, certainly before the period of greatest German influence in 1941–2.

40. *Domingo*, 11 December 1938.

41. Antonio Vallejo-Nágera, *Divagaciones intranscendentes* (Valladolid: Talleres Tipográficos Cuesta, 1938) pp. 105–6.

42. Carsten Humelbæk, *Inventing the Nation: Spain* (London: Bloomsbury Academic Press, 2015), p. 64. The promulgation of the Inquisition in Spain had caused a similar brain drain as most scholars, mathematicians and doctors were Jewish.

43. Preston, *Spanish Holocaust*, p. xviii.

44. Helen Graham, *The War and its Shadow: Spain's Civil War in Europe's Long Twentieth Century*, p. 48; Angela Cenarro, *El fin de la Esperanza: Fascismo y Guerra Civil en la Provincia de Teruel (1936–1939)* (Teruel: Diputación Provincial de Teruel, 1996), p. 75; Preston, *Spanish Holocaust*, pp. 318–22.

45. James Buchanan Given, *Inquisition and Medieval Society: Power, Discipline and Resistance in Languedoc* (Ithaca, NY: Cornell University Press, 2001), p. 78.

46. Preston, *Spanish Holocaust*, pp. 191–2.

47. Alfredo González-Ruibal, 'The Archaeology of Internment in Francoist Spain,' in Adrian Myers and Gabriel Moshenska (eds), *The Archaeology of Internment* (New York: Springer, 2005), pp. 53–74: p. 60, quoting Michel Foucault, *Surveiller et Punir* (Paris: Gallimard, 1975), p. 70.

48. Richards, *Time of Silence*, p. 55. See also Yannick Ripa, 'La Tonte Purificatrice des Republicaines Pendant la Guerre Civile Espagnole', *Identités Féminines et Violences Politiques (1936–1946). Les Cahiers de l'Histoire du Temps Present* 31 (1995), n.p.

49. *Arriba*, 1 August 1936, quoted in Carlos Fernández, *Antología de cuarenta años 1936–1975*, p. 13.

50. Haig A. Bosmajian, *Burning Books* (Jefferson: McFarland, 2006), p. 14 and p. 140.

51. Raquel Sánchez García, Ana Martínez Rus, *La lectura en la España contemporánea* (Madrid: Arco Libros, 2009), p. 82.

52. Tusquets quoted in Preston, *Spanish Holocaust*, p. 36.

53. Graham, *War and its Shadow*, p. 201, n. 20.

54. Javier Rodrigo, 'Exploitation, Fascist Violence and Social Cleansing: A Study of Franco's Concentration Camps', *European Review of History* 19:4 (2012), pp. 553–73: p. 558; for other forms of forced labour, see among others, Gonzalo Acosta Bono et al., *El canal de los presos (1940–1962). Trabajos forzosos: de la represión política a la explotación económica* (Barcelona: Crítica, 2004); Isaías Lafuente, *Esclavos por la patria: La Explotación de los Presos bajo el Franquismo* (Madrid: Ediciones Temas de Hoy, 2002).

55. González-Ruibal, 'The Archaeology of Internment', p. 56.

56. On Vallejo-Nágera see Michael Richards, 'Antonio Vallejo-Nágera: Heritage, Psychiatry and War', in Alejandro Quiroga and Miguel Ángel del Arco (eds), *Right-Wing Spain in the Civil War Era: Soldiers of God and Apostles of the Fatherland, 1914–1945* (London and New York: Continuum, 2012), pp. 195–224.

57. Rodrigo, 'Exploitation, Fascist Violence', p. 559.

58. González-Ruibal, 'The Archaeology of Internment, p. 60.

59. Domínguez Arribas, 'The Judeo-Masonic Enemy', p. 69.

60. In reality while Spain had not discriminated against Jewish refugees nor had it allowed them to settle in the country, even when they held Spanish passports. Jews who had reached Spain illegally during the first years of the Second World War, and those whose onward transit arrangements failed, had been imprisoned in the concentration camp of Miranda de Ebro or even turned back at the frontier, see Rohr, *Antisemitism and Opportunism*, also Haim Avni, *Spain, the Jews, and Franco* (English ed.: Philadelphia, 1982), and Antonio Marquina and Gloria I. Ospina, *España y los Judíos en el Siglo XX: la Acción Exterior* (Madrid: Espasa Calpe, 1987); also the more recent monograph by Bernd Rother, *Spanien und der Holocaust* (Tubingen: Max Niemeyer Verlag, 2001; Spanish transl. *Franco y el Holocausto* (Madrid: Marcial Pons, 2005)), and Josep Calvet's *Huyendo del Holocausto: Judíos evadidos del Nazismo a través del Pirineo de Lleida* (Lleida: Milenio, 2014). Rother concentrates on Spanish diplomatic responses to the Nazi persecution/deportation of the Jews, while Calvet focuses on the experiences of Jewish refugees who crossed the Pyrenees into Spain.

61. Álvarez Chillida, *El antisemitismo*, pp. 419–20.

62. Angela Cenarro, 'Memory beyond the Public Sphere: The Francoist Repression in Aragon', *History and Memory* 14:1 and 2 (2002), pp. 165–88.

63. Graham, *War and its Shadow*, p. 140.

64. Alejandro Baer, 'The Voids of Sepharad: The Memory of the Holocaust in Spain', *Journal of Spanish Cultural Studies* 12:1 (2011), pp. 95–120.

65. Luis Suárez, 'Memoria Histórica', *La Razón*, 5 May 2013.

## Further reading

Álvarez Chillida, G., *El antisemitismo en España: La imagen del judío (1812–2002)*, Madrid: Marcial Pons, Ediciones de Historia, 2002.

Domínguez Arribas, J., 'The Judeo-Masonic Enemy in Francoist Propaganda (1936–1945)', in Charles Asher Small (ed.), *Global Antisemitism: A Crisis of Modernity, Volume III Global Antisemitism Past and Present*, New York: Institute for the Study of Global Antisemitism and Policy, 2013, pp. 63–70.

Flesler, D., Linhard Tabea, A. and Pérez Melgosa, A. (eds), *Revisiting Jewish Spain in the Modern Era*, London, New York: Routledge, 2013.

González-Ruibal, A., 'The Archaeology of Internment in Francoist Spain', in Adrian Myers and Gabriel Moshenska (eds), *The Archaeology of Internment*, New York: Springer, 2005, pp. 53–74.

Preston, P., *The Spanish Holocaust: Inquisition and Extermination in Twentieth-Century Spain*, London, New York: W.W. Norton, 2012.

Rodrigo, J., 'Exploitation, Fascist Violence and Social Cleansing: A Study of Franco's Concentration Camps', *European Review of History* 19:4 (2012), pp. 553–73.

Rohr, I., *The Spanish Right and the Jews: Antisemitism and Opportunism*, Brighton: Sussex University Press, 2007.

# CHAPTER 5

## A COUP AGAINST CHANGE: REPRESS IN SEVILLE AND THE ASSAULT ON CIVILIAN SOCIETY

*Rúben Serém*

### An Andalusian class war

In April 1936, the director of the military conspiracy against the democratically elected Republican government of Spain, General Emilio Mola Vidal, issued his first set of secret instructions which read:

> It has to be borne in mind that the action has to be violent in the extreme so as to subdue as soon as possible the enemy which is strong and well organized. It goes without saying that all leaders of political parties, societies and trade unions not part of the movement will be imprisoned and exemplary punishment carried out on them in order to choke off any rebellion or strikes.[1]

In the city of Seville, the overwhelmingly pro-Republican capital of Andalusia, where the victorious Republican electoral coalition (the Popular Front) had collected 61.5 per cent of the vote in the February 1936 elections, Mola's instructions amounted to clear and murderous intent.[2] Mola was fully aware of this when he entrusted to the mentally unstable, militarily inept and uncontrollably violent General Queipo de Llano, described by historian Paul Preston as 'a monster', the truly monstrous mission of enforcing the military insurgents' will in Seville.[3] Before long, their military leadership, whose legitimacy was founded on a myth – that the 17–18 July 1936 *coup d'état* consisted of a pre-emptive strike against a Soviet-sponsored communist revolution[4] – was compelled to formulate a second myth to justify Queipo de Llano's genocidal regime in Spain's fourth-largest city: the legend of the 'miracle of Seville', according to which General Queipo and his *soldaditos* had taken the centre of Seville against enormous military odds.

If stripped of its mythical aura, the military rebellion was an action designed to reverse the recent electoral results and to achieve by means of violence the political demobilization of the pro-Republican masses. In Seville, a feudal conception of social relations and a morbid fear of change united the local (predominantly landowning) elites who had become increasingly alarmed in the preceding five years of the Spanish Second Republic. Accordingly, they had aligned themselves with the military nucleus which engineered the rising, the *Africanistas*, the military officers forged in Spain's savage ₒnial war in Morocco.[5] Central to this alliance was a mutual loathing of the democratic ₙallenge posed by the Republic. Patrician Seville was particularly incensed by what it considered as the Republic's endorsement of local workers' 'insolent' rejection of the Andalusian 'caste' system, whereby the lower strata of society were regarded as subhuman and virtually a race apart.[6] At the same time, the *Africanistas* dreamed about the restoration of Spain's lost empire, starting with a modern-day *Reconquista* of the metropolis itself, which would eliminate the 'internal enemy of the *Patria*' – identified as all pro-Republican constituencies in Spain.[7] In fact, the *Africanistas* came to regard the Republican 'other', and especially worker constituencies, as tantamount to a foreign intruder to be treated with the same racist contempt usually reserved for the indigenous Moroccan population.[8] General Mola encapsulated this Manichean worldview with brutal sincerity when he assured his liaison officer, Félix Máiz, that 'we are about to confront an enemy which is not Spanish and is already embedded in the vast majority of the vital institutions of the *Patria*'.[9] Mola was categorical about the need for 'exemplary punishments', a term that would be employed ad nauseam to rationalize the insurgents' plan to obliterate the Republic via the extermination of its representatives, a nihilistic strategy that was exemplified in the crushing of popular opposition to the military rebellion in Seville. Given the city's reputation as a Republican bastion, it featured prominently in insurgent wartime propaganda and myth-making. The insurgent press chief, Luís Bolín, gave free rein to his imagination, claiming: 'Russian ships had landed arms and ammunition along the Guadalquivir River; a Communist *putsch* had been set for the end of July or beginning of August'.[10] Far from being Bolín's own delirious fantasy, his colourful account was part of a deliberate propaganda strategy aimed at exaggerating (indeed inventing) the military threat posed by the radical left while playing down the insurgents' actual post-coup repression as mere 'exemplary punishments' for treason. In fact, given its support for the rebellion, the most treasonous and indeed dangerous socio-political constituency in Seville was the elite itself – headed up by wealthy landowners (some of whom were aristocrats) and supported by the institutional Catholic Church. On 15 May 1936, the local dockworkers prophetically denounced them as 'reactionary bosses who are seeking to provoke a class war'.[11]

The success of the conspiracy in Seville was assured by both the tireless subversive labour of its local director, Major José Cuesta Monereo, and the fanaticism of the local elites. The reclusive Cuesta wove a network of conspirators which cohered as an alliance against change, encompassing the entire garrison of Seville and the Civil Guard, as well as the far-right paramilitary organizations, the Falange and the Carlist *Requeté*.[12] Mindful of all this, Mola ordered Queipo de Llano to act as the visible head of a rebellion that needed no real further planning, as it had already been organized down to the last detail. Queipo had previously been associated with various republican conspiracies in the 1920s and in 1930 – as had numerous other officers. In essence these were a protest against proposed army reforms rather than any deep indication of republican political faith – added to which Queipo himself was personally disaffected from both the king, Alfonso XIII, and from the dictator who with royal patronage ruled Spain in the 1920s, General Miguel Primo de Rivera (1923–30). Then from 1931 under the Republic, Queipo once again became disaffected and started looking for other options, especially following the impeachment of his close friend, President Niceto Alcalá-Zamora, the monarchist-turned-republican, in May 1936. But even as Queipo cast around, he reassured the acting President Diego Martínez Barrio that he remained 'a man of honour and a republican from head to toe'.[13] Mola was all too aware of Queipo's political slipperiness and opportunism and refused to disclose any sensitive information to him until the coup was barely weeks away, at which point he briefed Queipo on his assignment. A few years later, in one of his many eruptions of pathological narcissism, Queipo portrayed the late General Mola (killed in an air crash in June 1937) as a hesitant leader who had only been willing to continue heading the conspiracy provided Queipo pulled off the feat of persuading another Republican-inclined senior officer, General Miguel Cabanellas, to side with the rebels.[14]

Needless to say, the fate of the plot did not rely on Queipo's powers of persuasion, nor on his volatile persona; nevertheless, Mola did hope to make use of his past republicanism to sway several high-ranking officers, most notably General José Fernández Villa-Abrille, the leader of the Second Military Division based in Seville. But Villa-Abrille rejected Queipo's proposal, nevertheless also refusing to denounce his friend and co-officer to the Republican authorities.[15] Queipo's failure to win over Villa-Abrille marked the end of his active participation in both the conspiracy and the coup. After the rebels had taken control of Seville's city centre (*sans* Queipo), then it devolved to the general to assume control, in order to impose Mola's instructions on the working-class districts of the city. Indeed, what had first impelled Mola to nominate Queipo to Seville was the general's notoriously violent personality, the only constant in his turbulent life – from his spectacular escape from a seminary, aged only fourteen, when he stoned a group of priests who had given pursuit, right through to his repeated wild threats in the years just before his own death in 1951, to 'crush' Franco's own brother-in-law, the still publicly (if not politically) influential former senior cabinet minister, Ramón Serrano Súñer.[16]

## Queipo and the myth against change

After forging a career in the bloody campaigns against indigenous rebels in the Spanish colonies of Cuba and Morocco, Queipo then became a rebel himself, setting out to oversee the internal colonization of southern Spain. In order to conceal this uncomfortable reality and to legitimize the violent overthrow from Seville of Spain's first democracy, the insurgents devised a multi-layered myth, which was presented by its main protagonist, Queipo himself, including a series of radio broadcasts which began as early as 23 July.[17] First, he vehemently denied that there had been any subversive military plot in Seville and instead declared that he had gallantly accepted what was to all intents and purposes a suicide mission in a city controlled by the radical left.[18] A compulsive fantasist, the general added that he alone initiated the army rebellion in Seville after single-handedly arresting his former friend, General Villa-Abrille and a number of other high-ranking officers who chose to remain loyal to the Republic – all this after a brief confrontation in which Queipo punched Villa-Abrille. In particular, Queipo presented Villa-Abrille's 'cowardice' as symbolic of the moral and ideological 'degeneracy' of the Republic.[19] Then the self-styled 'saviour of Seville' maintained that he had also almost single-handedly captured the nearby infantry barracks, going as far as to claim that he was temporarily isolated in the building surrounded by a crowd of hostile officers. Curiously, nobody dared to arrest him while Queipo pondered settling the stand-off 'with bullets', meaning he apparently entertained the idea of fighting the entire regiment, before somehow miraculously arresting the commander, Colonel Manuel Allanegui Lusarreta and his pro-Republican subordinates through a mixture of intimidation and bravado.[20] According to the insurgent account, the ideological superiority of Queipo's own ideal sustained him in accomplishing the near impossible, this military feat of epic proportions.

Reality differed considerably from the just-described myth. It would be the terrified testimony of three high-ranking officers before an insurgent court-martial which demolished Queipo's extravagant tale.[21] They revealed that Queipo did not punch but rather embraced General Villa-Abrille as both men entered into an amiable dialogue. Villa-Abrille's neutrality was tactical – he was alarmed by the anti-republican zeal displayed by his fellow officers and hoped that his stance would spare him from execution. Moreover, Queipo was never left alone in the infantry barracks. Not only was he flanked by several other insurgent officers, but it was also the case that a number of 'loyalist' officers urged Allanegui to throw in his lot with the rebels. Finally, Queipo never actually confronted Allanegui, but simply lured him into a trap by suggesting that Villa-Abrille should mediate their dispute. The Colonel agreed to pay a visit to Villa-Abrille at the Divisional Headquarters only to be unceremoniously detained upon arrival.

The first and most enduring version of the 'miracle of Seville' was Queipo's own in his 23 July radio broadcast.[22] Only a few months later, his fable of the 180 *soldaditos* overpowering 600 Assault Guards had become the more spectacular claim that the insurgents had also defeated an immense communist 'red army' numbering no less than 100,000 soldiers.[23] But this 'red army' existed only in Queipo's fertile imagination. The local leader of the conspiracy in Seville, the meticulous Cuesta Monereo, had ensured that no weapons fell into the hands of pro-Republican civilians by masterminding the lightning capture of the artillery depot. In addition the civil governor of Seville, José María Varela Rendueles, refused to arm the workers, a decision backed by the centrist republican mayor, Horacio Hermoso, who was no friend of the workerist left.[24] The only reason why, in the end, some civilians became armed was because the communist leader Manuel Delicado eventually talked the Republican Assault Guards into handing over eighty rifles to a crowd demanding arms against the coup.[25] These were the only weapons in the hands of the city's ad hoc Republican militia composed of civilian volunteers, with a core from the trade unions and pro-Republican political parties. Regardless, the insurgents cynically exploited the tale of the 'red army' to corroborate the equally fictional story of the imminent communist coup. What started as just another lie spread by the loquacious Queipo was rapidly subsumed into the insurgents' official history.[26] To safeguard the myth, they mounted a propaganda campaign to camouflage the fact that the 'miracle of Seville' was but an expertly planned *coup d'état* followed by a series of massacres carried out by a professional army numbering 6,125 operatives against Seville's civilian population. General Queipo's *soldaditos* consisted of the entire garrison of Seville, supported by the Army of Africa as well as members of the Civil and Assault Guard, *Requeté*, Falange and a further 187 volunteers unaffiliated to any existing political organization.[27] Vastly overwhelmed, loyal sectors of the Assault Guard managed to barricade themselves in Seville's main square, the Plaza Nueva, repelling successive rebel attacks until being finally shelled into submission by the Artillery Corps.

The despondent civil governor of Seville, Varela Rendueles, was left with no option but to negotiate the terms of his surrender with a surprisingly accommodating Queipo, who promised to spare the lives of all captured Republicans – only to later break his word. In a preview of the modus operandi of his personal dictatorship, and indeed of the insurgents' modus in general, Queipo turned the tables, holding those who had been attacked and were now defeated as responsible for the violence in Seville – targeting especially for blame the civil governor, Varela Rendueles.[28] Neither he nor any of the captured Republican authorities really grasped that this coup was something new and murderous. Indeed the only person in Seville who fully understood was, unsurprisingly, another *Africanista*, Lieutenant-Colonel Juan Caballero, who, in desperation, offered his own services to Queipo de Llano, hoping to save his life thereby. But the general shunned his proposal and Caballero was later executed.[29] Equally illuminating was the insurgents' obsession with crushing civilian opposition to the rising. Once again, the local elites demonstrated their determination to pursue a ruthless class war, using the army as an instrument. Large landowner and retired army captain Luis Alarcón de la Lastra set up a heavy machine-gun on one of the bridges that separated the city centre from the poverty-stricken district of Triana to cut down all attempts on the part of its population to reach the Plaza Nueva.[30] The first massacre took place when a crowd of workers tried to break into the artillery depot. The rebels sprayed them with machine-gun fire, killing fourteen. Another twelve corpses were discovered the next morning and left to decompose for several days to remind workers of the price of challenging their subordinate, even subhuman, status in the new insurgent Seville.[31]

## The victory of the elite

The key political objective of the military rebels on 18 July 1936 was to restore to the local landowning elites, in particular their core of wealthy landowners, the political dominance they had enjoyed prior to the Second Republic. For these elites, the success of the military coup did not merely represent the end of the intolerable affront that were the five years of Republican rule, but also the start of a much anticipated class war that would decimate worker sectors 'poisoned' by the 'Marxist virus'.[32] The oligarchy proposed to 'purify' Seville by means of mass killing targeted at all 'infected' groups, defined as all those that supported the Republic.[33] This discourse clearly possessed social-Darwinist and eugenic overtones. The insurgents rationalized the massacres that followed the military rising as a 'biological necessity'.[34] In particular, the gravest manifestation of the Republican 'disease' was the 'chaos' instigated by the triumph of the Popular Front in the February 1936 elections. For the military victors and their backers, this appeal to order reinforced their underlying belief that non-elite groups had no right to exercise power – so it was immaterial that the majority of the local population was pro-Republican. The insurgents claimed that the Republic was fundamentally 'disordered' and the originator of violence. Recent historical research has shown that in the months after the Popular Front elections of February 1936 there were thirty-four politically motivated assassinations in Seville.[35] Yet once the insurgents had taken the 'law' into their own hands, they were responsible for more than doubling this number of killings *in a single day*, when, on 18 August 1936, the military authorities executed seventy-three prisoners to 'celebrate' the first month of General Queipo de Llano's rule in the now 'peaceful' capital of Andalusia.[36]

The insurgent leadership in Seville enthusiastically embraced the binary worldview of the Andalusian landed classes (indeed more than a few of them were linked by the ties of family). As Paul Preston has noted, 'The near racist contempt of the southern landowners for their peasants had found an echo in the *Africanistas*. Their belief in their right of arbitrary power over the tribes of Morocco was comparable to the sense of near-feudal entitlement of the *señoritos*.'[37] To the elation of his aristocratic allies, Queipo de Llano confirmed that military victory would not stop the 'cleansing labour' initiated on 18 July; he made repeated incitements to rape, authorized his supporters 'to kill like a dog' any Republican they might come across and promoted extremists to positions of power, such as new Civil Governor Pedro Parias and part-time mayor, part-time warlord, Ramón de Carranza.[38] The chronically ill Parias and his four sons, all affiliated to the Falange, participated in both the rising and the ensuing repression in Seville.[39] Likewise, Carranza commanded a column named after himself (*Columna Carranza*) that laid waste to south-western Andalusia and joined the lethal march of the insurgent armies towards Madrid, until being reminded of his municipal administrative duties which obliged him to return to Seville. There the ruling families had rapidly voided all existing political institutions of their democratic content, using them as mere instruments to support Queipo's vicious domination.[40] Indeed, the first decision of the new Town Hall Committee, appointed on 19 July 1936, was formally to sack all municipal councillors; thereafter they released successive lists of workers who either had been, or were to be, 'repressed'.[41] Unsurprisingly, the first victims of these 'exemplary punishments' tended to be of modest social extraction. The first atrocities were carried out even before the pacification of the working-class neighbourhoods (*barrios*), such was the eagerness of both *Africanistas* and *señoritos* to 'put the clock back'.

## The pacification of Seville's worker districts

The first major military operation in the barrios took place a mere day after the dual appointment of Parias and Carranza as civil governor and mayor respectively. In celebratory mood, the new Mayor of Seville ordered the blanket shelling of the Gran Plaza worker district by mortar fire and the execution on the spot of anyone caught with weapons in hand, this despite loyalist workers having put up only a token resistance at best.[42] All existing doubts concerning the homicidal agenda of the new overlords of Seville were rapidly and brutally dispelled by their actions in the barrios. The swift capture of the Gran Plaza was followed by the slow and thorough obliteration of resistance in Triana over the following two days. The extreme imbalance of forces and firepower between insurgents and civilian Republican defenders was evident: the ratio was one rifle per twenty loyalists. Regardless, Queipo de Llano termed Triana an 'impregnable red fortress' in a contrived attempt at deflecting attention from the brutal insurgent methods which included 'punitive shelling of Triana', the 'severe punishment of the Marxist rabble' and the cold-blooded killing of wounded Republicans in Seville's municipal hospital.[43] On 21 July, three insurgent columns penetrated the 'fortress' of Triana, covered by artillery and anti-sniper fire, before splitting into smaller units that encircled the barrio. After taking military control, the rebels organized mixed groups of soldiers and Falangists to sweep the streets, murdering any loyalists they encountered. Once more, Ramón de Carranza led by example, giving a ten-minute deadline for all pro-Republican graffiti to be removed from the walls of Triana. His *compagnon de route*, the aristocratic Rafael de Medina, rejoiced as he watched the distressed residents struggling to complete the task before the set deadline. Republicanism was literally, physically wiped out in Triana.[44] Also obliterated were the very concepts of neutrality, the 'civilian' and 'prisoners of war' – here was the moral paradox of slaughtering the same civilians the new rulers of Seville were supposed to govern. A residential area was transformed into a war zone, shelled into submission, ravaged by a professional army and covered in white flags that announced the unconditional 'surrender' of its *civilian* population; all of which was cynically presented by the insurgents as a display of the 'pacifist attitude of its workers, freed from Marxist tyranny'.[45] Ultimately, extreme violence was employed irrespective of the level of resistance, for, as presaged in Mola's secret instructions, the insurgents were imposing a prior plan of extermination – mass killings whose aim was not merely military pacification but socio-political control.

The final military objective of the insurgents was the recalcitrant worker barrio of La Macarena. According to General Queipo, 'the punishment was exemplary'.[46] The massacre signalled the establishment of a pact of blood, a coalition sealed over the corpses of its victims. All members of this alliance exorcized their collective phobia of the Republican 'other' by taking part in the pacification of the barrio: the entire garrison of Seville, the Army of Africa (formed by the Foreign Legion and the Moroccan mercenaries of the *Regulares*), Civil Guards and Assault Guards (a minority of the latter also supported the rising, but many more were forced to fight for it under duress, following capture), and then the various paramilitary formations of Falange and *Requeté*, plus the local *Columna Carranza* and *Harca Berenguer*.[47] There were also other participating volunteers who were not enlisted in any of these military and paramilitary organizations, and even the institutional Catholic Church played its part, via a priest who blessed the advance of the insurgent army.[48] The assault against the barrios also served to reaffirm the fictive *casus belli* for the rising, the myth of the communist coup, which was now used to metamorphose the inhabitants of La Macarena (renamed the 'Sevillian Moscow') into a Soviet-sponsored 'red army'. The insurgents laying siege to the capital of Andalusia also claimed that they were surrounded by this 'red army' and therefore compelled to resort to extreme violence. According to this crude inversion of responsibilities, the workers and civilians of Seville had actually forced the insurgents to murder them en masse. General Queipo's first biographer made the extraordinary claim that over one in every three inhabitants of Seville were affiliated to this imaginary 'red army'.[49] Predictably, the entire population of the Andalusian capital, including women and children, were all included in the murderous clauses of the ambiguous proclamation of martial law (*Bando de Guerra*) of 18 July 1936 that established the death penalty for 'anyone who by any means disturbs daily life in the territory of this Division'.[50]

Unsurprisingly, the loyalists were too weak and lacking in arms to capture several isolated Civil Guard posts defended only by a handful of guards. The dearth of weapons in La Macarena was such that trade union leader Julián Arcas patrolled the barrio with an antique sabre. In despair, communist leader Manuel Delicado urged the unarmed workers to fight the rising by any means possible.[51] They had absolutely nothing to lose, for the insurgents showed no mercy towards the population of La Macarena. The entire area was subjected to a relentless two-day bombardment by land and air. On 18 July, Aviation Major Rafael Martínez Estévez had refused to obey direct orders from the civil governor to bomb the mutinous troops in the city centre on the grounds that it would cause extensive civilian casualties.[52] Yet only a few days later (22 July), Major Antonio Castejón Espinosa of the Foreign Legion initiated the most brutal colonial war tactics against the same civilians Martínez Estévez had previously sought to protect, as the insurgents began their eagerly anticipated internal colonization of Spain. Castejón launched a three-pronged attack and explicitly instructed the men under his command to encircle the entire district so as to maximize casualties.[53] Trapped within a tiny defensive perimeter, the panic-stricken population suffered another barrage of artillery fire while the Foreign Legion, supported by armoured vehicles, entered the barrio using women and children as human shields. Several infants died during the offensive, in which the Army of Africa tossed hand grenades into houses and randomly stabbed residents to death.[54] The weapon-starved loyalists, headed by Andrés Palatín, made a last stand at the strategically located orphanage, now converted into a military headquarters, hospital and refugee camp. The newspaper *La Unión* described the final assault as an 'apocalypse'. Palatín was captured and lynched. The Army of Africa employed heavy machine-guns and hand grenades, showing an absolute disregard for the lives of the many children, pregnant women and elderly people sheltering inside the orphanage, now officially 'purified' of the 'Marxist virus' in a operation explicitly described by reporter Cándido Ortiz de Villajos as the 'cleansing of La Macarena'.[55] Queipo's propaganda chief, Antonio Bahamonde, described the final assault on the San Julián quarter in the following terms: 'In San Julián the slaughter was tremendous. They forced all the men they found sheltering inside houses to go to the street and, without ascertaining whether they had taken part in the battle or not, executed them on the spot'.[56] As in Triana, the insurgents did not leave without first subjecting the surviving neighbourhood residents to a collective humiliation, in this case by ordering them to tear down the barricades with their bare hands. The day after the carnage, a reporter was sickened by the 'unbearable stench' of the corpses left to rot under the scorching Andalusian sun.[57]

### Jus ad bellum

The crushing of civilian resistance in the barrios was merely the opening stage of repression in Seville, whose institutionalization would be based upon the state of war (*Bando*) which had been declared on 18 July. To further this process, two days after the pacification of the city on 25 July, Queipo appointed the retired Captain Manuel Díaz Criado as Military Delegate for Andalusia and Extremadura. Also an *Africanista*, Díaz Criado was in many ways a mirror image of the mentally unstable Queipo – in that Díaz Criado's heavy drinking and notorious cruelty (including rape) also require clinical definition.[58] The implacable Queipo had warned the local population that the purification of Seville would continue – the subjugation of the working-class districts had been just the beginning of the 'cleansing'.[59] This was precisely what Díaz Criado went on to do. Nearly 3,000 people were assassinated during the retired captain's four-month reign of terror.[60]

It goes without saying that Queipo felt no qualms about the fact that the insurgents' own projected legitimacy for enacting Mola's murderous project rested entirely upon a lie: the myth of the communist coup and the 'miracle of Seville'. Queipo personally directed, via his macabre radio speeches, a defamation campaign aimed at presenting the democratic Republican leadership as extremists and traitors. (It is telling that Queipo's pathological radio tirades were subject to rigorous military censorship at the direct orders of the Seville coup's architect, Major Cuesta Monereo himself, because he understood the damage they would do to the insurgents' own cause – especially if reported internationally. He thus instructed the insurgent press to publish only highly edited versions.)[61] Nevertheless, many Republicans were subsequently arraigned, court-martialled and executed under the Kafka-esque terms of the *Bando de Guerra* for the crime of 'military rebellion' – i.e. rebelling against the rebellion.[62] Ramón Serrano Súñer would, much later, call this process 'back-to-front justice'.[63]

But read historically rather than mythically, both the military rising and the declaration of a state of war were pre-emptive, not reactive: there was no impending communist revolution, but there was a Republic in power which sought a redistribution of social and economic power within the country through peaceful legislative means. The coup and what followed were themselves the extremist instruments – designed physically to 'extirpate' Republicanism from Seville. This exterminatory policy was masked by a relentless propaganda campaign. First, this stressed their moral, rather than military might.[64] Second, the insurgents exaggerated the level of armed resistance to the rebellion in order to justify the carnage they had always intended to inflict in order precisely to impose their control on one of Spain's foremost urban centres.[65] The insurgent leadership asserted the myth that their uprising was part of a wider struggle between the 'Army of the *Patria*' against the 'Empire of Marxism', and identified the barrios as an integral part of this empire.[66] Looked at historically, what occurred in Seville between 18 and 23 July was a spontaneous mobilization of its civilian population in an attempt to prevent what they already correctly perceived as a coup against change, and a return to a rigidly hierarchized, if not also neo-feudal socio-political order. The insurgent mythology had the effect of dehumanizing entire residential neighbourhoods, which were treated as legitimate military targets. Ironically, it was the disproportionate and top-down nature of violence that most undermines the insurgents' own argument that the repression was merely a 'retributive' justice, whether 'exemplary' or otherwise. Queipo de Llano outdid his own promise of avenging every single insurgent fatality by executing ten Republicans. Twelve rebel sympathizers were killed in Seville between 19 and 23 July – killings which were themselves triggered by the rebellion – whereas the insurgents massacred 3,028 people between July 1936 and January 1937, in a city which was five hundred kilometres away from the main military front, located around the capital, Madrid.[67]

Removed from the main theatre of conventional war in Spain, Seville nevertheless remained a battlefield of critical importance for the insurgents. Their brutal modus operandi – the use of disproportionate force against what was essentially a civilian 'opponent' – laid bare the real *raison d'être* of the 17–18 July 1936 rebellion: to eradicate the economic, cultural and political reforms introduced by the Republic. Since the objectives of the rebellion were ambitious, so too then did their repression have to be. For instance, the suffering of the inhabitants of the economically depressed neighbourhood of Amate did not conclude with the atrocities perpetrated by the *Columna Carranza* and a 'razzia' (raid) carried out by the notorious paramilitaries of the *Harca Berenguer*. The quarter was again 'purged' during Díaz Criado's subsequent period of command and then plagued by famine, until it was finally razed to the ground on Queipo's orders in 1937.[68] But for the impoverished survivors of Seville's working-class constituencies, life under the rule of Queipo de Llano's kleptocratic state was often a living death.

## The second 'miracle of Seville': economic repression

The planned obliteration of the working-class districts was followed by an equally calculated economic assault against workers, but also, and crucially, against other sectors of civil society. For, as in Nazi Germany, so too in insurgent Spain, coercive policies were equally intended to discipline those being sculpted as regime insiders and patriotic subjects of the new state under construction. As the largest urban centre to fall to the insurgents at the start of the conflict, Seville not only functioned as their unofficial capital, but was also the principal testing ground for the rebels' state-building policies. On 24 October 1936, the aristocrat Maria Luis de Carlos of the *Plato Único* (single-course meal) organizing committee declared that 'Seville will again receive the honour of having been the initiator of such magnificent enterprises'.[69] Originally a Nazi-inspired fundraising campaign, the *Plato Único* turned out to be such a lucrative venture that it was eventually expanded to the rest of insurgent-held territory.[70] All revenue collected in Seville was transferred to the Auxilio de Invierno (Winter Aid), an aid agency also modelled on the Nazi *Winterhilfe* and an example of the growing symbiosis between insurgent Spain and the Third Reich.[71]

In Seville, physical and economic repression not only coexisted, but complemented each other to the point that they became the dual cornerstones of Queipo de Llano's rule. The surviving Republican population, as well as other civilian sectors whose politics may have been more amorphous were, in the words of Queipo's own propaganda chief, 'sentenced to abject misery. Misery that nobody dares to remedy, out of fear of being labelled a Marxist'.[72] The institutionalization of 'misery' was confirmed by three expropriationary decrees (*Bandos*) released by Queipo on 18 August, and 2 and 11 September 1936, whose function was to allow the insurgent authorities to take control of the belongings and wealth (including bank accounts) of anyone they deemed to have aided or abetted Republican 'rebellion' in any way.[73] Plunder gradually evolved into organized extortion which funded the insurgents' war of attrition and punished ideological enemies while at the same time rewarding allies, thus providing an additional form of bonding for the ruling coalition, in addition to the earlier mentioned 'pact of blood'. Queipo's justification for these economic measures was given as the fact that Seville had been 'spared' the ravages of war and was therefore morally obliged to support financially the new order, locally represented by Queipo. On 28 October 1936, the Falange's official newspaper, *FE*, published a blistering editorial: 'Many in Spain are starving: prisoners, those under siege, orphans, widows; many, they are many! Seville had the good fortune to be spared these and other horrors thanks to Providence and its instrument, the General' (Queipo).[74] The myth of the Soviet-sponsored revolution and the 'miracle of Seville' was regurgitated to pressure the local population into donating en masse to the perpetual fundraising campaigns. Needless to say, these donations were anything but voluntary and their coercive power went wide. For instance, a Falangist from Granada was temporarily expelled from the party for failing to meet the extravagant monetary demands of Seville's new ruling order. It later transpired that he had already donated the substantial sum of 25,410 pesetas to no less than fifteen different 'patriotic subscriptions'.[75] Press chief Bahamonde also revealed that the insurgents had fixed individual quotas for each town and village in Andalusia. The message was clear: anyone who did not collaborate would be labelled as 'unpatriotic' and regarded as an enemy of the state. Punishment included one or more of the following: a huge fine, job loss, social marginalization, potential torture/physical abuse and/or a prison sentence that could itself lead to extrajudicial execution.[76] Seville was experiencing an excruciating metamorphosis from nascent democracy into a kleptocracy which, in September 1936, claimed over one execution per hour – this a full two months after the conclusion of military operations in the city.[77] Against this background, the predictable success of the campaigns for 'patriotic subscriptions' was nevertheless conveniently interpreted by the insurgents as a spontaneous manifestation of popular support for the coup. According to this triumphalist rhetoric, each and every fundraising campaign functioned as a referendum acclaiming and ratifying Queipo's rule.[78] Thus, the 'miracle of Seville' was followed by a second 'miracle' that was the torrent of voluntary contributions by a contrite population looking to 'atone' for its Republican past or else, and often equally fearfully, to confirm its explicit allegiance to the new order.

## 'Re-educating' the masses: the depoliticization of the working class

So we see the direct relationship between the extortion perpetrated by the kleptocratic state in Seville and the formation of a specifically insurgent identity in what was still, during the first months after the rebellion, a time of military uncertainty (the coup had failed in most of urban, populous Spain). Aiding this too was Queipo's promotion of political polarization via the constant demonization of the Republican 'other' in his many propaganda campaigns.

While all components of the 'pact of blood' participated in the creation of Queipo's kleptocratic state (social and economic elites, army, paramilitary organizations (Falange and Requeté) and the institutional Catholic Church), the most prominent – and profitable – partnership, which developed into a de facto economic conglomerate, was that between the army and the Falange. It was they together who were responsible for extracting maximum 'value' from surviving worker constituencies. Concomitant with the 'exemplary punishments' targeting the masses for their stubborn Republicanism was the process of 'educating' them into accepting the new regime. In a secret report, the insurgents analysed the 'special' social structure of Andalusia, which they divided into three main groups – landowners, businessmen and landless peasants – and then proceeded to describe one of its most remarkable features: whereas the landless day-labourers could rearrange society without the remaining groups, landowners and businessmen 'cannot exterminate the third group [landless peasantry] because of its large numbers and the disastrous consequences such measure would entail'.[79] Since southern Spain's landowning elite depended for its very existence (or at least for its way of life) on the feudalistic exploitation of the poorer strata of rural society, then clearly it did not intend to eradicate the entire rural working class but rather to wipe out its union leaders and to make periodic examples of ordinary workers (by 'strategic' executions), and thus to terrorize the remainder into submission. The patronizing language used by all members of the ruling insurgent coalition indicated their profound contempt for the mass of impoverished rural labourers, regarding them as bestial and thus deserving of the brutal treatment meted out to them by the 'victors'.

The traumatized 'defeated' were now forced to prove their loyalty time and again to every single group that had participated in the pacification of Seville. The requisite 'expiation' came via the previously described extortion in forced donations, but also via slave labour and starvation wages. All the insurgents' campaign fundraising committees, without exception, were dominated by the ruling coalition. Queipo de Llano excused the absence of worker input by claiming quite unfeasibly that one of the many fundraising campaigns was the brainchild of a group of local workers.[80] The irascible general, who deeply resented popular resistance to his rule, could not conceal his delight at the re-establishment of slave labour in Seville through the many decrees bearing his signature, but which were nevertheless conceived by the economic elites backing him.[81] On 4 September, he disingenuously remarked that 'It is intriguing to note how, in such a short space of time, we managed to change the mindset of an enormous number of workers.'[82] They were almost certainly 'persuaded' by the twenty-six daily executions carried out in Seville during that same month. In his chilling radio broadcasts, Queipo read numerous letters from working-class organizations notifying him of their dissolution and the donation of all funds to one or more components of the ruling coalition. The most shocking example came from the dockworkers of Seville who, on 18 July, under communist leader Saturnino Barneto, barricaded inside the Hotel Inglaterra, had mounted an out-and-out defence against the insurgent onslaught.[83] But the dockworkers' subsequent fear is entirely understandable: while Barneto himself managed to escape from Seville, his mother, 72-year-old Isabel Atienza Lucio did not. She was taken prisoner in his stead and killed, after first being forced to witness several other executions.[84] On 11 September, an ecstatic Queipo read a letter from the dockworkers that read 'thanks to the aforementioned Army, we [the dockworkers] have forever emancipated ourselves from the rule of the gun which, in Marxist hands, had imposed itself in these docks'. They also apologized for the delay in producing their letter of thanks, by mentioning the 'absence of many co-workers' (many of whom were in hiding to try to avoid execution). The letter concluded: 'since we are unable to contribute with money or goods to the needs of the present circumstances, we happily offer our labour free of charge as many times as the authorities deem necessary'.[85] Sentenced to 'abject misery', the dockworkers offered their only remaining possession: their labour – and thus announced what would be another instrument of insurgent (and later Francoist) repression, the massive use of forced labour. Meanwhile, other working-class organizations continued to contribute feverishly to existing fundraising campaigns in the hope that General Queipo would eventually recognize that they had 'liberated themselves from Marxist infamy', in the hope that this might thus bring some relaxation of the physical violence, even if the donations meant near starvation.[86] To this end, the Sociedad Minera y Metalúrgica de Peñarroya (Peñarroya miners' union) submitted its eighteenth donation on 14 September 1937.[87] For their part, the insurgents regarded this institutionalization of slavery and the eradication of trade unions as indicative of the desired political demobilization of the masses, a key objective of the 17–18 July 1936 coup. The daily queues of famished workers begging for food scraps outside military buildings confirmed the successful re-establishment of a neo-feudal caste system in Seville.[88]

## The humanitarian catastrophe in the unofficial capital of insurgent Spain

In only a few weeks, General Queipo's policies pushed the capital of Andalusia to the brink of economic collapse, a cataclysm that could potentially have undermined the insurgents' own war effort. Ironically, they were now forced to deal with a humanitarian crisis of their own making. The most pressing problem was the many abandoned and starving orphans wandering the streets of Seville, a direct consequence of the mass killings in the barrios. In private, the rebels accepted their responsibility while showing neither regret nor remorse for their actions. On 20 August 1936, Major Ramón de Carranza wrote: 'Due to recent events, the San Julián neighbourhood, last stronghold of the Marxist hordes, has suffered the consequences of the [extremist] obsessions of its residents, leaving numerous children, innocent beings alien to this conflict, in the most extreme form of abandonment'.[89] The situation was so dire that on 7 August Queipo released order number 13 establishing an special 'Pro-Seville' postage stamp from which the money raised would go 'to remedy the misery of our brothers, especially the children, orphaned, abandoned and on occasions even exploited by professional beggars'.[90] The stamp proved to be a profitable enterprise. By 16 December the city authorities were earning an average of 676.20 pesetas per day from stamp sales. The situation of the orphans, however, remained unresolved. On 14 October 1937, the director of a local orphanage, the Casa Cuna, warned the city authorities of 'the serious problem caused by the presence of so many orphaned and vulnerable children' in Seville. But a year and a half later, in January 1939, many infants were still being abandoned by their emaciated mothers.[91] The insurgents had successfully annihilated the Republic in Seville but struggled to replace it with a functioning state.

The scale of the humanitarian catastrophe engulfing Seville was such that, as early as 2 August 1936, the impoverished general population of the city was officially exhorted to mitigate the effects of the insurgent repression by providing financial support for a new relief agency, the Junta de Auxilios Alimenticios a Necesitados (Committee for Food Aid to the Needy).[92] But it was not until 17 August that the Junta was even formally established (via decree 12), which indicates a lack of any sense of urgency, humanitarian aid not being a priority for Queipo and his entourage.[93] Ramón de Carranza, paramilitary chief and newly appointed Mayor of Seville, was the rather strange choice as head of the organization, whose main preoccupation turned out to be the minutiae of raising 'taxation and how to implement it to ensure getting the necessary funds in cash to cover future expenses'.[94] It was eventually agreed that the Junta would be financed by 'voluntary contributions from the residents of Seville to the subscription, now permanently open at the offices of the II [military] Division', and also by 'the release of a special stamp by the aforementioned *Junta* whose purchase would be mandatory'.[95] At the same time, the insurgents imposed extremely strict conditions on eligibility for free meals: only males aged between 18 and 60 could apply. In order to do so, they had to fulfil *all* the following conditions: be unemployed, registered as an active jobseeker, in possession of a special permit (issued by the authorities) and, crucially, have their loyalty to the new regime vouched for by a parish priest.[96] These clauses, which effectively excluded all Republicans, implied that the agency's much lauded philanthropic motivations were, in truth, ideologically exclusive, and designed primarily to ensure the availability of a labour force sufficient to cover essential requirements. The Junta's logic was again confirmed by its obsession with keeping applications to an absolute minimum, much to the despair of the malnourished population of Seville. In one of his frequent verbal outbursts, on 3 November 1936, Queipo admitted that as many as 3,000 applications from 'poor souls' without any apparent means of survival had been turned down because the Junta was unable to increase its meal production, currently standing at an alarmingly low 17,000 daily; on 6 November he went on to 'offer thanks for the sum raised on a voluntary basis from the salaries of all Sevillians, on my initiative'.[97] The reality was that, behind the façade of a relief agency, the Junta functioned as a corporate entity which had accumulated, by 30 November 1936, a respectable profit of 265,640 pesetas. The Junta was another way in which the 'pact of blood' was consolidated through the involvement of all the coalition's members in its 'enriching' labour; it was also part of the victory of a totalitarian regime over civil society in that the Junta also created a sophisticated surveillance apparatus to ensure the successful collection of its universal tax. Regarding the 'voluntary' nature of the contributions, the Junta's treasurer noted that by 30 November 1936 the revenue from private donations was almost equal to that raised through taxing all commercial transactions in the city – which gives some indication of the coercive power of Queipo's kleptocratic state. Last but not least, the Junta also punished ideological enemies by effectively imposing starvation, this being the effect of excluding all Republicans from these meals. Not even the magnitude of the humanitarian crisis consuming Seville could persuade the myriad forces pillaging the fourth-largest city in Spain to reformulate the Junta's priorities. After achieving the repressive and disciplinary goals it had been set, the organization was officially disbanded on 15 January 1937 and all its funds transferred to the Asociación Sevillana de Caridad.[98] As for the 'poor souls' referred to by Queipo, they were again subjected to an extreme form of collective degradation by being aided by the very same social groups that had earlier massacred them during the pacification of the working-class districts. To add insult to injury, the local elites, headed by the Catholic Church, now assumed responsibility for providing food and rudimentary education (little better than indoctrination) to the sons of their executed enemies, which only intensified the grief of surviving family members.[99] This was the crudest manifestation of the policy of (re)educating the masses: it was a socio-political vendetta which would endure until the very end of General Franco's dictatorship, especially through the abduction and trafficking of working-class babies.[100]

## Conclusion

This chapter has explored the meaning of the disproportionate force which the military insurgents deployed against the mainly civilian resistance in Seville. Even the trade union militias represented no credible threat to the triumph of the coup there, since the insurgents already had behind them the entire city garrison. Indeed they rapidly – and relatively bloodlessly – captured the city centre. Only then – and from a position of control – did the insurgents begin to use extreme violence, which was targeted overwhelmingly against the civilian population of the city's working-class neighbourhoods. This pattern suggests that the violence was premeditated, certainly that its purpose was other than military – what Preston has termed an investment in terror, and one 'bankable' for years to come.[101] It was designed to institute extreme forms of socio-political control and economic exploitation (asset stripping). From the time of the insurgents' takeover in Seville, they began to disseminate a series of obfuscating myths, foremost among which was that they had been a mere handful of soldiers triumphing against all the odds, a myth which for a long time helped obscure the origins and intent of their onslaught against the city's civilian population.

Mass executions, torture, rape, plunder, famine, social apartheid, slave labour, class war, public and collective humiliation, the annihilation of trade unionism, the abduction and 're-education' of Republican orphans and the appointment of a psychopath – General Queipo de Llano – to preside over terror: all this amounted to an apocalyptic response which used violence to halt democratizing social change and to impose a brutal hierarchy at once both old and new. As Helen Graham has written, 'Francoism, like Stalinism and Nazism, can best be defined as a regime that was at war with its own society'. The scale of destruction was extreme because so much had to be destroyed, both physically and psychologically, in order to reverse the incipient forms of democratic modernity emerging within the Second Republic.[102] Moreover, Seville had to lead by example, as the de facto capital of insurgent Spain. The dual purpose of the kleptocratic state was to use famine both as a weapon of war in itself, and also to fund a total war through which was being forged a totalitarian order. The rebels successfully depoliticized the Republican masses and reintroduced a form of social feudalism to twentieth-century Seville; but they failed to create the homogeneous society they sought, or indeed a functional one. By 30 September 1936, the Asociación Sevillana de Caridad was providing for the basic material needs of 47,784 residents out of a total of 267,192. While one of every five inhabitants of Seville was starving, the army fund alone collected in the city the astronomical sum of 16,625,825.25 pesetas during the remaining years of the battlefield war.[103] Although this unofficial capital of insurgent Spain never experienced the battlefield war itself, it was nevertheless subjected to an uncivil peace which claimed the lives of over 1 per cent of its population in only six months. All of this was the actual cost – both human and economic – of the insurgent assault on civilian society.

## Notes

1. Felipe Betrán Güell, *Preparación y desarrollo del alzamiento nacional* (Valladolid: Librería Santarén, 1939), p. 123. The translation cited here is from Paul Preston, *The Spanish Holocaust: Inquisition and Extermination in Twentieth-Century Spain* (London: HarperPress, 2012), p. 119.

2. José Gómez Salvago, *La Segunda República: elecciones y partidos políticos en Sevilla y provincia* (Sevilla: Universidad de Sevilla, 1986), pp. 222–3.

3. *Vanity Fair*, 26 July 2012; B. Félix Maíz, *Mola, aquel hombre: diario de la conspiración, 1936* (Barcelona: Planeta, 1976), p. 200.

4. For a magisterial scholarly debunking of this myth, see the work of Herbert Rutledge Southworth in *Conspiracy and the Spanish Civil War: The Brainwashing of Francisco Franco*

(New York: Routledge, 2002) and earlier in Southworth's classic, *El mito de la cruzada de Franco* (Barcelona: Debolsillo, 2008) – first published in French as *Le Mythe de la Croisade de Franco* (Paris: Ruedo Ibérico, 1964).

5.  Sebastian Balfour, *Deadly Embrace: Morocco and the Road to the Spanish Civil War* (Oxford: Oxford University Press, 2002).

6.  The pervasive influence of this caste system was so crushing that it created 'an inferiority complex that was all too human in Seville' in the words of Falangist leader Joaquín Miranda, cited in Maximiano García Venero, *La Falange en la guerra de España: la unificación y Hedilla* (Paris: Ruedo Ibérico, 1967), p. 178.

7.  José María Pemán y Pemartín, *Arengas y Crónicas de Guerra* (Cádiz: Establecimientos Cerón, 1937), p. 12.

8.  Preston, *The Spanish Holocaust*, pp. 20–3.

9.  B. Félix Maíz, *Alzamiento en España: de un diario de la conspiración* (Pamplona: Editorial Gómez, 1952), p. 54.

10. Luis Bolín, *Spain: The Vital Years* (London: Cassell, 1967), p. 177.

11. Letter from 'Obreros del Puerto de Sevilla' [Seville dockworkers] to the Minister of Labour, 15 May 1936, Centro Documental de la Memoria Histórica, PS Madrid, 385(2)/37.

12. Archivo Intermedio Militar Sur (AIMS), Legajo 5375, Carpeta 18; Antonio Olmedo Delgado and José Cuesta Monereo, *General Queipo de Llano: aventura y audacia* (Barcelona: AHR, 1957), p. 88; García Venero, *La Falange en la guerra de España*, p. 113; Guzmán de Alfarache, *¡18 de julio en Sevilla! Historia del alzamiento glorioso de Sevilla* (Sevilla: FE, 1937), pp. 40, 141–7, 177, 201.

13. Diego Martínez Barrio, *Memorias* (Barcelona: Planeta, 1983), p. 322; Joaquín Arrarás, *Historia de la segunda república española*, Vol. 4 (Madrid: Editora Nacional, 1968), pp. 108–9. For examples of Queipo's political cynicism and his participation in previous conspiracies, see his own memoirs, Gonzalo Queipo de Llano, *El General Queipo perseguido por la dictadura* (Madrid: J. Morata, 1930) and *El movimiento reivindicativo de Cuatro Vientos* (Madrid: Tip. Yagues, 1933) both *passim*.

14. Archivo de la Real Academia de Historia (ARAH), Archivo Natalio Rivas, Legajo II-8923; Arrarás, *Historia de la segunda república española*, Vol. 4, p. 299, 304–5; Félix Maíz, *Alzamiento en España*, p. 100; *Mola, aquel hombre*, pp. 133–4.

15. García Venero, *La Falange en la guerra de España*, p. 130; Guzmán de Alfarache, *¡18 de julio en Sevilla!*, pp. 42–8; Olmedo Delgado and Cuesta Monereo, *General Queipo de Llano*, pp. 84–94; José María Varela Rendueles, *Rebelión en Sevilla: memorias de su gobernador rebelde* (Sevilla: Servicio de Publicaciones del Ayuntamiento, 1982), pp. 76–80.

16. ARAH, Archivo Natalio Rivas, Legajo II-8923; Olmedo Delgado and Cuesta Monereo, *General Queipo de Llano*, pp. 10–13, 32.

17. These were Queipo's infamous radio 'charlas' (chats), with that of 23 July published in somewhat expurgated form in *ABC* (Seville), 24 July 1936. In this account, the General's initial objective was simply to 'talk up' his role in the local rebellion: he claimed that on 18 July his 180 rebel soldiers defeated the 600 Republican Assault Guards defending the Civil Government.

18. ARAH, Archivo Natalio Rivas, Legajo II-8923. This myth was the one providing the *casus belli* for the insurgents' July coup – as a pre-emptive strike against an imminent Soviet-sponsored revolution, spearheaded by native 'Marxist hordes'.

19. *ABC* (Seville), 18 July 1937; *La Unión*, 18 July 1937; *El Correo de Andalucía*, 18 July 1937; Queipo de Llano, 'Cómo dominamos a Sevilla', in *Estampas de la Guerra, Tomo Quinto, Frentes*

*de Andalucía y Extremadura* (San Sebastián: Editora Nacional, 1938), pp. 28–30; Guzmán de Alfarache, *¡18 de julio!*, pp. 62–3; Jorge Fernández-Coppel, *Queipo de Llano: memorias de la guerra civil* (Madrid: La Esfera de los Libros, 2008), p. 38; Olmedo Delgado and Cuesta Monereo, *General Queipo de Llano,* pp. 102–3.

20. *ABC* (Seville), 18 July 1937; *La Unión*, 18 July 1937; *El Correo de Andalucía*, 18 July 1937; Queipo de Llano, 'Cómo dominamos a Sevilla', pp. 30–1; Guzmán de Alfarache, *¡18 de julio!*, p. 66; Olmedo Delgado and Cuesta Monereo, *General Queipo de Llano*, pp. 103–6.

21. Archivo del Tribunal Militar Territorial Segundo, SUM 239/1938; 243/1938.

22. *ABC* (Seville), 24 July 1936.

23. Queipo's first biographer repeated this claim, Luis de Armiñán Odriozola, *Excmo. Sr. General D. Gonzalo Queipo de Llano y Sierra, Jefe del Ejército del Sur* (Ávila: Impresora Católica, 1937), pp. 28–31. Many (minor) variations of the myth appeared until Queipo presented the 'canonical' version on the first anniversary of the rebellion in *ABC* (Seville), 18 July 1937, and also in Gonzalo Queipo de Llano, 'Cómo dominamos a Sevilla'.

24. Hermoso, a member of Manuel Azaña's centrist republican party, had commented that he preferred a 'riding boot dictatorship' (*dictadura de bota de montar*) to one of 'peasant sandals' (*alpargatas*). Seville's 'riding boots' executed him on 29 September 1936. (In Spanish the expression 'riding boots' connotes the boots of social elites and cavalry officers.)

25. AIMS, Legajo 5363 (Cavalry); Legajo 5375, Carpeta 20; Manuel Delicado, 'Cómo se luchó en Sevilla', *Discurso pronunciado en el Pleno ampliado del C. C. del Partido Comunista de España, celebrado en Valencia los días 5, 6, 7 y 8 de Marzo de 1937*, p. 5; Juan Ortiz Villalba, *Del golpe militar a la guerra civil: Sevilla 1936* (Sevilla: RD Editores, 2006), p. 95; Varela Rendueles, *Rebelión en Sevilla*, pp. 115–17.

26. AIMS, Legajo 5363, Carpeta 1.

27. AIMS, Legajo 5364, Carpeta 1, 2; Legajo 5375, Carpeta 1–20; Legajo 5376, Carpeta 12; Legajo 5381, Carpeta 9; Archivo General Militar (AGM – Madrid), Zona Nacional, Armario 18, Legajo 1, Carpeta 68; Legajo 2, Carpeta 9; Legajo 6, Carpeta 2; Manuel Aznar, *Historia Militar de la Guerra de España* (Madrid: Editora Nacional, 1940), pp. 158–64; Guzmán de Alfarache, *¡18 de julio!*, pp. 72–88, 110–15, 130–7, 153–60, 223–69; Ana Martín Fidalgo, Enrique Roldán González and Manuel Martin Burgueño, *El Requeté de Sevilla: orígenes, causas e historia*, p. 50; Rafael de Medina Vilallonga, *Tiempo pasado* (Sevilla: Gráfica Sevillana, 1971), pp. 36–7; Luis Redondo and Juan de Zavala, *El requeté (la tradición no muere)* (Barcelona: AHR, 1957), pp. 461–9.

28. AGM, Armario 18, Legajo 1, Carpeta 68; Legajo 6, Carpeta 2; Legajo 18, Carpeta 25; AIMS, Legajo 5375, Carpeta 20; *ABC* (Seville), 18 July 1937; *El Correo de Andalucía*, 18 July 1937; '18 de Julio de 1936 en Sevilla', *Archivo Hispalense* 43:132–3 (1965), pp. 175–87: pp. 184–7; Guzmán de Alfarache, *¡18 de julio en Sevilla!*, pp. 104–9; Varela Rendueles, *Rebelión en Sevilla*, pp. 118–23.

29. Ortiz Villalba, *Del golpe militar a la guerra civil*, pp. 239–40.

30. Ibid., pp. 130.

31. AGM, Armario 18, Legajo 1, Carpeta 68; AIMS, Legajo 5375, Carpeta 14.

32. Queipo barked into the radio that: 'we must eradicate the marxist scum (*la canalla marxista*) from Spain, every last trace', reported in *El Correo de Andalucía*, 25 July 1936. An example of the 'pacification' of a village 'poisoned' by the 'marxist virus' in a newspaper report on events in El Pedroso (Seville): *La Unión*, 11 August 1936.

33. Cuesta Monereo claimed that even high-ranking military officers and police had become infected with the 'marxist virus' (thus 'explaining' the opposition of many army officers and

Assault Guards, as well as some Civil Guards, to the insurgents' coup), in Olmedo Delgado and Cuesta Monereo, *General Queipo de Llano*, p. 88.

34. José María García Márquez, 'El triunfo del golpe militar: el terror en la zona ocupada', in Francisco Espinosa Maestre (ed.), *Violencia roja y azul: España, 1936–1950* (Barcelona: Crítica, 2010), pp. 81–145: p. 135.

35. Eduardo González Calleja, 'La necro-lógica de la violencia sociopolítica en la primavera de 1936', *Melánges de la Casa de Velázquez* 41:1 (2011), pp. 37–60 (on open access at: http://dialnet.unirioja.es/ejemplar/287796).

36. Francisco Espinosa Maestre, 'Sevilla, 1936. Sublevacion y represion', in Alfonso Braojos Garrido, Leandro Álvarez Rey and Francisco Espinosa Maestre, *Sevilla, 36: Sublevación fascista y represión* (Brenes, Sevilla: Muñoz Moya y Montraveta, 1990), p. 253; on pre-coup killings of civilians, the right's accusations and the historiographical polemic over 'Republican disorder', Preston, *The Spanish Holocaust*, p. 122.

37. Preston, *The Spanish Holocaust*, pp. 164–5.

38. Ibid, pp. 149, 330; AGM, Zona Nacional, Armario 18, Legajo 6, Carpeta 1.

39. Archivo Municipal de Sevilla (AMS), Asuntos Especiales, 1938, n. 4.

40. AIMS, Legajo 5352, Carpeta 1; José Díaz Arriaza, 'La represión de Queipo de Llano sobre la administración local sevillana', in Juan Ortiz Villalba, *Andalucía: guerra y exilio* (Sevilla: Universidad Pablo Olavide, 2005), pp. 103–20; Julio Ponce Alberca, 'Política y administración local en la Sevilla de Queipo (julio-diciembre 1936)', *Archivo Hispalense* 84: 256–257 (2001), pp. 31–54: p. 35.

41. AMS, Actas de la Comisión Gestora del Ayuntamiento, 19, 31 July, 10 September 1936.

42. Medina Vilallonga, *Tiempo pasado*, pp. 38–40.

43. AIMS, Legajo 5375, Carpeta 14, 20; *El Liberal*, 4 August 1936; *La Unión*, 18 July 1937; Delicado, 'Cómo se luchó en Sevilla', pp. 5–7.

44. AGM, Zona Nacional, Armario 18, Legajo 18, Carpeta 18, Documento 1; Legajo 25, Carpeta 23; Antonio Bahamonde y Sánchez de Castro, *Un año con Queipo de Llano: memorias de un nacionalista: seguido de Noches de Sevilla de Jean Alloucherie y de El infierno azul de Edmundo Barbero* (Sevilla: Espuela de Plata: 2005), p. 80; Medina Vilallonga, *Tiempo Pasado*, pp. 42–3.

45. *ABC* (Seville), 24 July 1936.

46. *La Unión*, 23 July 1936.

47. The insurgents distributed weapons to any freelance right-wingers who presented themselves to the barracks, to such an extent that there were some 187 unaffiliated vigilante volunteers on 19 July alone; Medina Vilallonga, *Tiempo Pasado*, pp. 36–7.

48. AGM, Zona Nacional, Armario 18, Legajo 18, Carpeta 18; Legajo 35, Carpeta 23; *El Correo de Andalucía*, 22, 23 July 1936; *La Unión*, 23 July 1936; Candido Ortiz de Villajos, *De Sevilla a Madrid: Ruta libertadora de la columna Castejón* (Granada: Librería Prieto, 1937), pp. 27 and 45–50.

49. Armiñán Odriozola, *Excmo*, pp. 28–31; Nicolás Salas, *El Moscú Sevillano: Sevilla la roja, feudo del comunismo español durante la República y símbolo triunfal del frente popular en 1936* (Sevilla: Universidad de Sevilla, 1990). Armiñán Odriozola was a war correspondent with the insurgent armies and later a Francoist one in the Second World War. But his own political past (for a time he'd been a member of the clientelist and populist Radical (Republican) Party) led to him later falling victim to the Francoists' repressive hysteria: in 1944 he was investigated by Franco's Political Responsibilities Tribunal.

50. Gonzalo Queipo de Llano, *Bandos y órdenes dictados por Gonzalo Queipo de Llano y Sierra, General Jefe de la Segunda División Orgánica y del Ejército del Sur desde la declaración del*

*estado de guerra, 18 de julio de 1936, hasta fin de febrero de 1937, etc.* (Seville: n.p., 1937), pp. 5–6.

51. AIMS, Legajo 5375, Carpeta 12; *La Unión*, 22 July 1936; Delicado, 'Cómo se luchó en Sevilla', p. 5; Juan Ortiz Villalba, *Del golpe militar a la guerra civil*, p. 148.

52. AGM, Armario 18, Legajo 35, Carpeta 23; *El Correo de Andalucía*, 22, 23 July 1936; Varela Rendueles, *Rebelión en Sevilla*, pp. 112–13.

53. *ABC* (Seville), 24, 25 July 1936; *La Unión*, 23 July, 1 August 1936.

54. Archivo de la Diputación Provincial de Sevilla (ADPS), Sangre, Libro 133; *Heraldo de Madrid*, 25 August 1936; *Informaciones*, 7 August 1936; Edmundo Barbero, *El infierno azul* in the trilogy by Bahamonde y Sánchez de Castro, *Un año con Queipo de Llano*, pp. 371–2; Espinosa Maestre, 'Sevilla, 1936. Sublevación y Represión', p. 216.

55. *ABC* (Seville), 24, 25 July 1936; *El Correo de Andalucía*, 22 July, 3 August 1936; *La Unión*, 22, 23, 31 July, 1 August 1936; Ortiz de Villajos, *De Sevilla a Madrid*, p. 21.

56. Bahamonde y Sánchez de Castro, *Un año con Queipo de Llano*, pp. 79–80.

57. *El Correo de Andalucía*, 22 July 1936; *La Unión*, 22 July 1936; *ABC*, 24 July 1936.

58. On Criado's tenure as Military Delegate for Andalusia and Extremadura, see Bahamonde y Sánchez de Castro, *Un año con Queipo de Llano*, pp. 158–60, and Francisco Gonzálbez Ruiz, *Yo he creído en Franco: proceso de una gran desilusión (dos meses en la cárcel de Sevilla)* (Paris: Imprimerie Coopérative Étoile, 1938), pp. 51–2. Díaz Criado was eventually replaced in mid-November 1936, but this did little to change the generic policy of cleansing, even if it did reduce the 'scandal' of what Paul Preston has termed Díaz Criado's degenerate thuggery, P. Preston, 'The Psychopathology of an Assassin. General Gonzalo Queipo de Llano', in Peter Anderson and Miguel Angel del Arco Blanco (eds), *Mass Killings and Violence in Spain, 1936–1952: Grappling with the Past* (New York: Routledge, 2015), pp. 23–58: p. 41; also Preston, *The Spanish Holocaust*, pp. 142–4. More on Díaz Criado's violent track record in Francisco Espinosa Maestre's pathbreaking study, *La justicia de Queipo. Violencia selectiva y terror fascista en la II División en 1936: Sevilla, Huelva, Cádiz, Córdoba, Málaga y Badajoz* (Barcelona: Crítica, 2006, 2nd edn.), pp. 19–22. In May 1936, Criado had also been arrested for his involvement in a plot to murder Republican President Azaña: *ABC* (Madrid), 3 May 1936.

59. For Queipo's remarks on the need to eradicate 'marxist scum', see note 32 above.

60. Espinosa Maestre, 'Sevilla, 1936. Sublevación y Represión', pp. 252–6; Preston, *Spanish Holocaust*, pp. 142–5.

61. Cuesta Monereo's instructions of 7 September 1936, which also give his reasons, in Archivo General Militar (Madrid), Zona Nacional, Armario 18, Legajo 6, Carpeta 5.

62. Espinosa Maestre, *La justicia de Queipo*, pp. 59–90.

63. Ramón Serrano Súñer, *Entre el silencio y la propaganda, la Historia como fue: memorias* (Barcelona: Planeta, 1977), pp. 244–8; Preston, *Spanish Holocaust*, p. 473.

64. For example, Queipo told reporter Jean Alloucherie that the Holy Ghost had inspired him to seize Seville and save 'Western Civilization'. Jean Alloucherie, *Noches de Sevilla*, pp. 247–8.

65. For instance, on 22 July General Queipo claimed that twenty pro-rebel civilians were murdered in the San Marcos neighbourhood alone. *La Unión*, 22 July 1936.

66. AMS, Actas Capitulares de la Comisión Gestora del Ayuntamiento de Sevilla, 20 August 1936.

67. *La Unión*, 26 July 1936; Espinosa Maestre, 'Sevilla, 1936. Sublevación y Represión', pp. 252–7; 'Julio de 1936. Golpe militar y plan de exterminio', p. 67.

68. AGM, Zona Nacional, Armario 18, Legajo 18, Carpeta 18, Documento 1; AMS, Actas de la Comisión Gestora del Ayuntamiento, September 1936–July 1937; Sanidad y Beneficiencia, Junta de auxilios alimenticios a los necesitados.

69. *FE*, 24 October 1936.

70. *FE*, 24, 28 October 1936.

71. For the Auxilio Social see Angela Cenarro, *La sonrisa de Falange: Auxilio Social en la guerra civil y en la posguerra* (Barcelona: Crítica, 2006); *Los niños del Auxilio Social* (Pozuelo de Alarcón, Madrid: Espasa, 2009).

72. Bahamonde y Sánchez de Castro, *Un año con Queipo de Llano*, p. 125.

73. *Bando* n. 13, 18 August 1936 (*Confiscación de bienes de inductores a la violencia, propagandistas y rebeldes*), *Bando* n. 23, 2 September (*Inductores de la rebelión. Inmovilización de cuentas y valores*) and *Bando* n. 29, 11 September (*Confiscación de bienes. Y adiciones y aclaraciones al bando n° 13*), Queipo de Llano, *Bandos y órdenes dictados por Gonzalo Queipo de Llano y Sierra,* pp. 23–30.

74. *FE*, 28 October 1936.

75. José Antonio Parejo Fernández, *Señoritos, jornaleros y falangistas* (Sevilla: Bosque de Palabras, 2008), pp. 126–8.

76. Bahamonde y Sánchez de Castro, *Un año con Queipo de Llano*, pp. 129–31, 137.

77. Espinosa Maestre, 'Sevilla 1936. Sublevación y represión', p. 254.

78. *FE*, 4 December 1936.

79. AGM, Cuartel General del Generalísimo, Armario 4, Legajo 273, Carpeta 6.

80. *FE*, 15 November 1936.

81. These elite-devised economic policies impressed the insurgent leadership. For instance, Joaquín Benjumea Burín, from a major local landowning family, was appointed President of the Diputación Provincial de Sevilla in December 1936 and under his presidency, the Diputación collected astronomical sums from 'fundraising campaigns'. He was then appointed as Mayor of Seville between 1938 and 1939, and then subsequently served in several senior ministerial posts between 1939 and 1942. In 1951 General Franco ennobled him as the Count of Benjumea, from which time he also served as Governor of the Bank of Spain until his death in 1963. Nicolás Salas, *Joaquín Benjumea Burín, I Conde de Benjumea: su época y su labor, 1878–1963* (Sevilla: Guadalquivir, 1990).

82. *FE*, 5 September 1936.

83. '18 de Julio de 1936 en Sevilla', p.185; Saturnino Barneto, *Cómo luchan bajo la bandera de la I.S.R. los obreros del puerto de Sevilla* (n.p., n.d.).

84. Ortiz Villalba, *Del golpe militar a la guerra civil*, pp. 281–2.

85. *FE*, 12 September 1936.

86. *FE*, 16 September 1936.

87. AIMS, Legajo 5382, Carpeta 14.

88. AMS, Sanidad y Beneficiencia, Actas de la Junta de auxilios a los necesitados, 18 September 1936.

89. AMS, Hacienda, Expedientes generales, 1936, n. 71.

90. Queipo de Llano, *Bandos y órdenes dictados por Gonzalo Queipo de Llano y Sierra,* pp. 12–13.

91. ADPS, Casa Cuna, Legajo 39, 519.

92. AMS, Sanidad y Beneficiencia, Actas de la Junta de Auxilios a los Necesitados, 2 August 1936.

93. Queipo de Llano, *Bandos y órdenes dictados por Gonzalo Queipo de Llano y Sierra*, pp. 13–15.

94. AMS, Sanidad y Beneficiencia, Actas de la Junta de Auxilios Alimenticios a los Necesitados (n.d.).

95. Archivo Municipal de Sevilla (Seville), Sanidad y Beneficiencia, Junta de Auxilios Alimenticios a los Necesitados (n.d.).

96. AMS, Sanidad y Beneficiencia, Junta de Auxilios Alimenticios a los Necesitados; Actas de la Junta de Auxilios a los Necesitados, 2 August 1936; *FE*, 27 September 1936.

97. Queipo reported in *FE*, 4, 7 November 1936.

98. AMS, Sanidad y Beneficiencia, Junta de Auxilios Alimenticios a los Necesitados (n.d.).

99. *FE*, 1, 4 November 1936; Bahamonde, *Un año con Queipo de Llano*, p. 72.

100. *El País*, 24 December 2008.

101. Paul Preston, *Franco. A Biography* (London: HarperCollins, 1993), p. 783.

102. Helen Graham, *The War and its Shadow: Spain's Civil War in Europe's Long Twentieth Century* (Eastbourne: Sussex Academic Press, 2012), p. 103.

103. AIMS, Legajo 5382, Carpeta 13; AMS, Sanidad y Beneficiencia, Junta de auxilios alimenticios a los Necesitados; José Manuel Macarro Vera, *La utopía revolucionaria: Sevilla en la Segunda República* (Sevilla: Monte de Piedad y Caja de Ahorros de Sevilla, 1985), p.22.

## Further reading

Apart from Paul Preston's own work, there is little published in English on this topic, so also listed here is a selection of work in Spanish – comprising the best recent historical research, some older studies and the classic contemporary account by Bahamonde.

Preston, P., *The Spanish Holocaust: Inquisition and Extermination in Twentieth-century Spain* (London: HarperPress, 2012).

Preston, P., 'The Psychopathology of an Assassin: General Queipo de Llano', in P. Anderson and M.A. del Arco Blanco, *Mass Killings and Violence in Spain, 1936–1952: Grappling with the Past* (London: Routledge, 2015), pp. 23–58.

Serém, R., *Laboratory of Terror: Conspiracy, Coup d'état and Civil War in Seville (1936–1939)* (Sussex Academic Press, forthcoming).

### In Spanish

Álvarez Rey, L., 'Del rojo al azul: los inicios de la Guerra Civil en Sevilla', in L. Álvarez Rey (ed.), *Andalucía y la Guerra Civil: Estudios y perspectivas* (Sevilla: Universidad de Sevilla, 2006), pp. 161–89.

Bahamonde y Sánchez de Castro, A., *Un año con Queipo de Llano: memorias de un nacionalista: seguido de noches de Sevilla de Jean Alloucherie y El infierno azul de Edmundo Barbero* (Sevilla: Espuela de Plata, 2005). These three volumes were originally published as follows: *Un año con Queipo* (Barcelona: Ediciones Españolas, 1938); *Noches de Sevilla* (Barcelona: Ediciones Europa-América, 1937); *El infierno azul* (Madrid: Talleres del SUIG (CNT), 1937).

Barrios, M., *El último virrey: Queipo de Llano* (Sevilla: J. Rodríguez Castillejo, 1990).

Espinosa Maestre, F., 'Sevilla, 1936. Sublevación y represión', in A. Braojos Garrido, L. Álvarez Rey and F. Espinosa Maestre, *Sevilla, 36: Sublevación fascista y represión* (Brenes, Sevilla: Muñoz Moya y Montraveta, 1990).

Espinosa Maestre, F., *La justicia de Queipo. Violencia selectiva y terror fascista en la II División en 1936: Sevilla, Huelva, Cádiz, Córdoba, Málaga y Badajoz* (Barcelona: Crítica, 2006), pp. 29–37, 59–99, 175–202.

Gibson, I., *Queipo de Llano. Sevilla, verano de 1936 (Con las charlas radiofónicas completas)* (Barcelona: Grijalbo, 1986).

Gil Honduvilla, J., *Militares y sublevación, Sevilla 1936: causas, personajes, preparación y desarrollo* (Brenes: Muñoz Moya, 2010).

Ortiz Villalba, J., *Del golpe militar a la Guerra Civil: Sevilla 1936* (Sevilla: RD Editores, 2006).

Ponce Alberca, J., 'La represión de las organizaciones obreras durante la guerra civil y la posguerra', in L. Álvarez Rey and E. Lemus López (eds), *Sindicatos y trabajadores en Sevilla: Una aproximación a la memoria del siglo XX* (Sevilla: Universidade de Sevilla, 2000), pp. 157–77.

# CHAPTER 6

## NATURAL ALLIANCES: THE IMPACT OF NAZISM AND FASCISM ON FRANCO'S DOMESTIC POLICIES

*Angel Viñas*

It is obvious that the Franco regime was set upon creating new political institutions, on diffusing new ideological values and a new political culture. It was based on the reactionary tradition of the Spanish extreme right as well as on the new values of Fascism. Thus the Franco dictatorship was, in a way, the true expression of Spanish Fascism.[1]

The civil war in which Francoism was forged remains the single most important episode in the history of twentieth-century Spain. It was also a source of profound continental change in Europe and beyond (given the continent was, in the 1930s, still the pivot of global and imperial power internationally). With the opening of both public and to some extent private archives in Spain and abroad, the civil war and its aftermath are being rewritten, although not without difficulty. Under the current conservative government in Spain,[2] historical archives have been made less accessible, bucking what has been until now a broader European trend towards greater governmental accountability and democratic transparency. Inside Spain, the civil war and its long-term consequences continue to raise uncomfortable issues for society.

Franco's military victory in 1939 and his emergent dictatorship were substantially helped by the continuous military, financial, diplomatic and political assistance of both Hitler and Mussolini. The anti-democratic thinking of socially and politically conservative sectors in Spain, strengthened by their convergence in the coalition underpinning Franco's war effort, also became exposed to the allure of Fascism and Nazism. They were irresistibly drawn thereby to the idea of disciplining Spain's unruly masses by imitating Fascism's and Nazism's combination of force, ideology and the offer of material rewards (to some). The de facto alliance of the three dictators – reflected in various agreements during the civil war and also during 1939–40 – would shape the course of Spanish politics for almost forty years.

### Fascism, military rebellion and Franco

Far too many scholars, particularly in the English-speaking world, still sustain the view that the origins of the civil war were purely Spanish. In the emphasis on structural factors, foreign influences are discounted – except for that of the USSR, which was allegedly looking for opportunities to make Spain into a satellite. This assertion, redolent of the Cold War, but recently resurrected in Spain,[3] has turned out to be a shining example of what psychologists term 'projection', a defence mechanism for rejecting highly uncomfortable facts.

In the tumultuous spring of 1936 the Spanish left was not preparing a revolution and still less a civil war. The monarchists and leading military conspirators, however, were. Their intention was to restore the monarchy which had been supplanted by a Republic in April 1931. Between March and June 1936 secret negotiations took place in Rome for the purchase of modern war matériel.[4] Mussolini had had a jaundiced view of the Spanish Republic ever since its establishment.[5] He was friendly with a long list of opponents of the new Republican regime, sent military and civilian agents to Spain,[6] agreed in March 1934 to support a military uprising (which, in the event, did not materialize), and financed the minuscule Spanish Fascist party (Falange).[7] Once the conquest of Abyssinia had been achieved in spring 1936, he also found time to intervene in Spanish affairs once again.

On 1 July 1936, four contracts for the supply of aircraft were signed with the Società Idrovolante Alta Italia in Rome by Pedro Sainz Rodríguez, number three in Renovación Española, Spain's extreme-right monarchist party headed by José Calvo Sotelo. This aircraft company had excellent connections with the Fascist Air Ministry. These extremely detailed contracts provided for the supply to Spain's future insurgents of forty-three modern aircraft (15 Savoia bombers, 24 Fiat fighters and even 4 seaplanes), all ready for war, fully equipped with Regia Aeronautica crews, masses of bombs and ammunition and many spare aero engines.[8] A first batch was to be dispatched before the end of July. A few days after the contracts were signed a number of aircraft were moved from northern airfields towards the south of Italy. In Spain the long-prepared military coup began on 17 July.

Spanish monarchist and Carlist[9] agents had also toured other countries trying to buy weapons. As is well known, the monarchist General José Sanjurjo, then leader of the Spanish military conspiracy, paid a visit to Berlin. This took place in the context of the Nazi occupation of the Rhineland in March 1936 and Sanjurjo's presence received little attention. However, it has recently come to light that right after the July coup the military attaché in Paris, Major Antonio Barroso, was of the opinion that Hitler's advisor on foreign affairs, Joachim von Ribbentrop, knew of some (albeit vague) promises of support for Spain's military rebels that had been made by as yet unidentified sectors in Germany.[10] On 25 July Hitler took the personal decision to help Franco.[11] In the German case as in the Italian, the reasons for supporting the insurgents were mainly geostrategic and geopolitical – both dictators wanted to weaken France's position – although they disguised these intentions in a conveniently couched anti-Communist newspeak.

Franco was by no means intended at the outset to be the insurgents' top military leader. He was finally appointed, in late September 1936, because of five factors: Sanjurjo's death in a plane accident on 20 July left the conspiracy without a guiding authority; Franco was in command of the most professional of all the insurgents' military forces, the Army of Africa, mostly airlifted by German planes from Morocco to southern Spain in the summer; his proven monarchism; his military successes (albeit over a ramshackle peasant and militia-based resistance); and last, but by no means least, because he was the only recipient of Nazi and Fascist help. By the end of September/early October the Germans started planning what would be the only truly strategic innovation of the war, the shipment of a combined arms and aircraft-based contingent known as the Condor Legion.[12]

Of the two Fascist dictators, Mussolini was the first to show a sustained interest in Spain's domestic situation. On 14 September Rome instructed the Italian Consul General in Tangier to remind Franco of the social aspects of 'his' movement and of the need to win the hearts and minds of all Spaniards so as to put it on a safe basis. Franco should distance himself, he was told, from a mere military *pronunciamiento* (coup) (i.e. one identified predominantly with the old elites only) and work instead to achieve a 'national revolution' for the benefit of all sectors of the population. The Consul General had secret talks with Franco on 20 September and Franco readily agreed because, so he declared, Mussolini's ideas totally coincided with his own.[13]

The insurgents established a collective leadership (National Defence Junta, JDN) and on 28 July 1936 a state of war was declared following individual proclamations by rebel generals across the territory they controlled. All power was concentrated in military hands. Mindful of the need for a unified command they decided, with the prodding of monarchist General Kindelan, to trust Franco. JDN Decree 138 appointed him head of the state government and *Generalissimo* (supreme military commander). The version of the decree published on 2 October explicitly granted Franco all the powers of the 'new state'. He subsequently dropped the reference to 'the government', thus with one stroke emerging from *primus inter pares* to a position of singular control as head of state. Thus the origins of Franco's exalted position lay exclusively in an obscure process of co-option by self-appointed rebellious military leaders who took it upon themselves to speak for the 'true' Spain.

The JDN never confined itself to dealing only with military and personnel matters. From the very beginning, taking advantage of the state of war, it proceeded to dismantle the social, political and educational reforms introduced by the hated Republic.[14] Its crucial agrarian reform was reversed; co-education was abolished and Catholic religion and history were both introduced as mandatory subjects on the school syllabus. All but conservative political parties were abolished, along with trade unions. Trial by jury was ended. Civil servants were subject to ideological and political purges. In the midst of all the immediate pressures deriving from a military situation rapidly evolving in their favour, the JDN lost no time in flagging up its true socio-economic colours.

## Under friendly 'influence'

Franco, whose support base was still the Army of Africa, intensified this dismantling process under a new hybrid military-civilian institution, the Junta Técnica del Estado (JTE). It was supposed to take charge of the administrative running of the territory under the insurgents' control. For new ideological inspiration here Franco looked to the Falange. Already at the top, he was unwilling to be entirely dependent on monarchist or Carlist ambitions and thus leaned on to the Falange to bolster and expand his support base. Again the Italians were quick in perceiving that this could lead to many opportunities for influencing political and ideological developments in Spain. The Nazis were not so keen on getting involved in this way. They would concentrate more on securing economic compensation for their material assistance and eventually attempted to make the Spanish economy into a satellite of the Third Reich. Here they encountered resistance, but their military prowess and Franco's wartime dependence on their supplies overcame many difficulties.

Nazis and Fascists became embroiled in a fully fledged conventional war in Spain quite early on, once Soviet support for the beleaguered Republic started arriving by mid-October 1936. Prior to this, the military campaign had been a continuous success for the insurgents and a continuous retreat for the Republican forces. Thereafter, foreign intervention to a great extent shaped the political evolution of the two contending zones. The insurgents became increasingly influenced by Fascist/Nazi ideology mostly channelled by the Falange, but also by the increasingly fascistized conservative middle classes, many caught up in what they perceived – at least for a time – as a new national revolution in which they were to be the 'chosen' class.

For their part, the Republicans had been informed of Stalin's strategy of preventing an easy Fascist victory in Spain whilst encouraging them to seek a rapprochement with the democratic powers. Soviet assistance, discontinuous and intermittent, underlined Stalin's wish to play a relatively secondary role.[15] Nevertheless, inside Republican Spain, the Spanish Communist Party (PCE) grew exponentially, for reasons that were in an important part domestic – and to some extent comparable with the middle-class mobilization in Franco's zone – to become a new major *national* actor in the wartime Republic's political and military life.[16] But the Soviet Union did not meet with much success in its international strategy, as Britain (and France in its wake) maintained their distance and grew even warier of Soviet intentions in Spain as time went on. In contrast, in Franco's zone both Nazis and Fascists achieved their objectives and, as this chapter will show, their influence shaped his emerging dictatorship – while the Western democracies, and especially Britain, adopted a remarkably consistent laissez-faire (if not complaisant) attitude to Axis involvement in Spain.

As soon as military developments permitted, Franco unified all paramilitary forces in December 1936. Then in April 1937 all political parties were combined in a Fascist-style single party subordinated to Franco – the FET y de las JONS (or the Movement for short).[17] Political plurality was deemed incompatible with the anti-democratic goals being pursued by Franco as Spain's supreme military and political leader (Caudillo). On 4 August the statutes of the new party made Franco its 'national head, accountable to God and History only'. Franco would never relinquish this power. Indeed, later on, his leadership was portrayed as being the outcome of 'God's grace'.[18] Spain's institutional Catholic Church, dominated by religious and political integrists, was happy to endorse this fully, becoming a major component in Franco's new power base and, alongside the Falange, a crucial tool in the disciplining and control of the population.

Italian Fascists took credit for having inspired Franco's political unification of April 1937, but it would have also happened without any specific Fascist input. Even before the July 1936 coup, Spanish monarchists and sundry other conservative forces were thinking in terms of reshaping Spanish society by mobilizing it inside new forms of organization in order to control the population both politically and socially. In part at least these ideas drew on Fascist principles, but it was the extreme conditions of the civil war that enabled the project to be brought to fruition. In Spain, it was the fact of military vigilance which allowed the synthesis of integrist Catholicism and fascist disciplinary mechanisms to work in sync rather than in tension or opposition.[19]

Fascist ideology proper was put into practice by establishing new forms of (separate) worker and employer organizations, this in an attempt to destroy the socio-economic relationships modernized by the Republic. Workers were now to join the new 'National-Syndicalist' labour unions, the Centrales Obreras Nacional-sindicalistas (CONS): the idea was to indoctrinate and control them and to provide jobs and housing. The employers were to join their own equivalent – the Centrales de Empresarios Nacional-sindicalistas (CENS). Needless to say strikes and lock-outs were both strictly forbidden.[20]

The *Fuero del Trabajo* (Labour Charter) of 9 March 1938 was to be the first attempt to shape Francoist society in a Fascist mould. It was directly inspired by the Fascist *Carta del Lavoro* and the Nazi *Gesetz zur Ordnung der nationalen Arbeit*, to which a dash of reactionary and paternalistic Catholic social thinking was added. The historian Alejandro Andreassi has recently emphasized the importance of the Nazi input.[21] In the new structures created by the Labour Charter authority went on flowing downwards from the top as in a pyramid. The management of companies was to be shaped along Fascist lines with the employers acting as little Führers. Workers were to be subject to political and economic discipline under 'enlightened' leadership in new 'vertical unions' in which employers and workers were expected to strive for common goals as established by the state. The 'marxist' class struggle was to be abolished by decree.

All interests were made subservient to the service of the state, considered to be a totalitarian tool to achieve the integrity of the 'Fatherland'.[22] This 'verticalism' along with the political 'unification' of April 1937 was the earliest manifestation of the Spanish version of Hitlerian or Mussolinian *Gleichschaltung* (coordination) in socio-economic matters. Subsequently, Spain imported institutions equivalent to the Nazi *Hitlerjugend* (Frente de Juventudes, or Youth Front), *Bund deutscher Mädel* (Sección Femenina, the Women's Section of the Falange), *Winterhilfswerk* (Auxilio Social, wartime relief/welfare organization) and *Kraft durch Freude* (Educación y Descanso, worker education/welfare section, within the 'vertical unions'). All of them were adapted to specific Spanish circumstances.

The influence of Fascist and Nazi ideology varied according to the sector and type of organization. Generally it has been asserted that the most fascistized dimensions were in the socio-economic domain. However, more recent research into other aspects of domestic policy suggests that this assertion is too limited. Fascist principles were applied equally to other (overlapping) spheres too – those of organization, repression, the law, the economy and international affairs. This chapter will illustrate some of them.

## The allure of Nazi principles

The 1938 Labour Charter was only the most obvious example of the undiluted Francoist adaptation of Nazi and Fascist forms. However Franco and his politico-military coterie were also attracted in particular by other specific features of Nazi ideology. Not by the more outlandish elements to be sure (e.g. Nazi paganism), but certainly by those principles – including juridical, or at least quasi-juridical ones – which could be readily adapted and applied to the warlike, militaristic and fascistic regime they were intent on creating in Spain. Prominent amongst the most serviceable here was the concept of *Führerprinzip*, the fundamental idea that the Führer, i.e. in Spain's case the Caudillo, was the primary source of law, and therefore he was not bound by any constitution, nor by any laws deriving therefrom (as was the usual arrangement in European democracies). *Führerprinzip* thus buttressed Franco's political position, reinforced his powers and gave him a tool to shape his regime.

A country where people were expected to obey orders from above unencumbered by any other authority was a dream which the Fascist regimes were making more perfectly realizable by the day. Under the principle of *Caudillaje* (Spain's equivalent of *Führerprinzip*), Franco's will was all-encompassing. The nation's combined energies – political, social, economic and cultural – were to be mobilized under his leadership to fight the deadly forces of the 'anti-Spain', i.e. communism, socialism, freemasonry, liberalism, parliamentarism, separatism and atheism. It is significant that a political theorist like the Carlist Francisco Elias de Tejada immediately understood the Caudillo's aspirations. Franco was:

> not only the supreme authority of the new State but the *ultimate root of power on earth*. He is independent in his decisions, *rises above everyone else in his judgments*, cannot be contested over his orders [...] He is placed at the highest echelon in the hierarchy of service and sacrifice [...] *The old distinctions between powers break down before him* because *he is the supreme power. The procedural rules of old parliamentarism disappear before him* ...[23]

What does this mean? Simply that Franco's authority would be the main factor shaping the single party, the economy and the entire new state emerging from the war.

However, this approach had to be made 'legal'. The initial declaration of a state of war in July 1936 was not enough. Hitler's dictatorship had been rendered 'legal' by the Enabling Law of 1933 which was renewed by the puppet Reichstag in 1937 and 1939 (and in 1941 and 1943 by decree, this time without any temporal limit). Before the Labour Charter was promulgated, Franco, in the full exercise of his supreme power, had issued a Law on 30 January 1938 establishing a 'regular' government to replace the JTE. But he was not prepared to go too far. Article 17 foresaw that 'the head of state who assumes all powers according to the JDN decree of 29 September 1936 will wield supreme authority for issuing legislation of a general character'. Obviously Franco was intent on preserving his power as the primary lawmaker and law-giver. This is evident in his approach to 'parliament', government and lawmaking, which will now be discussed in turn.

## Subjugating 'parliament'

Franco did not dispense completely with a kind of 'parliament' – he decreed in July 1942 (via a Fundamental Law[24]) that provision be made for establishing a Cortes, just as other fascist regimes also retained or established some form of pseudo-'representative' body. Hitler used a Reichstag divested of all constitutionalism; Mussolini replaced Parliament by a Chamber of Fasci and Corporations. Franco's Cortes would merely be a sounding board for draft legislation which the dictator condescended to have discussed with a view to fine-tuning its detail. Holding to the *Führerprinzip* was specifically acknowledged in the preamble:

> Since the Head of State maintains his supreme authority for issuing legal norms of a general character, in the terms of the Laws of 30 January 1938 and 8 August 1939, the entity [Cortes] hereby created represents an efficient tool for collaborating in the above-mentioned function as well as a self-limiting point of departure for a more systematic use of said authority.[25]

The Cortes was never the real originator of major legislation in Franco's Spain. The Caudillo imposed his will on his bogus parliament not only in the early years but also well after the putative end of the dictatorship's fascist period. This happened both publicly and, more tellingly (and frequently) in secret. On at least two major public occasions – in 1958, and again in 1966 – the continuities with the *Führerprinzip* were evident in both procedure and content. The first occasion was in May 1958 when Franco presented to 'his' Cortes the Fundamental Law determining the 'basic characteristics of the National Movement' which 'by their very nature' were declared to be immutable and inalterable. Some of the most flagrantly fascistic terminology had, it is true, been replaced, but 'organic democracy' based on 'political representation' by families, municipalities and vertical 'unions' – and thus all redolent of fascist corporativism – was reaffirmed. The role of the Cortes was simply to pass the new Fundamental Law by acclamation – even if, as was not untypical of fascist regimes, there had been a fierce Darwinian struggle in private over the law's terms between the various sectors of the dictatorship's power base: monarchists, Carlists, Falangists, Catholics, and the new and influential caste of high-ranking bureaucrats.

The second occasion indicating that the *Führerprinzip* was alive and thriving was that of the presentation to the Cortes in 1966 of another Fundamental Law outlining the basic structure of the Francoist state. A preliminary draft had in fact been submitted by Franco's trusted luminaries some eight years previously, but it had languished until 1966 when the dictator decided to have it overhauled. Once he was happy with the revision, he placed it before the Cortes. Again it was accepted with alacrity and without a vote. Indeed the Cortes explicitly recognized 'Franco's courtesy' in bringing the law before 'parliament'.[26]

There is, then, far more juridical and political continuity between the forms and procedures of the 'late' dictatorship (*tardofranquismo*) and its originating fascism than is commonly accepted today.

## Franco's 'secret legislation': the beginning

After Franco's victory in the battlefield, the dictator reorganized his cabinet in August 1939 and set up a more regular administrative system. But for all this, he did not lift his arbitrary prerogatives nor the continuous existence of a state of war (which would itself last until 1948). His reorganization did not mean that the regime became any less dictatorial. Quite the contrary, for Franco took the greatest care that his 'legal' supremacy continued as before. This ambition was enshrined in article 7 of the Law of 9 August 1939. The formulation was suitably vague:

> As the supreme authority for issuing legal norms of a general character lies with the Head of State ..., and since the governmental function lies with him permanently, his resolutions may take the form of Laws or Decrees even without previous discussion in the Cabinet ...

A great deal of draft legislation was still formally tabled for cabinet discussion, but as no minutes were taken, it is difficult to say whether any real debate took place and within what terms. We do not know how often Franco had recourse to the powers enshrined in article 7 to circumvent discussion. In principle, nothing would have prevented him from issuing legislation without any cabinet discussion, though like Hitler or Mussolini, he would have had to rely on officials or government ministers because he was obviously not knowledgeable about all policy areas.

However under the *Führerprinzip* Franco had the power to enact 'legal norms' – effectively laws – in secret. He took up this option with great enthusiasm – and in so doing he contravened the absolutely fundamental principle that laws must be made public. By 30 November 1944 Franco had signed at the very least fifty-two secret Decrees, of which only a few have surfaced since.[27] Needless to say, all of them were mandatory – although only those ministers and officials in charge of the matters the secret legislation dealt with were aware of their existence, on a need-to-know basis.

In view of what has been outlined so far in terms of Franco's approach to parliament, cabinet government and lawmaking – all this after 1945 as well as before the defeat of the Axis – then one wonders about authors who still insist that his was a 'limited' form of authoritarianism rather than a modern, fascistized anti-constitutional dictatorship.[28] In fact, the Spanish dictatorship's conceptual framework, based on Franco as the source of all law, was a carbon copy of the theory which the well-known Nazi jurist Carl Schmitt (as well as others less-known) had first applied to justify Hitler's own authority: the Führer had to be free from any legal restraints so as to exercise his sovereign powers, i.e. to decide when to step outside the 'antiquated' rule of law.

Schmitt's doctrines had not been widely known about in Spain during the Republican period (1931–5) although some of his early writings had already been translated. After the July 1936 coup, a number of jurists and military lawyers were quick to draw the pertinent operational conclusions. In his wartime headquarters Franco could count on several reactionary legal experts who knew how to articulate the requisite combination of military and political imperatives. The best known are Lorenzo Martínez Fuset and Blas Pérez González, the latter destined to become an iron-hard home office minister in the 1940s. However, during the latter part of the civil war Franco's brother-in-law, Ramón Serrano Suñer, also a lawyer and deeply attracted to Fascist ideology, became another source of inspiration to the Caudillo. For the implementation of Franco's military-led and regulated repression from 1937, the Gestapo and even the SS were always keen to cooperate.[29]

The fusion of unlimited 'legal' power, the continuous war of the true Spain against the anti-Spain (for which Schmitt's allegory of friend versus foe as the basis of all politics was highly opportune), and the militaristic traditions of the most fervent Francoist officers, led to a wide-ranging, and secret, application of the *Führerprinzip*. Nor was this limited to the time of the civil war or the exceptional period of the Second World War. All sorts of 'imperative' requirements were marshalled to justify the continued application of the Nazi concept which proved so 'useful' in circumventing obstructive legal norms.

## The *Führerprinzip* in action after the Second World War

After the defeat of Fascism the most glaring and public features of the Spanish dictatorship became more of a burden to Franco than a manifestation of alleged Fascist 'modernity'. The Caudillo had to find a way of surviving in new times, now that his former political models had been swept from the international scene. This was first done by a whitewashing of the 'legal' framework of the dictatorship.

The first step was the promulgation of a 'constitutional' façade, the so-called *Fuero de los Españoles* of 17 July 1945, an assemblage of toothless principles in the form of a theoretical 'bill of rights' which was never properly translated into secondary legislation, i.e. laws, codes, statutes and regulations. The *Fuero* constituted Franco's third 'Fundamental Law' and while it might theoretically have offered a possible softening of fascistic elements, this did not happen in practice. International observers (including the British Ambassador Sir Ivo Mallet[30]) were well aware of that fact, as were many inside Spain. However, the Catholic Church, which had always looked with some suspicion on Nazi influence in Spain because of worries about the non-Christian and non-traditional dynamics inside Nazism, took it upon itself to 'redeem' Franco's regime. In so doing the Catholic Church not only helped the dictator internationally but also assured its own institutional prerogatives in postwar Spain. 'National Catholicism' (an updated version of the traditional Spanish amalgam of throne and altar which had been renovated in the civil war) exploded into domestic politics and overcame Falangist opposition to renovate the basis of Franco's state.[31] The Church derived significant benefits from allowing itself to be deployed as a state instrument. Nor was there any clash of interests here, since both state authorities and ecclesiastical hierarchy shared the same integrist ideological nationalism and the same belief in the need to 'purify', separate and subjugate Spain's 'eternal' enemies, among whom were numbered much of the domestic population.

With the Church on board at home, Franco then simply waited for the clash to happen amongst the victors of the Second World War – a clash eagerly anticipated by Nazi propaganda. Domestically, Franco continued his permanent balancing act between monarchists, Carlists, Falangists, Catholics and sundry conservatives which was to last as long as his regime. Simultaneously, after the Concordat with the Vatican in 1953, he was able to draw internationally on a new political legitimacy as a 'Christian' regime, further endowing the Church at home with exorbitant privileges, some of which still exist today in twenty-first-century Spain.

But this national-catholic mantle did not mean that the useful *Führerprinzip* was ever forgotten. Franco continued applying it with some persistence long after the turbulent times of the Second World War. Recent research in Spanish archives by the present writer has revealed a number of examples of this related to the circumvention of statutory norms and legislation.[32] In other words, when inconvenienced, Franco was quite ready to ignore even his own cosmetic system of 'checks and balances'. Whenever Franco's ministers ran into political or managerial difficulties they simply requested the use of the Caudillo's prerogatives, which immediately 'dissolved' all constraints imposed by established norms. Obviously, in such a system, the Cortes itself was viewed contemptuously as something that merely got in the way of the serious business of running the state.

Technically, therefore, the Franco regime must be characterized as a dictatorship ultimately based on the *Führerprinzip*, whether applied publicly or secretly. Franco went much further than Hitler and Mussolini, and he was more successful, in the sense that he maintained right up to his death in 1975 both his open and his secret role as lawmaker/fount of law. In view of this, it is difficult not to concur with the powerfully concise assessment made by Borja de Riquer, one of Spain's most distinguished contemporary historians, and with which this essay began: that the Franco dictatorship, in synthesizing within itself the old right and the new right, became the perfect expression of Spanish Fascism.

This is a far-reaching assertion, based on the empirical observation that Fascist modes and ideological influence were much more pervasive within Francoism and for far longer than is conventionally acknowledged, indeed throughout the dictatorship's four long decades. Their influence also went beyond the socio-economic sphere to influence, in varying degrees, many other aspects of Spanish life. Central here was the effect of Franco's secret legislation. Through it, the Nazi principle of 'working towards the Führer (Caudillo)', brilliantly depicted by Ian Kershaw, was also an active element in how policies were made in Spain. Some ministers took it upon themselves to obey the 'highest law' that was Franco by issuing their own secret rulings in order to circumvent existing legislation of a higher order. This meant that secret rulings were frequently used to get around the Civil Code of 1889 which would otherwise have taken precedence in the hierarchy of legal norms, and which Franco had never formally abolished. This secret legislation also underpinned Franco's repression – his institutionalized 'war' from 1939 against the 'internal' enemy who had been defeated on the field of battle during 1936–9.

## Secret legislation for after a war

The war years 1936–9 were, as is now commonly accepted, accompanied by massive violence against the civilian population. These various forms of violence, which continued long after Franco's military victory, were entirely in keeping with the original political aims of the coup itself – to restructure the population into an obedient and disciplined unit to be mobilized by and for the state. The population would never again fall prey to 'individual' desires, still less liberal or democratic ones such as had previously undermined the Fatherland. As the Falange's programmatic point, perfectly assimilated by Francoism, expressed it, Spain was *'una unidad de destino en lo universal'* ('united in an eternal purpose'): it was also a collectivity which was, after 1939, primed and mobilized for war against the 'enemy within'.

Franco's postwar repression was enacted on the basis of a number of well-known explicit legal measures, beginning with the Law of Political Responsibilities (9 February 1939) designed to punish its victims economically, while also extracting resources for the victorious coalition. It was followed by the Law for the Repression of Freemasonry and Communism (1 March 1940), in force until 1964 (when it was replaced by the infamous Tribunal de Orden Público (TOP)); the Law on State Security (29 March 1941); the new Code of Military Justice (17 July 1945) and the Decree-Law of 18 April 1947 against Banditry and Terrorism. All of this was published legislation, the study of whose effects is one of the most interesting and original areas of Spanish historiography today.

But neither these laws nor the state of war still in force from 1936 were considered by the dictatorship to be enough. In addition to this open legislation, as the historian Juan José del Aguila has shown,[33] Franco also took full advantage of the latitude offered by the *Führerprinzip*. In secret the Caudillo created in June 1940 a new special jurisdiction to deal with activities related to communism and espionage (always as defined by the dictatorship, of course). We still do not know how the remit of this new jurisdiction differed from the one covered by the published law of the same year. Immediately afterwards, the minister for the army, General Enrique Varela (the only general to be awarded Spain's equivalent of two Victoria Crosses), appointed as the head of this secret jurisdiction General Jesualdo de la Iglesia Rosillo, an appointment that was itself kept under wraps. General de la Iglesia's political preferences may be inferred from the fact that he was a year later awarded the Nazi 'Cross of Merit of the German Eagle with Stars and Swords', an honorary award usually bestowed on prominent foreigners (often diplomats). Very little is known about the activities of de la Iglesia, who was by then the oldest army general. His name seldom crops up and there is still a high degree of secrecy too about who succeeded him. Possibly it was the infamous Colonel (later General) Enrique Eymar who in spite of having no legal training at all was appointed by Franco on 24 January 1958 as Special Military Judge Against Extremist Activities.[34]

This secret institutionalization of the terror process is very important. In the case of Nazi Germany the *Sondergerichte* (Special Tribunals) were created by an open law on 21 March 1933[35] and duly published in the *Reichsgesetzblatt* (Reich Legal Gazette). But Franco went further than Hitler in making his measures a part of the secret, unpublished legislation. As in Nazi Germany, so too in Spain the military machine worked 'towards Franco'. General Varela and his successor, the intensely Germanophile General Carlos Asensio Cabanillas, also issued a great many pieces of low-level secret legislation dealing with numerous aspects of the treatment to be meted out to prisoners. Much of this legislation was in breach even of the 'legal' standards set by Franco. Ministerial decisions arbitrarily modified the sentences passed on prisoners convicted by the military courts. The destiny of huge swathes of the prison population was left to the whim of ministerial bureaucracy.[36]

The speed and scale of this repression was in itself part of Franco's brutal attempt at state and nation building – what Paul Preston has termed the 'politics of revenge' through which the Francoist political coalition and its social support base were forged. This 'constructive' brutality was also economic: Franco's core policies of the 1940s, his autarkic ones (which are to be discussed in the next section) were also instruments of repression – of social as much as economic repression, as was memorably demonstrated several years ago by historian Michael Richards' pathbreaking study.[37] Nonetheless, it remains the case that the very *economic* basis of autarky, and in particular, Franco's astounding tenacity in refusing for so long to relinquish it, even in the face of all the practical evidence of the damage it was doing to the national economy and in spite of the exhortations of his few remaining economists, itself constitutes prima facie evidence of the enduring influence of Nazi and Fascist ideology. These were to shape the dictatorship's economic policy, and through it the entire Spanish economic system, for more than twenty years – i.e. more than half the total span of the Franco dictatorship.

## The primacy of ideology: Franco's long dream of fascist autarky

Autarky means economic independence through self-sufficiency. That Franco should have sought to achieve such a goal, after a civil war which had bled the economy dry and exhausted the country's gold reserves, is inexplicable in rational economic terms (and above all in Spain which had always been highly dependent on external sources for its energy supplies). Franco wanted to emulate the fascist regimes and was dazzled by their example of militarized discipline in the economy. Autarky, then, was for Franco the key to becoming less dependent on Spain's two traditional trading partners, France and the UK, which as 'degenerate' liberal democracies he considered Spain's long-standing enemies.

During the civil war Franco had repeatedly alluded to economic self-sufficiency. Spain was in his view a country rich in natural resources which could provide for its own needs as soon as the structural balance of trade deficit was solved. Franco's references to this are numerous. In his well-known statements (18 August 1938) to Henri Massis in the right-wing French weekly *Candide*, the General remarked:

Spain is a privileged and self-sufficient country. We have everything we need to live and our production is big enough to ensure our existence. We have no need to import anything and this is why our standard of living is the same as before the war . . .[38]

Reality was, however, quite different and indeed quite unsusceptible to the military discipline the Caudillo had been used to imposing in earlier phases of his career. The Spain he had conquered by April 1939 urgently needed to import food from overseas because it was simply not in a position to feed its population. However, Franco's pipe-dream remained impervious to that reality (doubtless aided, though in a contradictory way, by the underlying conviction uniting his coalition that the defeated 'internal enemy' must be made to suffer materially in order to achieve the expiation of its (political) 'sins' – so the hunger which autarky created also became a political tool for repression). Nevertheless, Franco really believed that autarky could be achieved by restricting imports drastically (importing only crucial items that Spain could never hope to produce) and by mobilizing all domestic resources to achieve rapid industrialization and expanding exports. Even the coming of continental European conflict in 1939, which more sober-minded Spanish diplomats had foreseen since the end of the civil war, failed to dent Franco's confidence, much to the despair of his new Minister of Finance, José Larraz.

Larraz would (much later) reproduce in his memoirs Franco's ideas on economic policy such as he stated them in 1940: autarky *à outrance*; attacks on liberalism; the defence of a state-directed economy; anticapitalist attitudes (or at least anti-'Anglo' capital); the belief that Spain could become a great European power within ten years; a determination to engage in massive public works; the mechanization of the army; the vast expansion of the navy and air force.[39] (New secret laws were also used here to mobilize the necessary credits and resources for this expansion,[40] through which Franco, with the backing of Nazi Germany and Fascist Italy, was to join the fray against the 'decadent' democracies.) These endeavours were to be financed by printing money without any thought to the risk of inflation. Needless to say Larraz was deeply shocked. But the point is that Franco not only voiced these views, he also acted on them – opting merely to crisis-manage the inflationary consequences, including by means of another secret law (9 February 1939) which provided emergency monetary aid to exporters hit by the inflationary and other consequences of autarky.[41] (This law, which would remain in place until 1959, also opened the way for all manner of graft and corrupt practices which tied exporting enterprises to the dictatorship.)

Already by 22 March 1939, Francoist functionaries had prepared a memorandum for circulation to the various ministries outlining the goals of the 'new state' for cooperation with Germany. They involved the establishment of new industries and the modernization of existing ones. The aim was to nationalize all those industries deemed necessary to ensure autonomy in a foreign war. To achieve an even balance in Spain's international transactions was also a major goal. Planning was to be extended to the war industries, shipbuilding, transport, production of oil and fuels, cotton, nitrogen, machine tools and artificial fibres.[42]

On 25 October Franco passed the Law for the Protection of National Interest Industries, this with the intention of freeing Spain from the necessity of importing foreign goods. On 24 November there followed the Law for the Regulation and Defence of Industries whose goal was to create a prosperous industrial economy freed from foreign dependence. Though the goals remained distant, both laws would also remain in place until 1959. The most conspicuous Falangist luminaries were, or would become, ardent promoters of these new policies. Their names, and those of fellow travellers, were familiar to two generations of Spanish students and civil servants: Areilza, Ferrándiz Luna, Ferrer Calbetó, Fuentes Irurozqui, Vicente Gay, Gay de Montellá, Antonio de Miguel, Paris Eguilaz, Perpiñá Grau, to name but some. Autarky was to be inserted in a new international economic order, spearheaded by Germany and Italy, and of which Franco's Spain was to be an integral part. 'Autonomy, independence, economic sovereignty' were the watchwords. In consequence, imports were reduced to a minimum through a complex system of quotas, restrictive bilateral trade schemes, high levels of customs duties and the overvaluation of the peseta.

This approach went hand in hand with Franco's political and economic cooperation with the Fascist powers during the Second World War and was supported inside Spain by strict rationing measures and an immense network of regulatory interventions which destroyed both private initiative and any semblance of a normal economy – in addition to generating huge inequalities and raging starvation for many. For some of those Falangist luminaries like Gay de Montellá, all this meant that, as in the Third Reich, economic life – and in particular decisions about the allocation of scarce economic resources – was being subordinated to politics and ideology.[43]

In fact, the Second World War provided something of a reality check on such a perspective. Spain was economically exploited by Nazi Germany (to whom it exported food among other things) and was unable to dispense with overseas supplies of food, fuels or a wide range of other products. Domestic production collapsed, and famines became pervasive, in particular between 1941 and 1943. Not only was the much-vaunted economic self-sufficiency nowhere to be found, but catastrophic starvation loomed for large swathes of the population. Only material aid from the UK and the USA (and also from Perón's Argentina) kept this somewhat at bay – although the aid from the Western Allies was implemented strictly in order to control Franco and keep him from throwing in his lot entirely with the Axis powers. This ultimately he did not do – largely because of British countermeasures and Nazi military reverses on the Eastern Front. But geopolitical realities also played an important part (Spain could have been economically blockaded by the Western Allies), and here we can also trace back to 1939 a glimmer of the primacy, not of ideology but of economics: on the very day that Franco declared with much fanfare his civil war victory, 1 April 1939, he also signed a secret law recognizing as debts of the Spanish state the foreign credits he had obtained to finance his war effort from (mainly) Portuguese, Swiss and British banks.[44] Franco did this because, for all his Axis preferences, the scarcity of foreign currency meant that he still needed to obtain credits from these 'despised' sources.[45] Many of Franco's international financial transactions during the Second World War, especially those involving gold and silver, took place under cover of secret legislation.[46]

But inside Spain Franco's dream of autarky lived on. On 29 August 1941, he ordered the circulation to his ministers of a project creating a 'National Institute of Autarky', based on the Italian model of the IRI (Institute for Industrial Reconstruction). Modified by Franco's ministers, it became the INI (National Institute for Industry), and was responsible to the office of the Presidency of the Government (POG) and therefore to Franco. The INI's function was to invest in war industries and many other industrial activities. The POG became responsible for a dense network of interventionist measures in all economic sectors which would continue until the final demise of the dictator's autarkic dream in 1959.

## Conclusion: the enduring appeal of fascism

As the historian Ismael Saz has argued,[47] the Spanish dictatorship contained certain elements which brought it close to the fascist regimes, thereby differentiating it from authoritarian systems. However Francoism, precisely because it was much longer-lived than the fascist regimes of the 1930s and 1940s, eventually acquired a physiognomy which made it distinct from, and in the long run turned it into something other than, a mere copy of them.

This said, five simultaneous and long-lasting features of the Franco dictatorship point directly to the enduring presence of a strong fascist influence. The first and perhaps the most important one is the role of Franco, throughout, as the ultimate source of law. Second, is his charismatic exaltation as the providential man responsible for placing the 'Fatherland' on the path of grandeur and glory. Third is the façade of 'political representation for all Spaniards' through the curious artefact of 'organic democracy' and its reactionary presiding groups (the so-called Francoist (political) families: Falangists, monarchists, integrist Catholics (among which Opus Dei), and so on), all permanently at loggerheads with each other in ever-changing power constellations which shifted over the successive decades of the dictatorship. Fourth, there is the overarching presence throughout of political violence, be it under a 'state of war' (which lasted until 1948) or during the subsequent declarations of a 'state of alarm' which were used right up to the end of the regime in the 1970s, or in the overwhelming authority of the juridical and police apparatus. Fifth, and finally, one should note the continued existence of the 'vertical unions' throughout the dictatorship.

The simultaneous and permanent combination of these five features has never been found in any other political system in the Western world *that was not also fascist*. Obviously, the Franco dictatorship lasted almost forty years and was able to adapt to far-reaching changes in the international environment. A thoroughly and overtly fascist Spain would not have been able to survive the military collapse of the Axis powers, whereas a political system able in some regards to adapt, and in others effectively to 'disguise' itself, was much better placed. Furthermore, after 1945 Franco's survival did not present any real danger to the victorious liberal-capitalist democracies. These, faced with an existential enemy in the shape of the Soviet Union, would during the Cold War period experiment among themselves with new forms of political, military, economic and social cooperation and even, when necessary, with integration. Spain was left isolated in its political particularities, reliant on the sole but substantial support of the United States. For Franco this was more than enough.

The sociological, Weberian ideal-type characterization of the Franco dictatorship as a mere 'authoritarian regime', with all that conjures of mass political demobilization and elite factions, and which the US-based political scientist Juan J. Linz posited in the early 1960s, does not pass the test of empirical history. Francoism, born of modern mobilization in an all-encompassing, total (civil) war, was almost predetermined by this process and experience to emerge as a modern, mobilizing dictatorship – all the more especially because this solution also 'solved' the problem of political and social control identified by patrician and populist ultranationalists alike, particularly during the Republican democracy of the early 1930s. The discourse and practice of Francoism would, of course, assimilate and use traditionalist materials/agencies – first and foremost an integrist Catholic Church – but what this produced by way of a polity (and society) was something radically new, and in its brutal and bloody birth we would do well to remember the enduring influence on Franco of Europe's fascist regimes, Nazi Germany especially. Fascist influence was sometimes channelled by the Falange, but ultimately what was 'fascist' in Franco's Spain was not a component party, but the state and polity itself – and what it became in the 1940s it would remain in important measure right until the end.

## Notes

1. Borja de Riquer, *La dictadura de Franco* (Barcelona and Madrid: Crítica/Marcial Pons, 2010), p. 15.
2. At the time of writing (December 2014).
3. Luis E. Togores still defends this old *canard* in a number of books, for instance in *La guerra civil española* (Madrid: La Esfera De Los Libros, 2012).
4. This can be inferred from the credit of 500,000 pounds given to the conspirators by the Kleinwort Bank, London, in March 1936. Jehanne Wake, *Kleinwort Benson. The History of Two Families in Banking* (Oxford: Oxford University Press, 1997), p. 251. The negotiations themselves have not yet been documented. The Spanish banker and millionaire Juan March was behind this largesse.
5. Morten Heiberg, *Emperadores del Mediterráneo: Franco, Mussolini y la guerra civil española* (Barcelona: Crítica, 2004), pp. 31–8.
6. Mauro Canali, *Le Spie del regime* (Bolonia: Il Mulino, 2004), pp. 245–57.
7. This well-known sequence has been recently reiterated by José Ángel Sánchez Asiaín, *La financiación de la guerra civil española: Una aproximación histórica* (Barcelona: Crítica, 2012), pp. 77–91.
8. The primary evidence for this was found in a private archive in Madrid openly accessible: see Angel Viñas, 'La connivencia fascista con la sublevación y otros éxitos de la trama civil', in Francisco Sánchez Pérez (ed.), *Los mitos del 18 de Julio* (Barcelona: Crítica, 2013), pp. 79–181,

for copies of the original contracts and lists of matériel in Italian and their translations into Spanish.

9. Followers of a different dynastic line.

10. Angel Viñas, *Las armas y el oro: Palancas de la guerra, mitos del franquismo* (Barcelona: Pasado & Presente, 2013), pp. 389–404. Barroso's views were given to a wealthy American living in Paris, William T. Middleton, at whose home the attaché called on 24 July. Middleton refers to this episode in a letter of 28 January 1940 to Esteban Bilbao Eguia, then Franco's Minister of Justice.

11. Ángel Viñas and Carlos Collado Seidel, 'Franco's Request to the Third Reich for Military Assistance', *Contemporary European History* 11:2 (2002), pp. 191–210: p. 191.

12. It also comprised tanks, artillery and communications units.

13. Angel Viñas, *La soledad de la República: El abandono de las democracias y el viraje hacia la Unión Soviética* (Barcelona: Crítica, 2006), pp. 269–70. British Intelligence intercepted the Consul's report. It is published in *Documenti Diplomatici Italiani*, Series VIII, vol. V, doc. 58.

14. Carlos Barciela, 'El trágico final de la reforma agraria. La revolución "fascista" en el campo español', in Angel Viñas (ed.), *En el combate por la historia* (Barcelona: Pasado & Presente, 2012), pp. 335–54; Carlos Jiménez Villarejo, 'La destrucción del orden jurídico republicano', *Hispanianova* 7 (2007), pp. 1–30 (available from http://hispanianova.rediris.es).

15. Angel Viñas, *El escudo de la Republica: El oro de España, la apuesta soviética y los hechos de mayo de 1937* (Barcelona: Crítica, 2007), *passim*.

16. Fernando Hernandez Sanchez, *Guerra o revolucion: El Partido Comunista de España en la guerra civil* (Barcelona: Crítica, 2010). The PCE's function in domestic Republican politics/mass mobilization is also analysed throughout Helen Graham, *The Spanish Republic at War, 1936–1939* (Cambridge: Cambridge University Press, 2002), see pp. 75, 146–7 and esp. 183–6 and 375–6, 416–17.

17. This process is ably studied in Joan Maria Thomàs, 'La Falange, de la revolución al acomodamiento', in Viñas (ed.), *En el combate por la historia*, pp. 565–74.

18. To the extent that all Spanish coins were to be inscribed '*Caudillo por la gracia de Dios*' (Caudillo by the grace of God).

19. Ferran Gallego, *El evangelio fascista: La formación de la cultura política del franquismo (1930–1950)* (Barcelona: Crítica, 2014), and *idem.*, 'La evolución política de la zona sublevada', in Viñas (ed.), *En el combate por la historia*, pp. 313–34.

20. Maria Silvia López Gallegos, 'El proyecto de sindicalismo falangista: de los sindicatos autónomos jonsistas a la creación de las Centrales Obreras y de Empresarios Nacional-sindicalistas', in Ferran Gallego and Francisco Morente (eds), *Fascismo en España* (Barcelona: El Viejo Topo, 2005), pp. 43–67: pp. 55–62.

21. Alejandro Andreassi Cieri, 'Trabajo y empresa en el nacionalsindicalismo', in Gallego and Morente (eds), *Fascismo en España*, pp. 13–42: pp. 15–21.

22. Ibid., pp. 15–21.

23. Francisco Sevillano, *Franco: Caudillo por la gracia de Dios* (Madrid: Alianza, 2010), p. 170. My italics.

24. These laws were called 'fundamental' because they were considered to be the most important legal norms.

25. *Boletín Oficial del Estado*, 18 July 1942.

26. Glicerio Sanchez Recio, *Sobre todos Franco: Coalición reaccionaria y grupos políticos* (Barcelona: Flor del Viento, 2008), pp. 252–8.

27. According to Spanish practice, laws and decrees were numbered consecutively. Secret decree no. 42 is available at the Centro Documental de la Memoria Historica, Salamanca; Angel Viñas, *La otra cara del Caudillo. Mitos y realidades en la biografía de Franco* (Barcelona: Crítica, 2015).

28. This 'authoritarian' characterization of Francoism is still used by the current conservative prime minister in Spain, Mariano Rajoy. *El País*, 8 December 2013. It was also the preferred adjective of US diplomats in the late 1960s.

29. Manuel Ros Agudo, *La guerra secreta de Franco (1939–1945)* (Barcelona: Crítica, 2002), pp. 181–4, in which are published the secret arrangements signed on 31 July 1938 between the Nazi police and their Spanish counterparts. Their implementation/police collaboration is only now being researched: Patrick Bernhard, 'The Gestapo in Spain: German Police Collaboration with Franco's Regime and the Persecution of Jews, 1936–1944', presented at the Thirteenth Biennial Lessons and Legacies Conference, Boca Raton, Florida (USA), October 2014.

30. The National Archives (TNA) (London): FO371/13854, 'General Franco's plans for the future', 22 July 1958.

31. See Ángel Luis López Villaverde, 'Iglesia de la Cruzada. La elaboración del mito de la Cruzada', in Manuel Ortiz Heras and Damian A. González (eds), *De la Cruzada al desenganche: la Iglesia española entre el franquismo y la transición* (Madrid: Sílex, 2011) for a recent discussion, and Hilari Raguer, 'Nacionalcatolicismo', in Viñas (ed.), *En el combate por la historia*, pp. 547–63; for background José Manuel Cuenca Toribio, *Nacionalismo, franquismo y nacionalcatolicismo* (Madrid: Actas, 2008).

32. For example, on 13 April 1956 and 1 February 1957 Franco issued two secret Decree-laws to overcome obstacles arising from pre-existing legal norms. Since these latter were enshrined in formal laws (the highest form of legal norm), another law (or at least a Decree-law) was necessary to circumvent them.

33. Juan José del Aguila, 'La represión política a través de la jurisdicción de guerra y sucesivas jurisdicciones especiales del franquismo' and Francisco Moreno Gómez, 'Franco y su proyecto represivo de posguerra', both in *Hispania Nova*, special issue, November 2015 (available at http://hispanianova.rediris.es).

34. His appointment was not published in the Official Journal (*Boletín Oficial del Estado*) but in the Official Gazette of the Ministry of the Army (*Diario Oficial*) on 13 February 1958, seldom read outside of military circles.

35. Carsten Becker, *Justiz im Dritten Reich: Sondergerichte und Regimegegner* (Munich: Grin-Verlag, 2003) for a summary discussion of the Special Tribunals.

36. Gutmaro Gómez Bravo, 'Venganza tras la victoria. La política represiva del franquismo (1939–1948)', in Viñas (ed.) *En el combate por la historia*, pp. 575–92: p. 580, for a reference to other secret repressive instruments.

37. Michael Richards, *A Time of Silence: Civil War and the Culture or Repression in Franco's Spain* (Cambridge: Cambridge University Press, 2007).

38. www.generalisimofranco.com/Discursos/prensa/00028.htm (accessed 24 August 2015).

39. José Larraz, *Memorias* (Madrid: Real Academia de Ciencias Morales y Políticas, 2008), p. 182.

40. Manuel Ros Agudo (*La guerra secreta de Franco*, pp. 45–50) was the first historian to identify this kind of secret legislation.

41. The present author found this important secret law in AGA (Archivo General de la Administracion), MIC, box 1.

42. Angel Viñas, Julio Viñuela, Fernando Eguidazu, Carlos Fernández Pulgar and Senen Florensa, *Política comercial exterior en España (1931–1975)* (Madrid: Banco Exterior de España, 1979), pp. 295–7. This book was the first to make full use of Spanish government archives, just two years after Franco's death.

43. Francisco Comín and Miguel Martorell Linares, *La Hacienda Pública en el franquismo: La guerra y la autarquía (1936–1959)* (Madrid: Instituto de Estudios Fiscales, 2013), pp. 153–6.

44. This highly significant secret law was found in the (then) Confidential Archive of the Ministry of Finance. It was published by the present author in Viñas et al., *Política comercial exterior en España.* It has now become widely known.

45. Franco turned first to a Swiss bank where his supporter, the financier Juan March, had a leading interest.

46. For a recent overview see Angel Viñas, *La otra cara del Caudillo. Mitos y realidades en la biografía de Franco* (Barcelona: Crítica, 2015).

47. Ismael Saz, 'El franquismo. ¿Régimen autoritario o dictadura fascista?', in Javier Tusell, Susana Sueiro, Jose Maria Marin and Marina Casanova (eds), *El régimen de Franco (1936–1975)*, Vol. 1 (Madrid: UNED, 1993), pp. 189–202, *passim*.

## Further reading

### *In English*

Leitz, C., *Economic Relations between Nazi Germany and Franco's Spain: 1936–1945*, Oxford: Oxford University Press, 1996.

Leitz, C., 'Hermann Göring and Nazi Germany's Economic Exploitation of Nationalist Spain, 1936–1939', *German History* 14:1 (1996), pp. 21–37.

Preston, P., *The Politics of Revenge: Fascism and the Military in Twentieth-Century Spain*, London: Unwin Hyman, 1990.

Preston, P., *Franco. A Biography*, London: HarperCollins, 1993.

Preston, P. and Balfour, S. (eds), *Spain and the Great Powers in the Twentieth-Century*, London and New York: Routledge, 1999.

Richards, M., *A Time of Silence: Civil War and the Culture of Repression in Franco's Spain, 1936–1945*, Cambridge: Cambridge University Press, 1998.

Viñas, A., 'Franco's Dreams of Autarky Shattered: Foreign Policy Aspects in the Run-up to the 1959 Change in Spanish Economic Strategy', in C. Leitz and D.J. Dunthorn (eds), *Spain in an International Context 1936–1959*, New York and Oxford: Berghahn, 1999, pp. 299–318.

Viñas, A. and Collado Seidel, C., 'Franco's Request to the Third Reich for Military Assistance', *Contemporary European History* 11:2 (2002), pp. 191–210.

### *In Spanish*

Águila, J. J. del, *El Tribunal de Orden Público: La represión de la libertad (1963–1977)*, Barcelona: Planeta, 2001.

Aróstegui, J. (ed.), *Franco: la represión como sistema*, Barcelona: Flor del Viento, 2012.

Gallego, F., *El evangelio fascista: La formación de la cultura política del franquismo (1930–1950)*, Barcelona: Crítica, 2014.

Heiberg, M., *Emperadores del Mediterráneo: Franco, Mussolini y la guerra civil española,* Barcelona: Crítica, 2004.

Riquer, B. de, *La dictadura de Franco*, Barcelona: Crítica and Madrid: Marcial Pons, 2010.

Ros Agudo, M., *La guerra secreta de Franco (1939–1945)*, Barcelona: Crítica, 2002.

Viñas, A. (ed.), *En el combate por la historia*, Madrid: Pasado y Presente, 2012.

Viñas, A., *La otra cara del Caudillo: Mitos y realidades en la biografía de Franco*, Barcelona: Crítica, 2015.

# CHAPTER 7
## STATES OF WAR: 'BEING CIVILIAN' IN 1940s SPAIN

*Jorge Marco*

Translated from Spanish by Carl-Henrik Bjerstrom and Helen Graham

Life here is unbearable: one cannot talk, there is no freedom of expression or feeling since they 'liberated' us; this is a prison ... the police presence is massive. There are thousands of them, always patrolling city centre streets, day and night, with a rifle over their shoulder ... and that's without mentioning the executions, which still haven't stopped four years after the end of the war. People are executed daily on the pretext that they are reds, separatists, freemasons, anarchists, communists, republicans.

This is how one woman, who preferred to remain anonymous in order to avoid reprisals, described the Spanish postwar period. Her letter skirted postal censorship, crossed the Atlantic, and was published on 28 May 1943 in *España Popular*, an exile newspaper based in Mexico City.[1] It provided a detailed account of the anguished and desperate life of thousands of Spaniards under the Franco dictatorship. Spain was a prison, a great concentration camp, a police state which had declared war on its own citizens. The assassinations and executions by military tribunals formed part of everyday life in a Spain where a state of war (i.e. martial law) was maintained throughout the country until 1948 – twelve years after its declaration in 1936 and a decade after the end of the battlefield war. In those regions where there was strong anti-Franco resistance, martial law was maintained until 1951 – that is, for sixteen years. All of this means that, as historians, we need immediately to problematize the idea of 1940s Spain as 'peace time'.

The long duration and intensity of the state of war arose from the constant mobilization (from the end of the battlefield war) of state and society. Sections of the army, other state institutions and a large number of ordinary citizens voluntarily and enthusiastically supported this war which extended beyond the battlefield and consisted of a social and political purge of Spanish society. Chained columns of prisoners, executions, shots fired at dawn and the gathering of desperate and grieving widows before the prison gates: all feature among the dominant images of the darkest period of Spain's contemporary history. This period cast a long shadow of violence stretching across the rest of the dictatorship, which was only dismantled in 1977 – violence which the historian Paul Preston has defined as an 'investment in terror', given its successful prolongation through fear across the decades since.[2]

The Spanish war and postwar period gave rise to experiences similar to those suffered in many other places in Europe during the 1940s. Under the impulse of Nazi expansion (but not caused solely by it) Europe was torn asunder by a violent war of extermination conducted against (and between) civilian populations – conflicts shaped by underlying ethnic, ideological, cultural and social tensions. All across Europe societies were gripped by fear-induced images of internal and external enemies whom they sought to consign to segregation, expulsion or physical elimination. Nowhere in Europe was immune from this dynamic of social 'cleansing', often fuelled by ultranationalist projects and implemented not only during the Second World War, but also after it.[3]

In the Spanish case too, ultranationalism based on integrist Catholicism and an anti-communist discourse functioned as the ideological glue binding together the victorious coalition and its social support base across Spain. Ultranationalism, religion and anticommunism: these were exactly the same elements found at the heart of the violent conflicts across 1940s Europe. Even so, after 1945 the European metanarrative of the Second World War and postwar period always struggled to incorporate the Franco dictatorship to the new continental 'story', as was also the case with other southern European anomalies like the Salazar dictatorship in Portugal or the experience and outcome of the civil war in Greece.

The reasons for this difficulty are complicated but nevertheless clear today. After the Second World War a grand narrative was constructed in Europe, which located the origin of postwar Western parliamentary democracy in national efforts to resist fascism. This was a myth intended to draw a veil over an awkward reality, thereby legitimizing and thus stabilizing these new postwar regimes – but it was a myth that then lasted for decades. Beneath the resistance myth lay a darker, more complicated history of extensive collaboration with the Nazis, through which civilians in many European countries were complicit in the denunciations and mass deportations of others to Nazi concentration camps. Similarly, the grand narrative also glossed over the fact that post-1945 Western parliamentary democracy did not really confront or challenge the dictatorships or quasi-dictatorial regimes ruling in southern Europe.[4] Moreover, the regimes in Spain, Portugal and Greece had been given a political alibi by the new Cold War agenda: the West's omnipresent fear of communism thus permitted the establishing or survival of regimes founded on mass killing and imprisonment and/or the use of concentration camps – methods similar to those used by old and new enemies of the Western Allies (Nazi Germany and Soviet Russia), and now roundly condemned as the antithesis of Western politics and values.[5]

The durability of these extremely violent regimes inside Western Europe – most prominently Franco's Spain – clearly challenged the metanarrative of European antifascist resistance and postwar political 'civility', a problem most easily solved by excluding them from the narrative altogether. The paradox is even more striking when considered against the fact that the armed resistance to fascism in Europe had actually begun in Spain in 1936. Nine years later, while fascism had been defeated in most parts of the continent, it still ruled in Spain, and would continue to do so for another three decades.

During the 1940s, Spain's civilian population endured harsh conditions marked by extreme violence: mass killing, social segregation, confinement, punishment and forced displacement – processes which together constitute what Preston has recently termed the 'Spanish Holocaust', given its lengthy and dramatic consequences, both physical and psychological, for Spanish society.[6] But even under these asphyxiating conditions there emerged among the civilian population diverse forms of daily resistance against the huge power of the dictatorship. The most immediately obvious of these was armed resistance itself, perceived by those involved as an integral part of the armed antifascist resistance present across the war-torn continent. But alongside these irregular Spanish soldiers, there were also many 'irregular civilians' who engaged in acts of transgression and dissidence, just as others did elsewhere across the continent.[7]

This essay will focus on the civilian experience in Spain during the prolonged state of war, exploring different responses at the heart of a threadbare civil society, and also the different forms of violence and social control deployed against sectors of the civilian population by the Franco dictatorship. The civilian responses sometimes challenged the power of the dictatorship, explicitly or implicitly, and including on the symbolic or ideological plane. The cost of such acts, however small or apparently insignificant, could be very high, incurring even the death penalty. So the fact that they occurred indicates their importance in permitting the defeated some measure of self-esteem and integrity beyond mere survival. Contestation offered a means of keeping intact important remnants of their individual and collective identities, whose destruction – even of the most apparently harmless facets – remained a particular hallmark of Francoism.

## The forging of a new society of victors and vanquished

Officially, Spain's civil war ended on 1 April 1939 with Franco's declaration of victory. But the wave of violence continued to hit certain sectors of the civilian population. From the time of Francoism's birth in the bloodbath triggered by the military coup of 17–18 July 1936 and onwards, the dictatorship retained the use of explicit violence as an instrument of rule. Even though after 1948 its quantitative levels grew less, it was always on display, with the implicit threat of more should the survival of the regime be at stake. And as a popular saying had it: 'the dictatorship came into the world, as it left it – killing.' (On 27 September 1975, only one month before the death of the dictator, five activists from two organizations belonging to the anti-Francoist opposition were executed.) But the darkest period was undoubtedly the 1940s, the period in which Franco's 'investment in terror' was made.

This reign of terror extended from the war and through the 1940s because the objectives pursued by Franco and his coalition could not be reduced to the conventional goal of overthrowing Republican democracy. In Spain, as elsewhere across Europe, the desired reconfiguration went deeper. To this end, the memory and model of colonial war would be deployed against sectors of the civilian population within the metropolis itself – and most specifically against those who had previously, especially during the 1930s, challenged the older forms of social and political hierarchy preferred by the Franco coalition and many of its supporters.[8] Francoism's objective was to root out all forms of political culture and collective identity that had challenged the traditional order based on the power of the army, the Church, and landed elite. They were basically those named by the anonymous correspondent cited in the chapter epigraph as those being targeted by Francoist violence. She grouped them under the familiar political categories of that time – socialists, anarchists, communists, republicans, liberals and Basque, Galician and Catalan nationalists – but beyond those descriptors what they had in common was that they all bore within themselves the possibility of social change in Spain. It was for this reason that the dictatorship collectively labelled them 'red', despite their other considerable differences – thereby homogenizing them and identifying them as the 'enemy within', the anti-Spain to be exterminated.

'In a civil war, a systematic occupation of territory accompanied by the necessary cleansing is preferable to a rapid rout of the enemy armies which leaves the country still infested with enemies':[9] thus Franco explained his strategy in February 1937 to one of his Italian military advisers, Colonel Emilio Faldella, when being pressured by his Axis allies to bring the war to a swifter close. The battlefield dead during the war numbered at least 200,000 Spanish soldiers, of whom more than half were 'reds'.[10] At the same time as this 'natural' process of eliminating the enemy occurred on the military front, a systematic policy of extermination was also being implemented inside Francoist territory, through mass killing, including by quasi-judicial means – execution after court-martial. Extrajudicial murders were carried out by death squads composed of ordinary citizens (sometimes the victims' neighbours), together with army officers and Civil Guards (the militarized rural police), while the court-martial proceedings were by definition entirely under army authority. At least 100,000 'reds' were killed behind the lines in insurgent/Francoist territory during the period of the battlefield war, either by extrajudicial murder or by execution after court-martial.[11] This is a conservative estimate, as the lethal violence in the expanding territory controlled by the Francoists has not been completely mapped: moreover, the exact number of deaths caused by bombing raids on the big, Republican-held cities, and those occurring because of forced displacement both inside and outside the country remains unknown.[12] Even so, as Graham and Quiroga have observed, 'the [Spanish] regime murdered and incarcerated its own nationals on a scale that outdid anything that the Nazi state had undertaken within its pre-1938 borders'.[13]

Despite the extensive extermination carried out during the years of the battlefield war, the Francoist dictatorship continued its project of political cleansing and social purification thereafter. Around a million prisoners would pass through the regime's gaols and concentration camps, or other forms of penal servitude, like the Workers' Battalions and Disciplinary Battalions under military supervision. Thousands of prisoners died from the extreme overcrowding and the resulting sanitary conditions and epidemic disease, as well as from torture and malnutrition.[14] From 1939 to 1952, at least 20,000 'reds' who had survived the war were also killed in a deliberate and continuous elimination campaign. The majority of these were executed by sentence of the military courts, while others were killed under the legal cover of the so-called *Ley de Fugas* – this was a 'historic' form of extrajudicial murder in Spain (much used by the army and police under the Restoration monarchy) by which prisoners were shot while supposedly 'trying to escape'. Precisely because of the irregular forms of killing still involved after 1939, it is difficult to arrive at a definitive figure and some historians calculate it higher, at between 40,000 and 50,000.[15]

A comparison with the numbers of executions and assassinations in other Western European countries after the Second World War clarifies both the quantitative and qualitative differences between them and the exterminatory dimension of the Franco dictatorship in the 1940s. In France, the site of what is often called *l'épuration sauvage* (brutal purification), it is estimated that some 8,000 to 9,000 people were killed extrajudicially during the acute phase of the Liberation, while around 1,500 were sentenced to death by court-martial and executed in the postwar period, though the numbers are still contested.[16] In Italy, where insurrectionary violence was swifter and more implacable, historians estimate between 12,000 and 15,000 were killed in the final stages of the war, while those sentenced to death by court-martial after the war were fewer than fifty.[17] Not even what happened at the end of the Greek civil war can compare with the intensity of killing in Spain. In Greece, with a population at that time about a quarter the size of Spain's, approximately 50,000 'reds' were imprisoned and some 3,000 executed.[18]

These figures clearly indicate how Francoism needs to be distinguished from this postwar moment in Western Europe because for Spain this was not in any way an 'aftermath', rather it was the continuation of a process of targeted killing initiated during the battlefield war. In Spain war and postwar were not separated by any clear dividing line because they were parts of a continuum devised to 'cleanse' Spanish society of its internal enemies. Achieving this meant not only killing those the authorities labelled 'irredeemable', but also exerting brutal forms of social control on those left alive and categorized as 'redeemable' even though they had been 'misled' (by the Republic and its ideas). These people were to be segregated, punished and forcibly re-educated – or in the regime's Catholic discourse, 'converted': it was a means of 'destroy[ing] in order to subjugate'.[19] This involved lengthy prison terms, during which prisoners would undergo intensive 're-education' supervised and disciplined by the Catholic Church, author and implementer of Franco's entire 'social redemption' programme.[20] The repercussions – psychological and otherwise – of many aspects of this process remain live and painful issues in twenty-first-century Spain, probably the most notorious of which was the 'eugenic' forcible removal of children from their biological parents, in which the Church and its personnel were heavily implicated.[21] Even physical elimination and forcible re-education were not considered sufficient by the Franco dictatorship. In addition to the killings, court-martials and exile (half a million people in 1939),[22] the regime deployed a whole legal arsenal to segregate and exclude the defeated – they purged the professions, sacked people deemed 'the enemy' in all sectors of the economy, and via a new system of political courts expropriated the property of thousands. All who had fought in the Republican Army, or had been active within the labour movement or identified with organizations favouring social change were stigmatized as the defeated and subjected to forms of repression and social control across every aspect of their lives – and livelihoods.[23] The dictatorship even used hunger and food rationing as instruments of punishment and a means of revenge against the defeated. In a country where even the authorities themselves admitted that 'one seems to have come to a country of beggars; everywhere one goes one sees only ragged people and emaciated faces,'[24] the consequences of such punitive strategies were doubly devastating. Though there are scant official records, and no statistics, by a conservative estimate 200,000 people died of hunger between 1939 and 1945, most of whom were workers or peasants described by the regime as 'disaffected'.[25]

This social and spatial rift between victors and vanquished in the villages, towns and cities and which had been actively deepened by regime policies, was now a chasm and could be sensed in every quotidian gesture. Walking down the street, waiting in rationing queues or at the prison gates, everyone else was free to insult the defeated, hit them with impunity, or force them to sing the fascist anthem and to make its salute with outstretched arm. As in other parts of Europe, women were subjected to gendered violence, for example being forced to appear in public with shaved head and a small red ribbon tied to a remaining lock of hair.[26] This constant humiliation of the defeated, stigmatized daily, became one of the most sophisticated and effective methods of psychological torture in the regime's considerable 'postwar' arsenal. But it must be remembered that the politics of punishment, segregation and social exclusion were not only implemented from 'above', but were also actively pursued from 'below'. Tens of thousands of ordinary Spaniards across the country supported the dictatorship enthusiastically, making themselves complicit in the repression by denouncing neighbours, friends and even family members.[27]

## Surviving imprisonment

At the end of military hostilities in April 1939, many Republican civilians as well as soldiers who had fought in the Republican Army still thought that they could return to their previous lives, but they were soon confronted by a reality which quickly made them realize that nothing was going to be the same as before. Republican soldiers passed, at the point of demobilization, virtually en masse into internment camps where they were to be classified.[28] The authorities took their time here, determined that those they sought for elimination would not escape them. The rest of the soldier-internees were classified either as needing re-education through imprisonment, or as able to return home under the supervision of local authorities.[29] The prolonged situation of mass internment generated great social unease, which the authorities were well aware of. The fact too that the prisons themselves were also overflowing with political detainees also provoked regime fears of a popular insurrection potentially gaining momentum in conjunction with antifascist guerrilla action, and especially in a context where the war in Europe was now turning in the Allies' favour. These fears were indicated in official reports, which ultimately recommended freeing a significant proportion of prisoners in order to contain the build-up of social tension within safe limits. The repression had to be constant, but also carefully regulated, so that it would not provoke a social explosion.[30]

According to official sources, the release of a great number of prisoners in 1940 reduced the number of inmates to 270,000, but these figures only included those with a confirmed custodial sentence, not those held on remand in ad hoc detention centres, or other buildings converted to prison functions, of which there were very many at this time in Spain.[31] Although the official figures are still disputed, with most historians believing the number of prisoners was under-recorded, there were certainly more releases in subsequent years, which, according to official figures, reduced the prison population to 124,000 in 1943 and 42,000 in 1946.[32] Whatever the precise totals of prisoners, it is plausible to interpret the prison releases as based in a fear of unrest, as the Francoist authorities themselves stated. By contrast, the idea that the dictatorship rapidly lost interest in punishing the defeated, as suggested by some authors,[33] does not fit with the extensive and integrated processes of social cleansing developed in the postwar period, nor with the fact that these prison releases were sometimes deployed as a means of freeing up space for new waves of prisoners detained under new state security laws. But the notion that the dictatorship became less interested in punishment does not convince, primarily because we know that these releases did not result in the prison system being scaled down, but rather in its expansion beyond the prison walls into society (towns and villages) as the process and forms of Francoist surveillance were expanded and transformed.

The prison releases produced some sense of relief at first, but the defeated quickly realized that it did not lessen the dictatorship's coercive power over their lives. Youths who had been held in preventive detention but not brought before the military courts were sent directly, without trial, to forced labour camps known as Workers' Battalions. The system of forced labour was maintained in Spain right up until the 1960s, using prisoners for infrastructural construction of bridges, reservoirs, roads or even football grounds, in addition to erecting colossal fascist monuments such as Franco's own Valley of the Fallen.[34] Official reports themselves indicated how the process of classifying Republican conscripts as either 'loyal', 'indifferent' or hostile ('*desafecto*'), introduced to identify who should be sent to prison or labour camps, was 'deepening rifts and reopening political wounds in all towns and villages. ... Today, these families have seen their relatives being conducted by the Civil Guard to Workers' Battalions and they ask themselves when this division of Spaniards into castes will end'.[35]

Francoist labour and concentration camps were designed with the aim of humiliating and dehumanizing the prisoners, but life in the camp universe also revealed an acute tension between the rulers' strategies of domination and everyday resistance.[36] The camp at Bustarviejo, near Madrid, was operational between 1944 and 1947 and at this time various family members of the prisoners came to live around its perimeter, building small huts for shelter. This situation seems to have been common at various Spanish internment camps, although we need further research here. The massive imprisonment of men from 1939 had condemned thousands of families to misery, especially in cases where the prisoner was the main breadwinner. This was the reason why some families tracked down the camp where their relative was being held and set up makeshift living quarters for themselves nearby.

The Francoist authorities acquiesced to these family settlements, but this sprang not from generosity but calculation and pragmatism. In a situation where prison break-outs were common, the simple presence of family members around the camp acted as a deterrent. In fact, the authorities tended to place family members in locations of high altitude, so that some visual contact was possible, albeit from a distance.

The visible presence of family members outside the camp provoked a complex set of emotional and psychological responses in the prisoners. On the one hand it allowed them to establish a link with the outside world, which strengthened them in the face of the grinding, dehumanizing routine of the camp. But on the other hand they suffered from acute depression when reflecting on the circumstances of their loved ones, which also reaffirmed the gravity of their own situation. The authorities would also place the inmates in situations which involved painful public humiliation. One of the daily domination strategies most commonly employed in Francoist internment camps was the instalment of open-air latrines, which forced prisoners to attend to their needs before the eyes of other prisoners. This situation was made worse by the presence of family members, who were forced to witness their emaciated relatives – often suffering from serious intestinal problems – endure this degradation daily.[37] The objective was to erode the prisoners' sense of self-worth, until both their spirit and will were utterly broken. The use of constant harassment as a means of brutalization would do serious psychological damage to both prisoners and family members, subjected as they were to this regime of humiliation.

Nevertheless, the prisoners did find ways to show dissent, which allowed them to maintain a degree of psychological composure both for themselves, and before their families and fellow inmates. At times this kind of resistance relied on the 'weapons of the weak',[38] such as the simple creation of leisure objects which granted prisoners brief moments of distraction.[39] At other times, mundane routines of hygiene and self-care took on deep importance in an abnormal and nauseating environment, thus helping to reaffirm human dignity and the basic principles of resistance. This was the case, for example, with political prisoners in Barcelona's prison for women, as observed by Mavis Bacca Dowden, a British woman detained in Spain and transferred to the Barcelona gaol in 1939.[40]

On other occasions the practices of resistance could be more overt, which entailed the risk of paying a high price. Triniatrio Rubio, a prisoner in a labour camp, recalled how 'we tried to commit small acts of sabotage. This was our way of rebelling. We put the small explosive devices [used in building work] on the rails, we broke the handles of picks and spades, ... we peed on the dynamite before lighting the fuse and told the foreman that the explosive had failed, we derailed railway wagons instead of making them stop'.[41] Adelaida Abarca, another prisoner in the postwar period, remembered years later how in 1940 she and fellow inmates commemorated the proclamation of the Second Republic on 14 April (1931) inside the prison walls. In order to evade punishment, she and two other friends each wore a jumper of a single colour – one red, one yellow and the third purple – which together made up the colours of the Republican flag. The three came down to the prison courtyard together and began their exercises. When the rest of the prisoners realized what the three friends had done, they began to applaud and say 'long live the Republic' in hushed voices.[42] Small acts of symbolic resistance like this allowed prisoners to survive psychologically, as well contributing to the process of making antifascist identities inside prison.

## Surviving outside prison

The daily experience of stigmatization imposed enormous psychological pressure on the defeated, especially given their demoralization and the poverty to which so many were consigned.[43] Not only had their relatives and friends been killed or imprisoned, but the shadow of guilt and suspicion hung over them too. Any gesture, no matter how insignificant, was charged with a meaning corresponding to the narrative of victors and vanquished. No one could escape the asphyxiating atmosphere suffused with hate, exclusion and vengeance. As the letter-writer quoted at the beginning of this chapter expressed it: Spain itself was one huge prison.

In such circumstances, humour became for the defeated a form of catharsis – both a means of easing the pressure and, at the same time, a form of veiled protest. Criticism of the punitive politics of food became a common topic for jokes targeted against the dictatorship. The phrase 'less Franco and more white bread' was frequently repeated after official news broadcasts on the radio, and came to form part of the collective imaginary of a whole generation.[44] In this way the civilian population expressed moral condemnation of the regime's speculative food policies which, in the words of Gregorio Marañón, the Spanish physician, essayist and public figure, to Italy's Ambassador to Spain in 1946, 'sucks the blood out of the people'.[45]

One of the jokes appearing in the exile press in a section entitled 'Humour: a weapon of the popular struggle' told the story of a man who returned to a shop to ask the assistant to rewrap his churros (fried doughnuts) in a different sheet of newspaper, one that did not feature Franco's photograph, because 'that guy is capable of sucking out all the oil'.[46] But popular humour also alluded to the police state and the widespread sense of anxiety permeating society. This is reflected in another joke where a police officer arrests a traveller for having commented out loud when reading his newspaper: 'What a shitty government!'; the traveller replied that he did not mean Franco's but the British government, but the police officer insisted on arresting him, because 'you said "shit government", and we all know that Franco's is the shittiest government in the world, so I'm really going to have to arrest you'.[47] This kind of black humour challenged the cultural certainties of the dictatorship and disrupted its hegemonic discourse, posing a threat of which the Francoist authorities were well aware: 'We have to confront the secretive battle of the comment, the joke, of an irony so subtle that it trickles down to places it must not reach, acquiring there the potential to break our resolve', thus warned a leading Francoist in 1950.[48]

Humour was typically a controlled form of protest used in private contexts, but spontaneous outbursts of dissidence could occasionally be seen in public. These were often triggered by alcohol, which overrode the usual mechanisms of self-control. Carmen García Puga was a 68-year-old woman who lived in a small town in the south of Spain.[49]

Her husband, a socialist, had died in prison in 1940 after spending a year incarcerated. She was old and alone, without any means of support, given the local authorities had classified her 'hostile' (*desafecto*) and denied her a widow's pension. One night in 1941, weary of her situation and spurred on by alcohol, she dared to enter one of the local taverns. Her interruption into this space broke two social taboos: this was a place reserved for the victors and for men. But Carmen did not limit her transgression to this violation of segregated public space. After asking to be served a brandy, before the customers' astonished gaze, she began to argue with the tavern keeper about the miserable life she had to endure because of Franco. He responded by praising the dictator, to which Carmen replied: 'The only thing Franco ever does for us is to screw us over! Thanks to him, we're all fainting away!' – a reference to the raging hunger being endured by ordinary working people. Two neighbours immediately denounced Carmen for insulting the Head of State. Soon afterwards a military tribunal sentenced her to two years and four months in prison.

This kind of clash was not uncommon, particularly from 1943, when Allied troops gained the upper hand in the Second World War and antifascist optimism rose exponentially in Spain. Many sectors of the population thought that the defeat of fascism in Europe would bring the immediate overthrow of Franco's dictatorship and the restoration of democratic freedoms. The Francoist authorities themselves were alarmed by the ever more frequent public expressions of enthusiasm for likely Allied victory and its consequences in Spain.[50] Rumour was so pervasive that they even considered setting up a network spreading disinformation in an attempt to counteract the effects of the rumour mill.[51] But on more than one occasion this jubilant atmosphere triggered public reactions which had terrible consequences. On the night of 1 May 1945, 28-year-old Manuel César came out into the street in an inebriated state, in all likelihood after having celebrated International Workers' Day and the now certain victory of the Allies at home in the company of family and friends. As he walked past a group of soldiers, and he shouted jubilantly: 'Now we've taken Berlin!' the response was immediate and lethal; the soldiers beat him to death in the street with complete impunity.[52]

The only safe attitude the defeated could adopt was submissiveness and the public declaration that he or she was 'grateful' for the clemency shown by the regime in not inflicting a more severe punishment. Any other response was considered a symptom of rebelliousness and defiance of the new social order. Taking their cue from what the victors expected, thousands of desperate people wrote directly to the dictator asking him to intervene. In these letters one can see how the defeated, often having recourse to the 'weapons of the weak', adopted a submissive tone, expressed shame, and guilt, as were expected of them. Dolores S. wrote not to Franco but to his wife, perhaps hoping for some form of mutual female understanding. She asked for mercy for her husband, who had been sentenced to death by the military courts. In her heart-rending letter she described the miserable conditions in which she lived together with her two-year-old baby and fifteen-year-old son, disabled in a work accident. Dolores exhibited the requisite contrition concerning the past political activities of her husband, who was a victim of 'the accursed influence the propaganda of red leaders had on simple workers ..., [an influence] not easily counteracted by the humble advice of a wife'.[53] The misery and repression heaped on the defeated forced them to adopt this submissive attitude daily, whether it was genuine or not, just in order to survive. Such was the case of Miguel I. G., a fifteen-year-old youth who wrote to Franco asking for his protection so that he could feed his family. His father had been executed by a military tribunal and now he had to take care of his mother and five siblings: he concluded his letter 'May God protect Your Excellency many years to come'.[54]

In this oppressive environment, any voice or message reaching in from abroad provided a ray of light. Hope was kept alive especially by *La Pirenaica*, a radio station run by the exiled Spanish Communist Party (Partido Comunista de España, or PCE), and listened to by broad swathes of Spanish society for whom the station, because it represented 'outside', was endowed with an authority and credibility that maintained its huge listener levels for years – indeed the station operated from the 1940s right up to 1977 and the final dismantling of the Franco regime. In listening to Radio *Pirenaica*, everyone understood the risks they ran if discovered, but despite this threat thousands of people not only listened, but also went a step further and became its informal correspondents, clandestinely sending reports from Spain which detailed the conditions of hunger and state terror oppressing the country, articles which were then broadcasted to the station's numerous listeners.[55] The dictatorship too was aware of *La Pirenaica*'s influence inside Spanish society, and it even installed machinery to generate interference to disrupt its reception. But the authorities also used more direct dissuading tactics, such as imposing severe and exemplary punishments with the intention of blocking its expansion. In 1945, for example, Alfonso Martínez, a sailor on the Cartagena naval base, was sentenced to death and executed simply for having been caught listening to *La Pirenaica*.[56]

Similar risks obtained in listening to, or being involved with, other clandestine media. Hundreds of leaflets, newspapers and journals were published and distributed across Spain, reaching even the prisons. The peak of such activities came between 1942 and 1946, when many Spaniards placed their hopes for change inside the country on the resolution of the European conflict. *English Dispatch*, a bulletin with reports on the Second World War taken from the BBC, was distributed across the whole of Andalusia. Consequently thousands of people knew what was happening in Europe without having to negotiate the Francoist propaganda disseminated by the official news agency. But the measures taken by the dictatorship against the clandestine distribution networks were swingeing. In 1941, for example, the police dismantled the *English Dispatch* network in Almeria, arresting thirty-seven people, all of whom were members of various republican, socialist, communist and anarchist organizations. Eight were sentenced to death and executed, the rest were given prison sentences.[57]

The era that followed Franco's declaration of battlefield victory was not 'peace', then, but the institutionalization of that victory. All Republican sectors remaining inside Spain experienced this process, not least through the daily experience of feeling unsafe: the authorities were not a source of protection or security – quite the contrary, it was the authorities and the state which threatened them, which saw them as in some way 'irregular' or suspicious and which could at any time bring down further punishment, including death. It was to escape this certainty (or indeed the uncertainty) that many men in at-risk categories, or who had already suffered punishment or been threatened, left their homes to join the guerrilla, the phenomenon which encapsulated par excellence the 'irregular civilian'.

## The road to the sierra

During the battlefield war of 1936–9, there was some guerrilla activity linked to the Republican Army, and also to neighbourhood groups who had fled their villages when they were occupied by Francoist forces. But when we speak of armed anti-Francoist resistance, we usually mean specifically those armed groups which emerged after the end of the battlefield war, and thus between 1939 and 1952. This anti-Francoist resistance was a fundamentally rural phenomenon: the majority of guerrilla fighters were peasants and their operations occurred primarily in the mountains – even if there were small nuclei of urban guerrilla in Barcelona, Madrid, Granada and Malaga. In the 1939–52 period most guerrilla fighters were connected in some way to socialist, anarchist or communist organizations, but ultimately it was the communist guerrilla which came to play the biggest role.

This armed resistance in Spain would never operate on the same scale as the resistance in other European countries, but it functioned in similar ways and was invested with the same broad antifascist goals and objectives.[58] Between 1939 and 1952, it mobilized around 8,000 guerrilla fighters, to whose numbers we can add a further 8,000 to 9,000 Spanish fighters who, after involvement in the French resistance, crossed the border back into Spain to participate in the operation at the Val d'Aran in November 1944. Its objective was to establish a free zone and provisional government on the Spanish side of the border, and thence to trigger an armed insurrection across the country, in tune with the others occurring elsewhere in Europe. But this operation, which could have changed the future of Spain, ultimately failed as a result of poor Allied support and a rapid counter-response by the Francoist Army.

Armed resistance in Spain after 1939 went through three stages. Between 1939 and 1942 the first armed groups were formed by those hundreds of men who left their villages to avoid being targeted by Francoist state violence. At first their aim was not so much actively to fight the dictatorship as to stay alive, to keep death (Franco's forces) at arm's length. These first groups, created more or less spontaneously and in response to state coercion, lacked coordination and remained essentially defensive in their tactics. Then from 1943 the situation changed radically. This change was triggered both by Allied advances in the Second World War, which in turn acted as a spur to resistance in Spain, and also by a change in the strategy of the PCE. From its exile base, the PCE sent back to Spain a large number of units with serious military experience, mostly acquired in the French resistance. Using these units, plus the older 'spontaneous' armed groups from

1939–42, plus some new recruits, the PCE managed to construct across Spain a highly organized and disciplined National Guerrilla Army. This guerrilla network would continue to grow even after the end of the Second World War in 1945. However, the fundamental problem for the armed resistance in Spain was one of timing: its strength peaked in 1947, just at the moment when the new Cold War order crystallized internationally. The political climate it generated cut off the anti-Francoist resistance totally, and Franco, sensing that the tide was turning, unleashed against it a campaign of extermination carried out by the army, until, in 1952, the PCE took the decision to demobilize the guerrilla force completely.[59]

When the first guerrilla fighters fled to the sierras between 1939 and 1942 they all had one rudimentary goal – survival. Many remembered their experience in Francoist internment camps and how it had driven them to despair, even to the edge of madness. Every night in those camps, after sunset, the names of those to be executed at sunrise would echo in prisoners' ears. The daily reading of these death lists was one of the most harrowing rituals of the 'postwar' period. It is difficult to convey afterwards, and with mere words, the feelings of emptiness, disgust and sadness that subsequently plagued the prisoners. Not to feature on the list oneself, though a relief, was scant consolation, since it meant that others who were comrades, friends or family members had been chosen instead. This macabre and fearful 'execution lottery' was a sophisticated form of psychological torture and its barbed effects would leave many survivors permanently scarred. Faced by it daily, some decided to take the risk of escaping to seek refuge in the mountains. At that time, the mountains, precisely because of their inaccessibility, offered the only free spaces still beyond the reach of the dictatorship. Thus it was a dynamic of sheer desperation, and especially the desire to get away from the inhumane world of the camps, that led to the formation of the first guerrilla groups.[60]

Immediately after any camp escape, the authorities would initiate a 'hunt' for the 'escapees'. Between 1939 and 1943 the Civil Guard were in charge of these, assisted by locally recruited paramilitaries, but from 1940 both the army and the Brigada Político-Social (political police) played an active role pursuing the guerrilla. From 1944, full counterinsurgency operations were deployed with more sophisticated methods, making use of military and civilian intelligence, and also by using counter-guerrilla groups. These state forces of various types would bring back from their 'expeditions' the bodies of those they had caught (whether camp escapees directly or guerrilla fighters) which they then exhibited in public, as a matter of policy, in order to spread terror among the civil population. The message was simple and direct: the fate of all those who flee to the mountains is death.[61] But the fate of the thousands of go-betweens (*enlaces*) who aided the guerrillas was not much easier. These go-betweens represent the clearest example of 'irregular civilians': they were friends, relatives and neighbours who, along with the clandestine political opposition, provided an extensive support network for the guerrilla. Their main function was to provide the practical support and local information which the guerrillas needed to survive. Between 1939 and 1952 approximately 60,000 go-betweens were arrested, though it is still not known how many of them were themselves then killed using the *Ley de Fugas*.[62] The Civil Guard and paramilitary groups habitually used torture to extract information. At the start of 1941, for example, an official report admitted that a group of soldiers had thrown boiling oil in the ears of a go-between and then applied lethal torture: he died in his house a couple of days later.[63]

The levels of physical violence and the constant psychological pressure which the authorities inflicted on people suspected of helping the guerrilla often led the *enlaces* to join the guerrilla groups themselves. This was much facilitated by the fact that these local networks of go-betweens already had strong social links to those in the guerrilla stretching back to before the civil war – they were friends, neighbours, sometimes family members, all of which reinforced the political affinities, guaranteeing a high degree of loyalty and support throughout the postwar period.[64] In this supporting role too, women were crucial, although they were almost totally excluded from the armed guerrilla units themselves. The Republic of the 1930s, notwithstanding its limitations, had opened up for many women new political opportunities.[65] One might surmise that this experience of expanded horizons was what prepared them for a new political role in supporting the guerrilla resistance. But as historian Mercedes Yusta has argued, earlier Republican change mainly affected urban women, while those women who predominated as go-betweens were from rural backgrounds. Thus their function as *enlaces* originated more often in previous bonds of family loyalty which were then extended in new and extreme circumstances to the public sphere and the field of politics.[66] Nonetheless, this still means that this rural environment was being socially transformed and its female inhabitants along with it.

The activities of these rural women, who reported on army movements or offered food or refuge to the guerrillas, challenged the official discourse denouncing the men in the mountains as 'bandits and criminals'. The guerrillas themselves also sought to combat this discourse by disseminating their own propaganda and, above all, by letting their conduct and actions speak for them. In particular here, the PCE imposed strict discipline and meted out severe punishments to those who transgressed the boundaries of political action. The punishment for acts considered not political but criminal could even include death. The Agrupación Guerrillera de Granada (Granada Guerrilla Detachment) executed one of its members for having kept back the money seized by the unit in one of its actions. The Agrupación had formal written rules, and they were clear: any action that was not clearly part of their political goals had to be eliminated.[67]

But even more effective than self-discipline, it was the myth-making by the civilian population which created the mystique around the guerrilla. Heroic and legendary stories transmitted in popular verse, ballads and oral narration became the most powerful 'weapon of the weak' against the overbearing hegemonic discourse of Francoism.[68] On occasion the dictatorship too grew alarmed by these legends and rumours which revived and cherished the very identities the authorities had tried so hard to eradicate. At times they felt they were fighting more against a phantom hiding in popular myth than against a real guerrilla army. This was perhaps the guerrillas' greatest achievement – for while the state's weapons could and did defeat the armed resistance, they were unable entirely to wipe out the hopes and dreams which sustained the myth.

## Conclusion

For the defeated, surviving Franco's extended state of war involved searing, often horrific experiences which for many left a permanent mark on their lives. The same too can be said of their children, the second 'war generation', who decades later would be the protagonists of Spain's democratic transition in the 1970s. For them too guilt and shame were the enduring psychological effects of the dictatorship and still strongly felt as they faced the political challenges of the future – though there were also counter-sentiments, including sometimes a sense of pride in having dissented, even if in the most insignificant of ways or even only in one's own mind. But if there was a single powerful feeling pervading the transition period, that was fear: a fear that had been spread daily by the dictatorship since the 1940s right up to its last days, and which has survived long beyond the regime's own demise.

At the end of 1977, six months after Spain had held its first democratic elections for over forty years, and as the last institutional remnants of the dictatorship were being dismantled, a group of neighbours in a small town in Toledo province came together to exhume the remains of ten villagers who had been extrajudicially killed in October 1937 by local pro-insurgent (Falangist) vigilantes, effectively the villagers' own neighbours. The organizers contacted the relatives of the dead so that they could participate in the event. Privately they all expressed their gratitude that it happened, but several declined to attend 'for fear of what might happen'. The son of one of the murder victims even requested that the organizers not mention his father by name during the commemorative ceremony. After the war, he, as an orphaned child, had been adopted by one of the most powerful Francoist families in the village and had rebuilt his life on the basis of disowning his father's identity and his own past. Having made a career in the Civil Guard, this child, now an adult, could feel only shame when he thought of his murdered father – or at least these were the terms in which he articulated it to the organizers of the commemoration.[69]

This short anecdote clearly shows how the power of Franco's four-decade-long rule was capable of permeating and reconfiguring even the family identities of the defeated. It is possible to find testimonies pointing to a radically different outcome – circumstances could vary, and though the odds were invariably against the defeated, much could still depend on the resources they could draw on, and on the memory work they could perform, from their subaltern position. Long after the death of Franco, one young man remembered how his mother had managed to recover the shirt that his father had worn on the day of his execution and how, for years after, she had taken strips from it, sewing them into the linings of his and his brothers' clothing.[70] For decades they wore these small pieces of the shirt in the seams of their trousers or under their sleeves. In this case then, and in others too, nothing, not even the oppressive atmosphere of the dictatorship, was able to wipe out the sons' and wife's memory of a beloved father and husband. But it was not only a question of love, the son recalled. In preserving the memory of their father they were also keeping alive his desire for, and dreams of, social change, the things which had cost him his life.

## Notes

1. To avoid censorship they wrote using invisible ink, or in code; or else letters destined for exile political organizations were enclosed in envelopes addressed to 'innocuous' family members or commercial businesses. This meant they often eluded the censor's gaze, even though this tactic meant some risk. See Armand Balsebre and Rosario Fontova, *Las cartas de La Pirenaica: Memorias del antifranquismo* (Madrid: Cátedra, 2014), pp. 78–80.

2. Paul Preston, *The Spanish Holocaust: Inquisition and Extermination in Twentieth-Century Spain* (London: Harper Press, 2012), pp. 469–517.

3. Mark Mazower, *Dark Continent: Europe's Twentieth-Century* (London: Penguin Books, 1998), pp. 157–84, 215–48; Donald Bloxham and A. Dirk Moses, 'Genocide and Ethnic Cleansing', in Donald Bloxham and Robert Gerwarth (eds), *Political Violence in Twentieth-Century Europe* (Cambridge: Cambridge University Press, 2011), pp. 87–139.

4. Helen Graham and Alejandro Quiroga, 'After the Fear was Over? What Came after Dictatorships in Spain, Greece, and Portugal', in Dan Stone (ed.), *The Oxford Handbook of Postwar European History* (Oxford: Oxford University Press, 2012), pp. 502–25.

5. Ibid., p. 506.

6. Preston, *Spanish Holocaust*, p. xi.

7. Indeed the term was first coined for France, see H.R. Kedward, *In Search of the Maquis: Rural Resistance in Southern France, 1942–1944* (Oxford: Oxford University Press, 1994), p. vi.

8. Preston, *Spanish Holocaust*, pp. 34–51; Sebastian Balfour, *Deadly Embrace. Morocco and the Road to the Spanish Civil War* (Oxford: Oxford University Press, 2002); Enzo Traverso, *A sangre y fuego. De la Guerra Civil europea, 1914–1945* (Valencia: PUV, 2009).

9. Paul Preston, *Franco: A Biography* (London: Fontana Press, 1995), p. 222.

10. A higher figure of 275,000 (not including either the Moroccan or Italian troops in Franco's forces) is given in Julio Alcaide Inchausti, 'Las secuelas demográficas del conflicto', in E. Fuentes Quintana (dir.), *Economía y economistas españoles en la guerra civil*, Vol. II (Madrid: Círculo de Lectores, 2008), pp. 374–5; the figure of 200,000 in Preston, *Spanish Holocaust*, p. xi.

11. Santos Juliá (coord.), *Víctimas de la Guerra Civil* (Madrid: Temas de Hoy, 1999), p. 411; for an updated set of estimates of the extrajudicially killed, covering the entire major period of Francoist repression, from 17–18 July 1936 until the end of the 1940s, see Francisco Espinosa Maestre, 'La represión franquista: un combate por la historia y la memoria', in Francisco Espinosa Maestre (ed.), *Violencia roja y azul, 1936–1950* (Barcelona: Crítica, 2010), pp. 17–78, see especially the tables pp. 77–8, and the comments on the existing figures for the Francoists' extrajudicial and quasi-judicial killings as *minimum* ones on pp. 35–6, 40.

12. Preston, *Spanish Holocaust*, pp. xvi–xx.

13. Graham and Quiroga, 'After the Fear was Over?', p. 506.

14. Carme Molinero et al. (eds), *Una inmensa prisión: Los campos de concentración y las prisiones durante la guerra civil y el franquismo* (Barcelona: Crítica, 2003), pp. 160–2; Javier Rodrigo, *Cautivos: Campos de concentración en la España franquista, 1936–1947* (Barcelona: Crítica, 2005).

15. Preston, *Spanish Holocaust*, p. xi gives the lower figure of 20,000 and the higher range is in Juliá, *Víctimas de la Guerra Civil*, p. 411.

16. Henry Rousso, 'The Purge in France: An Incomplete Story', in Jon Elster (ed.), *Retribution and Reparation in the Transition to Democracy* (New York: Cambridge University Press, 2006), pp. 93–112.

17. Philip Morgan, *The Fall of Mussolini* (New York: Oxford University Press, 2007), p. 167, 216–26; Tony Judt, *Postwar: A History of Europe since 1945* (New York: Penguin Books, 2005), p. 47–8.

18. David H. Close, 'The Reconstruction of Right-Wing State', in David H. Close (ed.), *The Greek Civil War, 1943–1950: Studies of Polarization* (London: Routledge, 1993), pp. 156–89: p. 168.

19. Jacques Semelin, 'What is "Genocide"?', *European Review of History* 12:1 (2005), pp. 81–9: pp. 85–8.

20. Rodrigo, *Cautivos*, pp. 127–46; Gutmaro Gómez Bravo and Jorge Marco, *La obra del miedo: Violencia y sociedad en la España franquista, 1936–1950* (Barcelona: Península, 2011), pp. 65–9, 269–91; Helen Graham, *The War and its Shadow: Spain's Civil War in Europe's Long Twentieth Century* (Brighton: Sussex Academic Press, 2012), pp. 103–24.

21. Ricard Vinyes, 'Las desapariciones infantiles durante el franquismo y sus consecuencias', *International Journal of Iberian Studies* 19:1 (2006), pp. 53–73; in English, see the following: Giles Tremlett, 'Spain's "Stolen Babies" Attempt to Blow Lid Off Scandal', *The Guardian*, 5 January 2015 (http://www.theguardian.com/world/2012/jan/05/spain-stolen-babies-scandal); Giles Tremlett, 'Spain Seeks Truth on Baby-trafficking Claims', *The Guardian*, 27 January 2011 (http://www.theguardian.com/world/2011/jan/27/spain-baby-trafficking-claims); Raphael Minder, 'Spain Confronts Decades of Pain Over Lost Babies', *New York Times*, 7 July 2011 (http://www.nytimes.com/2011/07/07/world/europe/07iht-spain07.html?_r=0) [accessed 23 August 2015].

22. Geneviève Dreyfus-Armand, *El exilio de los republicanos españoles en Francia: De la guerra civil a la muerte de Franco* (Barcelona: Crítica, 2000).

23. Julio Aróstegui (coord.), *Franco: la represión como sistema* (Barcelona: Flor del Viento, 2012).

24. Jefatura Provincial del Movimiento. Jaén, January 1940. 51/20.519 (Archivo General de la Administración: AGA).

25. Michael Richards, *A Time of Silence: Civil War and the Culture of Repression in Franco's Spain* (Cambridge: Cambridge University Press, 1997), pp. 7, 142–4; Miguel Ángel del Arco Blanco, 'Hunger and the Consolidation of the Francoist Regime', *European History Quarterly* 40:3 (2010), pp. 458–83.

26. Yannick Ripa, 'La Tonte Purificatrice des Republicaines Pendant la Guerre Civile Epagnole', *Les Cahiers de l'Histoire du Temps Present* 31 (1995), n.p.: http://www.ihtp.cnrs.fr/spip. php%3Farticle246&lang=fr.html [accessed 14 January 2016]; Enrique González Duro, *Las rapadas : El franquismo contra la mujer* (Madrid: Siglo XXI, 2012), pp. 181–5; Fabrice Virgile, *Shorn Women: Gender and Punishment in Liberation France* (Oxford: Berg, 2002).

27. Peter Anderson, *The Francoist Military Trials: Terror and Complicity, 1939–1945* (London: Routledge, 2009), pp. 63–119.

28. Rodrigo, *Cautivos*, pp. 127–46.

29. Ángela Cenarro, 'La institucionalización del universo penitenciario', in Molinero, *Una inmensa prisión*, pp. 133–53.

30. Jefatura Provincial del Movimiento. Málaga, August 1940. 51/20.556 (AGA).

31. *Anuario Estadístico de España 1946–1947*, Vol. II (Madrid: Imprenta Nacional, 1947), pp. 1240–1; Gutmaro Gómez Bravo, 'The Origins of the Francoist Penitentiary System, 1936–1948', *International Journal of Iberian Studies* 23:1 (2010), pp. 5–21: p. 8.

32. *Anuario Estadístico de España 1946–1947*, Vol. II, p. 1240–1; Ricard Vinyes, 'El universo penitenciario durante el franquismo', in C. Molinero et al. (eds) *Una inmensa prisión*, pp. 160–2; Gutmaro Gómez Bravo, *El exilio interior: Cárcel y represión en la España franquista, 1939–1950* (Madrid: Taurus, 2009), pp. 24, 76–80; Julián Casanova et al., *Morir,*

*matar, sobrevivir: La violencia en la dictadura de Franco* (Barcelona: Crítica, 2004), pp. 24, 123–4; Graham, *The War and its Shadow*, pp. 109–110, 201–2.

33. Julius Ruiz, *Franco's Justice: Repression in Madrid after the Spanish Civil War* (Oxford: Oxford University Press, 2005), pp. 224–9.

34. Isaias Lafuente, *Esclavos de Franco: La explotación de los presos bajo el franquismo* (Madrid: Booket, 2004); Gonzalo Acosta Bono et al. (eds), *El canal de los presos, 1940–1962: Trabajos forzados: de la represión política a la explotación económica* (Barcelona: Crítica, 2004); Gareth Stockey, *Valley of the Fallen. The (N)ever Changing Face of General Franco's Monument* (Nottingham: Critical Cultural and Communications Press, 2013).

35. Jefatura Provincial del Movimiento. Jaén, June 1940. 51/20.519 (AGA).

36. Alfredo González-Ruibal, 'The Archaeology of Internment in Francoist Spain (1936–1952)', in Adrian Myers and Gabriel Moshenska (eds), *The Archaeologies of Internment* (New York: Springer, 2011), pp. 53–74.

37. Alfredo González-Ruibal, *Arqueología de un campo de concentración: Informe de las excavaciones en el campo de concentración de Castuera (Badajoz, España), 1939–1940* (Madrid: CSIC, 2010).

38. James C. Scott, *Weapons of the Weak: Everyday Forms of Peasant Resistance* (Connecticut: Yale University Press, 1985).

39. González-Ruibal, *Arqueología*, p. 35.

40. Ricard Vinyes, *Irredentas. Las presas políticas y sus hijos en las cárceles franquistas* (Madrid: Temas de Hoy, 2010), p. 144.

41. Lafuente, *Esclavos de Franco*, p. 287.

42. Tomasa Cuevas, *Cárcel de mujeres*, Vol. II (Barcelona: Sirocco Books, 1985), p. 263.

43. Antonio Cazorla, *Fear and Progress: Ordinary Lives in Franco's Spain, 1939–1975* (Chichester: Wiley-Blackwell, 2010), pp. 17–56.

44. Rafael Cruz, *Protestar en España, 1900–2013* (Madrid: Alianza, 2015), p. 146. The slogan can be seen in the film *Las 13 rosas*, for example, where it appears printed in a pamphlet published by the anti-Francoist opposition. See Igor Barrenetxea Marañón, 'Las 13 rosas: el cine como reconstructor de memoria', *Bulletin of Spanish Studies* 89: 7–8 (2012), pp. 9–21: p. 16.

45. Cited in Miguel Ángel del Arco Blanco, 'El estraperlo: pieza clave en la estabilización del régimen franquista', *Historia del Presente* 15 (2010), pp. 65–78: p. 71.

46. *Cultura y Democracia*, 4 (México DF, April 1950), pp. 95–6.

47. Ibid., p. 95.

48. Sainz Orrio, leader of the *Sindicato Vertical* (official trade union), reproduced in *Cultura y Democracia*, 4 (México DF, April, 1950), p. 95.

49. Consejo de Guerra 1.075/1.740 (Archivo del Tribunal Togado Militar de Almería).

50. Jefatura Provincial del Movimiento. Málaga, April 1944. 51/20.646 (AGA); Jefatura Provincial del Movimiento. Almeria, June 1945. 51/20.660 (AGA).

51. Jefatura Provincial del Movimiento. Málaga, August 1940. 51/20.556 (AGA).

52. Óscar J. Rodríguez Barreira, *Migas con miedo: Prácticas de resistencia al primer franquismo. Almería, 1939–1953* (Almería: Universidad de Almería, 2008), p. 140.

53. Antonio Cazorla, *Cartas a Franco de los españoles de a pie, 1936–1945* (Barcelona: RBA, 2014), pp. 169–70.

54. Ibid., p. 201.

55. Armand Balsebre and Rosario Fontova, *Las cartas de la Pirenaica: Memorias del antifranquismo* (Madrid: Cátedra, 2014).

56. Luis Zaragoza, *Radio Pirenaica: la voz de la esperanza antifranquista* (Madrid: Marcial Pons, 2008), p. 393.

57. Rodríguez Barreira, *Migas con miedo,* p. 109–17.

58. Jorge Marco, 'The Long Nocturnal March: The Spanish Guerrilla Movement in the European Narrative of Antifascist Resistance', in P. Anderson et al. (eds), *Grappling with the Past: Mass Killing and Violence in Spain* (New York: Routledge, 2014), pp. 173–92.

59. Secundino Serrano, *Maquis: Historia de la guerrilla antifranquista* (Madrid: Temas de Hoy, 2002).

60. Jorge Marco, *Hijos de una guerra: Los hermanos Quero y la resistencia antifranquista* (Granada: Comares, 2010), p. 83–98.

61. See Jorge Marco, 'Una Corea en pequeño: Contrainsurgencia y represión de la guerrilla en España, 1939–1952', *Contenciosa* 1 (2013), pp. 1–20.

62. Francisco Moreno Gómez, *Historia y memorias del maquis* (Madrid: Editorial Alpuerto, 2006), pp. 231–3.

63. Jefatura Provincial del Movimiento. Córdoba, January 1941. 51/20.548 (AGA).

64. Jorge Marco, *Guerrilleros y vecinos en armas: Identidades y culturas de la resistencia antifranquista* (Granada: Comares, 2012), pp. 81–102; Ana Cabana, *La derrota de lo épico* (Valencia: PUV, 2013), pp. 169–227.

65. Helen Graham, 'Women and Social Change', in Helen Graham and Jo Labanyi (eds), *Spanish Cultural Studies. An Introduction: The Struggle for Modernity* (Oxford: Oxford University Press, 1995), pp. 99–115.

66. Mercedes Yusta, 'Rebeldía individual, compromiso familiar, acción colectiva: las mujeres en las resistencia al franquismo durante los años cuarenta', *Historia del Presente* 4 (2004), pp. 63–92.

67. Marco, *Guerrilleros y vecinos en armas,* pp. 120–3.

68. Ibid., pp. 175–9; Cabana, *La derrota de lo épico,* pp. 252–5.

69. Interviews by the author with Luis Maroto (21 July 2014), Jesús Herrera (16 June 2014) and Francisco Pleite (6 June 2014), neighbours in the town of Bargas (Toledo).

70. Marco, *Hijos de una guerra,* p. 440.

## Further reading

Anderson, P., *The Francoist Military Trials: Terror and Complicity, 1939–1945,* London: Routledge, 2009.

Anderson, P. and Arco, M.Á. del (eds), *Grappling with the Past: Mass Killing and Violence in Spain,* New York: Routledge, 2014.

Cazorla, A., *Fear and Progress: Ordinary Lives in Franco's Spain, 1939–1975,* Chichester: Wiley-Blackwell, 2010.

Graham, H., 'Gender and the State: Women in the 1940s', in H. Graham and J. Labanyi (eds), *Spanish Cultural Studies: An Introduction,* Oxford: Oxford University Press, 1995, pp. 99–115.

Graham, H., 'Popular Culture in the "Years of Hunger"', in H. Graham and J. Labanyi (eds), *Spanish Cultural Studies: An Introduction,* Oxford: Oxford University Press, 1995, pp. 182–95.

Graham, H., *The War and its Shadow: Spain's Civil War in Europe's Long Twentieth Century,* Brighton: Sussex Academic Press, 2012.

Marco, J., *Guerrilleros and Neighbours in Arms: Identities and Cultures of Antifascist Resistance in Spain*, Brighton: Sussex Academic Press, 2016.

Preston, P., *The Spanish Holocaust: Inquisition and Extermination in Twentieth-Century Spain*, London: HarperPress, 2012.

Richards, M., 'Terror and Progress: Industrialization, Modernity and the Making of Francoism', in H. Graham and J. Labanyi (eds), *Spanish Cultural Studies: An Introduction*, Oxford: Oxford University Press, 1995, pp. 173–81.

Richards, M., *A Time of Silence: Civil War and the Culture of Repression in Franco's Spain*, Cambridge: Cambridge University Press, 2007.

Richards, M., *After the Civil War: Making Memory and Re-Making Spain since 1936*, Cambridge: Cambridge University Press, 2013.

Serrano, S., *Maquis. Historia de la guerrilla antifranquista*, Madrid: Temas de Hoy, 2002.

# PART III

## MAKING MEMORY: HISTORY AND THE FUTURE OF DICTATORSHIP

# CHAPTER 8
## STORIES FOR AFTER A WAR: SOCIAL MEMORY AND THE MAKING OF URBAN AND INDUSTRIAL TRANSITION IN 1960s SPAIN
*Michael Richards*

Between the end of the battlefield war in Spain in 1939 and the post-Franco *political* transition to democracy in the 1970s, Spain underwent a profound *social* transition from relative backwardness to modernity. This was a transition created not by the state, from above, but rather one which came out of society, from below, as specific groups responded to the military conflict of 1936–9 and to the long dictatorship born of it. Claims by historians and other commentators that General Franco prepared the way for the political transition are contradicted by the dictator's carefully laid plans for a continuation of Francoism after his demise.[1] Such claims have rested upon generalized observations of changes introduced by Franco's governments under international pressure to make Spain appear more open, including legislation for collective bargaining in industry in 1958 and the Press Law of 1966.[2] The claims also apparently derive substance from the evident contrast between social conditions in the war-ravaged 1940s and the qualitatively different consumer society of the early 1970s. But the claims fail to analyse how it was that these social and cultural changes occurred (or Franco's role in driving them) – changes which, in retrospect, we can view as laying the foundations of the democratic transition.[3]

A distinction is therefore required between the Franco dictatorship, on the one hand, and Spanish society during the Franco years, on the other. The groundwork for modernization and democratization occurred during the Franco era, though regime contributions to this were, in many respects, *reactive* – being mostly responses to the threat posed by social unrest from the early 1950s onwards, which was in itself partly caused by the regime's own repressive economic strategy of the 1940s.[4] Autarkic state intervention aggravated food shortages and the Francoist authorities colluded in the growth of a huge black market which benefited the victors; by the beginning of the 1950s ever-rising prices meant economic and political crisis loomed. One regional Civil Governor declared early in 1951 in an internal memo that 'the people are exhausted ... The current system of intervention has completely failed; we must try other more efficient and flexible ways ... What is important to me is saving the regime'.[5] The formation of Franco's fifth government in July 1951 was hailed by the regime as a reorganization of the state, though it followed anxious and heated discussion in the Council of Ministers (the cabinet): Franco had been pressed for cabinet reconstruction and he had resisted, wanting to rely on repression rather than reform.[6] The most significant change was the creation of a separate Ministry of Commerce, detached from the Ministry of Industry, making trade much less dependent on the industrializing strategy of autarky. This marked a liberalizing turn in economic policy that recognized the need to meet the barest necessities of the population.[7]

A key underlying force impelling modernization (and ultimately democratization) during the years of the dictatorship came thus through indirect social pressure 'from below'. Change would be forced upon Francoism by the process through which rural and urban working-class constituencies adapted to the repressive world created during the civil war and the decade of its institutionalization following Franco's military victory in 1939. This socially modernizing pressure, beginning in the immediate aftermath of the war, was centred on migration from the countryside to the cities, a demographic shift in which the migrants' aim was to escape en masse the dire political, economic and social consequences of the victors' control imposed politically across the towns and villages of Spain after Franco's victory. The postwar social and political settlement – which was never dignified by a formal peace agreement – was based both on direct state coercion, violence and imprisonment, as well as on the co-opting of other sectors of civil society as participants in the repression; other key components included the reversal of land reform and ensuing primitive capital accumulation by landowners (prominent amongst 'the victors'), the suppression of free political parties and trade unions, and the dominance of an ultraconservative institutional Catholic Church in social and cultural matters, alongside the Falangist state party.

The manual labour and material hardships of those who migrated to the cities would amount to the sacrifice of one generation in the interests of the next, and this became a fundamental basis of economic modernization in Spain. Rural migrants would become the pliant labour force to create the industry which leading Francoists deemed to be indispensable – a labour force which would compensate for the regime's lack of capital investment, and also compensate for its imposition of economic protectionism which would contribute to this very lack, thus 'sacrific[ing] the comforts of a generation'.[8] At the same time, collective identities – political, social and cultural – were restricted and atomized, as the destruction of a civil public sphere forced the entire population inwards to the private, domestic sphere. At the same time, social sectors targeted for punishment by the regime were also impelled outwards towards reliance on the city as a promised land of relative anonymity, safety and a viable economic future. The resulting great process of migration, and its causes and modernizing consequences, are areas of Spain's postwar experience that have largely been neglected by historians. This neglect has been, in part, because of an anxiety among critically minded historians that any exploration of this process, however carefully qualified, would end by allowing Francoism to take the credit for modernization and thereby lay spurious claim to be the 'antechamber of democracy'.[9]

Postwar urbanization has been explored by economic historians, geographers and sociologists who have mainly focused on the unprecedented massive population shift of the 1960s. This focus has resulted in the shift being linked inextricably to what the Franco government called the 'economic miracle', occurring during the second half of the 1960s.[10] Much of the historiography has followed that lead, imposing an orthodox chronology on the Franco years, which simply splits the era in two: 'early Francoism' and 'late Francoism', around the pivot point of 1959, when the aforementioned strategy of economic liberalization was finally forced in full upon Franco by his ministers of industry and commerce.[11] This was a pragmatic response to several threats, not least that posed by a population shift that had in fact been in train since the 1940s and which would continue and increase in the 1960s. So, though it hardly appeared so at the time, the war of 1936–9 had in fact marked a social watershed in Spain: it was the outcome of the war with its brutal segregation of the population, rather than the later decision by Franco to accept economic liberalization, which marks the real point of social rupture and transformation in Spain. Once we can understand that, then we can also recover the essential continuity linking the civil war, its repressive aftermath, the 'Spanish miracle', consumerism and the transition to democracy. The clearest way to perceive this whole is by viewing the history of post-1939 Spain 'from below', and especially by examining it from the perspectives of the migrants themselves, in particular through their social memories of the war, as articulated in the accounts they gave after it, including of the punishments visited upon them.

## Intimate violence, state-building and migration

Within communities all over Spain, the convulsions of the civil war presented the opportunity for a violent backlash against the socially reforming legislation which had been fundamental to the Second Republic's programme for change, including land redistribution and secular forms of primary education. This backlash was particularly notable in the war's aftermath in rural communities – where in the 1930s the majority of the Spanish population lived. Throughout rural Spain the defeated were made to pay for the Republic's earlier attempt to redistribute power and wealth. This process of punishment and control was facilitated by the very nature of how village society worked: everyone knew everyone else's business, and what had been done by whom, and where benefits might be gained or old scores settled by 'elaborating' stories about others which were shaped – indeed 'written' – by the new, highly charged ideological atmosphere of war. In many communities kinship relations had been fractured by the pre-war and wartime process of class conflict and political and social mobilization.[12] Once 'liberated' by Francoist forces, many individuals were willing to align themselves with the local power brokers put in place by the victorious Francoist coalition both during and after the military conflict, either because this made them 'safe' (if their own past appeared insufficiently 'pure' (i.e. Francoist)), or else because they saw material opportunities to be gained in so doing. Those with power were responsible for identifying liberals and leftists for punishment and the local authorities welcomed and encouraged people to denounce their own neighbours. The result was often that local Republicans were forced to sell possessions and give up their homes, while opportunists who were not politically compromised could take advantage.[13]

Political denunciation became key for co-opting support; it was one important element of the war culture which continued throughout the 1940s, pervading communities and, ultimately, from which state-building would be achieved.[14] Reporting on 'enemies of the *Patria*' was publicly encouraged by the 'liberating' authorities as a civic duty. The Head of Public Order in newly occupied Lérida (Catalonia) published an instruction in July 1938, which succinctly reinforced the point: 'Whoever does not denounce those not worthy of forming part of the New State will be considered a poor citizen.'[15]

Women from Republican families often bore the brunt of discrimination and exploitation in the aftermath because husbands and fathers of military age were absent – either because they had been killed during the battlefield war or in the political repression; or because they were undergoing the stringent process of state categorization (demobilized Republican soldiers were classified for execution, internment or release); or else were in hiding or participating in the underground guerrilla resistance. These women left alone in villages across Spain had to confront particular, gendered forms of violence at the hands of the new Francoist (often Falangist) local authorities, or the representatives of major Francoist interest groups (such as landowners). The gendered dimension, which re-enacted control over the women it targeted, was a means of legitimating and strengthening the new state order by 'responding' to conservative fears over what had gone before. For traditionalists, social cohesion had been disrupted by Republican reforms – in particular because this cohesion rested on the harmonizing, subordinate role of women as wives and mothers. The transgressive demands of Republican women for greater freedom, political rights and social equality had upset this conservative 'balance' which had to be restored. Thus women perceived as having transgressed traditional gender norms were targeted by violence aimed at 'purging' them and which simultaneously permitted those inflicting it a form of catharsis. More than this, the violence was also *publicly* performed through rituals aimed at purifying the entire community, defined as 'contaminated' by the women's transgression.[16] Many women were singled out for such punishments which included head shaving, forced castor oil ingestion and ritual procession through the streets for public vilification. The intention was that the community would be brought together, at the expense of Republican scapegoats, and could thus project its own collective commitment to the new Franco state under construction, and in particular to the national-Catholic ideology underpinning it and for which the war, as a 'crusade', had been fought.

Many scapegoated victims moved away from their villages in the aftermath of these traumatizing events: evading the official controls and police surveillance which severely hampered free movement at that time, they escaped to the relative anonymity of the city during the early postwar years.[17] Indeed mass migration had begun even during the years of battlefield war between 1936 and 1939, because these repressive practices were imposed incrementally throughout the war as territory fell to the Francoist armies. By the second half of 1937, some three million refugees, including thousands from the south – mostly women, children and the elderly – had been evacuated to the safety of Republican Catalonia. The population of the Republic, which by this time comprised only two-fifths of national territory, had increased by 25 per cent above its pre-war level.

Among those who chose migration, a major motive force was the fear (or indeed the near certainty) of being ostracized in their local community of origin. One woman,

'Antonia', from rural Granada, who had led the PCE-inspired Popular Frontist organization, Mujeres Antifascistas (Antifascist Women), in her economically polarized pueblo, was imprisoned in Málaga after the city was taken by the Francoists in February 1937. She remained in gaol until 1942 and once released, never returned to her village, declaring that she would prefer even to stay in prison than to go back.[18] Another, the daughter of a shepherd from rural Córdoba who had been executed by the Francoist authorities during the war, migrated to Madrid at about the same time to escape from the village where her father's property had been taken from the family in spite of the wishes expressed in his final letter.[19] Another migrant declared that 'when the 'Nacionales' (Francoist forces) entered the village [her father] had to sell his olive trees and an embargo was placed on his property'. She and her husband had to resort to illegal black market labour in order to survive, collecting *esparto* grass in the countryside, exchanging it for olive oil and selling this to those who could afford to pay.[20] Ruin like this, through forced eviction or confiscation of a plot of land, was frequently brought about because of a denunciation within the community, leaving migration as the only way out for the person targeted – as, crucially, the only way for him or her to recover a livelihood.[21]

Migration of those targeted by the authorities was therefore a reaction to an economic vulnerability which was linked inextricably to the pre-war ideological patterning of political conflict between 1931 and July 1936 and the subsequent political repression which formed the basis of Francoist power 'on the ground'. Migration involved movement from one's village to the nearest substantial town, and – more usually – to larger industrial and commercial centres. The brutal uprooting of those amongst the rural poor from rural Burgos to Barcelona, for example, was engendered by the conflict and its repressive aftermath.[22] But urbanization was a broad and complex 'dance of the Spaniards'[23] during and after the war – thus while some groups of rural poor were fleeing Burgos province, others were arriving in its 'capital' city. The President of Acción Católica there complained in April 1954 about the 'overwhelming exodus' from rural areas to towns and cities, stating that 90 per cent of those given charity in the city of Burgos were not locals, and that 'many thousands of these are families of political prisoners who arrived during the period of the liquidation of the civil war'.[24] According to his plea to be rid of them, these families were 'fearful of returning to their villages where they committed their crimes', though what lay behind that formulation, and the real reasons for their flight, as we have seen, was to do with the wartime/postwar reconfiguring of local power by the victors across rural Spain.

These reasons are reflected in numerous stories told after the war by those who became migrants. When a woman whose Republican father and uncle had been imprisoned during the war returned from a place of safety to her small community in rural Santander, she was not welcomed. Neighbours warned her to take refuge with all possible haste at her grandparents' house and other residents of the pueblo soon arrived at the door accusing them of being 'Communist Reds'. The message was that they ought to have left when the 'liberators' had come 'to rescue the *Patria* from communism'. The underlying motive for this social participation in repression was related to their confiscated property, and to the desire of denouncers unequivocally to display their alignment with the new regime. Ideology thus went hand-in-hand with opportunism. This woman's mother was ordered to present herself to the local Falange to participate in celebrating Franco's victory. The daughter understood that this meant ritualized humiliation and she even risked going to the Guardia Civil to protest: 'the majority of the pueblo knew that we were good people, but at that time nobody dared to speak up for us'.[25] It subsequently became impossible for the family to continue living in the village and, in the end, she would escape with the help of friends who offered refuge in Catalonia, a region which from the time of the war until the 1970s would attract hundreds of thousands of people fleeing persecution and poverty. The condition of being socially excluded was passed on from one generation to the next. When the daughters of local Republicans in one pueblo in the province of Zaragoza (Aragón) were paraded through the streets, with shaven heads to be condemned, one liberal-minded woman had protested, for which she was denounced and later (in August 1936) executed by firing squad.[26] Then her own daughter was taunted as the child of 'Reds', a form of discrimination from which she fled by migrating to Barcelona as soon as she could.

The most economically humble classes of the Spanish countryside were not the only sector of society to suffer the consequences of the war, but in material terms they bore the brunt collectively more than other social groups. The forced movement of young men through obligatory military service of two years (introduced in August 1940) – many deployed on public works projects – was also to become a significant factor in postwar migration.[27] Virtually all those called up were deliberately stationed outside their home regions. This meant that many lost whatever civil employment they had secured, but it also opened up the possibility of making a new start far from home.

At the sharp end of state repression, the masses in rural poverty who possessed little or no social or cultural capital would become central actors, though silently, of the social change which was to follow. Migration led them to the margins of urban life, often to an existence in deeply degrading conditions, to self-constructed dwellings in spontaneous communities, produced from found or cheaply produced materials: homes with no floors, electricity, water or sanitation. They were permanently vulnerable because they were prone to be cleared forcefully by the police at any moment and the occupants returned to the countryside.[28] These shanty towns were called *chabolas* in much of the country, including Madrid, and *barracas* in Barcelona.

At the most obvious level, this was an existence propelled by little more than trying to ensure material survival. One Catholic priest, commenting in the 1950s, understood that for migrants 'poverty diminished their faculties, reduced their horizons, and erased their initiatives. Many, since childhood, have developed in an atmosphere of hatred and despair . . . deceived by those who treated them badly in their place of origin and compelled them to leave'.[29] But migration to the margins of cities was also seen by some observers as in itself a form of rebellion, reflecting the active agency of migrants through 'spontaneous urbanization' and their 'clandestine building'.[30] These informal and illegal communities, where the scrutinizing gaze and repressive measures of the pueblo could be avoided, were perhaps the only form of resistance possible for rural migrants 'ruined by Francoism'.[31] The underground communist opposition hoped that migrant slums would form a new focus of political resistance, though the constant daily struggle of their inhabitants merely to survive severely restricted such possibilities.[32] Even as active agents, migrants were viewed by the state as inherently inferior – the *chabola*, it was said, 'suits some individuals better than a proper living space'[33] – and all (in theory) were entered onto the census, not least so previous political allegiances could be checked. Shanty towns were also subject to periodic clearances by the police. As a result, according to the criminalizing language of the authorities, 'some subjects lost their lairs'.[34] Some 9,000 individuals were expelled from Barcelona in the 1950s, and many more whose dwellings had been destroyed were placed in temporary barracks, the site of wartime and postwar political executions which reminded many of the people who were sent there of previous periods spent in wartime or postwar concentration camps.[35] The misery of these conditions could only be put up with because in most cases migrants had little to return to.[36]

Catholic diocesan institutions calculated that there were 439,000 individuals living in these conditions in Madrid as early as 1952 and up to 600,000 by the end of the decade. The estimation in 1940 had been 10,000.[37] By the end of 1947, in seventeen of Spain's largest large cities there were 797,992 individuals living in similar informal migrant communities with little by way of basic facilities, including 60,000 families in Barcelona and 40,000 in Valencia. So, well before the 1960s, migration was already huge and sustained: it was also viewed by some as a contribution to developmental change. The strong preference of officialdom to disperse the dangerously burgeoning worker concentrations of Barcelona[38] was rejected by certain sociologists (even ones within the Falange) who during the 1940s criticized government attempts to prevent migration. They argued that the 'liberation' from the countryside of a section of the agricultural population 'constitutes precisely one of the indexes of the social-economic progress of a nation'.[39] The deleterious effects on the physical growth of children born in the shanty towns during the period 1948–53 – even compared with those who remained in the poverty-stricken southern countryside – were nonetheless dramatic.[40] To officials, the migration, which would carry on during the 1950s and become a flood in the 1960s, had already had an 'asphyxiating' effect on urban municipalities as early as 1944.[41] In 1956, 20 per cent of Madrid's inhabitants were living in self-assembled dwellings (*chabolas*) or caves on the margins of the city. The state could not keep pace: in 1957 the housing deficit was estimated to be 1,067,452 family units.[42] By 1970, the number of *chabolas* in the country as a whole stood at some 110,000, where 600,000 people lived, and the number in the capital by 1973 had risen to 35,000. By the 1970s, 47 per cent of all Madrid shanty dwellers were found in the area of Vallecas on the southern periphery of the city, the total population of which in 1976 stood at over 300,000, which was more than the population of Córdoba, or Murcia or Valladolid.

## Social memory and the origins of the transition

Through the testimonies and memories of those rural migrants who arrived in Spain's cities during the period from the 1940s to the 1960s we can elucidate the postwar process of urban and industrial transition. Migrants' recollections – in oral or (more occasionally) written form – sought to 'make sense' of their postwar lives in relation to the war, its aftermath, and the consequences both brought for them. Their incorporation into urban society and the industrial labour force was achieved through interactions with a developing labour movement, a new emerging liberal intelligentsia and newly radicalized worker priests, as well as through the harsh encounter with Franco's authoritarian state, and, by the 1960s, also with a growing new (especially urban) middling class which prioritized its own needs and material aspirations, supporting Francoism as the bringer of modernity with social peace. These social interactions, and the need of migrants and worker constituencies generally to find solutions to practical problems ignored by the state, would lead to the development of a new political and civic culture focused on democracy.[43]

The considerable reluctance of the new migrant constituencies to discuss the recent past related quite directly to their own experiences in their rural towns or villages of origin. Nevertheless, oblique references abound in the period from the 1940s to the 1970s to 'denunciation', 'shaming', loss of 'honour', 'falling into disgrace', and the often unbearable 'harsh criticisms' or 'sanctions' of neighbours, which made 'remembering past events upsetting' – all of which help the historian penetrate the relative silence of these decades, and reinforce our understanding of how flight was an active strategy which 'separated them from a sorrowful past'.[44] Leaving old communities behind did not necessarily mean that migrants had been involved in actual crimes, but, as we have seen, merely that either they themselves or their family members had been identified with the Republic, and had often as a result transgressed the dominant national-Catholic ideology of much of rural Spain, situating themselves beyond the confines of the inflexible framework of custom, especially those (as we have seen) connected with purity and shame. Some of the migrants' recollections also highlight how the conflict had been a kind of culture war, fought over the possibility of broadening individual horizons and freedoms which thus demanded the reduction of the power of an ultraconservative Church, especially over primary education. The son of an executed Republican mayor in a small southern (Badajoz) village recalled from a 'cultured' Barcelona in the late 1970s, where there was an organized worker and labour movement boosted by thousands of rural migrants, how in a community 'without culture' (his rural pueblo) many people had a very superficial attitude to politics, adopting labels impetuously as best suited their own needs or desires at a given moment: 'Ah, I'm a socialist, or I'm this, or I'm that.' When, after the military coup in 1936, villagers wanted to kill the parish priest, his father the mayor had intervened, arguing for maintaining legality and order. Notwithstanding this, the mayor would later be killed by the village elites (their power re-established in full by victorious Francoism), 'the same *señores* (gentlemen) he had served all his life'.[45] Another landless labourer, born in 1917, who fought for the Republic and migrated from Badajoz to Barcelona in 1956, described the rural system he had known as 'feudal' and the workers as 'the slaves of the powerful', the *caciques*, who had long controlled the situation politically. Challenging this had been a root cause of the war in which he had fought, been captured and imprisoned, and in which his father had been killed.[46]

The impoverishment of so many migrants was, as we have seen, closely related to this political context, many suffering imprisonment for their previous political affiliations. In the small town in Huelva in south-west Spain studied in the 1960s by anthropologist George Collier, some 35 per cent of those on the defeated side in the civil war migrated in the period 1937–50 compared to 25 per cent in the town at large.[47] It was recalled that many of those who left in the 1940s and 1950s, in this depopulation, had earlier been locked up. One migrant, interviewed many years later, put it simply: 'we came from the war … from the prisons'.[48] A migrant inhabitant of industrial Sabadell (Barcelona) explained the process:

> What kind of people came here? All the disinherited, those who did not even have a place to drop dead in their town of origin. We were people who had a restlessness and a tendency towards the left because we had been obliged to leave our homes (*nuestras tierras*[49]) … Sabadell was an epicentre for reception of people from all parts, from every place, and naturally very few fascists came because they were well accommodated in their place of origin.[50]

Migrants recalled in the postwar era how the war had changed everything. The daughter of the Republican woman from rural Aragón discussed earlier who was executed by the insurgents in August 1936, had herself been discriminated against and had suffered greatly afterwards. She would view her own departure from the pueblo as a form of escape:

> When I was eighteen I came here to Barcelona, which was when my life became resolved … When I came here I began to see how I was a person. I had a position in a house in which, although I worked as a servant … they treated me very well … I renounced my pueblo because they exploited me more and they treated me badly. There you were virtually a slave of the *señorial* families. Here I was much more protected and at ease as a person.[51]

The woman from rural Santander also cited earlier, whose family home had been sacked and occupied by neighbours, similarly sought refuge far away, as she explained: 'It should not seem strange that my family loves Catalonia so much, because it opened its arms to us in those moments in which our own *tierra* offered us only hatred'.[52] During the Catalan floods of October 1940 she would meet her future husband, a Republican political prisoner held in Barcelona who was assigned to help with reconstruction work. There she would become one of many in the immediate postwar years who had arrived in the city as political detainees, or to be close to them, and who remained thereafter. Although the relative anonymity and facelessness of urban existence was daunting, it was also liberating. Rural communities were intimate ones; villagers were constantly under the observation of their fellows, which formed part of village sociability, but it was also about surveillance and control – glances and expressions also carried their own sub-texts related to rigid understandings of power and subordination.[53]

Many young women migrants found work as domestic servants and older women as seamstresses in middle-class homes.[54] For thousands of rural migrants, many of them born during the first fifteen years or so after the end of the military conflict, the city was 'a promised land', a perception reinforced by stories relayed back to rural pueblos and working-class suburbs of the south in the 1950s and 1960s by earlier migrants of the immediate postwar era.[55] But villagers' 'fantasies' about life in the city, with migrants largely ignored by the municipal authorities, obscured an often grim reality.[56] When women from the countryside arrived and sought positions in the houses of the wealthy classes, they would be asked to produce papers to show a 'clean' record of moral and political behaviour. Gaining a certificate of good conduct was difficult and some were accused of being 'Reds' and the door was slammed shut.[57] At the same time, other forms of social control began to appear in the urban environment – for example, religious missions were launched to give guidance and instruction through courses of spiritual exercises to 'those without God', and these were aimed at domestic servants and those working in the large factories.[58] They also provided the crucial certificates of good conduct which attracted a good attendance, thereby allowing these Catholic lay missions to claim a working-class religious resurgence. The families of prisoners or those 'redeeming' their political crimes through hard labour made a living as best they could and many depended on the Falangist welfare organization, Auxilio Social (Social Assistance). In Barcelona, in the immediate aftermath of the war, one news report relayed an example of urban social control when it indicated how thirty-four Auxilio children aged from ten to thirteen years, 'all belonging to Marxist families', were 'reintegrated' through baptism under the guidance of the New State.[59]

The causal links connecting successive waves of migration from the 1940s to the 1960s can also be traced through the new social connections forged by inward migrants to the city. One of the first working men with whom the trade unionist and Communist Party activist José López Bulla became acquainted, when he himself migrated as a young man from rural Andalusia to industrial Barcelona in 1965, was the son of a leftist shot by Falangists in Perchel, a working-class neighbourhood of Málaga devastated by the wartime repression in 1937 and from which refugees and then migrants had left in successive train from 1937 onwards.[60]

Inward migration to the city of Barcelona in the four-year period from 1961 to 1964 would total 443,222.[61] Following the general trend for industrial towns in Barcelona province during the postwar period, the population of Mataró, where López Bulla volunteered in a social centre offering support to migrants, grew by 20 per cent in the period 1955–60 and by more than 40 per cent from 1960 to 1965, to almost 60,000. The 77 per cent growth between 1960 and 1970 would be twice the rate of increase in Barcelona as a whole.[62] By the mid-1960s some 44 per cent of residents were born outside Catalonia and almost half the total migrants in the year 1966 came from Andalusia. Even so, the influx to Mataró was relatively small compared to other burgeoning manufacturing towns around Barcelona, such as Hospitalet de Llobregat. Some 50,000 people arrived there during the five years from 1961 to 1965; from a total population of 50,000 in 1940, Hospitalet would expand to 240,000 by 1970.[63] Social marginalization was an inevitable structural consequence of this rapid expansion: the most recent arrivals, again mainly from Andalusia, lived furthest from the centre.[64]

Achieving any measure of social integration was difficult and some migrants reported that it took time for them to feel they had made the right decision in leaving their pueblo. There were memories which recurred, even in dreams, decades later.[65] Economic and social relationships in the city were different to those of rural Spain, though there were also continuities. Work and income were still based on the 'clocking' of daily life and depended on the labour power not only of men but also of women and children.[66] Economic exploitation did not, of course, come to an end: migrants to the city took on the jobs many Catalans did not want to do, and thereby fuelled economic reconstruction.[67] There was also discrimination against migrants to deal with. 'Outsiders' had in the past been blamed for revolutionary violence in Barcelona.[68] The derogatory term *charnego*, used by some to describe those from rural society outside Catalonia, circulated to mark the difference between insiders and outsiders, a situation reinforced by spatial segregation of the shanty communities.[69] The positive feeling of migrants towards Catalans and Catalonia, which has already been noted, was a counterbalance to this discrimination. It was in part founded on an appreciation of a common work ethic and migrants' willingness to adapt.[70] In the new urban landscape it also became possible to express a shared class identity and consciousness, which had become impossible in the rural south since the civil war. The early postwar migrants also arrived in Catalonia at a time when the region was being repressively 'castilianized'.[71] Knowing that many Catalans had also suffered the effects of the civil war grievously contributed, at least for a time, to a new sense of solidarity.[72]

The perception of migrants was that Catalonia offered the prospect of cultural development, where incomers might aspire to a life that was more than mere material survival. In rural society, compared to the city, the repressive force of tradition still weighed heavy. Young women, once married, seemed rapidly to age, though the process at times began with a father's death: 'I began to dress in mourning when I was 18 and didn't cease to until I married at 25'.[73] In the city, people dressed every day 'as though it were Sunday': 'everyone wore shoes'.[74] More than 60 per cent of the active immigrant population were unskilled labourers who had known only rudimentary schooling until the age of nine or ten, because they were needed for work to supplement their family's income. One recalled that 'we were not children as they are now' (1979), and nor did the need for child labour immediately cease once migrants arrived in the city.[75] But there were important underlying structural differences which made life in the city, even with its hardships, much more bearable, and particularly in psychological terms. In the countryside, status was conferred primarily through ownership of land, while in the city one could progress in diverse ways, through professional qualifications, commercial success or trade union activism.[76] This was far harder of course in practice than it was in theory, but, nevertheless, it was possible. Moreover, social mobility came to be within the reach of some migrants because for perhaps the first time they had a regular income. By the end of the 1960s, as long as the wage could be stretched far enough, consumer goods could even be purchased – all of which allowed for the creation of a new perspective on life, freed from the constraints still existing in the village, with everyone more or less beholden to the local landowning elite, even if that power might now be exercised with a greater degree of paternalism.[77] In contrast, too, to how the rural black market of the 1940s and 1950s had functioned, the law was relatively more impartial in the city – whereas in the villages, even in the later Franco decades, it still accorded the prerogative of power to landowners and their retainers.[78] In urban society, public space also meant something different – diversity and the possibility of free activity, instead of signifying dependency, as it did back in the pueblo, for example, where men and women would assemble on the village square in the early hours hoping to be hired for a day's work.[79] Instead of sterile migrant resentment focused on the single dominant landowner backed by the Civil Guard, the sound and fury of a busy, anonymizing factory was, in effect, an ally of the workers, pushing society onward. By the late 1960s, it was possible in the environment of the city to declare oneself a leftist; although if one went beyond words, by organizing or associating collectively, or publishing leftist ideas, this could still end in a prison term: nonetheless, at a time of boom, economic progress increasingly *required* channels of negotiation between capital, labour and the state precisely in order to ensure uninterrupted production.

Gradually, a new political and civic culture would develop. In urban and industrial Madrid and Barcelona migrants and labour leaders would meet, discuss and organize in collaboration with Catholic-Marxist activists, interacting thus with a Church which was quite different to the political norm in rural parishes.[80] In the socially complex city, the roots of an associational culture which functioned between family and state were being laid before the 1960s. This development, parallel to the coming-of-age of a critical postwar intellectual generation, encompassed trade unions (though these were formally illegal and often suppressed), labour lawyers, sections of the Church, and an emerging liberal intelligentsia (which included an increasingly critical and politically engaged literary movement). This interaction encouraged the inculcation of a level of human respect towards migrants and in turn increased a sense of their own worth.[81]

The critical social realist literary movement of the 1950s was composed of young writers who were themselves 'children of the war', born in the period 1925–8. The work produced by such writers as Ignacio Aldecoa, Carmen Martín Gaite, Ana María Matute and Juan Goytisolo, amongst others, was widely read and influenced the thinking of the educated and literate younger generations about the war and its legacy.[82] Their critique of the self-censoring ethos of National-Catholicism was affected profoundly by what they saw of the plight of the defeated and the hardship of migrants in the postwar period. These social realist writers drew on war memories as a way of making sense of the shanty towns and their broader historical significance, as too did political dissidents, progressive sociologists and social psychologists, leftist lawyers and radicalized worker priests.[83] These dissenting voices had emerged in part out of the protests of university students in 1956 – many would join the PCE's clandestine opposition movement in the 1960s – but their dissent had its origins in their observation of the marginalized shanty communities.[84]

In 1956 the writer Carmen Martín Gaite, for example, published an evocative short story exploring postwar social conscience faced with the migratory influx, and which was based on her own earlier experiences volunteering at a charitable clinic in the Madrid shanty town of Vallecas. The story described how a Madrid doctor, influenced by the prevalent received image of migrants, is summoned to the *chabolas* to treat a young girl of a migrant family from Jaén:

> he knew above all that there were so many of them, swarms, which multiplied with each day, emigrating from even poorer places and that they spread, hidden in the backstreets, like a contagion, their dwellings of earth and sun-dried bricks ... They were so many that they advanced towards the better part of the city, invading and contaminating it.[85]

Martín Gaite not only locates the bleak rudimentary and itinerant existence of the migrants on the margins between an urban culture which was future-oriented and represented enlightenment, and the rural void which they had left behind: she also expresses conventional bourgeois responses to population movement in the aftermath of the war, torn between fear of the breakdown of the social order and a sense of conscience.

While young intellectuals, such as the Catholic-Marxist writer and political activist Alfonso Carlos Comín, understood their radicalism as consistent with religious faith, others rejected Catholicism entirely. For the socially committed who did not reject religion, there were already in existence (from the second half of the 1940s) Catholic lay organizations of working-class men and women, such as the HOAC – which was formally controlled by the Church, but more preoccupied with immediate, temporal questions of social justice, and which was accused by the Franco regime of allowing internal 'communist infiltration'.[86] But increasingly by this time, younger priests and lay reformists were reorienting religion towards belief and practice lived in the world, and were in favour of accepting – and even encouraging – greater social dynamism.[87]

Alfonso Comín, born in 1933, had been six when his father died on wartime service for the Francoist side. His father had represented the Carlists as a parliamentary deputy during the Second Republic and there had been conspiratorial political meetings against the government in the family home, and the term 'red' was heard constantly 'to refer to this or that person'.[88] Growing up in the 1940s, Comín would react against such polarizing terms and was soon helping to establish urban social centres within migrant communities, the result of collaborative efforts between priests, self-educating migrant workers and young middle-class lay Catholics. Watched carefully by the police, these centres were locales in which a daily witness to poverty took place, as well as being spaces where practical advice, education and assistance was given.[89] The pioneer was the Jesuit priest (and, later, clandestine Communist Party member), Father José María Llanos, who had established in Madrid the prototype for later social centres in the migrant slums. Several leading radical priests, including Father Llanos, were former Francoists who had as seminarists been indoctrinated against 'Reds', which had seemed to have a logical basis in the anticlerical purge of priests in Republican territory during the war.[90] But by the 1950s, Llanos had turned against the ideological narrative of the civil war as crusade. The Catholic social centres were able to shelter beneath the socially progressive ideas emanating from the Second Vatican Council in the early 1960s, and they became forums for discussion groups about social justice, human rights, political action and economic policy, as laid out in various encyclicals of Pope John XXIII between 1961 and 1967.[91] The fact that the response of the Franco regime to these various initiatives was to see the migrants as an active threat also suggests that they were protagonists in a social process, rather than helpless victims. For the regime, the 'threat' was again viewed historically – and pathologically: as one reform-minded insider commented, 'it cannot seem strange that, in certain moments, this type of individual produces revolutionary situations, bloody and destructive, because the deformation which structures his life bring him towards moments of desperation.'[92] Accordingly, those seen as 'abetting' them also became the target of state action: for example, four Catalan priests were sentenced to a year's imprisonment for their part in a demonstration in May 1966, which included delivering a letter of protest about migrants' conditions to both the Archbishop of Barcelona and the city's police chief.[93]

The principal Catholic lay organization, Acción Católica (AC), was also active in missionary work amongst the migrants, and in the 1960s it began to respond to the reforming messages from Rome. For example, in 1962 the National Women's Council of AC established a Civic-Social Commission, and in 1966 distributed a questionnaire about 'citizenship formation' to its various sections. The responses indicated social commitment was a high priority of members who repeatedly emphasized matters of 'social conscience' and 'worldly commitment'.[94] The AC groups worked alongside autonomous oppositionist and neighbourhood associations in the 1960s.[95] Although the 'urban revolution' (mass migration) had produced a challenge for pastoral and evangelical work which the Church would ultimately find unmanageable without state intervention, the Second Vatican Council had given impetus to highly significant reform within the Spanish Church. While, for radicals, the Council's decrees on religious freedom were 'safe-conducts (*salvoconductos*) for some to defend themselves with religious arguments against a state which legitimated itself religiously', as far as the Franco regime was concerned, the decrees encouraged 'subversion'.[96]

These very debates point up the structural continuity between the civil war and its repressive aftermath, the ensuing mass migration, and subsequent calls for toleration and reform. Looking back from 1978 at the response in Spain to the Vatican-led Catholic reforms of the 1960s, the Archbishop of Madrid, Cardinal Vicente Enrique y Tarancón, who by that point had become a figurehead of forward-thinking Catholicism, drew attention to the migration of working-class people to Spain's cities as having exerted a key influence on the Church:

> Large sections of the working population, notably enlarged by industrial expansion, profoundly jolted in their consciences by the cultural consequences of migration and up-rooting, explicitly demonstrated their lack of confidence and distance with respect to a Church which since the time of the civil war, without looking for origins longer ago, they viewed as indifferent to their problems, spiritually and materially removed from their ways of living and even in opposition to their aspirations.[97]

Various housing plans produced high-rise solutions: poorly constructed *chabolas verticales*, as they were popularly called, were insufficient to tackle the problem – indeed the national housing deficit was calculated as 3.7 million in 1972, with 52 per cent of the country deemed as badly housed.[98] A report from the Instituto Nacional de Estadística (National Institute of Statistics) in early 1969 claimed that there had been a marked increase in meeting people's basic needs, 'which has much to do with the current consumer society', but it also indicated that 34 per cent of homes in Spain still had no running water and 68 per cent of rural families were without electricity.[99] The refusal of the local and central state to take any responsibility for remedying these structural deficiencies would become a primary motive behind the campaigns of urban neighbourhood associations in the later 1960s, whose protests would gradually develop into broader campaigns in the 1970s in favour of democracy and an amnesty for detained political opponents of the regime.[100]

## Conclusions

It was from within these grass-roots networks of neighbourhood, Catholic, women's and trade union associations, and the cooperative social, cultural and political relationships they forged that a civic culture gradually re-emerged in Spain, one which would later support the transition to democracy. At the same time, it was within this world of rapid urbanization and accompanying social marginalization that there was nurtured and sheltered a more complex social memory of the war and its consequences. Although there appeared to be a pervasive social stasis in the 1940s, once we look at the demographic roots of the beginning of industrial take-off in the 1950s, we can see that it was dependent on the availability of a pliant, cheap and largely migrant workforce which, as a social phenomenon, had its origins in the civil war itself and in the war's repressive and hungry aftermath.

For the landless poor, who had been amongst the most solid supporters of the Second Republic, defeat in the war had destroyed the revolutionary myths of the 1930s, a blow which would reinforce their impulse for flight from the countryside.[101] This socio-psychological rupture reinforced a dissociation from the past more broadly, as links with the culture and forms of identity of the pueblo and with previous generations were broken. Although large-scale urbanization in Spain had begun in the pre-civil-war period, between 1910 and 1930 – a process which itself helps explain the arrival of the Second Republic in 1931 – the outcome of the civil war supposed a break, with the victorious Franco coalition attempting to turn the clock back. However, with defeated constituencies faced by unprecedented levels of economic exploitation, social discrimination and violence in the countryside, clandestine migration took off again from 1939, a process which was in some respects also a continuation of the movement of wartime refugees which had begun right back in the in the summer of 1936, as the insurgent forces began to control and conquer territory.

The 1940s constitute a social watershed because they saw the start of the definitive modernization of Spain from below: not through the grandiose autarkic strategy of the

Franco state, but through a rebellious and self-motivated transfer of labour power which would become a veritable flood by the 1960s. This also provoked a social response from sectors of Spain's urban middling classes: not all, as this sector was complex and fragmented, with some parts translating their new-found affluence, especially of the later 1950s onwards, into political support for Francoism. But some more established and/or more liberal urban middle-class sectors still held the memory of support for the Second Republic's democratic political revolution in 1931 and, either by necessity or also out of social conscience, they began to interact with the burgeoning migrant workforce. In the face of this change, they began to re-prioritize democratic ideals and demand action from the state to provide the basis of an integrative, peaceful and more just social order.[102] This combined process from below would form the social basis of Spain's transition to democracy.

## Notes

1. Paul Preston, *Franco: A Biography* (London: HarperCollins, 1993), pp. 782–7.

2. Raúl Morodo, *La transición política* (Madrid: Tecnos, 1993), pp. 79–86.

3. For a recent statement of Franco's legacy (his 'monument') as 'prosperity' and 'organic solidarity' in Spain, see Stanley Payne and Jesús Palacios, *Franco: A Personal and Political Biography* (Madison: University of Wisconsin Press, 2014), p. 515. According to this interpretation, the Caudillo was 'the country's definitive modernizer'; the creator of post-1975 'peaceful coexistence', an analysis which neglects Franco's divisive postwar economic strategy of autarky, and is devoid of any sense of the dictatorship's legacy of fear, including the attempted military coup to halt democratization in February 1981.

4. Michael Richards, 'Falange, Autarky and Crisis: The Barcelona General Strike of 1951', *European History Quarterly* 29:4 (1999), pp. 543–85.

5. Civil Governor of Asturias, Francisco Labadie Otermín, 13 February 1951, Archivo General de la Administración, Secretaría General del Movimiento; Secretaría Política; 51/19018. For his criticisms Labadie was accused by one Minister of being a 'demagogue' and his dismissal proposed: Labadie letter, 26 April 1951.

6. The National Archives (TNA) FO371/96158/WS1016/41, 16 May 1951.

7. Pablo Martín Aceña and Francisco Comín, *INI: 50 años de industrialización en España* (Madrid: Espasa Calpe, 1991), p. 111.

8. Manuel Fuentes Irurozqui, 'Prefacio', in Mihail Manoilescu, *Teoría del proteccionismo y del comercio internacional* (Madrid: n.p., 1943), pp. xiii–xiv.

9. E.g. Ofelia Ferrán, 'Memory and Forgetting: Resistance and Noise in the Spanish Transition: Semprún and Vázquez Montalbán', in Joan Ramón Resina (ed.), *Disremembering the Dictatorship: The Politics of Memory in the Spanish Transition to Democracy* (Amsterdam: Rodopi, 2000), pp. 191–224: p. 193; Josep Ramoneda, 'Memoria, amnesia, perdón', *El País*, 7 November 1997.

10. E.g. Salustiano del Campo Urbano, Manuel Fraga and José Velarde Fuertes, *La España de los años 70: la sociedad, la economía y la política*, 3 vols. (Madrid: Editorial Moneda y Credito, 1972).

11. E.g. Abdón Mateos and Álvaro Soto, *El final del franquismo, 1959–1975. La transformación de la sociedad española* (Madrid: Historia 16, 1997); Nigel Townson (ed.), *Spain Transformed: The Late Franco Dictatorship, 1959–75* (Basingstoke: Palgrave, 2007).

12. Jaume Botey Vallès, *Cinquanta-quatre relats d'immigració* (Barcelona: Diputació de Barcelona, 1986), p. 69; Carlos Gil Andrés, *Lejos del frente: La guerra civil en la Rioja Alta* (Barcelona: Crítica, 2006), p. 448; George A. Collier, *Socialists of Rural Andalusia: Unacknowledged Revolutionaries of the Second Republic* (Stanford, CA: Stanford University Press, 1987), p. 31.

13. E.g. Francisco Lara Sánchez, *La emigración andaluza* (Madrid: Ediciones de la Torre, 1977), p. 193; Alfonso Lazo, *Retrato de fascismo rural en Sevilla* (Seville: Universidad de Sevilla, 1998), p. 59; Collier, *Socialists*, pp. 9, 23–4, 41–4. Denunciation has been defined as 'the volunteered provision of information by the population at large about instances of disapproved behaviour': Robert Gellately, *The Gestapo and German Society: Enforcing Racial Policy, 1933–1945* (Oxford: Clarendon Press, 1990), p. 130. For an overview in Spanish rebel zone: Angela Cenarro, 'Matar, vigilar y delatar: la quiebra de la sociedad civil durante la guerra y la posguerra en España (1936–1948)', *Historia Social* 44 (2002), pp. 65–86; Peter Anderson, 'In the Interests of Justice? Grass-roots Prosecution and Collaboration in Francoist Military Trials, 1939–1945', *Contemporary European History* 18:1 (2009), pp. 25–44.

14. E.g. Francisco Espinosa Maestre, *La guerra civil en Huelva* (Huelva: Diputación de Huelva, 1996), pp. 374–8; Vicente Gabarda Ceballán, *Els afusellaments al País Valencià (1938–1956)* (Valencia: Universitat de València, 1993), pp. 44–50; Francisco Sevillano Calero, 'Consenso y violencia en el "Nuevo Estado" franquista', *Historia Social* 46 (2003), pp. 159–71; Francisco Cobo Romero and Teresa María Ortega López, *Franquismo y posguerra en Andalucía oriental* (Granada: Universidad de Granada, 2005), p. 125.

15. Mercè Barallat, 'La repressió en la postguerra civil a Lleida', in *El primer franquisme a les terres de Lleida (1938–1950)* (Lérida: Institut d'Estudis Ilerdencs, 2002), p. 69.

16. E.g. Ricard Vinyes, Montse Armengou and Ricard Belis, *Los niños perdidos del franquismo* (Barcelona: Plaza y Janés, 2002), pp. 90–1; Botey Vallès, *Relats*, p. 75; Jordi Roca i Girona, *De la pureza a la maternidad. La construcción del género femenino en la postguerra española* (Madrid: Ministerio de Educación y Cultura, 1996), p. 30; Alfonso Bullón de Mendoza and Álvaro de Diego, *Historias orales de la guerra civil* (Barcelona: Ariel, 2000), pp. 154, 178, 189–90; Francisco Moreno Gómez, *Córdoba en la posguerra* (Córdoba: Francisco Baena, 1987), p. 304; José Sánchez Jiménez, *Vida rural y mundo contemporáneo* (Barcelona: Planeta, 1976), p. 247; Giuliana Di Febo, *Resistencia y movimiento de mujeres en España, 1936–1976* (Barcelona: Icaria, 1979), pp. 96–7. On women and repression, see also Helen Graham, *The War and Its Shadow: Spain's Civil War in Europe's Long Twentieth Century* (Eastbourne: Sussex Academic Press, 2012), especially pp. 53–73.

17. E.g. Gil, *Lejos*, pp. 218–9; Ronald Fraser, *Blood of Spain: The Experience of Civil War, 1936–1939* (Harmondsworth: Penguin, 1979), p. 150; Víctor Morales Lezcano and Teresa Pereira Rodríguez, *Memoria oral de una transformación social* (Madrid: UNED, 1997), pp. 39, 79, 107, 120–2; Carlota Solé, *Los inmigrantes en la sociedad y en la cultura catalanas* (Barcelona: Península, 1982), pp. 66, 78–84, 97; Richard Barker, *El largo trauma de un pueblo andaluz* (Seville: Ayuntamiento de Castilleja del Campo, 2007), pp. 119–20.

18. Angelina Puig i Valls, 'La guerra civil española: una causa de l'emigració andalusa en la dècada dels anys cinquanta?', *Recerques* 31 (1995), pp. 53–69: p. 65.

19. Personal testimony, Carlos Elordi (ed.), *Los años difíciles* (Madrid: Aguilar, 2002), pp. 196–7.

20. Testimony, Puig i Valls, 'La guerra civil', p. 57. Also, Botey Vallès, *Relats*, p. 78; Miguel Siguán, *Del campo al suburbio: un estudio sobre la inmigración interior en España* (Madrid: CSIC, 1959), p. 89.

21. E.g. Botey Vallès, *Relats*, pp. 71–2.

22. E.g. Botey Vallès, *Relats*, p. 75.

23. José Palanca, 'Hacia el fin de una epidemia', *Semana Médica Española* 4: 2 (1941), pp. 431–40: p. 432.

24. Archivo de Acción Católica de Madrid (AAC), Caja 93, 'Secretariado de migración – propuestas (1952–1954)', Carpeta 93-1-2, report, 27 April 1954.

25. E.g. Elordi (ed.), *Años difíciles*, pp. 308–10. See also Jesús Gutiérrez Flores, *Guerra civil en Cantabria y pueblos de Castilla* (Buenos Aires: Libros en Red, 2006).

26. Elordi, *Años difíciles*, pp. 182–7. Also Julián Casanova, Angela Cenarro, Julita Cifuente, María del Pilar Maluenda and María del Pilar Salomón, *El pasado oculto: Fascismo y violencia en Aragón, (1936–1939)* (Madrid: Mira, 1992), p. 398.

27. E.g. María González Gorosarri, *No lloréis, lo que tenéis que hacer es no olvidarnos: la cárcel de Santurrarán y la represión franquista contra las mujeres* (San Sebastián: Ttartalo, 2010), pp. 119–24; José López Bulla, *Cuando hice las maletas: un paseo por el ayer* (Barcelona: Península, 1997), p. 21; Botey Vallès, *Relats*, p. 99; Francisco Candel, *Los otros catalanes* (Barcelona: Península, 1965), p. 118; Siguán, *Del campo al suburbio*, pp. 89, 101; Collier, *Socialists*, p. 191.

28. 'El pueblo "sin permiso" desapareció ayer', *ABC*, 16 July 1955. See also Siguán, *Del campo*, pp. 59, 69, 94, 98.

29. Florentino del Valle, 'La inmigración en Madrid', in Semanas Sociales, *Los problemas de la migración española* (Madrid: Semanas Sociales, 1959), p. 390.

30. Siguán, *Del campo*, p. 245.

31. Candel, *Otros*, p. 121; Solé, *Inmigrantes*, p. 65.

32. E.g. *Nuestra Bandera*, May 1950, pp. 413–14.

33. Cited in *Libertad Española* 7, 16 August 1956, p. 8.

34. 'El pueblo "sin permiso"'; Antoni Batista, *La Brigada Social* (Barcelona: Empúries, 1995).

35. Esperanza Molina, *Los otros madrileños* (Madrid: El Avapiés, 1984), p. 24; Botey Vallès, *Relats*, pp. 97–8.

36. Botey Vallès, *Relats*, p. 99.

37. *Libertad Española* 7, 16 August 1956, p. 8; Valle, 'Inmigración', p. 377.

38. E.g. the Third Industrial Congress of the Falangist syndicates, December 1944: Alberto Ribas i Massana, *L'economía catalana sota el franquisme* (Barcelona: Edicions 62, 1978), pp. 118–24, 135–42.

39. Cristóbal Gómez Benito, *Políticos, burócratas y expertos: un estudio de la política agraria y la sociología rural en España (1936–1959)* (Madrid: Siglo XXI, 1996), p. 240.

40. José María Basabé Prado, 'Efectos del ambiente suburbial sobre el biotipo del inmigrante', *Estudios Geográficos* XXVII:105 (1966), pp. 579–605.

41. José Antonio Martín Fernández to Ministerio de Gobernación, 'Informe – Valores municipales', May 1944, AGA, SGM, Vicesecretaria; 52/14146.

42. Valle, 'Inmigración', p. 382.

43. Santos Juliá, 'Obreros y sacerdotes: cultura democrática y movimientos sociales de oposición', in Javier Tusell et al. (eds), *La oposición al régimen de Franco*, Vol. II (Madrid: UNED, 1990), pp. 147–59.

44. Siguán, *Del campo al suburbio*, pp. 76–80, 114.

45. Botey Vallès, *Relats*, pp. 74–6.

46. Botey Vallès, *Relats*, pp. 49–50. On deserted '*caciques*', p. 53.

47. Collier, *Socialists*, pp. 171–2, 175. See also, Morales and Pereira, *Memoria*, pp. 79, 107, 120, 122.

48. Morales and Pereira, *Memoria*, p. 154. Also Candel, *Otros*, pp. 115–17; Carmen Martín Gaite, *Esperando el porvenir: homenaje a Ignacvio Aldecoa* (Madrid: Siruela, 1994), p. 93.

49. The sense is of [home]land, which reflects the fusion of 'home' with a specific local territory in what was still an overwhelmingly rural culture and popular imaginary.

50. Cited in Xavier Domènech Sampere, 'La otra cara del milagro español: clase obrera y movimiento obrero en los años del desarrollismo', *Historia Contemporánea* 26 (2003), pp. 91–112. Also, for example, on 'Los Olivos' in the Aracena valley in Huelva, Collier, *Socialists*, p. 20; Sebastian Balfour, *Dictatorship, Workers and the City: Labour in Greater Barcelona since 1939* (Oxford: Clarendon Press, 1989), pp. 31–2.

51. Personal testimony, Elordi (ed.), *Años difíciles*, pp. 187–9. Also Mercedes Vilanova, 'Las fronteras interiores en la sociedad de Barcelona, 1900–1975', in *Historia, Antropología y Fuentes Orales* 1:16 (1996), pp. 123–39: p. 133.

52. Elordi, *Años difíciles*, p. 310. Also Solé, *Inmigrantes*, pp. 83–5 and pp. 65–9.

53. López Bulla, *Cuando hice*, pp. 25–7, 45. Also Botey Vallès, *Relats*, p. 119.

54. E.g. Puig i Valls, 'La guerra civil', pp. 64–7; Siguán, *Del campo*, pp. 98, 116, 251–2; Jesús María Vázquez, *El servicio doméstico en España* (Madrid: INP, 1960).

55. López Bulla, *Cuando hice las maletas*, p. 21. See also Solé, *Inmigrantes*, p. 103; Botey Vallès, *Relats*, p. 99; Candel, *Los otros catalanes*, p. 118.

56. López Bulla, *Cuando hice*, p. 79. On the peripheral migrant suburbs, see Rogelio Duocastella et al., *Mataró: estudio socio-económico y de planificación de servicios sociales* (Barcelona: ISPA, 1967), Vol. I, p. 11; 5.1–5.3, 6.5–6.6 and Vol. II, 9.21–22.

57. E.g. María Encarna Nicolás Marín, 'Actitudes de la sociedad murciana en la etapa 1936–1978', in José Manuel Trujillano and Pilar Sánchez Díaz (eds), *V Jornadas Historia y Fuentes orales. Testimonios orales y escritos. España, 1936–1996* (Ávila: Fundación Cultural Santa Teresa, 1998), p. 123.

58. Aurelio Orensanz, *Religiosidad popular Española, 1940–1965* (Madrid: Editora Nacional, 1974), p. 10.

59. *La Vanguardia Española* (*Suplemento Gráfico*), 11 August 1939, p. 2; 12 August 1939, p. 2; 16 August 1939, p. 4.

60. López Bulla, *Cuando hice*, p. 141. Also J. Piquer y Jover, 'Consideración etiológica sobre algunas fallas del juicio moral en la disciplina del niño abandonado de la postguerra española', *Actas Españolas de Neurología y Psiquiatría* IV: 2–3 (1943), pp. 159–67: p. 166.

61. (No author), *Conversaciones sobre inmigración* (Barcelona, 1966), p. 40.

62. Duocastella et al., *Mataró*, Vol. I, p. 0.11; Raimon Bonal, *Mataró 1974* (Barcelona: Caritas Interparroquial, 1974), pp. 13–14.

63. The period 1950–80 saw a 423 per cent rise in population (70,000 to 300,000). See Clara Carme Parramón, 'Polític cultural i migracions, l'Hospitalet, 1960–1980', in Carles Santacana (ed.), *El franquisme al Baix Llobregat* (Barcelona: L'Abadia de Montserrat, 2001), pp. 483–505: p. 484. On similar levels in Sabadell, Solé, *Inmigrante*, p. 79; on vast influx to Badalona, *Conversaciones sobre inmigración*, p. 141.

64. Angels Pascual, 'El impacto de la inmigración en una ciudad de la comarca de Barcelona: Hospitalet', in Antoni Jutglar et al. (eds), *La inmigración en Cataluña* (Barcelona: Edición de Materiales, 1968), pp. 71–8: p. 74.

65. López Bulla, *Cuando hice*, pp. 47, 52. On forced migration within Spain as 'exilio', Armando López Salinas, *La Mina* (Barcelona: Destino, 1960), p. 39. On dreams, Botey Vallès, *Relats*, p. 49.

66. López Bulla, *Cuando hice*, pp. 49, 50–3. Also Pilar Díaz Sánchez, *El trabajo de las mujeres en el textil madrileño* (Málaga: Universidad, 2001), pp. 92–166.

67. Botey Vallès, *Relats*, pp. 114–15, 143; Candel, *Otros*, pp. 89–90; Lara, *Emigración*, pp. 195–6.

68. E.g. Fraser, *Blood*, pp. 141, 149.

69. Many believed the postwar influx was politically provoked by the state to dilute Catalan (and Basque) identity. Candel, *Otros*, pp. 120–1; 'Emigración, un tema para denuncia', *Boletín HOAC* 705, cited in Lara, *Emigración*, pp. 202–3.

70. Duocastella et al., *Mataró*, Vol. I, 5.19, 5.29; Solé, *Inmigrantes*, pp. 66, 78, 86; Botey Vallès, *Relats*, p. 122.

71. Candel, *Otros*, p. 79. The civil war formed a political, social and cultural barrier: 'the Catalonia of before was distinct from that of now (1964)': Candel, p. 84.

72. López Bulla, *Cuando hice*, pp. 115–16, 125–9, 130–3.

73. Botey Vallès, *Relats*, p. 89.

74. On *alpargatas* (rope sandals) hung around the neck in the countryside to save them from wear and put on the feet when entering the village at the end of the working day, see López Salinas, *La Mina*, pp. 12–13. Also Botey Vallès, *Relats*, pp. 56, 59–60, 64.

75. 'Gracia', born Zamora, 1933 in Botey Vallès, *Relats*, p. 61. See also pp. 53–8; Duocastella et al., *Mataró*, Vol. I, pp. 1.12, 1.14–15, 1.18; Candel, *Otros*, p. 31; López Bulla, *Cuando hice*, pp. 34–5, 119.

76. Miguel Siguán, 'Actitudes y perspectivas de la inmigración', *Conversaciones*, p. 144.

77. José María Marín et al., *Historia política, 1939–2000* (Madrid: Istmo, 2001), p. 160.

78. Botey Vallès, *Relats*, p. 71.

79. Memories: Morales and Pereira, *Memoria oral*, pp. 130–1; Botey Vallès, *Relats*, p. 90.

80. On rural Church, see J. Sánchez Jiménez, 'La jerarquía eclesiástica y el estado franquista: las prestaciones mutuas', *Ayer* 33 (1999); and urban priests dissociated from political and economic power: e.g. Botey Vallès, *Relats*, p. 86; Solé, *Inmigrantes*, p. 76. On left and Catholics: Carlos Castilla del Pino, *Casa del olivo* (Barcelona: Tusquets Editores, 2004), pp. 180, 350.

81. López Bulla, *Cuando hice*, pp. 20, 70–5; Botey Vallès, *Relats*, pp. 97, 141. On migrants' own sense of inferiority: e.g. Siguán, 'Actitudes y perspectivas', p. 143.

82. E.g. Piñero Valverde, 'Mi viejo álbum', in María Guadalupe Pedrero and Concha Piñero, *Tejiendo recuerdos de la España de ayer* (Madrid: Narcea, 2006), p. 59.

83. These included the social psychologist Miguel Siguán: Castilla del Pino, *Casa del olivo*, p. 353.

84. See, e.g. Marcos Ana, *Decidme cómo es un árbol* (Barcelona: Umbriel, 2007), pp. 37–8.

85. Carmen Martín Gaite, 'La conciencia tranquila', in Martín Gaite, *Cuentos completos* (Madrid: Alianza, 1981), pp. 309–24: pp. 314–15.

86. Basilisa López García, *Aproximación a la historia de la HOAC, 1946–1981* (Madrid: Alianza, 1995), pp. 49–60.

87. José María Llanos, *Ser católico y obrar como tal* (Bilbao: Mensajero, 1968), pp. 20–1, 31–8, 175–98.

88. Alfonso Carlos Comín, 'Fe en la tierra' (1975), in Comín, *Obras*, Vol. II (Barcelona: Fundació Alfons Comín, 1987), p. 302.

89. Batista, *La Brigada Social*, pp. 202–3. Also López Bulla, *Cuando hice*, p. 136; *Documentación Social: Los Centros Sociales* (Madrid: Caritas Española, 1958), p. 5.

90. E.g. Alberto Iniesta, *Recuerdos de la Transición* (Madrid: PPC, 2002).

91. *Ecclesia*, 23 January 1965, p. 16; 6 February 1965, pp. 19–20; Dionisio Ridruejo, 'El santo y su milagro' (1964), *Entre literatura y política* (Madrid: Seminarios y Ediciones, 1973), p. 153. See also Joaquín Ruiz Giménez, in *Vida Nueva*, reprinted in *Apostolado Seglar* 205 (1966), n.p.

92. See 'El fin del suburbio', *Cuadernos para el Diálogo* (*CPED*) 4 (1964), p. 4.

93. *La Vanguardia Española*, 6 March 1969, p. 6.

94. 'Resumen de las contestaciones recibidas al cuestionario sobre formación cívico-social' (1966), AAC, Caja 95, Carpeta 95-1-7.

95. See, e.g. Pamela Beth Radcliff, *Making Democratic Citizens in Spain: Civil Society and the Popular Origins of the Transition, 1960–78* (Basingstoke: Palgrave, 2011).

96. Olegario González de Cardedal (ed.), *Iglesia y política en España* (Salamanca: Sígueme, 1980), p. 35. Also *CPED* 1 (1963), pp. 26–7.

97. Enrique y Tarancón, 'La iglesia en España hoy', *Iglesia y política*, p. 72.

98. Mario Gómez-Morán y Cima, *Sociedad sin vivienda* (Madrid: Euramérica, 1972), cited in *FOESSA: estudios*, p. 421; Ramón Tamames, *Estructura económica de España* (Madrid: Alianza, 1980), pp. 572–3, 578; Jaume Fabre and Josep M. Huertas, 'Crònica d'una suburbialització', *L'Avenç* 88 (1985), pp. 45–9.

99. *La Vanguardia Española*, 18 January 1969, p. 7.

100. E.g. Juan Mayoral et al., *Vallecas: las razones de una lucha popular* (Madrid: Mañana, 1976), pp. 36, 97–112.

101. Juan Martínez Alier, *Labourers and Landowners in Southern Spain* (Totowa, NJ: Rowman and Littlefield, 1971), esp. pp. 31–2, 234–8; Miguel Bernal, 'Resignación de los campesinos andaluces: la resistencia pasiva durante el franquismo', in David Ruiz et al., *España franquista: Causa General y actitudes sociales ante la dictadura* (Castilla-La Mancha: Universidad, 1993), pp. 145–59.

102. Santos Juliá has persuasively argued a similar case, though his thesis focuses specifically on the 1960s, without making a direct connection to the preceding two postwar decades: 'Orígenes sociales de la democracia en España', *Ayer* 15 (1994), pp. 165–88.

## Further reading

Anderson, P., *The Francoist Military Trials: Terror and Complicity, 1939–1945*, London: Routledge, 2010.

Balfour, S., *Dictatorship, Workers and the City: Labour in Greater Barcelona since 1939*, Oxford: Clarendon Press, 1989.

Graham, H., *The War and Its Shadow: Spain's Civil War in Europe's Long Twentieth Century*, Eastbourne: Sussex Academic Press, 2012.

Preston, P., *Franco: A Biography*, London: HarperCollins, 1993.

Richards, M., *After the Civil War: Making Memory and Re-making Spain since 1936*, Cambridge: Cambridge University Press, 2013.

# CHAPTER 9
## DISREMEMBERING FRANCOISM: WHAT IS AT STAKE IN SPAIN'S MEMORY WARS?

*Julián Casanova*

Translated from Spanish by Linda Palfreeman and Helen Graham

General Francisco Franco and the victors in the civil war of 1936 to 1939 set in motion and consolidated a fear-based state founded on military law and courts martial. The new Franco regime had, from the beginning, the monopoly of violence, with extraordinary mechanisms of terror sanctioned and legitimized by often legally highly questionable 'laws'. But even these norms were violated, thus increasing the extent and effectiveness of the terror. This procedural system, fully erected once the war on the battlefield had ended, maintained its continuity throughout the dictatorship. Torture was legalized with the *Fuero de los españoles* (the Spanish Charter), the pseudo-constitutional political text stating the 'rights' of the Franco regime, adopted on 17 July 1945, the ninth anniversary of the military uprising. Prisoners were kept in police stations for days, humiliated and tormented. There were times when no detention was even registered.

Franco's dictatorship was, in short, a regime of terror that, like all modern terror systems, rested not only on state power but also on the support of some sectors of society who helped the state to violate systematically the human rights of other sectors of the Spanish population. There is no doubt about the definition and existence of these political crimes. The democratic transition of the later 1970s and early 1980s, however, forgave them, amnestying the perpetrators of Francoist state violence (police and army personnel above all) and closing the subject without any public discussion. But in recent years, in the absence of any restorative initiative from state or government, there has developed in Spain a bitter debate about historical memories and over the question of compensation for victims of the dictatorship; almost four decades after the death of Franco there are also calls for 'retributive justice' against those still living who were responsible for these crimes.

Franco's forty-year dictatorship always remembered its victory in the civil war. The fact that it remained militarily undefeated is important in explaining its political durability, and even 'charisma'. From its first days, it began to create places of memory which it embedded physically across Spain and psychologically within Spanish society. This regime-driven production of public remembrance began even before the end of the military conflict of 1936–9 when, on 16 November 1938, a decree by the Head of State proclaimed 20 November to be 'national mourning day', in memory of the execution of José Antonio Primo de Rivera, the leader of the Spanish fascist party, the Falange, on that same day in 1936. The decree established, 'in agreement with the church authorities', that 'the walls of every parish will bear an inscription containing the names of the Fallen during this Crusade, victims of the Marxist revolution'.

This was the origin of the appearance of plaques in churches, carrying commemorative inscriptions of '*caídos por Dios y por la Patria*' ('fallen for God and Fatherland'). The traveller can still see these mounted on or carved into the ancient stone of Romanesque, Gothic and Baroque monuments in many places across Spain. And, although it was not prescribed in the decree itself, the majority of these inscriptions are headed by the name of José Antonio, thereby converted into the sacred symbol of all those who died for the insurgent cause. All were named as 'martyrs of the Crusade' because Franco's side declared its cause to be not only political but also religious. Indeed, as was categorically declared by Aniceto de Castro Albarrán, Canon of Salamanca, in his book *Guerra Santa* (also published in 1938), all the victims of what he termed the 'Russian barbarism' were to be considered religious victims, not only the clergy. These included 'the most prominent Catholics, the most pious people, the most rightist apostles, all those, in short, whose martyrdom signified, exclusively, religious hatred and persecution of the Church'.[1] With this reading, the Franco coalition was imposing a highly sectarian version of the civil war which singled out one category of the dead – those it defined as 'religious martyrs' – for special state honours. Needless to say, the category is highly contentious, not least because many priests and lay Catholics had also been killed by Franco's forces for opposing the 'Crusade'.

After the war, during Franco's uncivil peace, the victors settled accounts with the defeated, reminding them for decades who were the patriots and who were the 'traitors'. Streets, public squares, schools and hospitals in hundreds of towns and cities bore thereafter (in many cases to this day) the names of military insurgents, high-ranking fascist leaders and pro-insurgent Catholic politicians. Some names are much repeated, such as those of the generals who led the July 1936 rebellion against emergent democracy in Spain – Franco, Yagüe, Millan Astray, Sanjurjo. Also frequently featured alongside José Antonio Primo de Rivera are other figures from the fascist firmament – notably Onésimo Redondo, one of the most uncompromising founders of Spanish fascism and of its use of violence, who was killed in fighting at the start of the conflict on 24 July 1936, in the Guadarrama mountains north of Madrid.[2]

There are provinces that surpass all others, such as Murcia in the south-east of Spain, where it is difficult to find a single town which has not kept Francoist symbols on streets, monuments, crosses and gravestones. It was in Murcia, during the Second Republic, that José Ibáñez Martín, Franco's first Minister of Education (1939–51), began his political career and where, in his honour, several schools bear his name. It would not be unusual for a school to bear the name of an education minister, were it not for the fact that this particular minister, along with his team of ultra-Catholic functionaries, began his career by purging from their jobs and punishing with fines thousands of teachers associated with the Republic, thereby turning the Spanish school system into a form of war booty to be distributed among regime-identified Catholic families, Falangists and other former Francoist combatants.

The final consecration of the memory of the victors of the civil war came, however, with the construction of the *Valle de los Caídos* (Valley of the Fallen), 'the glorious pantheon of heroes', as this monument, part-mausoleum, part basilica, was called by brother Justo Pérez de Urbel (professor of History at the University of Madrid, apologist of Franco's 'Crusade' and appointed as the first mitred abbot of the abbey of the Valle de los Caídos). It was inaugurated on 1 April 1959, after nearly twenty years in construction, during which time thousands of 'captive reds' laboured there as political prisoners. This was a site intended to portray the grandeur of Franco's cause and to withstand the passage of time and fading memory, an eternal tribute to the sacrifice of 'the heroes and martyrs of the Crusade' who were embedded at the base of the regime's political legitimacy.[3]

The other dead, the many thousands of compatriots categorized as 'red traitors' who had been extrajudicially killed during the war and its institutionalized aftermath did not officially exist, either because their deaths had never been registered, or else because the cause of death had been falsified. 'Skull fracture' or 'gun-shot wound' were euphemisms frequently appearing in the official records of the deceased – and this was a cover-up in which some bishops and priests were highly complicit. The bodies of these other dead were abandoned in fields, under cemetery walls and in mass graves. So their families, their children and grandchildren, are still looking for them today, aided now by various associations and forums for what is termed 'the recovery of historical memory'. They want, quite simply, remembrance and dignity, much less indeed than has already been accorded the hundreds of 'martyrs of the cross' – i.e. those commemorated for decades by the Francoist state – for whom the Spanish Catholic Church and the Vatican have assiduously sought (and still seek) beatification.

Streets, monuments, symbols, rituals and victims, all this and much more remains in Spain today as a direct legacy of Franco, four decades after the dictator's death – just as the legacy is present too in numerous political figures of the dictatorship still active in politics or public life today and who have never relinquished their authoritarian convictions. Others in Spanish society, with contrasting beliefs, want, via the historical memory campaign, to bring into the spotlight events and people that official history has still not documented – particularly in the cases of atrocity and violations of citizens' rights (some with still lasting effects today). Still other groups proclaim themselves tired of hearing so much about the history and memory of the war and the long ensuing dictatorship. What is certain however, is that the past has erupted into the present, with books, documents and other public tributes today giving particular prominence to the experience and memories of *survivors* of these traumatic experiences.

With regard to the Franco dictatorship, we are now in the 'age of memory', which has brought a return to the hidden and repressed past that is so uncomfortable for many. But we must bear in mind too that this is *memory*, not history – memory as the social reconstruction of the past and which, as is the way with the workings of memory, sometimes distorts what historians have discovered. Again, the problem goes back to Franco's dictatorship – precisely because of its lengthy repression and the way it perpetrated its own massive manipulation of Spain's recent past, it left what we might call a 'barbed' memory. For that very reason, and like everything repressed, it has returned under a rather different guise, updated by those who have inherited the memory.

Traumatic pasts, wars and dictatorships often cause conflicts between different memories, both of individuals and groups, and between different ways of looking at history. Although Spaniards commonly believe that not agreeing over the past and having (sometimes bitterly) conflicting memories of it, is a peculiarity of their own country and culture, in reality, similar fractures have occurred (and still occur) in all countries which have suffered criminal political regimes – such as, among others, Nazi Germany, Stalinist Russia, the military dictatorships of Chile and Argentina or Franco's Spain. And both history and memory, far from being neutral ground, become a political and a cultural battleground. This is the present situation in Spain, eighty years after the start of the civil war and forty years since the death of Franco.

It is the extraordinary persistence, immediacy even, of this 'long ago' unresolved past in Spain today which marks the country out, rather than the fact itself of having had one. For such difficult 'dark mid-twentieth-century' pasts are themselves common across Europe, which emerged in the 1940s from the series of civil wars that had been fought beneath the carapace of Nazi conquest and occupation between 1938 and 1947. After the military defeat of the Third Reich, punishment and avenging violence targeted those who had fought or collaborated with the Nazis. But in Spain, where fascism was still triumphant in the form of Francoism, the tables were turned and it was Spain's antifascist resistance groups which bore the brunt of the violence. Also in Spain, and crucially unlike elsewhere, the vengefulness of 'victorious' social groups could count on full state backing.

It was the fact that in Spain repression was directed by a state representing a fascist coalition with strong social support and under the control of the militarily undefeated Franco, which explains the huge difference of what then superseded in Spain, compared to the rest of the sphere emerging as Western Europe. The process of punishing actual flesh and blood Nazis was swiftly and hugely curtailed, under various pressures, not least the political requirements of the developing Cold War.[4] But everywhere else there still came about a public political acceptance that Nazism itself, in the form of the Third Reich as a state system, had been a political evil, responsible for mayhem and mass killing across the continent. In Spain, however, there was no such public recognition: after all, Franco had been a sworn ideological (and material) ally of the Axis, and after 1945 he offered political refuge to many Nazis and fascists from across Europe. Even in the 1960s and 1970s Franco's erstwhile alliance with Hitler was honoured, including by means of the public silence drawn. Indeed, even after the negotiated end of the dictatorship in the later 1970s, this silence continued more or less – so there has never been in Spain, to this day, any process of explicit denazification. For years the population was denied any possibility of a critical knowledge of the recent past – either its own, or Europe's more broadly.

The transition to democracy in Spain, following Franco's death in November 1975, was itself a highly controlled process, guided by a Francoist political elite and rigidly supervised by a vehemently pro-Franco army, backed by civilian Falangists, thousands of whom still had the right under Spanish law to carry arms. The price demanded by this powerful coalition for its support of institutional change was an amnesty for itself, and public silence over the recent past. Because of this demand, but also for other complicated reasons which went deep into Spanish society (and which were also largely symptoms of

Francoism's enduring power) this 'pact of silence', as it has famously become known, was broadly accepted. What this meant was that the first two decades of Spanish democracy (until the later 1990s) were marked by high levels of public and civic indifference to the cause of the victims of the civil war and the dictatorship. Certainly there was no lead from government, not even after the social democratic PSOE entered a long period in power in October 1982, for it too accepted that a public silence was the most convenient option. Thus it was that the struggle to unearth the hidden past, to bring that knowledge into the public sphere and on the basis of it to call for the recognition of, and justice for, the many thousands of people who had suffered under the Franco dictatorship, never became hallmarks of the transition years, despite the efforts of many historians (right from the start of the post-Franco era) to analyse what this hidden past contained, to understand it and to transmit its knowledge to future generations.

This public silence began to be disrupted, albeit slowly, in the second half of the 1990s, after the work of the aforementioned historians had unearthed new data on Francoist violence both during the war of 1936–9 and afterwards. But what made the key operational difference here was the broader influence of a changing environment internationally from 1989, with the rise of important debates on human rights and on how to deal justly with the memories (and the still-living victims) of wars and dictatorships. All of this was of course happening in the wake of the formal end of the Cold War, with the disappearance of the Soviet Union and the entire East European bloc. This new context also allowed the emergence into the public sphere in Spain of previously silenced histories and memories. (Though, of course, this collective social memory was not something simply preserved and transmitted, it was also being actively remembered anew.) Part of civil society began to mobilize itself, associations for what was termed the 'recovery of historical memory' were created, mass graves were opened in search of the remains of the extrajudicial dead who were never registered, and the descendants of those killed by the Francoists began to question publicly what had happened, why this story of death and humiliation had been hidden, and who had been the executioners (though this public questioning was much more likely to be by the victims' grandchildren rather than their children, who were too affected by the fear which was Francoism's most ineradicable legacy). The past was determined to stay in the present, but these new initiatives to restore and preserve the memory of the victims, and above all to give them public recognition and moral reparation, would encounter many new obstacles.

Just as the mayhem committed by the military insurgents from July 1936, and then afterwards by the Franco dictatorship, was coming to the knowledge of a broader public in Spain and beyond, this caused a backlash from influential Francoist or neo-Francoist sectors, some of whom had substantial media resources at their disposal in Spain (writers, journalists and broadcasters for example). They have since taken up and recycled, under the guise of 'history', the old Francoist myths and canards – for example, that the military coup of July 1936 was carried out to forestall a 'communist revolution'; that what rightists and 'decent people' did, in launching or supporting it, was to oppose a 'judeo-masonic-bolshevik' plot seeking to undermine traditional Spanish values; and that the Second Republic was governed by 'Soviet-inspired terror'. (In some regards, then, the Cold War myths remain alive.) Faced with this media onslaught, behind which is a present-centred political agenda, professional historians' research-based and conceptually nuanced and sophisticated analyses of the complex period of the 1930s – as one of social reform and modernizing change with all the attendant tensions and problems – is reduced to two crude questions: which 'side' provoked the war, and who killed the most and with most malice? Once again propaganda replaces history and although there is nothing new in this neo-Francoist revisionism, it carries on repeating its usual platitudes about red terror, anticlericalism, the International Brigades, *checas* (political prisons) and 'Soviet domination'. What is new of course is the late twentieth- and twenty-first-century context in which these Francoist and neo-Francoist forces have emerged – one of the increasing prominence across Europe since 1989 of populist and ultraconservative nationalism which has, in turn, created inside Spain a hospitable climate for such explicit recycling of Francoist propaganda.

The weapons used to disseminate this propaganda today in democratic Spain are many and powerful. Firstly, a new brand of pseudo-historians has appeared whose function has been to devise new formats for the old Francoist myths about the war, circulated via books carefully 'prepared' to appeal to a general and mass readership, but whose underlying content serves only the interests of the extreme right and those nostalgic for the dictatorship.[5] In order to create a market niche for themselves, these purveyors of fables first have to draw attention to themselves. Their rather tricksy technique has been to declaim from the rooftops that the history done by professional historians over the last two decades is a 'false', 'revengeful' one undertaken 'in the interests of the political left'. (Again one notes the extremely reductionist, binary thinking here – itself a product of Francoism.) Their mass market books are repackaged myths based on limited secondary sources and which carefully edit out any awkward data or facts that do not fit their preconceived and hackneyed narrative.[6] Hackneyed though it is, they all base their aggressive marketing on a single message – that what they have to say is new and innovative, and that they are the David facing the 'Goliath' of university historians who allegedly exert a stranglehold on history – all of which is of course yet another wily form of self-publicity, declaimed with an eye to making a media splash. It is also more than a little ironic, given that no jobbing university historian could dream of commanding even a tiny part of the media resources such authors have at their disposal via conservative (including Church-run) media networks, whose journalists, media pundits and presenters publicize, review and applaud their books and opinions, while piling outrageous insults upon anyone who counters them.

But for all the considerable impact of this advertising, aggressive marketing and the media-circus influence of certain sorts of news network, these things alone cannot explain the huge public success and impressive sales figures of some of these pseudo-history books. They are simpler and much easier to read, of course, than the ones written by professional historians in Spain (especially as there has never been a tradition in Spain of writing narrative history for a broader public). But this is far from the entire explanation. What their commercial success indicates is that there are still many in Spain who view Franco's dictatorship positively, not only for general reasons of religious or political conservatism, but because it is to the dictatorship that they owe their own, or their family's social position. In other words, they belong to a transgenerational cohort of Spaniards who still, to some degree, derive their identities from Franco's long-ago invented tradition of 'the martyrs' and who have found in this connection not only psychological solace (the 'martyrs' were sometimes family members) but also much tangible material benefit from their subsequent alignment with the long-running regime, and who, of course, never themselves suffered any violence or persecution at the hands of Franco's state. These social sectors (present more or less across Spanish territory, but more heavily concentrated in the historic Francoist heartlands of Old Castile) had already settled into the new post-1975 era of parliamentary democracy and had, in a fairly superficial fashion, 'composed' their memory for the new times. But then, suddenly, as if by means of some new Judeo-Masonic conspiracy (conspiracy theories remain a key part of their mindset), a clutch of history books appeared detailing military and Falangist violence that had been blessed by the Catholic Church,[7] along with some historical documentaries and the excavation of mass graves to find the remains of those killed by Franco's forces – all of which disrupted their composure, by forcing them to face not only the lethal violence perpetrated by Franco's order which they still remembered so fondly, but also that their own nostalgia and sense of well-being and contentedness – both past *and* present – were in effect now irremediably compromised by the new knowledge they were struggling to deny. All this has made them avid for the other 'history', the one they had always known – delivered across decades by the Francoist educational system and media – and which felt psychologically comfortable, even if it was, quite literally, myth not history: the pious incantation, that Franco and his dictatorship had been beneficial for Spain, because it freed them from something much worse, the 'red tyranny', and because, after the 'normal' punishment meted out to the Republicans for a war they had provoked, what Franco brought was economic development, modernization, roads and reservoirs.

It does not matter that today historians, economists and sociologists can demonstrate irrefutable empirical evidence that the civil war was triggered by a violent coup against the Republic, or that both the war and the dictatorship born of it profoundly damaged Spain's ability to develop a functioning and integrated civil society, especially the possibility of the population living together and developing forms of civic tolerance. But for these new propagandists, what matters is not explaining history in all its complexity, but rather combating with a preconceived Francoist memory of old, the new memory of harm/damage done emerging into the public sphere via the civic memory associations. Two different memories again, two experiences of the past, remembering some things and forgetting others. All things considered, the narratives of the historical memory movement are much closer to the reality of the past than are the myths and memories shaped under the Franco dictatorship, but both still replicate the dictatorship's obsession with binary judgements and with reducing the past to overly clear categories – a symptom which is itself the greatest indication that present-day Spain's cultural assumptions are still crucially inhabited and inflected by Francoist categories.

It is moreover memory, not history, which currently constitutes the axis of public debate in Spain, so historical understanding, acquired via the rigorous primary research of the 1980s, has been relegated to the hinterland of discussion (readers will recall the earlier comment that in Spain today the media foregrounds protagonists' experience of trauma, rather than explanations of how and why it occurred). The most significant events of the civil war have now already been researched and the most relevant questions are resolved, but that story is not the exclusive territory of historians and, in any case, what historians teach in universities and in their books by way of archival- and document-based retrospective analysis is not the same as the material that has shaped the perceptions of the majority of Spanish citizens who were born during the Franco dictatorship or in the first years of the transition to democracy – i.e. what they listened to in the broadcast media (news, documentaries) entering their homes, or what they saw at the cinema or read in secondary-school textbooks or other kinds of literature. Added to which, millions of people in Spain have never actually studied the civil war at school, either because they did not progress to middle-school certificate level (*bachillerato*) or because their teachers avoided the subject in history lessons.[8] All of this supposes a challenge for finding ways of developing a history- rather than memory-based approach for managing public remembrance, a particularly acute issue now in the twenty-first century as many countries witness a general shift to new cultures of remembrance.

And what of the history of the civil war as opposed to the doubly fraught memory of it generated under the Franco dictatorship and perpetuated since? During the first two decades of transition and democracy, uncovering the history of the civil war and the dictatorship was almost exclusively the work of a diverse group of historians who located new sources and discussed the different ways of interpreting them, thus opening up a professional debate, and started to think about Spain's war in the light of similar conflicts in other societies, both in Europe and beyond.

The victors' versions of the war became obsolete and empirically unsustainable. With the exception of quite technical military history, an area in which Francoist authors have always felt comfortable, almost everything else that was known by the mid-1990s, some sixty years on from the start of the war, was known either as a result of the work of foreign historians of Spain, especially British and Americans, the first to challenge the myths of the Crusade using the methods of empirical history; or else the new knowledge derived from a generation of professional historians inside Spain who entered the university system at the end of the dictatorship and during the first years of the democratic transition.

Such research, disseminated in academic circles, at specialist history conferences, in scholarly books and journals, modified and substantially enriched the knowledge of that long period of war and dictatorship that dominates the twentieth-century history of Spain. At the same time, however, this historical work circulated only among specialists who largely remained disconnected from a broader popular audience in Spain. This is not entirely unusual, given the high degree of specialism that has generally been the hallmark of professional historiography in the West today. But in Spain it was a very pronounced – even hermetic – division. With the 1990s explosion of memory, this changed – but of course what is now in the spotlight and the subject of great public polemic is not history but the narratives of memory. Even so, this raises the question as to whether it was the lack of mainstream circulation of the new historical knowledge in the 1980s which explains the absence then in Spain of any 'history war' similar to what occurred in (the then West) Germany.[9] Obviously there are many other differences between Francoism and Nazism, not least the scale of international responsibilities incurred. But there is a valid comparison to be made regarding the domestic dimension, with conservatives in 1980s West Germany seeking to rehabilitate German nationalism, as their equivalents now do in Spain through their attempts to rehabilitate Francoism. And indeed the emergence in the 1990s of a Francoist backlash in response to the emergence of the civic memory associations excavating the history of Francoist state violence, does suggest that this backlash occurred precisely because the 'other history' had left the groves of academia and begun circulating in the mainstream, where it was 'disturbing' the comfort zone of broad swathes of Spanish society which were (and are) still sociologically Francoist. (After all, actual Francoism, by the dictatorship's later decades, was relatively permissive of *elite* intellectual dissent, but extremely interventionist when it came to blocking any critical opinion with the potential for mass market dissemination.)

In any case, by the second half of the 1990s in Spain there had occurred a reversal of the earlier 'pact of silence', with opinion and remembrance to the fore in public debate. The term 'historical memory' began to be applied to everything that disseminated any aspect of the violence and horror of either the war or the dictatorship – whether general books or the testimonies of protagonists or witnesses, or, indeed as the media frenzy increased, the term came to be applied to any book that talked, however superficially, about the civil war or Francoism. As a result, historians too were catapulted into the public eye, but at the same time they found themselves competing with a flood of totally indiscriminate information and opinion, quite removed from the scrupulous empirical historical methodology and tools of analysis which guide the work of professional historians (and of the best 'amateurs' too) when they come to interpret their sources.

In recent years, then, a very clear tension has arisen between on the one hand the work of historians conducting empirical investigation (often working in universities, but also as freelance scholars) and on the other the recollections and memories of the protagonists, of those who claim to have been ones, or of their descendants. What the public in Spain today 'knows' of the war or Franco's dictatorship is increasingly conditioned by what is transmitted about them in the pages of the press or on radio or television programmes. Information and opinion blur the boundaries between historians, who follow a recognized professional methodology, and the history buffs and enthusiasts. As a result of the dominance of memory and opinion, interest in more methodological and theoretical reflection has decreased, while we have seen a flood of – mostly acritical and ill-informed – 'subjectivity' and 'feeling' when it comes to writing on historical topics. As a counterweight to all this, especially the white noise of the media, for the remainder of this present chapter, this analysis will focus on what the empirical research of historians has thus far allowed us to know about the nature of repression and political violence in Spain during the civil war and the Franco dictatorship; additionally, it will consider the controversies that have developed around what is called 'historical memory'.

If we judge developments in the history of the war and the dictatorship by the empirical yardstick of work done over the last fifteen years, then there has been no more fertile ground than the studies of repression and political violence. Before the 1990s, empirically rigorous studies on this broad and important topic were scarce, which has been argued by some to confirm that there was indeed something of silence and 'forgetting', pacted or otherwise, during the initial post-transition years. Compared to other major areas of research on the civil war, when the first research began on political violence, during the early 1990s, everything remained to be achieved – from mapping and quantifying the phenomenon, to developing an adequate theoretical and interpretative framework for the research. The syntheses produced in 1986 for the fiftieth anniversary of the beginning of the civil war, and a decade after the death of Franco, had few real possibilities of making in-depth studies of the topic, while, in contrast, they were able to offer both rigorous empirical data, and an interpretation for other themes, for example, on the mechanics of the military uprising, the international dimension of the war, its major battles and the politics of both the Republican and insurgent zones.[10]

By the time the sixtieth anniversary of the war's commencement was commemorated in 1996, research into political violence had advanced by leaps and bounds, as was evidenced only two years later by the publication of a milestone multi-author book synthesizing the crucial – and very substantial – empirical research undertaken to date, entitled *Victims of the Civil War*.[11] Since then, the historiography on political violence during the civil war and under Franco has increased exponentially.

The chief merit of this now extensive literature is that it provides an accurate and comprehensive picture of political violence behind the lines in both insurgent and Republican territory, and then, after Franco's military victory in 1939, across all of Spain during the institutionalization of his terror state during the 1940s. It is thanks to this historiography that we know the origins and objectives of this violence, the ideological perspectives of those 'involved' (though we know more about the victims than the perpetrators) its different phases and its consequences. We now have a sophisticated theoretical frame in which to place the various manifestations of terror and, as a result of the interplay between empirical research and the main theories of political violence, we know a very great deal about the story of the 'annihilation of the other' which began with the military coup of 17–18 July 1936. A substantial qualitative shift within Spanish historiography had to occur to allow this team of young (and not so young) historians to decipher the history, myths and memories both of the 'red terror' (violence in Republican territory) and fascist violence in the insurgent zone. They also investigated the violence triggered by ideas of class, or by a desire to impose rigid gender norms in Franco's Spain, and violence deployed to exterminate the other (for example via the obsessive and lethal persecution popularly targeted on the clergy in the wartime Republican zone), or that targeted by the insurgents against many groups (including priests) in the name of 'God and fatherland'.[12]

The repertoire of arguments, assumptions, questions and proven facts supplied by these studies is very substantial, pending a complete map of the statistics of repression (which will not add much to what we already know qualitatively). It has been further augmented by a flood of testimonies, documentaries and news stories. Nothing has been left out – from the extrajudicial killings by vigilantes who took their victims from home or out of prison (the *paseos* and *sacas* respectively), to the quasi-judicial executions carried out after sentences passed by Francoist military tribunals or (albeit for a much shorter time span) by popular tribunals in the Republican zone in the early part of the war, and to detailed accounts of the brutality of prisons and Francoist concentration camps.[13] Silence and 'forgetting' have also been cultivated in the huge annals of Republican exile literature, usually written by activists who filled their accounts with their own exploits, disputes, the reasons the war was lost, but who never addressed the Republican-zone violence of which they had often been perpetrators or witnesses. In recent years all of this has given way to a sheer overabundance, to the multiplication of studies of little relevance, and to the fragmentation of this 'historical memory' into hundreds of works, associations and opinions expressed in the so-called discussion forums on the Internet, which often become little more than channels for insult and slander.

Another of the characteristics of this extensive literature is the overwhelming presence of local and regional history, which also hallmarks Spanish history/historiography more generally, for structural reasons that go deep into that history itself but which have not been lessened by the experience of Francoism, or indeed much since. Many of these local and regional studies have been undertaken beyond the university sector, by researchers working in their own home towns/areas, without any institutional financial support, and whose driving goal has been to give a thorough account of the violent actions by the military insurgents and their civilian supporters in their own particular locality (whether large village, small town or entire province/region). What gives these studies their particular rationale, indeed what makes them invaluable nationally, is that it is only through records held locally or regionally that we can calculate with any degree of accuracy the exact figures for the Francoist repression. Used cumulatively, these studies offer a national map of Franco's repression over the whole of Spain. In this world of local studies and local historians, conceptual debates are rare – and it is the arithmetic of extrajudicial killings, the raw figures, which often become the main focus of disputes, as researchers criticize those of their fellows who are perceived not to have been 'thorough' enough, or who have apparently not computed all the dead. This is for many what the recovery of 'historical memory' means – a never-ending task where, no matter how much is achieved, there will always be something left to do.[14]

When all these investigations began, there also arose a clear clash of opinions, (rather than debate) regarding the logic of this violence, and especially about whether the insurgents' violence was part of a premeditated plan of extermination of those groups they considered 'out of control', or inimical to the kind of traditional, hierarchized society they wished to impose. Historians also still disagree over whether terms such as genocide or holocaust can be applied to what happened in insurgent territory immediately after the coup. But one clearly useful by-product of these debates is that they have facilitated a fruitful comparative consideration of the events in Spain, looking at how they are similar and how different to the uses of extreme violence against civilian populations elsewhere in wartime Europe in the 1940s.

There is fairly widespread agreement among specialist historians of the repression on the periodization of the massive violence that was triggered by the coup of 17–18 July against the Republic – forms of violence which were then institutionalized and continued by Franco's dictatorship after the end of the military conflict on 1 April 1939. What some time ago the present writer denominated the 'hot terror' was inextricably linked to the summer and autumn of 1936 – it was a form of terror symbolized by mass killings, designed to eliminate instantaneously the enemies of the 'Glorious National Movement'. The same strategy was used thereafter too throughout the battlefield war of 1936–9: whenever the insurgents/Francoists took new territory (as they did cumulatively across the years of the war), there would be a new phase of the 'hot terror' in the newly conquered territory. But more than a consequence of the battlefield war, as is sometimes believed, this 'hot terror' actually preceded it. It was present right from the days immediately after the coup, which from the outset used unrestrained murder as a tool – both civilian-on-civilian and summary executions by military personnel. It was a strategically designed plan which, where it failed, provoked a sudden revolutionary response, which was fierce (i.e. armed) in those cases where its protagonists were able to lay their hands on weapons, and directed against both the military rebels and all those civilian sectors considered to be the rebellion's natural political allies.[15]

These mostly extrajudicial killings were gradually reined in by 1937, and as the Republican state reconstructed itself after the fragmenting blast of the coup, then it sought to re-establish its own state monopoly on violence, reinstituting 'legal' repression via the court system (although proper judicial normalization would take some months more). In Francoist territory the extrajudicial killings had from the start been under military control – in the sense that the military authorities could have stopped them at any time (there was no fragmentation of power in military-held territory). But in the insurgent zone too there was a general progression from hot to 'cold' – or quasi-legal terror, authorized by courts martial and military tribunals.[16]

Once the military conflict of 1936 to 1939 had ended in Franco's victory, multiple forms of punishment were imposed by the victors. First, during the final weeks of the military conflict and for the first few weeks after Republican surrender at the end of March 1939, there was random retaliatory violence, with *in situ* killings without trial – i.e. a continuation of the 'hot terror' that had never entirely disappeared from the Francoist zone across 1936–9. Franco's unconditional victory meant the centralized application of violence under military control: this was the beginning of institutionalized terror legitimized by the repressive legislation of the new state. This state of terror existed within a formal state of war which was maintained in force until 1948. It transformed Spanish society, destroyed whole families and flooded daily life with coercive practices, with punishment and fear – as other authors in this volume have also analysed. The threat of being persecuted, humiliated, the need to acquire 'personal guarantees' and good reports simply in order to be able to survive, applied to huge swathes of the Spanish population – indeed to anyone who could not demonstrate an unwavering allegiance to the Movement or a past that was free of Republican associations – these very loosely defined, and of course the definition of what 'Republican associations' actually meant was entirely the victors' to decide.

Those who had, via a military uprising, provoked the war, had won it, and now they began administering that victory by means of their new state under construction. Central to its legitimacy was the idea they disseminated right from the start, that it was, irrefutably, the Republic and those associated with it who were responsible for all the disasters and 'crimes' that had occurred in Spain since 1931. Projecting 'blame' solely onto the defeated Republicans freed the victors from the slightest suspicion and gave them carte blanche to inflict punishment. Franco, the Head of State and fount of all authority, expressed this using the religious lexicon that the institutional Catholic Church had presented to him on a platter: 'The suffering of a nation at a point in its history is not a whim; it is spiritual punishment, the punishment that God imposes on a crooked life, an unclean history.'[17]

The weight of the Church and of authoritarian forms of Catholicism in shaping the Franco regime as it emerged from the war, has led some authors to argue that, rather than the physical extermination of the 'enemy', what the victors wanted from that war was their 'redemption' and 'atonement for sins' – i.e., something very different from the Nazi principle of racial extermination. According to the British historian of Spain, Julius Ruiz, since the empirical research confirms an inverse correlation between Franco's bureaucratization of repression and the number of victims (from 1940 the number of shootings decreased overall), then we cannot speak of a 'cumulative radicalization' of Francoist violence as we can in the case of Nazism.[18] For Ruiz, Franco more or less ended the repression in 1940, and while his dictatorship did not seek reconciliation, it adapted to its circumstances, something which kept Franco away from a systematic plan to eliminate the other. As an argument, however, this is too vague on many key points – and most crucially of all, *it ignores the chronology of Francoism* which was born in war, unlike Nazism which ended in it – hence any discussion of what 'radical violence' means and the chronology of its occurrence is necessarily going to be different. And as Rúben Serém shows empirically in this volume, in his study of the military coup of July 1936 and its aftermath in Seville, a deliberate policy of premeditated killing of civilian constituencies deemed 'the enemy' or 'the other' was the manifest outcome of that military coup itself.

In similar vein, Paul Preston's recent major work, *The Spanish Holocaust*, by far the best documented research on the different manifestations of violence in civil war Spain, has as its underlying thesis the existence of a prior plan of extermination among the military rebels. Preston implicitly compares Francoist violence with that inflicted by the Nazis. Spain hardly had a 'Jewish problem', of course – but as Preston indicates, Spanish 'antisemitism without Jews' was not about real Jews but rather an abstract construction of a perceived international threat. He devotes the first two chapters of *Spanish Holocaust* to examining the roots of the escalating hatred and violence, in particular the theories and arguments of fascists, army officers and authoritarian Catholics, who alleged the existence of a Jewish-Masonic-Bolshevik plot and with it justified the extermination of the left.[19]

Historians' debates about the civil war and the Franco dictatorship, which have also now extended to the themes of memory, only infrequently reach beyond specialist academic circles in Spain. Even so, it is an indication of just how 'live' and unresolved the emotional underpinnings of these academic subjects remain in Spain today, that whenever they do emerge from the university tutorial or specialist history books into the broader public sphere, there is no possibility of edifying reflection, but rather the instant eruption of bitter media polemic. This is especially the case where the subject is Francoist violence itself, where even the most dispassionate and basic statement by professional historians of what is incontrovertible – that the Franco state, born of the military coup and the civil war, established extraordinary mechanisms of terror which it sanctioned and legitimized by laws, remaining in place and essentially the same until the dictator's death forty years later – is likely to cause deep public discomfiture and malaise. What this indicates is that in Spain a great deal is still invested by many in the reputation of Franco and Francoism, even all these years after the dictatorship's formal end.

The return to power of the social democratic party (PSOE) in March 2004, under the leadership of José Luis Rodríguez Zapatero, opened up a new phase in this public polemic. For the first time in the history of post-1977 democracy in Spain, which was already thirty years old by the time Zapatero came to power, a national government opted to take an initiative to repair a historic injustice. This was the main significance of the bill introduced in late July 2006, and known as the Law of Historical Memory. With this law, the subject of memory acquired an unprecedented public profile: the past was to become a civic lesson for the present and the future. The law itself did not broach the different interpretations of the past, it did not attempt to define responsibilities or apportion blame. Nor did it propose, as had already happened in several other countries, to create a Truth Commission to identify the mechanisms by which death, or other violence, including torture were inflicted, or to identify the victims and perpetrators.

The Spanish law, finally adopted on 31 October 2007 in modified form, was a minimal measure, but it did open the way for moral reparation and for the legal and political recognition of the victims of the civil war and Francoism. On the basis of the law, in October 2008 Judge Baltasar Garzón initiated an investigation into the circumstances of the deaths and the whereabouts of tens of thousands of the victims killed by Franco's forces, including civilian vigilantes, during the war. Many of the bodies had been abandoned by their murderers in holes by the roadside, or by cemetery walls, or else buried in mass graves – all the victims of killing without any judicial proceedings. Neither the Spanish state nor any other constituted political authority since the democratic transition had taken seriously the legal and political recognition of these victims, so it fell to a judge to do it, the same judge who had previously sought the arrest of the former Chilean military dictator Augusto Pinochet and also gaoled hundreds of members of ETA who had been involved in the perpetration of violence.

But instead of allowing Garzón's legal initiative to take its course, and thus permitting that past of degradation and political murder to be investigated, instead of putting into the public realm an analysis of why it had happened, not least in order to learn civic lessons from it, other state and political actors in Spain (including other judges as well as politicians and sections of the media) began a campaign against Garzón which culminated in May 2010 in his suspension and disbarment. The legal challenge to Garzón was long and involved, but in essence he had been blocked for daring to investigate the crimes of the dictatorship. With the economic crisis and the victory of the Popular Party in the general elections of November 2011, the public finance attached to the Memory Law, including for forensic or other related investigations, ceased and the law became a dead letter, for lack of money and, above all, of government will. Meanwhile, during those same years, several hundred priests and other religious personnel 'martyred' during the civil war were beatified. So nothing had really changed since Franco: honour and glory for some and silence and humiliation for others. More recently, in 2013, it fell to an Argentinian judge to take up the cause of Franco's victims, seeking the extradition of still-living perpetrators through the application of the universal jurisdiction of human rights.[20]

What is it, then, that is at stake in Spain today with all these conflicts involving the history and memory of the civil war and Franco's dictatorship? In the first place, the need to educate today's society about the history of the twentieth century. This is particularly urgent in Spain, in order to debunk and go beyond the myths – and outright lies – disseminated for so long by the Franco regime and which still have a significant presence in Spanish society, for a number of reasons, including the activities of media pundits and propagandists masquerading as historians, both linked to powerful networks of right- and ultra-right-wing media. Neither did the Second Republic 'cause' the civil war, nor was the dictatorship of Franco necessary to defend Spain from its internal or external enemies. Without the military uprising of July 1936, there would not have been a civil war in Spain, and in the long and cruel dictatorship of Franco resides, ultimately, the great exceptionality in the history of twentieth-century Spain, when compared to the other Western capitalist countries. It was the only formal dictatorship of interwar Europe (along with that of Antonio de Oliveira Salazar in Portugal) which survived the Second World War. Hitler and Mussolini were dead, but Franco continued for another thirty years. The dark side of Europe's mid-twentieth century of civil wars and internecine hatred and discrimination, which was largely curtailed in Western Europe with the outcome of the Second World War, was to have a much longer life in Spain.[21]

Few still believe that the aim of the historian is to present their readers with the 'untainted and unpainted truth', or that the past exists entirely independently of the minds of individuals and that what the historian has to do, therefore, is to present it in an entirely neutral manner.[22] That the facts of history never reach us in a 'pure' state was shrewdly observed many years ago by the British historian Edward H. Carr, and has since become axiomatic.[23] But even if absolute truth is unattainable, historians should strive to discover conditional and relative truths. And we already have some important relative truths, and indeed quite a few certainties, about the civil war in Spain. After the past four decades of empirical historical research and theoretical deepening, we have been able to reconstruct the key, complex events and the no-less-complex lives of those who suffered, experienced or witnessed them.

All this has been the result of the empirical rigour of dozens of historians who have researched constantly in archives and libraries. Without all these thousands of documents and books, we would know little of this history. In addition to revealing the horror generated by the war and the dictatorship and compensating the victims who have been marginalized for so long, we must also enshrine archives, museums and the education system (schools and universities) as the three crucial components of public policy on memory.

In order to achieve this for the civic welfare of subsequent generations, we have to counter politically loaded attempts from some sectors of the state and the media to encourage ignorance about the past rather than the promotion of knowledge. One highly specious 'argument' currently circulating seeks to posit the severity of Spain's current economic crisis as a reason why citizens should look away from the past. But those arguing this only ever do so with regard to the history of the civil war and Francoism. Their memory fatigue is very selective indeed: for the same commentators are keen to remember (indeed reinvent) other historical episodes to suit their own political interests – the history of the *Reconquista* (the Christian conquest of Muslim kingdoms in Spain/Iberia), or of the fifteenth-century Catholic Monarchs who unified Spain under Castile, or the conquest of an empire in the Americas, or the grandeur of the imperial monarchy of the early modern period, or the glorious War of Independence (1808–14). This is of course a history raid – plundering the past to serve their own marvellous present as politicians. But the general direction of this manipulation is more alarming still, and points up the particular difficulty of Spain's memory juncture after 1989, in being caught between two opposing currents.

First, there came a small space for civic initiatives which helped open up information about and commemoration of the difficult past, thus also chiming with developments elsewhere, such as the emergence of truth commissions and other civil rights initiatives for restitution and justice – including in South Africa and South America which gathered momentum after 1989 and which were intended as a foundational basis for rebuilding democracy and healing collective memory after the fall of dictatorships. But in Spain this then came hard up against a very contrary current, also building after 1989, with the collapse of the antifascist consensus in Europe and the return and ascendancy of populist ultranationalism across the continent (especially though not exclusively in central/east Europe – with interwar fascist leaders being rehabilitated as good patriotic nationalists, because they were 'anti-communist', so this was the last act of the Cold War reintegration of former Nazis), and which has given courage to those in Spain who want to resurrect similar forms of ultranationalism reminiscent of the Franco years.

In Spain this tendency is now gravely obstructing the vital development of robust and salutary civic policies on memory and public remembrance/commemoration. Such policies, which would necessarily be based on archives, museums and education, will not be possible for as long as state and political authorities in Spain refuse to acknowledge publicly the country's traumatic recent past and for as long as political, legal and moral reparation for the victims of Francoist state violence is denied and blocked by powerful groups in Spain's judiciary, political system and media. Thousands of Spanish families are still waiting for the state to offer them the means of discovering what happened to their relatives who were murdered and deposited in the earth without trial, evidence or judicial trace, and yet who remain so strongly in the memory of their living descendants, as is almost always the case with the violently disappeared.

It is the right and proper task of the democratic state to undertake a complete census of those who were extrajudicially killed and to provide information about where they were executed and where their remains lie. By the same token – and this is perhaps stated less often than it needs to be – nor can the memory of the victors of the Spanish civil war be neglected, abandoned or destroyed. Here historians frequently part company with many other advocates of the 2007 Memory Law, in that they see the Francoist map of remembrance, all the places of memory constructed across Spain by the dictatorship, as themselves a vital part of historical memory – not least as proof that what defined the Franco regime historically was its – perhaps unique – fusion of militant religion and patriotism, forged in war and maintained throughout the long ensuing dictatorship as the lodestone and legitimator of the Franco state, and also as the solace of its social base. These things too are crucial components of Spain's history and cannot be consigned to oblivion.

Beyond the testimony literature of those people who endured Franco's violence, future generations will know history mainly through conventional history books and whatever documents, photographic and audiovisual material we are able to preserve and bequeath to them. This will involve the preservation of archives and state support for historical scholarship, as well as a civic environment which protects and promotes the free exchange of information and open debate. These are the requirements for excavating and recording the history of those parts of the recent past which are still to be opened up. Remembrance and opinion; commemoration and heritage; these are something else.

## Notes

1. Aniceto de Castro Albarrán, *Guerra Santa: El sentido católico del Movimiento Nacional Español* (Burgos: Editorial Española, 1938), p. 33.

2. On Onésimo Redondo's responsibility in fomenting a climate of violence in pre-coup Valladolid, see Paul Preston, *The Spanish Holocaust: Inquisition and Extermination in Twentieth-Century Spain* (London: HarperPress, 2012), pp. 44–7 and cf. pp. 189–92.

3. Quotation from Justo Pérez de Urbel, 'La guerra como Cruzada religiosa', in *La Guerra de Liberación Nacional* (Zaragoza: Universidad de Zaragoza, 1961), p. 71.

4. Hundreds of thousands of former Nazis, especially in Germany and Austria, avoided any sustained punishment. By 1948 the prosecutions were ending; by the 1950s they were a thing of the past. See István Deak, Jan T. Gross and Tony Judt, *The Politics of Retribution in Europe: World War II and Its Aftermath* (Princeton: Princeton University Press, 2000), p. 12; Donald Bloxham, 'British War Crimes Policy in Germany, 1945–1957: Implementation and Collapse', *Journal of British Studies* 42: 1 (2003), pp. 91–118.

5. Thoroughgoing analyses by professional historians of these neo-Francoist productions in Enrique Moradiellos, 'La intervención extranjera en la guerra civil: un ejercicio de crítica historiográfica', in Enrique Moradiellos (ed.), 'La Guerra Civil', *Ayer* 50 (2003), pp. 199–232; Francisco Espinosa, *Contra el olvido: Historia y memoria de la guerra civil* (Barcelona: Crítica, 2006), and Alberto Reig Tapia, *Anti-Moa: La subversión neofranquista de la Historia de España* (Barcelona: Ediciones B, 2006).

6. The author and book which epitomizes the trend is Pío Moa, *Los mitos de la guerra civil* (Madrid: La Esfera de los Libros, 2003).

7. There is a discussion of this historiography later in this chapter, with examples also cited in notes 10, 11, 12, 13.

8. Jesús Izquierdo and Pablo Sánchez, *La guerra que nos han contado: 1936 y nosotros* (Madrid: Alianza Editorial, 2006). A good summary of the changes in school history text books is in

Carolyn P. Boyd, 'De la memoria oficial a la memoria histórica: la Guerra Civil y la Dictadura en textos escolares de 1939 al presente', in Santos Juliá (ed.), *Memoria de la Guerra y del Franquismo* (Madrid: Taurus, 2006), pp. 79–99.

9. 'Vergangenheit, die nicht vergehenwill' (The past which refuses to be forgotten') was the title of the article written by the conservative German historian, Ernst Nolte, in the *Frankfurter Allgemeine Zeitung*, 6 June 1986. Nolte and others, including Andreas Hillgruber, provoked a debate over the uniqueness of the Holocaust. For them it was only one case among many genocides, and a 'reply' to and copy of Stalinist terror: their stance began the famous *Historikerstreit*, or 'historians' dispute' in the Federal Republic of Germany.

10. General Ramón Salas Larrazábal's *Perdidas de guerra* [War Losses] appeared in 1977, published by Planeta in Barcelona. The author, not only a historian but also a Francoist army officer, considered his work as offering a definitive set of figures on the repression. The first academic responses to it tended to focus on critiquing Salas' methodological and interpretive assumptions: see Alberto Reig Tapia, 'Consideraciones metodológicas para el estudio de la represión franquista en la guerra civil', *Sistema* 33 (1979), pp. 99–128 and also Reig Tapia's book, *Ideología e historia (sobre la represión franquista y la guerra civil)* (Madrid: Akal, 1984). The first critical work based on new empirical data came in 1985 with Josep María Solé i Sabaté, *La repressió franquista a Catalunya, 1938–1953* (Barcelona: Edicions 62, 1985) and Francisco Moreno, *La guerra civil en Córdoba* (Madrid: Ed. Alpuerto, 1986), although Solé i Sabaté had already by 1983 published, with his co-author Joan Villarroya, *La repressió a la guerra i a la postguerra a la comarca del Maresme (1936–1945)* (Barcelona: Biblioteca Serrador, 1983). At the same time, books were also appearing which presented material and testimonies from specific towns, villages or local areas across Spain, including many harrowing accounts of victims and also statistics on the Francoist repression based on detailed local investigation which were substantially larger than those figures cited in Salas Larrazábal's book. Among the first in this new wave of works were Antonio Hernández Gracia's *La represión en La Rioja durante la guerra civil* (Logroño: Universidad de Logroño, 1984, 3 vols.), and, especially noteworthy, the study by the collective Altaffaylla Kultur Taldea, *Navarra 1936: De la esperanza al terror* (Estella: Altaffaylla Kultur Taldea, 1986, 2 vols.) – both these books, as with many of the empirically crucial new studies of the Francoist repression, were financed and published by the researchers and writers themselves, because at that time established publishers had little interest in the topic, and not only because they doubted it was a commercial proposition but also because they were wary, even fearful, of the subject in itself – yet again evidence of the after-effects of the dictatorship, a decade on from its formal end. The mid-1980s also saw the publication, or re-publication, of revised works of synthesis by established British or American scholars such as Hugh Thomas or Gabriel Jackson, which also included new discussions of the Francoist repression, but overview ones based on published secondary sources. This was also the case for Paul Preston's own book, *The Spanish Civil War 1936–1939* (London: Weidenfeld and Nicolson, 1986), published to mark the fiftieth anniversary of the war, in which he discussed in a number of the chapters aspects of the repression in both the Republican and Francoist zones.

11. Santos Juliá (ed.), *Víctimas de la guerra civil* (Madrid: Temas de Hoy, 1999). (With chapters by Julián Casanova, Josep María Solé y Sabaté, Joan Villarroya and Francisco Moreno.)

12. For the most recent figures on political repression behind the lines in the two war zones, along with the principle sources thereof, see the pocket edition (*edición de bolsillo*) of Santos Juliá (ed.) *Víctimas de la guerra civil*. For the Francoist repression which ensued after military victory in 1939, and which was often a direct continuation of the repression perpetrated by the military rebels during the battlefield war, see Julián Casanova (ed.), *Morir, matar, sobrevivir: La violencia en la dictadura de Franco* (Barcelona: Crítica, 2002) (chapters by Francisco Espinosa, Conxita Mir and Francisco Moreno); an overview of the different forms

of this repression in Conxita Mir, 'Violencia política, coacción legal y oposición interior', in Glicerio Sánchez Recio (ed.), 'El primer franquismo (1936–1959)', special issue of *Ayer* 33 (1999), pp. 115–45; Angela Cenarro, 'Muerte y subordinación en la España franquista: el imperio de la violencia como base del "Nuevo Estado"', *Historia Social* 30 (1997), pp. 5–22; Javier Rodrigo, 'La bibliografía sobre la represión franquista. Hacia el salto cualitativo', in *Spagna Contemporanea* 19 (2001), pp. 151–9. The repression that occurred in the Republican zone, about which the Franco dictatorship produced many propagandistic texts and martyrologies, has been the object of close study, and also theorization, in recent years by a number of historians using methodologies derived from both social science and cultural history. A good overview in José Luis Ledesma, 'La "santa ira popular" del 36: La violencia en guerra civil y revolución, entre cultura y política', in Javier Muñoz Soro, José Luís Ledesma and Javier Rodrigo (eds), *Culturas y políticas de la violencia. España siglo XX* (Madrid: Siete Mares, 2005), pp. 147–92. On the complicity of the institutional Catholic Church in the Francoist repression, and also anticlerical violence, see Julián Casanova, *La Iglesia de Franco* (Barcelona: Crítica, 2005) which contains an extensive bibliography for both topics.

13. A thematic overview in Carme Molinero, Margarida Sala and Jaume Sobrequés (eds), *Una inmensa prisión. Los campos de concentración y las prisiones durante la guerra civil y el franquismo* (Barcelona: Crítica, 2003).

14. A recent summary in Angela Cenarro, 'Miradas y debates sobre la violencia franquista', *Ayer* 91:3 (2013), pp. 241–53.

15. Julián Casanova, 'Rebelión y revolución', in Santos Juliá (ed.), *Víctimas de la guerra civil*, pp. 57–177.

16. Julio Prada analyses the notion of 'legality', preferring to term it the 'judicialization of terror', which, in the last analysis, was epitomized by the military repression implemented via the system of military courts/courts martial, *La España masacrada: La represión franquista de guerra y de posguerra* (Madrid: Alianza, 2010).

17. Franco's speech in Jaén, 18 March 1940.

18. Julius Ruiz, 'A Spanish Genocide? Reflections on the Francoist Repression after the Spanish Civil War', *Contemporary European History* 14:2 (2005), pp. 171–91: pp. 175–6.

19. Preston, *Spanish Holocaust*, pp. 42–51. My review of it in *International Journal of Iberian Studies* 25:3 (2012), pp. 215–25. As well as being much reviewed, Preston's book also attracted its share of vituperation, something which follows a common pattern in Spain, where supposed 'debates' on the subject of historical memory especially, are no such thing but rather occasions for gratuitous insult: a good example in Pedro Carlos González Cuevas, 'Paul Preston: el ocaso de un hispanista', http://www.nodulo.org/ec/2011/n112p13.htm [accessed 23 August 2015].

20. In December 2011, the Argentinian judge, María Romilda Servini de Cubría, first requested from the Spanish government a list of those who had been politicians or senior army officers during the Franco dictatorship (defined as the period up to the first democratic elections of June 1977). In September 2013 Servini went on to serve extradition requests for four still-living Spanish citizens implicated in torture during the last years of the dictatorship and the opening period of the transition. In November 2014 two cabinet ministers were added to the list. From a situation of there being no possibility of retributive justice in the Spanish case, one seems now to have opened up.

21. This is dealt with in the introduction and epilogue of Julián Casanova, *A Short History of the Spanish Civil War* (London: I.B. Taurus, 2011).

22. The 'untainted and unpainted truth' was coined by John P. Bury in his inaugural lecture of 1902 when he succeeded Lord Acton as Regius Professor of Modern History at Cambridge.

Fritz Stern (ed.), *The Varieties of History. From Voltaire to the Present* (New York: Vintage Books, 1973 [1956]), pp. 210–23.

23. Edward H. Carr, *What is History* (Cambridge: Cambridge University Press, 1961), although the observation had already been made by American historians of the 'New History' in the early twentieth century.

## Further reading

Anderson, P., *The Francoist Military Trials. Terror and Complicity, 1939–1945*, London: Routledge, 2009.

Barahona de Brito, A., Aguilar, P. and González Enríquez, C. (eds), *Las políticas hacia el pasado. Juicios, depuraciones, perdón y olvido en las nuevas democracias*, Madrid: Istmo, 2002.

Casanova, J., 'Franco, the Catholic Church and the Martyrs', in Anindya Raychaudhuri (ed.), *The Spanish Civil War. Exhuming a Buried Past*, Cardiff: University of Wales Press, 2013, pp. 8–19.

Casanova, J. and Gil Andrés, C., *Twentieth-Century Spain. A History*, Cambridge: Cambridge University Press, 2014.

Deak, I., Gross, J.T. and Judt, T., *The Politics of Retribution in Europe: World War II and Its Aftermath*, Princeton: Princeton University Press, 2000.

Graham, H., *The War and its Shadow: Spain's Civil War in Europe's Long Twentieth Century*, Eastbourne: Sussex Academic Press, 2012.

Groppo, B. and Flier, P. (eds), *La imposibilidad del olvido. Recorridos de la Memoria en Argentina, Chile y Uruguay*, La Plata, Argentina: Ediciones Al Margen, 2001.

Judt, T., *Postwar: A History of Europe since 1945*, London: William Heinemann, 2005.

Muños-Rojas, O., *Ashes and Granite. Destruction and Reconstruction in the Spanish Civil War and Its Aftermath*, Eastbourne: Sussex Academic Press, 2011.

Preston, P., *The Spanish Holocaust. Inquisition and Extermination in Twentieth-Century Spain*, London: HarperPress, 2012.

Richards, M., *After the Civil War. Making Memory and Re-Making Spain since 1936*, Cambridge: Cambridge University Press, 2013.

Stone, D., *Goodbye to All That? The Story of Europe since 1945*, Oxford: Oxford University Press, 2014.

Viejo-Rose, D., *Reconstructing Spain. Cultural Heritage and Memory after Civil War*, Eastbourne: Sussex Academic Press, 2011.

Wodak, R. and Borea, G.A. (eds), *Justice and Memory. Confronting Traumatic Pasts. An International Comparison*, Vienna: Passagen Verlag, 2009.

# BIBLIOGRAPHIES

# CHAPTER 10

## BIOGRAPHIES FOR A CAUDILLO AFTER A WAR: A BIBLIOGRAPHICAL COMMENTARY ON BIOGRAPHIES OF FRANCO

*Enrique Moradiellos*

Translated from Spanish by Alison Pinnington and Helen Graham

In January 1936, the British Ambassador to Madrid, Sir Henry Chilton, in his routine annual report to the Foreign Office on 'leading personalities' within the Spanish arena, wrote a brief biographical note on 'el general de División Francisco Franco'. In it, he stressed the professional merits already achieved by the rising figure of the young general, and also Franco's clear preference for traditionalist social and political order, making him a decided opponent of revolutionary change; but Chilton also indicated what was then Franco's canny, careerist aloofness from any formal political commitment to either monarchist or Republican politics:

> Born at Ferrol on the 14th [*sic*] December 1892. An infantry officer who served with great distinction in Morocco, where he commanded the Foreign Legion from 1923 to 1926. He played a conspicuous part in the occupation of the Ajdir sector, for which he was promoted to Brigadier-General. On creating the General Military Academy at Saragossa in 1928, General Primo de Rivera appointed him its first Commandant. When this academy was closed under the first Republican Government, General Franco was appointed to the 15th Infantry Brigade. In 1933 he became Military Commander of the Balearic Islands. In February 1935 he was appointed Commander-in-chief, Morocco, but was called home in May, after Sr. Gil Robles had become War Minister, to be chief of the Central General Staff. He was promoted to his present rank in March 1934. A fearless officer, clever tactician, popular commander, General Franco is one of the most prominent officers in the Spanish Army, and has now the almost unique record among senior officers of being as much appreciated by Republican War Ministers as he was formerly by Ministers under the Monarchy. He is regarded as a 'national power'. He acted as principal adviser to the War Minister in many aspects of the military campaign in October 1934 in Asturias. General Franco belongs to a family of distinguished soldiers. His brother, Don Ramón, is the well-known airman.[1]

If in the middle of 1936 Franco was simply a distinguished general, just three years later he had become the Caudillo of Spain, the most important and decisive political and institutional figure within the political regime built by the military insurgents and their civilian allies. In his hands were concentrated a wide range of executive, legislative and judicial powers unparalleled in modern Spanish history. It was a process that began on 1 October 1936 when the Junta de Defensa Nacional transferred to Franco the 'absolute powers of the State' as Generalísimo and leader of the Government.[2] Ultimately, Franco's authority as Caudillo would rest not on traditional legitimacy (by succession), nor rational or democratic (by election), but on 'charisma' – as the Francoist politician and jurist Torcuato Fernández-Miranda would explain years later, in 1960, with a reasoning clearly indebted to the political categories both of Max Weber and Carl Schmitt:

> The authority (Jefatura) of the Spanish State, born of the national uprising (of July 18 1936), resides in the person of Generalísimo Franco, by virtue of the institution of the *caudillaje*. The Generalísimo is Head of State as leader of the Crusade. . . . *El caudillaje* is an exceptional title of authority, individual, and therefore unrepeatable, that rests on a right enshrined by proclamation and through outstanding support. . . . The process of permanent civil war, latent or explicit, in Spanish life since the time of Fernando VII, reached its worst moment in the anarchy of the Second Republic, making civil war inevitable. From that war there arose out of the National Movement, inspired by the support of *la España nacional*, the leader, or Caudillo, of the Crusade, in the person of Francisco Franco. In him is located the authority of the New State.[3]

Given that Franco constituted the cornerstone of the political system created during the war and formalized after the victory of 1939, it is not surprising that a plentiful biographical literature appeared inside Spain. While they varied to some extent in format and scope, these were obviously apologetic works, and for the most part they were produced with official support. Indeed, the almost forty years of Franco's personal dictatorship were enough to generate a very extensive body of biographical literature, though these are far better characterized as hagiographies than biographies. Only after Franco's death and with the dismantling of the institutions of the dictatorship, including its censorship apparatus, was it possible to publish serious or scholarly biographies of the dictator, because only then did the requisite array of primary sources begin to be available inside Spain – even if not necessarily always easily. Up until then, however, there was censorship: the regime was concerned from the outset with monitoring and controlling everything written about its origins in the civil war and about Franco's own history. To facilitate the task of the censors, described in the legal preamble as engaged upon a work of 'moral rectitude and political accuracy' dating back to the 1936 military rising, two censorship measures were implemented in 1941: one, an order from the Ministry of the Interior on 8 March 1941 required that publishers and presses present half-yearly work schedules to ensure that only 'interesting and useful works' were authorized to appear; the other, a decree of the Presidency of the Government of 23 September 1941, 'established the need for the prior approval of the Ministry of the Army for works relating to the war of liberation or its origins.'[4]

## Praising a Caudillo: Francoist biographies

Amongst the raft of apologetic biographies of Franco, it is the very first one that stands out and whose influence has been most enduring. Entitled simply *Franco*, it was written by the journalist Joaquín Arrarás Iribarren in 1937 in Burgos, then Franco's general headquarters.[5] Arrarás had known Franco for many years, and was involved in press and propaganda work for the insurgents from the beginning: it seems likely that Arrarás was the author of the biographical notes on Franco which were published in various media when he was appointed as Generalísimo and Head of State on 1 October 1936.[6] Arrarás's biography, just over three hundred pages long, focused on Franco's life before the start of the war, and immediately and for the period of the civil war became recognized as the official version of the new Head of State's life. A great commercial success, by October 1939 the book was already in its eighth edition and had been translated into English, French, German and Italian, as well as other editions in Spanish in several Latin American countries.[7] *Franco* served as a source of inspiration and information for newspaper reports and other subsequent biographies, largely thanks to its grandiloquent and obsequious style, as evidenced by its final fawning paragraphs:

> Ambition, of any kind, does not motivate General Franco, when he embarks on an undertaking (to save Spain). Neither does he care about command, which he does not crave, nor human vanities, which he disregards, or material advantages, which do not interest him. In his prime he has reached those peaks which rarely crown prestigious men and cap a glorious military career.... Franco, Caudillo of the Faith and of Honour in this solemn period of history, who accepts the most glorious and overwhelming of responsibilities.... Franco, Crusader of the West, elected Prince of Armies in this tremendous hour, to allow Spain to accomplish the destiny of the Latin race. And may Spain crush the Antichrist of Moscow and the Cross prevail over the hammer and sickle.[8]

Similarly hagiographical was General José Millán Astray's biography *Franco, Caudillo*, published in 1939 after the defeat of the Republic.[9] The disabled war veteran, founder of the Foreign Legion and Franco's former military commander in Morocco, Millán Astray had turned to propaganda work in Franco's HQ during the war, and this book was largely an extension of a brief sketch of Franco he had made in 1936 in a speech to cadets of the *Academia de Estado Mayor* (General Staff training school) in Valladolid during the war.[10] Like Arrarás's biography, Millán Astray's depicted the heroism of Franco's military and personal journey up to the beginning of the civil war, but in this case the book followed Franco right up to his military victory in 1939. It exhibited the same providential and hagiographic spirit and an identical phobia against what it described as the Marxist-liberal-democratic and Masonic enemy.

The year 1939 also saw a biography appear aimed at younger readers. This was part of a series called the 'Children's Library' and the volume on Franco was written by the journalist Víctor Ruiz Albéniz, who had been a war correspondent under the nom de plume of El Tebib Arrumi. This book, *La Historia de El Caudillo: Salvador de España* (*The Story of the Caudillo: Saviour of Spain*)[11] had begun life two years earlier, in 1937, as a propaganda brochure.[12] *La Historia de El Caudillo* was headed by an official portrait of Franco with the three obligatory acclamations, 'Franco, Franco, Franco! Arriba España!' ('Spain arise!'), and the caption: 'To courage and intuition, Franco added the dedication that soon gave him the status of first authority in military circles.'

With the defeat of the Italian–German Axis in 1945, these biographies, which indicated Franco's close relations with Hitler and Mussolini, became something of a liability, and this situation was not improved by new attempts such as that by Fernando de Valdesoto (the nom de plume of the journalists Joaquín Valdés Sancho and Oriol Fernando Soto), entitled *Francisco Franco*, or that of the prolific primary school inspector Ángel Pérez Rodrigo, *Franco: Una vida al servicio de la Patria* (*Franco: A Life of Patriotic Service*).[13] These works were politically at odds with the new postwar situation internationally, which posed something of a political problem for the dictatorship. It was not until journalist Luis de Galinsoga (former editor of the daily *ABC* and at that time editor of the Barcelona-based *La Vanguardia Española*) and Lieutenant Francisco Franco Salgado-Araujo (Franco's cousin and head of his military household) published *Centinela de Occidente: Semblanza biografica de Francisco Franco* (*Sentinel of the West: A Portrait of Francisco Franco*) in 1956, that a biography took care to play up Franco's Second World War contacts with the Allies, although still ignoring both their equivocal nature and Franco's strong preference for the Axis.[14] This biography also substantially airbrushed out Franco's anti-democratic diatribes and antisemitism in favour of a more internationally palatable and serviceable general anticommunism. The book's underlining of an anti-Communist profile, along with the projection of an equally vehement profession of Catholic faith which aligned itself with Vatican peace initiatives, served to soften and to some extent occlude the anti-democratic animus exhibited by the Franco regime during the brief period of international ostracism it suffered between 1945 and 1948.

As its title and date of appearance indicate, this new biographical portrait of Franco reflected the circumstances of the Cold War and Spain's military dependence on the United States following the dictator's sanctioning of the installation of American military bases inside Spain from September 1953. The degree of courtly flattery contained within the work can be seen even in a brief perusal of the chapter headings: 'Impassive before the siren song' (to explain the non-entry of Spain to the war, on Hitler and Mussolini's side, in 1940); 'Head unbowed before indignity' (to describe Franco's response to the international condemnation of his regime in 1945 and the veto against Spain joining the UN); 'El Pardo, Axis of the West and mediator with the East' (the chapter, whose title refers to the royal palace of El Pardo near Madrid, Franco's residence as Head of State, charted the gradual rehabilitation of the dictatorship by the Western powers from the beginning of the Cold War in 1947); and so on up to the high point of December 1955, when Spain formally joined the UN, which the authors Galinsoga and Salgado-Araujo celebrated with these words, concluding both the chapter and the book:

And the United States, the most powerful nation on earth, has realized, to its benefit and that of the whole world, that this tip of Europe, which could have been the bridgehead for communism, has become one for the diametrically opposed political camp, thanks to the presence in the Palace of El Pardo of the vigilant and far-sighted Generalísimo Franco. 'I am the sentry who watches while others are sleeping.' Thus, while the statesmen of the United Nations were sleeping, the Sentinel of the West kept watch . . .[15]

This was a text which perfectly encapsulated the vast public distance travelled by the Franco dictatorship, towards its modus vivendi with the new world power, a USA which Franco and his political old guard would nevertheless continue to view as in thrall to a freemasonry as vitiating and inimical to Spanish values as communism.[16]

Nearly a decade later, in 1964, a new biography of Franco appeared in the form of a documentary film. It was part of the official propaganda campaign orchestrated by the Minister for Information and Tourism, Manuel Fraga Iribane, to commemorate what was termed the 'twenty-five years of peace of Franco'. The writer José María Sánchez Silva and the filmmaker José Luis Sáenz de Heredia had produced a very simple text as the script for the film that was made and distributed widely that year, and for many years afterwards, as *Franco, ese hombre* (*Franco, that Man*).[17] Later the text, without any major changes, was published in book form under the same title, and with a substantial set of photographs included.[18] Its tone was in keeping with the official mood of those times, the years of economic growth (known as the 'years of development', *años de desarrollo*), which generated in those sectors of Spanish society who benefited therefrom (particularly the new urban middling classes) a sense of material well-being and acceptance of the regime. The portrait of Franco emphasized above all a 'man who gave [Spain] peace, work and prosperity'. The 'Victorious Caudillo' became the 'Caudillo of Peace', less heroic and more humanized, in civilian dress, with hobbies and a family life enjoyed amidst numerous grandchildren, and the recipient of support from a Spanish people 'united as never before with the man who won the war against communism, who miraculously preserved our neutrality and who was building a better and fairer Spain'.[19] In this sense, both the book and the film formed part of a new propaganda strategy by the Franco regime which now sought to appeal not so much to its original source of legitimacy, the military victory of 1939, but to a new, modernizing legitimacy derived from the socio-economic development of the 1960s.

The last major laudatory biography written during the period of the dictatorship traced Franco's career up to the start of the 1970s, and was the work of the prolific regime historian Ricardo de la Cierva. First published in the form of fifty-two collectable instalments, *Francisco Franco: un siglo de España* (*Francisco Franco: A Century in Spain*) it then appeared in book form in two volumes.[20] Certainly, given its documentary and testimonial base (la Cierva repeatedly interviewed Franco for the work), its photographic accompaniments (in colour), its length and detail, and a certain literary flourish, the work was a great improvement on previous official biographies. Nevertheless, the critical objectivity and political distance la Cierva claimed to be deploying (the work was advertised as a 'critical biography') was nowhere in evidence, and certainly la Cierva's work was, in the end, no less favourable to Franco than earlier official versions, portraying him as the venerable and humane leader.

With la Cierva's work, the regime's attempt at political aggiornamento had, in terms of Franco biographies, gone as far as it could. After the dictator's death in November 1975, subsequent Franco biographies written from a sympathetic perspective, were, in terms of their empirical and documentary contribution, lesser works – except perhaps for la Cierva's own second Franco biography published in 1982.[21] This took the account right up to the dictator's demise and la Cierva even sought to offer what he considered to be a historical verdict on Franco:

> He was the iron surgeon dreamed of by Costa.[22] He was not a scholar but a man of great professionalism and highly cultured, though he never boasted of it. . . . This historian sincerely thinks that if, God willing, democracy is consolidated in Spain, Franco will have been right about the most important objective of all.[23]

Of the pro-Franco biographies that appeared in the post-Franco era, some are particularly worthy of note: one, for the personality of its author, the veteran journalist Manuel Aznar (*Franco*, 1975), and others for their media impact, including those of the writer and former army officer, Ángel Palomino Jiménez (*Caudillo*, 1992); and the one written by present-day Spain's most controversial Francoist political commentator, of chequered ideological past, Pío Moa (*Franco: un balance histórico*, 2005).[24] The line taken in these three books is summed up in the subtitle of Palomino's biography: 'A unique man who recent history has been determined to conceal.' A further noteworthy and 'authorized' biography is the one by the medievalist Luis Suárez Fernández, *Francisco Franco y su tiempo* (1984), originally published by the Francisco Franco Foundation (FNFF) in eight volumes and then reissued two years later in twenty collectable parts with extensive photographs included.[25] Suárez Fernández had been a senior educational policy adviser to the dictatorship in the 1960s at the height of its developmentalist phase, and his insider status meant he had access to unpublished documents from Franco's private archive which is not open to the public,[26] and still less to independent historians – although in 2006 the FNFF did make available some documentation which was microfiched and deposited in the main archive of the Spanish civil war, the Centro Documental de la Memoria Histórica in Salamanca. In this sense of having used documents not generally available, Suárez Fernández's biography is a quite singular work, although it also manages to surpass even la Cierva as an apologia. Indeed there is no critical perspective at all: even la Cierva commented that 'the splendid historical and documentary study by Professor Suárez does not contain a single criticism of the errors of Franco and ignores the final degradation of the regime.'[27] Or, as the French Hispanist Bartolomé Bennassar (speaking for many contemporary and later historians) wrote: '[Suárez Fernández] is assiduous in the art of the pious omission.'[28]

Finally, an essential subset of the laudatory biographical literature on Franco is that produced by non-Spanish authors, an output which was well-received and indeed cultivated by the dictatorship. Some of these foreign works were published during the civil war as part of the propaganda campaign abroad, including Rudolf von Timmermans's *General Franco* (1937), Georges Rotvand's *Franco et la nouvelle Espagne* (1937), and Paolo Antoldi's *Chi e Franco* (1939).[29] However, many more appeared in the 1960s and were published directly in Spain at a time when economic boom was coinciding with a certain regime 'rebranding' of itself as technocratic rather than totalitarian, which was of course more acceptable to Western public opinion. These include the book by French author Claude Martin, *Franco, soldado y estadista* (1965) (*Franco, Soldier and Statesman*); and two biographies by British writers, George Hills' *Franco: el hombre y su nación* (1968) (*Franco, the Man and his Nation*) and Brian Crozier's *Franco: historia y biografía* (1969) (*Franco*).[30] Obviously, these books had a considerable propaganda value for the dictatorship at a time of economic and socio-cultural (although not yet political) integration into Europe. Their existence allowed the Franco regime to point out that there were foreign authors (and, as such, putatively impartial) whose work praised the Spanish leader both as a soldier and a statesman.

## Denouncing a Caudillo: anti-Francoist biographies during the years of the dictatorship

During the period of the dictatorship itself, anti-Franco biographies could not of course be published inside Spain. Among the defeated and fragmented anti-Franco opposition in exile it would obviously take some time before any substantive work on Franco appeared. Indeed this was an elusive goal, given that the condition of exile itself removed writers from the context they sought to analyse, generating anachronisms in perspective and sometimes negative- or counter-myth making. Nevertheless, from early on there were many articles, verbal sketches and caricatures, along with passing references to the life and character of Franco in the various journals and newspapers of the exiled anti-Franco forces (and also some, though rather fewer, among the materials circulated clandestinely and at great risk by the anti-Franco opposition inside Spain). In all possible formats – text, drawings, photographs and cartoons – this production demonized and schematized the life and character of Franco. He appeared as a cunning traitor; the mere puppet of Hitler and Mussolini or of capitalists and landowners; an ambitious, cruel and bloodthirsty dictator; an inquisitorial Catholic fanatic; and also, more curiously, as a castrated or effeminate male. The words of the exiled writer Arturo Barea in his novel *La forja de un rebelde* (*The Forging of a Rebel*) (1951) commenting on the cruelty Franco showed to both his own soldiers and enemies during his time in Morocco at the head of the Legion, serve as an example here: 'everyone hates him, just as the convicts hate the bravest killer in their gaol, he's obeyed and respected, he imposes himself on all the others, exactly like the most hardened killer imposes himself on the whole gaol'.[31] Also well-known were the vehement and acute critiques of the prominent Spanish liberal, writer and former diplomat, Salvador de Madariaga, against 'the cynical hypocrite who usurps power' in Spain as 'the leech of the West' (a witty riposte to Galinsoga and

Salgado-Araujo's *Sentinel of the West*) collected in Madariaga's widely circulated book *General, márchese usted* (1959) (*General, you must leave*):

> Franco is a devout and vulgar reactionary unable to conceive of or appreciate freedom. He is an ambitious and selfish man who failed to leave when, with Hitler's suicide, he became a terrible political burden for his homeland. ... The most important thing for Franco is Franco.... Franco is a Sancho Panza, whose ambition is to eat and sleep well. But the temptation [to make the comparison] should be resisted because that would be unfair to Sancho.[32]

However, it was not until the 1960s that a biography *stricto sensu* was produced by one of the members of the democratic opposition: Luis Ramírez's *Francisco Franco: historia de un mesianismo* (1964).[33] Behind this protective pseudonym was the Basque journalist and writer, Luciano Rincón Vega, who in 1971 would be tried and sentenced to six years in prison by the Tribunal de Orden Público for having dared in the biography to insult the Head of State politically and intellectually 'with his evident disrespect, imputing to Franco ideas and attitudes inconsistent with reality, exhibiting blatant contempt for his person.'[34] The Ramírez book was published by the exile publishing house par excellence, Ruedo Ibérico. Founded in 1961 in Paris by five Spanish Republicans and directed by the anarchist José Martínez, its huge cultural and historical significance has not yet been fully understood or recognized.

Ramírez/Rincón's book was a huge success in anti-Franco circles both in exile and also inside Spain, enjoying several reissues (three by 1973) and shaping the characterization of Franco among his opponents both inside and outside Spain. His version of Franco's character was made even clearer when the book's subtitle was modified after Franco's death, to *Francisco Franco: La obsesión de ser; la obsesión de poder* (*Franco: The Obsession with Self and with Power*) (1976).[35] The Ramírez/Rincón's portrait of Franco was a mordant one:

> Who is this man? A Messiah, a chosen one. ... Franco is no longer a man; he is a slave to his own messianism, as he was before to his ambition and as a consequence of his sad spiteful impotence. But he is a Messiah before whom you have to close your eyes so as not to see his limits.... He is a Messiah without personality, boastful, shy, mediocre, to whom time has not given poise or confidence in his public actions, hesitant to speak, always with an interpreter because he is not a master in any language.[36]

After the death of Franco in 1975, the process of democratic transition made the publication of more or less critical or hostile biographies and biographical sketches possible in Spain (this essay will not consider later cinematic representations of Franco, such as the documentary, *Caudillo*, made in 1977 by leading Spanish film director, Basilio Martín Patino).[37] Of all these later biographical sketches in textual form, it is worth mentioning the booklet written by the sociologist Amando de Miguel in collaboration with Anna Úbeda and Jaime Martín, published in 1976 as *Franco, Franco, Franco,* and which used as its title the Francoist triple acclamation with ironic intent.[38] One could also argue that it is within this genre of anti-Franco texts that we should also broadly locate the well-known literary fiction of the writers Francisco Umbral (*La leyenda del César visionario* (*Legend of the Visionary Caesar*), 1991), Manuel Vázquez Montalbán (*Autobiografía del general Franco*, 1992), José Luis de Vilallonga (*El sable del Caudillo* (*The Caudillo's Sword*), 1997), Juan Luis Cebrián (*Francomoribundia*, 2003) and Albert Boadella (*Franco y yo ¡Buen viaje, Excelencia!* (*Franco and me: Bon Voyage, Your Excellency!*), 2003).

All of these, included in the stormy literary subgenre of 'dictator novels', give voice to an elderly protagonist (or to his sword) who reviews his own life (sometimes with occasional interventions by other narrators by way of counterpoint). These books met with a considerable reader response in Spain and all went through several reprints. Something about their style or perspective was evocative – and they were also translated into many other European languages. Their general tone is encapsulated by the opening lines of Francisco Umbral's book (Burgos and Salamanca being Franco's two civil wartime capitals and also the epitome of imperial, traditionalist, time-locked Spain):

> In a Burgos Salamanca-like in its tedium, and laden with imperial architecture, in a cold-silver, Salamanca reminiscent of Burgos, Francisco Franco Bahamonde, small-time dictator, snacks on chocolate and passes death sentences. Yours is a youth not salvaged by African summers or Legionary nights, despite the legend, but a youth that is sinking, like a flower in a swamp, in the creamy softness of premature flabbiness and fat, as if the virile root of the military man, winner of a war, were sinking, obliterated by a bloody peace, beneath the flattery of the barracks and the chocolate of nuns. The voice, when he gives an order trembles with hypocritical remoteness and sounds high-pitched, minute and effeminate. The Generalísimo, less Caudillo than ever, who in his solitary lunch hour, in conversation with his dead, with the record and history of every man that he is about to kill or imprison, keeps the red beret of the *Requeté* [Carlist militia] on his head, like a night cap, devoid of the bravura of such a headdress, and occasionally applies a napkin to his trimmed moustache, outmoded and black, while calmly reading reports of the repression, couched in the language of barracks bureaucracy and violent trickery.

## Judging a Caudillo: a historiographical review of Franco biographies

The end of the Franco regime also opened the way for an avalanche of works and accounts by witnesses and protagonists of the dictatorship. This flow of testimonies provided a new set of observations (albeit obviously highly constructed and mediated ones) on the character and private life of Franco. In this respect, the publication in 1976 of *Mis conversaciones privadas con Franco*, the work of his secretary and first cousin, Lieutenant General Francisco Franco Salgado-Araujo, offered a window on the dictator's domestic and family routine and his working life (Salgado-Araujo's own memoir was published a year later: *Mi vida junto a Franco*).[39] 1977 saw the publication of two other revealing accounts: Ramón Serrano Suñer's *Entre el silencio y la propaganda: La historia como fue* (*Between Silence and Propaganda: History as it was*), is essential for its perspective on the years 1936–45 when the Generalísimo worked closely with Serrano Suñer, his brother-in-law (*cuñado*), and known popularly as the 'Cuñadísimo' (Supreme-Brother-in-Law), in what was a play on Franco's own title. Serrano Suñer, who was Franco's interior minister and then foreign minister for a time during the Second World War, was the key figure in developing the Spanish dictatorship's relationship with the Third Reich. Also published in 1977 was the first volume of memoirs by former cabinet minister, Laureano López Rodó, *La larga marcha hacia la monarquía* (*The Long March to the Monarchy*) – a crucial book for tracing the planned political evolution of the dictatorship.[40] Slightly later memoirs – all published (like the foregoing) by the Barcelona-based publishing house, Planeta, which became a privileged vehicle for this literature with its series 'Espejo de España' ('Mirror on Spain') – included the memoirs of Franco's sister, Pilar Franco Bahamonde, *Nosotros, los Franco* (*We, the Francos*) in 1980, the recollections of his ex-Ministers in *Franco visto por sus ministros* (*Franco as seen by his Ministers*) in 1981, and the testimony of his personal physician, Dr Vicente Gil (*Cuarenta años junto a Franco* (*Forty Years with Franco*)), in 1981.[41] On the basis of these new eyewitness accounts and supplemented by archive materials, a historiographical review of Franco became more feasible.

Aside from scattered and minor contributions in newspaper articles or research journals, the first serious work of historiographical synthesis was published in 1985, ten years after Franco's death, by the historian Juan Pablo Fusi, in his now famous short biographical essay, *Franco: Autoritarismo y poder personal* (*Franco: Authoritarianism and Personal Dictatorship*).[42] For his careful treatment and his use of the new documentation (among others, the previously mentioned memoirs of Francisco Franco Salgado-Araujo and Laureano López Rodó), Fusi's essay made a definite and decisive break with previous biographies. This was made clear by the author's preliminary 'warning', since he was well aware that the task he had posed himself was difficult and probably thankless:

> Francoist hagiography has always evaded the Franco regime's most interesting problem: its lack of genuine moral legitimacy, in the eyes of the liberal and democratic world, due to its origins in military insurrection and civil war and its authoritarian, repressive character. Anti-Francoist demonology – often, despite appearances, a kind of academic escapism – evades equally disturbing problems of its own, such as the willing and sincere acceptance of Francoism by a very broad spectrum of Spanish society, the system's almost inviolable stability over several decades, the weakness of the opposition and the remarkable transformation of Spain … between 1939 and 1975.[43]

The year 1992 (the centenary of Franco's birth) saw two further biographical works, differing in scope and perspective. First, the American historian of modern Spain, Stanley G. Payne's *Franco, el perfil de la historia*;[44] the second, Javier Tusell's exhaustive study of Franco during the civil war years, *Franco en la Guerra civil*.[45] Payne's work amalgamates the social and political context of the dictatorship (the subject of an earlier study, *The Franco Regime* (1987)) with a summary of the public and private life of the dictator which concentrated on Franco as modernizer. Tusell's biography opens with the question, 'How does a person become a dictator?'. His portrait of Franco in the final stages of his political ascendancy as leader in the midst of a civil war was based on a large array of new and highly revealing archival material (from the personal archives of numerous of Franco's high-ranking political collaborators, through official Spanish foreign ministry papers to state archives in Italy, Portugal and the UK). For Tusell, this material demonstrated convincingly that 'only the civil war' and Franco's sheer brutality had generated the circumstances which allowed an otherwise merely methodical and competent military officer to reach the heights of absolute personal power. In Tusell's own words, his book

> is a fragment of the biography of a man who was, perhaps, above average of the Spanish generals of the era, who had no political aspirations nor pretensions to hold an office of that nature, but through his own will in exceptional military circumstances became dictator until his death. . . . His dictatorship was the product of three years of a civil war more bloody and cruel than any witnessed in Western Europe since the religious conflicts of the seventeenth century. That – bloodletting – was an important factor in understanding what then followed.[46]

However, despite Tusell's significant contribution, still, a hundred years after Franco's birth, we did not possess a general biography which incorporated all of the available sources. True, by then there were some useful syntheses on Franco's persona, or studies of some of the other most crucial stages of his political or military career had appeared: the French Hispanist Philippe Nourry's interesting work on Franco's life up to 1937, that is, up to his emergence as Caudillo; the Galician journalist Carlos Fernández Santander's general biography; the psychiatrist Enrique González Duro's attempt at a psychological, and almost psychoanalytical, analysis; and the idiosyncratic and amusing biography by the journalist and social chronicler Jaime Peñafiel.[47] But there was nothing on Franco comparable to the comprehensive biographies of other modern European dictators, such as Allan Bullock's masterful *Hitler: A Study in Tyranny*, Renzo de Felice's opus, *Mussolini*, or Marc Ferro's portrait of Marshall Pétain.[48]

This gap was filled impressively in 1993 when Paul Preston published his much anticipated *Franco: A Biography*, after nearly a decade of research.[49] It was immediately hailed as a canonical reference work, and quickly translated into Spanish the following year,[50] where it also received resounding critical acclaim[51] and equally remarkable sales figures (between April and June there were four successive editions of the book). The same intellectual impact followed its translation into four other languages, in addition to multiple subsequent reissues, including a revised and much expanded edition in 2002.

Indeed, the publication of this biography was a publishing milestone, as well as a major cultural event in Spain where it attracted huge coverage in the press and broadcast media. The work was monumental both in its scale and as the fruit of exhaustive research – suffice it to say that the English edition had 787 pages of lucid and elegant text, plus 132 pages of rich and detailed explanatory notes, along with another thirty-three pages of bibliographical, documentary and newspaper sources. Comprising twenty-eight substantial chapters, Preston narrates with verve the successive phases of the life of Franco from his childhood in El Ferrol (Galicia) to his prolonged demise in a Madrid hospital. Preston assesses Franco as 'a brave and outstandingly able soldier between 1912 and 1926, a calculating careerist between 1927 and 1936, a competent war leader between 1936 and 1939 and a brutal and effective dictator who survived a further thirty-six years in power'.[52]

Ultimately, Preston's *Franco* has set a gold standard for the field, exemplifying the study of the figure of Franco within a historiographical frame rather than, as in earlier periods (discussed here) as either hagiography/political legitimation or else as political denunciation of a Manichean and rather schematic type (although as earlier sections of this essay also attest, both of these types of work continue to be published). New historiographical work since the mid-1990s has harvested additional perspectives, as a result of new testimony and/or archival findings. In 1995 two very valuable but markedly contrasting works were published: first, the iconoclastic study by political scientist Alberto Reig Tapia, entitled *Franco 'caudillo': mito y realidad* (*Franco 'caudillo': Myth and Reality*), which tore apart, with evident irony, many of the alleged political and diplomatic virtues of Franco, and subjected to forensic examination the ideological doctrines adduced to claim Franco's possession of a 'charismatic' mandate, as a substitute for the evident absence of any democratic one. Second, the more canonical biography by the French Hispanist, Bartolomé Bennassar.[53] The historical and biographical interest in Franco continues, as evidenced by the reprinting or revised editions of the works of Preston, Payne, Bennassar, Reig Tapia and Fernández Santander, and also by the work of a new generation of biographers, a number of whose texts have offered other perspectives and some of which have also been very successful commercially: the French Hispanist Andrée Bachoud's *Franco ou réussite d'un homme ordinaire* (1997), immediately translated into Spanish as *Franco o el triumfo de un hombre corriente* (1998) (*Franco or the Triumph of an Ordinary Man*); the Spanish historian Fernando García de Cortázar's very accessible *Fotobiografica de Franco: Una vida en imágenes* (*Photobiography of Franco: A Life in Images*) (2000); Gabrielle Ashford-Hodges' thought-provoking psychological analysis, *Franco: a Concise Biography* (2002); José Luis Rodríguez Jiménez's work *Franco: retrato de un conspirador* (*Franco: Portrait of a Conspirator*) (2005); and Enrique Moradiellos' *Francisco Franco: Crónica de un Caudillo casi olvidado* (*Francisco Franco: Chronicle of an almost-forgotten Caudillo*) (2002).[54] One might also include here the mainstream (and commercially very successful) publishing experiment, 'Cara y cruz' ('two sides of the coin') which included in its series a volume on Franco, with two essays by historians of diametrically opposed views, Ángel Palomino (with a text entitled '*Por España, frente al comunismo*' ('For Spain, against Communism')) and Paul Preston (whose text was entitled 'Los mitos del gran manipulador' ('The Myths of the Great Manipulator')).[55]

If anything, we can say that the latest contributions to the study of Franco tend to focus on particular aspects of his character or specific stages of his career. For example, there have been abundant studies on his military role with an abiding controversy about their accuracy: according to the Cavalry Colonel Carlos Blanco Escolá, Franco was a poor strategist and an even worse politician, but for Cavalry General Rafael Casas de la Vega, Franco was 'a good soldier' whose military and political work deserves respect and admiration, while Juan Blázquez Miguel comes down somewhere in the middle – although it is also the case that the criteria used by Blanco Escolá and Casas de la Vega are at times underpinned by quite different assumptions.[56] Moving from the military to the political sphere, Francisco Sevillano Calero has studied the charismatic and providential 'cult of personality', while Laura Zenobi has examined the background and process of building that cult of personality.[57]

Many of the myths spun by Francoist hagiography have now been completely debunked by professional historians using the common methodology of the discipline which allows for nuanced and sophisticated assessment based on a thorough examination of all the available primary and secondary sources. As this volume has amply attested, this debunking of myths to date includes the three which were most dear to Franco himself: his assumed role of providential Crusader who saved Spain from communism; his much vaunted ability as the statesman who cunningly deflected Hitler's demands and kept Spain formally neutral in the Second World War; and Franco as architect of modernity whose own particular policies made possible the economic and social modernization of the 1960s. In contrast to these myths, the historiographical assessment of the dictator is clear, the empirical case overwhelming. But as the great Italian historian and philosopher, Benedetto Croce, famously reminds us, history is always about our own times too, and we see this in the emergence today of new and polemical biographies of Franco.[58] While the past remains the past, the history which encapsulates it is also a live dialogue with the present, and sometimes possessed of future goals too: as such, it is never 'over'.

## Notes

1. Sir Henry Chilton, *Records on Leading Personalities in Spain*, 7 January 1936. Reproduced in Enrique Moradiellos, 'The Gentle General: The Official British Perception of General Franco during the Spanish Civil War', in Paul Preston and Ann L. Mackenzie (eds), *The Republic Besieged: Civil War in Spain, 1936–1939* (Edinburgh: Edinburgh University Press, 1996), pp. 1–20: pp. 1–2.

2. *ABC* (Seville), 2 October 1936.

3. Torcuato Fernández-Miranda Hevia, *El hombre y la sociedad* (Madrid: Doncel-Delegación Nacional de Juventudes, 1960), pp. 188–90.

4. Published in *Boletín Oficial del Estado*, 15 March 1941 and 25 September 1941.

5. Joaquín Arrarás Iribarren, *Franco* (San Sebastian: Librería Internacional, 1937).

6.  See for example the article 'La figura del Caudillo', in *El Eco de Santiago. Diario de la tarde* (Santiago de Compostela), 1 October 1936.

7.  English: trans. J. Manuel Espinosa (London: Geoffrey Bles, 1938). Italian: trans. Cesare Giardini (Milan: Bompiani, 1937). French: trans. Jeanne Sabatier and Luis Blanco (Paris: Les Editions de France, 1937). German: trans. Christel Oloff (Berlin-Hamburg: Hoffmann und Campe Verlag, 1937). A second English version was published in Milwaukee, edited by Bruce Publishing Co. (1939). During the war there were also versions in Danish, Dutch and a little later it was translated into Portuguese and Hungarian. In Latin America there were editions in Argentina and Chile before the end of the war.

8.  Joaquín Arrarás Iribarren, *Franco*, 8th edn. (Valladolid: Librería Santarén, 1939), pp. 304 and 314. The front page of the Toledo newspaper *El Alcázar*, 22 October 1937, used a large photo of Franco and under it, in capital letters, it copied one of Arrarás' titles: 'FRANCO. LEADER OF FAITH AND HONOUR. CRUSADER OF THE WEST. PRINCE OF THE CONQUERING VICTORS. CONQUEROR OF A NEW SPAIN'.

9.  José Millán Astray, *Franco, Caudillo* (Salamanca: Quero y Simón Editores, 1939). On Millán Astray himself, see Paul Preston, 'The Bridegroom of Death: José Millán Astray', in his *Comrades: Portraits from the Spanish Civil War* (London: HarperCollins, 1999), pp. 11–42.

10. José Millán Astray, *El Caudillo Franco y nuestro glorioso Estado Mayor: Conferencia a los cadetes de la Academia de Estado Mayor en Valladolid* (Valladolid, 1936).

11. El Tebib Arrumi (pseud.), *La Historia de El Caudillo: Salvador de España* (Madrid: Ediciones España, 1939).

12. El Tebib Arrumi, *Héroes de España: Siluetas biográficas de las figuras más destacadas del Movimiento Salvador. El Caudillo, S.E.D. Francisco Franco Bahamonde* (Ávila: Imprenta Católica, 1937).

13. Fernando de Valdesoto (pseud.), *Francisco Franco* (Madrid: Gráficas Espejo, 1945); Ángel Pérez Rodrigo, *Franco: Una vida al servicio de la Patria* (Madrid: Hijos de Ezequiel Solano, 1947).

14. Luis de Galinsoga and Francisco Franco Salgado-Araujo, *Centinela de Occidente. Semblanza biográfica de Francisco Franco* (Barcelona: Editorial AHR, 1956).

15. Ibid., p. 463.

16. Paul Preston, *Franco: A Biography* (London: HarperCollins, 1993), pp. 563–4, 597–8. As Preston indicates (p. 564, no. 6), as late as 1969 Franco was regaling his ministers with stories of masonic conspiracies against Spain. Preston also summarizes here the gist of Franco's earlier writings on the subject, under the (not at all concealing) pseudonym of Jakim Boor.

17. Nancy Berthier, *Le franquisme et son image : Cinéma et propagande* (Toulouse: Presses Universitaires du Mirail, 1988); Magí Crusells, 'Franco en el cine documental español', *Historia Contemporánea* 22 (2001), pp. 215–31. See also the articles by Vicente Sánchez Biosca and Ángel Quintana in *Materiales para una iconografía de Francisco Franco*, special issue of *Archivos de la Filmoteca* (Valencia) 42–3, Vol. 1 (2002–2003), pp. 141–61 and pp. 177–89 respectively.

18. José Luis Sáenz de Heredia and José María Sánchez Silva, *Franco, ese hombre* (Madrid: Lidisa, 1975).

19. Ibid., pp. 150–1.

20. Ricardo de la Cierva, *Francisco Franco: un siglo de España* (Madrid: Editora Nacional, 1972 and 1973).

21. Ricardo de la Cierva, *Franco* (Barcelona: Planeta, 1982, and reissued in 1986).

22. Joaquín Costa was an intellectual and reformer, and part of the Generation of 1898.

23. Ricardo de la Cierva, *Franco* (Barcelona: Planeta, 1986), p. 507.

24. Manuel Aznar, *Franco* (Madrid: Prensa Española, 1975); Ángel Palomino Jiménez, *Caudillo* (Barcelona: Editorial Planeta, 1992); Pío Moa, *Franco: un balance histórico* (Barcelona; Planeta, 2005). On Moa, see Helen Graham, 'New Myths for Old', *TLS*, 11 July 2003.

25. Luis Suárez Fernández, *Francisco Franco y su tiempo*, 8 vols. (Madrid: Fundación Nacional Francisco Franco, 1984); Suárez Fernández, *Franco: La Historia y sus documentos* (Madrid: Urbión, 1986).

26. This private archive contains documentation from Franco's lengthy period as Head of State and amounts to more than 27,000 documents totalling some 300,000 pages: see María Concepción Ybarra Enríquez de la Orden, 'Al servicio de la Historia: El Archivo de la Fundación Francisco Franco', in María Concepción Ybarra Enríquez de la Orden (ed.), *Testigos de la Historia II* (Madrid: Fundación Carlos de Amberes, 2009), pp. 113–35.

27. De la Cierva, *Franco*, p. 17.

28. Bartolomé Bennassar, *Franco* (Madrid: Edaf, 2000), p. 23.

29. Rudolf von Timmermans, *General Franco* (Olten, Switzerland: O. Walter, 1937); Georges Rotvand, *Franco et la nouvelle Espagne* (Paris: Les Éditions Denoël, 1937); Paolo Antoldi, *Chi e Franco* (Rome: Augustea, 1939).

30. Claude Martin, *Franco: soldat et Chef d'Etat* (Paris: Editions dels Quatre Fils Aymon, 1959), republished as *Franco: soldado y estadista* (Madrid: Fermín Uriarte, 1965); George Hills, *Franco. The Man and his Nation* (London: Robert Hale, 1967), swiftly republished as *Franco: el hombre y su nación* (Madrid: Editorial San Martín, 1968); Brian Crozier, *Franco* (Boston: Little, Brown and Co., 1967), republished as *Franco: historia y biografía* (Madrid: Magisterio Español, 1969).

31. Arturo Barea, *La forja de un rebelde* (Buenos Aires: Losada, 1966 [1951]), p. 409.

32. Salvador de Madariaga, *General, márchese usted* (New York: Ediciones Ibérica, 1959), pp. 10–11. Madariaga did not take his own advice, since he made the comparison with Sancho Panza in the same satirical, critical tone in a later work: his '*novela-fantasía*' entitled *Sanco Panco* (Mexico, D.F.: Editora Latino Americana, 1964), in which he coined the expression 'Leech of the West'.

33. Luis Ramírez, *Francisco Franco: historia de un mesianismo* (Paris: Ruedo Ibérico, 1964). It rapidly appeared in French translation, with the equally expressive title: *Vie de Francisco Franco: Régent du royaume d'Espagne par la grâce de Dieu* (Paris: Maspero, 1965).

34. Jon Juaristi, 'Fallece el escritor Luciano Rincón', *El País*, 5 September 1993. See the anonymous article entitled 'Luciano Rincón y Luis Ramírez', published in *Cuadernos de Ruedo ibérico* 33/35 (1972).

35. Luis Ramírez, *Francisco Franco: La obsesión de ser; la obsesión de poder* (Paris: Ruedo Ibérico, 1976).

36. Luis Ramírez, *Francisco Franco. Historia de un mesianismo*, pp. 257–8.

37. See on this theme the contributions of Alicia Salvador, Román Gubern, Nancy Berthier and Sonia García López in the monograph entitled *Materiales para una inconografía de Francisco Franco* in the journal *Archivos de la Filmoteca* (Valencia) 42–3, Vol. 2 (2002–3).

38. Amando de Miguel, Anna Úbeda and Jaime Martín, *Franco, Franco, Franco* (Madrid: Ediciones 99, 1976).

39. Francisco Franco Salgado-Araujo, *Mis conversaciones privadas con Franco* (Barcelona: Planeta, 1976); *Mi vida junto a Franco* (Barcelona: Planeta, 1977).

40. Ramón Serrano Suñer, *Entre el silencio y la propaganda. La historia como fue* (Barcelona: Planeta, 1977); Laureano López Rodó, *La larga marcha hacia la monarquía* (Barcelona: Noguer, 1977).

41. Pilar Franco Bahamonde, *Nosotros, los Franco* (Barcelona: Planeta, 1980); Ángel Bayod (ed.), *Franco visto por sus ministros* (Barcelona: Planeta, 1981); Vicente Gil, *Cuarenta años junto a Franco* (Barcelona: Planeta, 1981).

42. Juan Pablo Fusi Aizpurúa, *Franco. Autoritarismo y poder personal* (Madrid: El País, 1985).

43. Fusi, *Franco*, pp. 15–16. A good indication of the book's reception was its immediate translation into English with a preface by the eminent British historian of modern Spain, Raymond Carr: *Franco: A Biography* (London, Unwin Hyman, 1987).

44. Stanley G. Payne, *Franco: el perfil de la historia* (Madrid: Espasa Calpe, 1992). In 1993 this biography was already in its eighth edition, indicating its wide circulation.

45. Javier Tusell Gómez, *Franco en la Guerra civil* (Barcelona: Tusquets, 1992).

46. Tusell, *Franco en la guerra civil*, pp. 12, 385–6. Previous quotations on pp. 9 and 11.

47. Philippe Nourry, *Francisco Franco: La conquista del poder* (Madrid: Júcar, 1976); Carlos Fernández Santander, *El general Franco* (Barcelona: Argos Vergara, 1983); Enrique González Duro, *Franco: Una biografía psicológica* (Madrid: Temas de Hoy, 1992); Jaime Peñafiel, *El general y su tropa: Mis recuerdos de la familia Franco* (Madrid: Temas de Hoy, 1992).

48. Allan Bullock, *Hitler. A Study in Tyranny* (London: Odhams Press, 1952); Renzo de Felice, *Mussolini* (Turin: Einaudi, 1965–81, 5 Vols.); Marc Ferro, *Pétain* (Paris: Fayard, 1987).

49. Paul Preston, *Franco: A Biography* (London: HarperCollins, 1993).

50. Paul Preston, *Franco, Caudillo de España* (Barcelona: Grijalbo, 1994).

51. See for example the review by one of Spain's leading modern historians, Santos Juliá, *El País-Babelia*, 22 January 1994.

52. Preston, *Franco: A Biography*, p. xviii.

53. Alberto Reig Tapia, *Franco 'caudillo': mito y realidad* (Madrid: Tecnos, 1995); Bartolomé Bennassar, *Franco* (Paris: Perrin, 1995): Spanish edition, *Franco* (Madrid: Edaf, 1996).

54. Andreé Bachoud, *Franco ou réussite d'un homme ordinaire* (Paris: Fagard, 1997), Spanish edition *Franco o el triunfo de un hombre corriente* (Madrid: Juventud, 1998); Fernando García de Cortázar, *Fotobiografía de Franco: Una vida en imágenes* (Barcelona: Planeta, 2000); Gabrielle Ashford Hodges, *Franco: A Concise Biography* (New York: St Martin's Press, 2002) and in Spanish translation, *Franco: Retrato psicológico de un dictador* (Madrid: Taurus, 2001); José Luis Rodríguez Jiménez, *Franco: Retrato de un conspirador* (Madrid: Oberon, 2005); Enrique Moradiellos, *Francisco Franco: Crónica de un Caudillo casi olvidado* (Barcelona: Ediciones B, 2002).

55. Paul Preston and Ángel Palomino, *Francisco Franco* (Barcelona: Ediciones B, 2003); French edition (Paris: Grancher, 2005). A few years later, Paul Preston published an expanded version of his contribution as *El gran manipulador: La mentira cotidiana de Franco* (Barcelona: Ediciones B, 2008).

56. Carlos Blanco Escolá, *La incompetencia militar de Franco* (Madrid: Alianza, 2000); Rafael Casas de la Vega, *Franco, militar* (Madrid: Fenix, 1995); Juan Blázquez Miguel, *Auténtico Franco: Trayectoria militar, 1907–1939* (Madrid: Almena, 2009).

57. Francisco Sevillano Calero, *Franco, Caudillo por la Gracia de Dios, 1936–1947* (Madrid: Alianza, 2010); Laura Zenobi, *La construcción del mito de Franco: De Jefe de la Legión a Caudillo de España* (Madrid: Cátedra, 2011).

58. Stanley G. Payne and Jesús Palacios, *Franco. A Personal and Political Biography* (Madison, WI: University of Wisconsin Press, 2014).

# CHAPTER 11
## CUMULATIVE BIBLIOGRAPHY OF THE WORK OF PAUL PRESTON

This bibliography includes all material published in English but excludes US editions and translations into Spanish or other languages. (All of Paul Preston's books have been translated into Spanish, some in successive, revised editions.) It also excludes prologues, prefaces and introductions to books and dictionary and encyclopaedia entries. It does, however, include publications in Catalan and Spanish which are not available in English, and books which have been substantially expanded in their Spanish versions. It contains only first editions, except in cases where subsequent editions contain significant revisions and inclusion of new material.

## Books

*The Coming of the Spanish Civil War: Reform, Reaction and Revolution in the Second Spanish Republic 1931–1936*, London: Macmillan, 1978. 2nd English edition revised and expanded, London: Routledge, 1994.

*Las derechas españolas en el siglo veinte: autoritarismo, fascismo, golpismo*, Madrid: Editorial Sistema, 1986.

*The Triumph of Democracy in Spain*, London and New York: Methuen, 1986.

*The Spanish Civil War 1936–1939*, London: Weidenfeld & Nicolson; New York: Grove Press, 1986. 2nd English edition revised and expanded, with amended title, *A Concise History of the Spanish Civil War*, London: Fontana Press, 1996. Further expanded and updated version published as *The Spanish Civil War: Reaction, Revolution and Revenge*, London: HarperCollins, 2006.

*The Politics of Revenge: Fascism and the Military in 20th Century Spain*, London: Unwin Hyman, 1990.

*Franco: A Biography*, London: HarperCollins, 1993.

*¡Comrades! Portraits from the Spanish Civil War*, London: HarperCollins, 1999.

*Doves of War: Four Women of Spain*, London: HarperCollins, 2002. Spanish version (including a biography of Carmen Polo) published as *Palomas de Guerra: Cinco mujeres marcadas por el enfrentamiento bélico*, Barcelona: Plaza y Janés, 2001.

(With Ángel Palomino) *Francisco Franco*, Barcelona: Ediciones B, 2003.

*Juan Carlos: A People's King*, London: HarperCollins, 2004.

*Tres años que desafían el olvido: La Guerra Civil. Las fotos que hicieron historia*, Madrid: La Esfera de los Libros/JdeJ Editores, 2005.

*Botxins i repressors: Els crims de Franco i dels franquistes*, Barcelona: Editorial Base, 2006.

*We Saw Spain Die: Foreign Correspondents in the Spanish Civil War*, London: Constable, 2008.

*El gran manipulador: La mentira cotidiana de Franco*, Barcelona: Ediciones B, 2008.

*El holocausto español: Odio y exterminio en la guerra civil y después*, Barcelona: Editorial Debate, 2011.

*The Spanish Holocaust: Inquisition and Extermination in Twentieth-Century Spain*, London: HarperCollins; New York: W.W. Norton, 2012.
*The Destruction of Guernica*, London: HarperPress, 2012.
*The Last Stalinist: The Life of Santiago Carrillo*, London: William Collins, 2014.
*The Last Days of the Spanish Republic*, London: William Collins, 2016.

## Edited books

*Spain in Crisis: Evolution and Decline of the Franco Regime*, Hassocks: Harvester Press, 1976.
*Leviatán: antología*, Madrid: Ediciones Turner, 1976.
(With D. Smyth) *Spain, the EEC and NATO*, London: Royal Institute of International Affairs and Routledge and Kegan Paul, 1984.
*Revolution and War in Spain 1931–1939*, London: Methuen, 1984.
(With H. Graham) *The Popular Front in Europe*, London: Macmillan, 1987.
(With F. Lannon) *Elites and Power in Twentieth-Century Spain: Essays in Honour of Sir Raymond Carr*, Oxford: Clarendon Press, 1990.
(With A. Mackenzie) *The Republic Besieged: Civil War in Spain 1936–1939*, Edinburgh: Edinburgh University Press, 1996.
(With I. Saz) *Dynamism and Conflict: Valencia 1808–1975*, Glasgow: University of Glasgow/ Carfax Publishing, 1998.
(With S. Balfour) *Spain and the Great Powers*, London: Routledge, 1999.

## Articles

'Alfonsist Monarchism and the Coming of the Spanish Civil War', *Journal of Contemporary History* 7:3–4 (1972), pp. 89–114.
'El accidentalismo de la CEDA: ¿aceptación o sabotaje de la República?', *Revista Internacional de Sociología*, 2ª época, 30:3–4 (1972), pp. 242–53.
'The "Moderate" Right and the Undermining of the Second Republic in Spain 1931–1933', *European Studies Review* 3:2 (1973), pp. 369–94.
'The Assassination of Carrero Blanco and its Aftermath', *Iberian Studies* 3:1 (1974), pp. 33–8.
'Spain's October Revolution and the Rightist Grasp for Power', *Journal of Contemporary History* 10:4 (1975), pp. 555–78.
'The Dilemma of Credibility: The Spanish Communist Party, the Franco Regime and After', *Government and Opposition* 11:1 (1976), pp. 65–84.
'The Origins of the Socialist Schism in Spain 1917–1931', *Journal of Contemporary History* 12:1 (1977), pp. 101–32.
(With Eduardo Sevilla Guzmán) 'Dominación de clase y modos de cooptación del campesinado en España: la Segunda República', *Agricultura y Sociedad* 3 (1977), pp. 148–65.
'The Struggle Against Fascism in Spain: The Contradictions of the PSOE Left', *European Studies Review* 9:1 (1979), pp. 81–103.
'The Stability of Democratic Spain', *Contemporary Review* 234:1 (1979), pp. 89–114.
'La crisis política del régimen franquista', *La Gaceta* (Mexico City) 99 (1979), n.p.
'The Spanish Constitutional Referendum of 6 December 1978', *West European Politics* 2:2 (1979), pp. 246–9.
'Demócrata por encima de todo: Indalecio Prieto y la creación del Frente Popular', *Revista del Ministerio de Obras Públicas y Urbanismo* 305 (1983), pp. 37–41.

'Con o contra OTAN: una elección falsa', *Ideas para la Democracia* 1 (1984), pp. 361–3.

'Los orígenes de la transición: dictadura, terrorismo y cambio social', *Sistema* 68–69 (1985), pp. 131–40.

'Costruire barricate contro il fascismo: Azaña, Prieto e il Fronte Popolare in Spagna', *Ricerche di Storia Politica* (Bologna) II (1987), pp. 41–64.

'The Decline and Resurgence of the Spanish Socialist Party during the Franco Regime', *European History Quarterly* 18:2 (1988), pp. 207–24.

'General Franco Re-assessed: Inertia and Risk, World War and Cold War, 1939–1953', *Journal of the Association for Contemporary Iberian Studies* 1:1 (1988), pp. 3–11.

'Revenge and Reconciliation: The Spanish Civil War and Historical Memory', in 'From Counter Revolution to Historical Accommodation', *Harvard University Center for European Studies Working Papers Series* 13 (1989), pp. 31–48. http://www.people.fas.harvard.edu/~ces/publications/docs/pdfs/CES_13.pdf [accessed January 2016]

'Persecuted and Persecutors: Modern Spanish Catholicism', *European History Quarterly* 20:2 (1990), pp. 285–92.

'Franco et ses généraux (1939–1945)', *Guerres Mondiales et Conflits Contemporains* 162 (1991), pp. 7–28.

'El discreto encanto del general Franco', *Journal of the Association of Contemporary Iberian Studies* 4:1 (1991), pp. 4–16.

'Recent Spanish Labour History', *Bulletin of Hispanic Studies* LXVIII (1991), pp. 507–11.

'Franco and Hitler: The Myth of Hendaye 1940', *Contemporary European History* 1:1 (1992), pp. 1–16.

'General Franco as a Military Leader', *The Transactions of the Royal Historical Society* 6th Series, 4 (1994), pp. 21–41.

'The Victor and the Vanquished: Franco and Azaña', *International Journal of Iberian Studies* 9:2 (1996), pp. 69–77.

'A Pacifist in War: The Tragedy of Julián Besteiro', *Journal of Iberian and Latin-American Studies* 2:2 (1996), pp. 179–208.

'La venjança de Franco, el justicier', *Papers del Museu d'Història de Catalunya* 10 (2004), pp. 6–13.

'The Answer lies in the Sewers: Captain Aguilera and the Mentality of the Francoist Officer Corps', *Science & Society* 68:3 (2004), pp. 277–312.

'Two Doctors and One Cause: Len Crome and Reginald Saxton in the International Brigades', *International Journal of Iberian Studies* 19:1 (2006), pp. 5–24.

'Censorship and Commitment: Foreign Correspondents in the Spanish Civil War', *International Journal of Iberian Studies* 20:3 (2007), pp. 231–41.

'El impacto de 1968 en España', *Pasajes de Pensamiento Contemporáneo* 30 (2009), pp. 109–15.

## Chapters in books

'The Anti-Francoist Opposition: The Long March to Unity', in P. Preston (ed.), *Spain in Crisis: Evolution and Decline of the Franco Regime*, Hassocks: Harvester Press, 1976, pp. 126–82.

'Manuel Azaña y la creación del Frente Popular 1933–1936', in V.A. Serrano and J.Mª San Luciano (eds), *Manuel Azaña: Homenaje*, Madrid: Ediciones Edascal, 1980, pp. 269–85.

'The Historiography of the Spanish Civil War', in R. Samuel (ed.), *People's History and Socialist Theory*, London: Routledge and Kegan Paul, 1981, pp. 190–96.

'The PCE's Long Road to Democracy 1954–1977', in R. Kindersley (ed.), *In Search of Eurocommunism*, London: Macmillan, 1981, pp. 36–65.

'Spain', in S. Woolf (ed.), *European Fascism*, London: Methuen, 1981, pp. 329–51.

'La crisis del franquismo', in *Historia 16, Extra: Historia de España XXV*, Madrid, 1983, pp. 89–129.

'The PCE in the Struggle for Democracy in Spain', in H. Machin (ed.), *National Communism in Western Europe*, London: Methuen, 1983, pp. 154–79.

'The Agrarian War in the South', in P. Preston (ed.), *Revolution and War in Spain 1931–1939*, London: Methuen, 1984, pp. 159–81.

'Fear of Freedom: The Spanish Army after Franco', in C. Abel and N. Torrents (eds), *Spain: Conditional Democracy*, London: Croom Helm, 1984, pp. 161–85.

'El PCE en la transición', in J. Sinova (ed.), *Historia de la Transición*, 2 Vols., Madrid: Información y Prensa S.A., 1985, Vol.1.

'Guerrilleros contra Franco', in J. Sinova (ed.), *Historia del Franquismo*, 2 vols., Madrid: Información y Prensa S.A., 1985, Vol.1.

'Franco and the Hand of Providence', in J.M. Merriman (ed.), *For Want of a Horse: Choice and Chance in History*, Lexington, MA: Stephen Greene Press, 1985, pp. 149–58.

'The Creation of the Popular Front in Spain', in H. Graham and P. Preston (eds), *The Popular Front in Europe*, London: Macmillan, 1987, pp. 84–105.

'Los Frentes Populares y la lucha contra el fascismo', in J.A. Fernández Villa (ed.), *Mineros, sindicalismo y política*, Oviedo: Fundación José Barreiro, 1987, pp. 53–77.

'The Legacy of the Spanish Civil War', in S.M. Hart (ed.), *¡No Pasarán!' Art, Literature and the Spanish Civil War*, London: Tamesis, 1988, pp. 11–19.

'Populism and Parasitism: The Falange and the Spanish Establishment, 1939–1975', in M. Blinkhorn (ed.), *Fascists and Conservatives: the Radical Right and the Establishment in Twentieth Century Europe*, London: Unwin Hyman, 1990, pp. 138–56.

'Spain', in A. Graham and A. Seldon (eds), *Government and Economies in the Postwar World: Economic Policies and Comparative Performance, 1945–85*, London: Routledge, 1990, pp. 125–53.

'Decay, Division and the Defence of Dictatorship: The Military and Politics, 1939–1975', in F. Lannon and P. Preston (eds), *Elites and Power in Twentieth-Century Spain: Essays in Honour of Sir Raymond Carr*, Oxford: Clarendon Press, 1990, pp. 203–28.

'Materialism and Serie Negra', in R. Rix (ed.), *Thrillers in the Transition: 'Novela negra' and Political Change in Spain*, Leeds: Trinity and All Saints College, 1992, pp. 9–16.

'El "Contubernio" en la historia de la oposición al franquismo', in J. Satrústegui et al. (eds), *Cuando la transición se hizo posible: El 'Contubernio' de Munich*, Madrid: Editorial Tecnos, 1993, pp. 38–41.

'The Urban and Rural *Guerrilla* of the 1940s', in H. Graham and J. Labanyi (eds), *Spanish Cultural Studies. An Introduction: The Struggle for Modernity*, Oxford: Oxford University Press, 1995, pp. 229–37.

'The Great Civil War: European Politics, 1914–1945', in T. Blanning (ed.), *The Oxford Illustrated History of Modern Europe*, Oxford: Oxford University Press, 1998 (first pub. 1996), pp. 148–81.

'El largo adiós: 1969–1975', in S. Juliá, J. Pradera and J. Prieto (eds), *Memoria de la transición*, Madrid: Taurus, 1996, pp. 79–82.

'Mussolini's Spanish Adventure: from Limited Risk to War', in P. Preston and A. Mackenzie (eds), *The Republic Besieged: Civil War in Spain 1936–1939*, Edinburgh: Edinburgh University Press, 1996, pp. 21–51.

'El Ejército', in R. Carr (ed.), *Historia de España Menéndez Pidal Tomo XLI La Época de Franco (1939–1975): Volumen I Política, Ejército, Iglesia, economía y administración*, Madrid: Espasa Calpe, 1996, pp. 301–82.

'The Myths of José Antonio Primo de Rivera', in R. Stradling, S. Newton and D. Bates (eds), *Conflict and Coexistence. Nationalism and Democracy in Modern Europe*, Cardiff: University of Wales Press, 1997, pp. 159–95.

'De Franco al Rey', in M. Agís Villaverde (ed.), *Conferencias do Foro Universitario: V Centenario da Universidade de Santiago de Compostela*, Santiago de Compostela: Universidade de Santiago de Compostela, 1999, pp. 147–60.

'La guerra civil: defensa antifascista de la República', in J. Ruiz Portella (ed.), *La guerra civil ¿dos o tres Españas?,* Barcelona: Ediciones Áltera, 1999, pp. 29–54.

'Introduction: Spain and the Great Powers' (with S. Balfour), in S. Balfour and P. Preston (eds), *Spain and the Great Powers in the Twentieth Century,* London: Routledge, 1999, pp. 1–12.

'Italy and Spain in Civil War and World War, 1936–1943', in S. Balfour and P. Preston (eds), *Spain and the Great Powers,* London: Routledge, 1999, pp. 151–84.

'La historiografá de la guerra civil española: de Franco a la democracia', in J.L. de la Granja, A. Reig Tapia and R. Miralles, *Tuñón de Lara y la historiografía española,* Madrid: Siglo XXI, 1999, pp. 161–74.

'Franco's Foreign Policy 1939–1953', in C. Leitz and D. J. Dunthorn (eds), *Spain in an International Context, 1936–1959,* New York: Berghahn Books, 1999, pp. 1–18.

'Herbert R. Southworth: luchador por la verdad', in J.L. de la Granja et al. (eds), *Herbert R. Southworth: Bizitza eta Lana Vida y obra,* Gernika-Lumo: Ayuntamiento de Guernica, 2001, pp. 47–60.

'El papel de Mussolini en la guerra civil europea', in J. Casanova (ed.), *Guerras civiles en el siglo XX,* Madrid: Editorial Pablo Iglesias, 2001, pp. 29–49.

'El contexto europeo y las brigadas internacionales', in M. Requena Gallego and R. María Sepúlveda Losa (eds), *Las Brigadas Internacionales: El contexto internacional, los medios de propaganda, literatura y memorias,* Cuenca: Universidad de Castilla-La Mancha, 2003, pp. 15–20.

'Las víctimas del franquismo y los historiadores', in E. Silva, A. Esteban, J. Castán and P. Salvador (coords), *La memoria de los olvidados: Un debate sobre el silencio de la represión franquista,* Valladolid: Ámbito Ediciones, 2004, pp. 13–24.

'Fascismo y militarismo en el régimen fascista', in J. Tusell, E. Gentile and G. di Febo (eds), *Fascismo y franquismo cara a cara. Una perspectiva histórica,* Madrid: Biblioteca Nueva, 2004, pp. 277–97.

'Les raons del desenllaç de la guerra', in J.M. Solé i Sabaté (ed.), *La guerra civil a Catalunya. 3 Catalunya, centre neuràlgic de la guerra,* Barcelona: Edicions 62, 2004, pp. 10–25.

'Espanya i la segona guerra mundial', in J.M Solé i Sabaté (ed.), *El franquisme a Catalunya (1939–1977) 1. La dictadura totalitària,* Barcelona: Edicions 62, 2004, pp. 32–42.

'The Monarchy of Juan Carlos: From Dictator's Dreams to Democratic Realities', in S. Balfour (ed.), *The Politics of Contemporary Spain,* London: Routledge, 2005, pp. 27–38.

'Filiberto Villalobos y la tercera España', in R. Robledo Hernández (coord.), *Sueños de concordia: Filiberto Villalobos y su tiempo histórico 1900–1955,* Salamanca: Caja Duero, 2005.

'Una contribució catalana al mite del contuberni judeo-maçonic-bolxevic', in C. Güell and J. Sobrequés i Callicó (coords), *Aproximació anglosajona a la historiografía catalana del segle XX,* Barcelona: Publicacions de la Residència d'Investigadors, 2005, pp. 9–23.

'Entre la ficción y la biografía', in J. Parra Ramos (ed.), *Literatura e Historia,* Jérez de la Frontera: Fundación Caballero Bonald, 2006.

'La Reina Sofía: La consorte que vino de Grecia', in I. Morant, G. Gómez-Ferrer et al. (eds), *Historia de las mujeres en España y América Latina. IV Del siglo XX a los umbrales del XXI,* Madrid: Ediciones Cátedra, 2006, pp. 391–412.

'El traidor. Franco y la segunda República, de general mimado a golpista', in A. Egido León (ed.), *Memoria de la segunda República: Mito y realidad,* Madrid: Biblioteca Nueva, 2006, pp. 85–116.

'Amenazados, ametrallados e inspirados. Los corresponsales extranjeros en la guerra civil española', in C. García Santa Cecilia (ed.), *Corresponsales en la guerra de España,* Madrid: Fundación Pablo Iglesias/Instituto Cervantes, 2006, pp. 19–40.

'Razones para la resistencia: la represión franquista en zona nacional', in R. Miralles (ed.), *Juan Negrín: Médico y Jefe de Gobierno 1892–1956,* Madrid: Ministerio de Cultura/Sociedad Estatal de Conmemoraciones Culturales, 2006, pp. 265–74.

'1934–1940. Les interpretacions anglosaxones de Lluís Companys', in J. Maria Solé i Sabaté (ed.), *Lluís Companys. President de Catalunya. Biografía humana i política*, Barcelona: Generalitat de Catalunya/Enciclopedia Catalana, 2006, pp. 223–33.

'No Simple Purveyor of News. George Steer and Guernica', in *Picasso-Gernika: 70 aniversario*, Gernika-Lumo: Ayuntamiento de Gernika-Lumo, 2007, pp. 304–11.

'"No Soldier": The Courage and Comradeship of Dr Len Crome', in J. Jump (ed.), *Looking Back at the Spanish Civil War: The International Brigade Memorial Trust's Len Crome Memorial Lectures, 2002–2010*, London: Lawrence and Wishart, 2010, pp. 31–44.

'The Crimes of Franco' in J. Jump (ed.), *Looking Back at the Spanish Civil War: The International Brigade Memorial Trust's Len Crome Memorial Lectures, 2002–2010*, London: Lawrence and Wishart, 2010, pp. 177–97.

'Franco, a vingança do Justiceiro', in E. Lemus, F. Rosas and R. Varela (coords), *O Fim das Ditaduras ibéricas (1974–1978)*, Lisboa: Edições Pluma, 2010, pp. 19–39.

'Theorists of Extermination', in S. Amago and C. Jérez Ferrán (ed.), *Unearthing Franco's Legacy: Mass Graves and the Recuperation of Historical Memory in Spain*, Notre Dame: University of Notre Dame Press, 2010, pp. 42–67.

'Juan Tusquets: A Catalan Contribution to the Myth of the Contubernio Judeo-Masónico-Bolchevique', in A. Quiroga Fernández de Soto and M.A. del Arco Blanco (eds), *Right-Wing Spain in the Civil War Era. Soldiers of God and Apostles of the Fatherland*, London: Continuum, 2012, pp. 177–94.

'Esperanzas e ilusiones en un nuevo régimen: la República reformista', in A. Viñas (ed.), *En el combate por la historia: La República, la guerra civil, el Franquismo*, Barcelona: Pasado y Presente, 2012, pp. 53–72.

'Bajo el signo de las derechas: las reformas paralizadas', in A. Viñas (ed.), *En el combate por la historia: La República, la guerra civil, el Franquismo*, Barcelona: Pasado y Presente, 2012, pp. 73–86.

'Manuel Azaña', in A. Viñas (ed.), *En el combate por la historia: La República, la guerra civil, el Franquismo*, Barcelona: Pasado y Presente, 2012, pp. 739–58.

'Francisco Franco', in A. Viñas (ed.), *En el combate por la historia: La República, la guerra civil, el Franquismo*, Barcelona: Pasado y Presente, 2012, pp. 773–90.

'Ramón Serrano Suñer', in A. Viñas (ed.), *En el combate por la historia: La República, la guerra civil, el Franquismo*, Barcelona: Pasado y Presente, 2012, pp. 887–902.

'The Great Manipulator: Francisco Franco', in D. Baratieri, M. Edele and G. Finaldi (eds), *Totalitarian Dictatorship New Histories*, London: Routledge, 2014, pp. 83–102.

'The Psychopathology of an Assassin: General Gonzalo Queipo de Llano', in P. Anderson and M.A. del Arco Blanco (eds), *Mass Killings and Violence in Spain, 1936–1952: Grappling with the Past,* London and New York: Routledge, 2014, pp. 23–58.

## Pamphlets

*The Spanish Right under the Second Republic*, Occasional Publication No.3 of the Graduate School of Contemporary European Studies, Reading, 1971.

*Salvador de Madariaga and the Quest for Liberty in Spain*, Oxford: Clarendon Press, 1987.

*El Cid and the Masonic Super-State: Franco, the Western Powers and the Cold War*, London: Publications of the European Institute, London School of Economics, 1993.

*The Attlee Government and Franco,* The Socialist History Society, Occasional Papers Series: No.7, London, 1998.

*The Crimes of Franco*, London: International Brigade Memorial Trust, 2005.

# CODA

# CHAPTER 12
## INTERVIEW WITH PAUL PRESTON

This informal interview with Paul Preston was undertaken ostensibly for an online journal commission – since he was unaware that this book was being prepared in his honour. The interview is consciously set in a different register to the rest of the book, in order to offer an insight into Paul's background, the particular cultural and intellectual influences which shaped him and also the intricacies and contingencies of research, writing and publishing.

**Helen Graham (HG):** You're from Liverpool, as am I, and it would be interesting to hear something about how you think that kind of culture and way of seeing the world has influenced you. In what ways it has that made you the historian you have become?

**Paul Preston (PP):** I was born in 1946, a little over a year after the end of the Second World War and Liverpool, a target because it was the port for supplies coming in from the US, was really badly hit by the Blitz. Our house, which was a council house in which I lived much of my early life, had actually been hit although not totally destroyed, and as I was growing up the adults still talked a lot about the Blitz. And I can remember kids' games when I was very young were often British against Germans. You know, we'd do things like we used to put our gabardines – our raincoats – on, tie the top button, so it became a cloak, and then we'd be aeroplanes, you know Spitfires versus Messerschmitts. But after the kind of kids games playing Brits versus Germans, I used to read a lot about the Second World War, which I guess came from that early ambience. One of my hobbies was making aircraft models of the Second World War. So when I got into Oxford, I mean going to university, the thing I most wanted to study was the Second World War, particularly about the origins, how it happened, which I suppose, down the track, says a lot about my eventual interest in the Spanish civil war. Since there were very few contemporary history courses on offer, Oxford was not intellectually a particularly happy experience – I mean there were some great things, I used to go to Isaiah Berlin's lectures, which were mind-boggling, and those by Keith Thomas on political philosophy were also terrific. However, at the end of it I hadn't got to study the things that I was interested in. And towards the end, I knew I wanted to do research. But the possibilities were limited because the only languages I knew were Latin and French, and I really didn't want to do French history. The other thing I should say is that, in my day, when I went to Oxford, there were very few working-class people there, and one of the things that again hit me when I was there was that my biggest ambition when I arrived – and this is very much about being from a working-class family from Liverpool –was to be a schoolteacher. It never occurred to me that anything else was possible. Whereas most of my contemporaries just assumed they'd be going into the diplomatic service or into government at a fairly high level, others assumed that they'd be going into their fathers' merchant banks or business. That perhaps consolidated the left-wing orientation with which I'd arrived although I was not particularly political. 1968 rather passed me by. Anyway I was pondering 'what can I do, if I'm accepted to do postgraduate work?' As I said, I wanted to do something on twentieth-century Europe but I was not attracted by French history, so that left some minor issue regarding British foreign policy which didn't particularly excite me. And then I saw an advert. The University of Reading was starting a graduate school of contemporary European studies which was clearly aimed at rivalling Nuffield and St Antony's.

I applied and was awarded a scholarship funded by Sir George Weidenfeld, whom I got to meet. So I went to Reading to do an MA on contemporary Europe. A major attraction was that it was possible to choose subjects that were entirely interwar, which is what I was most interested in. And the structure of this particular degree was two taught courses plus (unusually) two dissertations. So what I chose to do was the Spanish civil war, about which I knew very little. I mean at that stage, I'd read Hugh Thomas's book *The Spanish Civil War* (1961), and I'd read Gerald Brenan's *The Spanish Labyrinth* (1943): that was my total knowledge. So I knew very little. And I also chose a course on interwar left-wing literature, which was mainly French – André Gide, Louis Aragon and others but also British and American writers. For the interwar left-wing literature, I did a dissertation on John Steinbeck's *In Dubious Battle* (1936). I was a huge fan of Steinbeck and I'd read literally everything written by him by the time I was sixteen. *The Grapes of Wrath* probably contributed to my growing leftist thinking. I probably couldn't read him now. So anyway, that was one dissertation. And the other, for the course on the Spanish civil war was actually published as a pamphlet called *The Spanish Right in the Second Republic* which, looked at now, seems pretty dreadful.

Anyway, so I got to Reading and I was doing the Spanish civil war with Hugh Thomas in a tiny weekly seminar of only four people doing the course. Hugh Thomas was a wonderful teacher. He was incredibly charismatic, entertaining and would occasionally bring in people he knew to speak to us. These included Admiral Sir Peter Gretton who wrote a book about the siege of Bilbao and Peter Elstob who had been in Spain during the civil war and wrote a novel and later a book about the Condor Legion. The consequence was that I got hooked on the Spanish civil war very quickly, read everything I could in English, and after about four weeks had more or less exhausted what there was in English. So of course I had to learn Spanish, and I started hanging out with Latin American students, of whom there were many at Reading, more in fact than Spaniards. I also did what you're not supposed to do, which is to take the book I most needed to read, and read it with a dictionary – but anyway, between one thing and another, I got a bit of a background in the language. To me actually, in memory, looking back, the experience with Thomas was fantastic and I later became his personal assistant. As a result of knowing him socially, I met some fascinating people, including the Cuban novelist Guillermo Cabrera Infante with whom I became friends and Ramón Serrano Suñer whom I interviewed numerous times for my Franco biography.

As a kind of appendix to what I was saying on Spain, my family were very Labour although not particularly *political*. The men were trade unionists but not militant. It would have been great if there was a time machine to go back and ask my grandfather and my father about their awareness of the Spanish civil war, if any. When I was born [1946], my father was twenty-four, so he would have been only fourteen when the Spanish war broke out. My grandfather of course had fought in the First World War, as did a great-uncle who came to live with us. I used to spend hours talking to them about the war and their experiences. They would mostly talk about occurrences and events, I was of course thirteen or fourteen years old, and they tended to play down the horrors.

**HG**: And do you think there's any connection between coming from Liverpool, working on Spain . . . from the fringes of England to the fringes of Europe . . . a sort of anti-centre thing?

**PP**: That is something I do think about quite a lot. When I was a teenager, my contemporaries had an intense awareness of Liverpool as an entity. It was nothing to do with politics, it was to do with popular culture – The Cavern, the Beatles and all that, and the football, you know, first Everton and then Liverpool were the dominant teams at the time. And one grew up thinking that Liverpool was the centre of the universe. It's the town the Americans have heard of. Going back to what you said about being on 'the fringes of England', there was actually no sense of being English. Our identity was about being from Liverpool. It was a really strong sensation. And what started me thinking about this, and this is really weird, is that – obviously as you know I'm a massive collector of and enthusiast for classical music. What surprised me was how utterly bowled over I was by English classical music when I got to hear it. There are things that I absolutely adore that are the quintessence of English patriotic music like Parry's *Jerusalem*, virtually all of Elgar and Vaughan Williams, the English pastoral, Finzi, and so on. Given what I said about Liverpool, they are perhaps things that should have been alien. They're all things with which I would perhaps have expected to have an affinity if I'd gone to an English public school and been brought up to that. But I wasn't. And my affection for it is a purely emotional reaction that has no intellectual basis. And yet I absolutely adore what Ernest Newman called the 'cowpat school' – meaning English pastoral. If people ask me in Spain about Englishness (I have a lot of interviews like this), I have to admit that I don't particularly feel English and yet I love so many aspects of English, Irish, Welsh and Scottish culture.

**HG**: Moving on to talking a bit more about your work – looking at it as a whole, your preferred genre seems to be biography. What is it that always draws you back to biography?

**PP**: Well, it wasn't a conscious choice. My first book – which was basically the PhD thesis which became *The Coming of the Spanish Civil War* – at the time it came out, if I'd been asked to write a review of it I'd have said it was a social history, that I'm a social historian interested in social movements, specifically the correlation between social movements and their political manifestations. And indeed it is a book about the sectors of society represented by the two big mass parties in 1930s Spain. Put crudely, the mass-Catholic CEDA represented landowners and industrialists and the Socialist PSOE represented miners, industrial workers and landless peasants. The book is roughly about how the clashes played out at a local level between workers and industrialists, say, in Asturias, or between landless labourers and landowners in Andalusia and Extremadura, and how those clashes fed through the two parties into the central political arena in Madrid. But one of the things that I was aware of retrospectively was, when I was writing it, how much I was interested in the personalities of the leaders – José María Gil Robles of the CEDA, and the principal Socialists, Indalecio Prieto, Francisco Largo Caballero and Julián Besteiro as well as other minor protagonists, many of whom I wrote about in more detail in later books.

And then I wrote the first version of the book on the Spanish civil war, and after that I wrote the book on the transition to democracy. Again the same was true, especially in the book on the transition, which is a not dissimilar kind of book, but less social, more political. A lot was about Machiavellian political manoeuvring, much of it by people I had actually met, so it was inevitable that there would be a lot of emphasis on the personalities. I got very interested in Adolfo Suarez, his rise and fall, and in Juan Carlos. I suppose the big revelation came because I'd been commissioned to write a book on Franco. And I first of all resisted that for a long time, and there was this pressure from the publisher: 'You have done the Republic; you've done the Spanish civil war. You're writing for an English audience: you've got to do Franco', and I didn't particularly want to do Franco. But I finally agreed, and then when I started I quickly got hooked. The politics of his rise and how he stayed in power were obviously crucial, but I was surprised by just how fascinated I was by the personality and his psychology, and by trying to fathom this enigma, the 'sphinx without a secret'. But, even after writing *Franco*, I wouldn't have said that my vocation was as a biographer. However, because of the success of *Franco*, I was commissioned to write a biography of Mussolini. I started work on it and absolutely loved it. I did a lot of work in Italian archives, worked on it for about four years, but I was head of department and under a lot of pressure from the publisher.

Franco had taken about a decade and Mussolini was going to take the same or more. I suddenly thought: I'm running out of time here and my Spanish publisher was trying to get me to finish quickly so that I could do a biography of King Juan Carlos, as the obvious next Spanish figure. To cut a long story short, I produced *Comrades: Portraits from the Spanish Civil War*, which was an attempt to tell the story of the Spanish civil war through nine lives ranging from the extreme right to the extreme left. It was a big success in Spain – and I loved doing it and learned the pleasures of doing short biographies. I realised that there are so many people whose lives are fascinating about whom a four- or five-hundred page book would not be fascinating, but whom I think you can capture imaginatively in sixty to a hundred pages. Anyway, my idea when I wrote *Comrades* (which consists of nine lives) was that I do three volumes, and I thought that twenty-seven lives would 'cover' the Spanish civil war for readers, and I had a whole series lined up. My English publisher was horrified when I told him that I wanted to do the second volume of *Comrades*. So I offered him a book just about women in the Spanish civil war. He agreed and I set out to do the book which eventually became *Doves of War* – which I still think is a great title. The reason for making the suggestion was that, by absolute serendipity, I had come by the papers of the Spanish feminist Margarita Nelken, the papers of the English Communist Nan Green, I had met the daughter of the Falangist Mercedes Sanz Bachiller, who had introduced me to her mother, and I'd got the diaries of Priscilla Scott-Ellis. So I did these four lives of the people, two right-wingers, one English one Spanish, Priscilla Scott-Ellis and Mercedes Sanz Bachiller, who was still alive and who gave me access to her papers, and two left-wingers, Margarita Nelken and Nan Green, and I got to know Margarita's family very well, and Nan Green – of course, I knew her son Martin very well, so I was very involved with all of them, got to feel I knew them. So there were these four and Mrs Franco, who was there mainly to please the Spanish audience. The book did relatively well in Spain and is still one that, at book fairs and literary festivals, women want to talk about. However, when I delivered the English version, the publishers loved it but thought that it was too long and wanted me to lose around one hundred pages. I was shocked at the prospect of a complex editing job when it was suggested that I just drop Mrs Franco. So I said, it's funny you should say that, because in Spain lots of people have said to me, why is this book called 'Doves of War' when one of them's a vulture?! So I came home and thought about it overnight, and then realised it's actually a better book without Mrs Franco. Here, it was *Doves of War: Four Women of Spain* – whereas the Spanish version was translated as 'Doves of War: five lives "marked" (meaning 'seared') by the Spanish civil war', because they all were in different ways and, apart from Mrs Franco, tragically so. So in the course of doing *Comrades* and *Doves of War*, I realised that what I really love doing, if only the publisher will let me, is biography. When *Doves of War*, a work of research based entirely on primary sources, was reviewed by one of Spain's most influential historians, the late Javier Tusell, he took me to task for 'writing about unimportant people'. A priceless comment, although not, of course, in the way Tusell intended. It confirmed me in the determination to go on writing about 'unimportant people'.

After the self-indulgence of *Comrades* and *Doves of War*, I had to face up to the fact that I had contracts to write biographies of Mussolini and Juan Carlos. I started on Juan Carlos initially seeing it as a chore but, again, I just got hooked on the personality and what such an extraordinary career meant to the man who experienced it. What I liked doing most was his childhood, and how it affected him and what it must have been like to have been a child brought up in such horrible circumstances . . . well, to be the child of royalty with absent parents and all of that. When it became known in Spain that I was doing the book, I was offered the chance to interview him but there was a price, which was that the royal household be allowed to vet the manuscript, and so I refused. So in fact I only got to meet him afterwards (of course I had met him before, but not while I was writing the biography) – so then I met him afterwards, and to my astonishment he'd loved the book. When I went to see him, he said welcome to the palace and I said to him well, I'm here with some trepidation, since I assumed that I had been summoned to the palace to have my head chopped off. And he said why do you think that? And I said well that's why people are usually summoned to palaces! But anyway my book must be amazingly painful for you, and he said – and I was deeply moved by his reply – which was that 'No, you gave me back my life'. 'What?', and he said, 'People in this country think I was just parachuted onto the throne, silver spoon in the mouth, and your book shows what I had to go through . . .' Well, I'm summing up a long conversation . . . Well, I won't say we became friends, but I saw him a few times after and we'd always have a good laugh; he has an amazing sense of humour. But again, writing that book I felt this . . . the great thing was the connection with the *biografiados*, with the person, and that was something that obviously I'd felt very strongly too with the others.

After the Juan Carlos biography, I got deeply involved in the research for *The Spanish Holocaust* – which would not be biographical, though there are biographical sketches in it: where I was able to I would go into lives but I was much more interested in the bigger picture of the violence and so on. And then there came a point in the course of *The Spanish Holocaust* that I couldn't take it any more: I'd started working on it ages before, collecting material, and it got so gruesome I had to take a break. Again, something serendipitous happened. Salvador Clotas, the director of the Socialist Party archive, the Fundación Pablo Iglesias, rang me and invited me to do part of the catalogue for an exhibition on foreign correspondents in the Spanish civil war. And I said 'well, I'm really busy, how long are you thinking of?' And he said fifteen to twenty pages would be fine since the catalogue would consist mainly of reproduced articles and of photographs. So I agreed for two reasons. First of all, I realised that I needed a break from the Spanish Holocaust work. However, more importantly, my revered mentor Herbert Southworth had always talked about many of the people in the exhibition, Jay Allen, his closest friend, Louis Fischer, Herbert Matthews and all these newspapermen he had known and worked with. So it was like linking back to Herbert, and I started on it and, in the end I wrote forty pages. I got back to Salvador Clotas and said look, I'm really sorry, I've written all this, and he said, no, that's what I wanted but I didn't want to put you off, by saying so. And by then I was just totally into it and couldn't leave it alone. As I acquired more and more papers, the whole thing ballooned into my book *We Saw Spain Die* . . . well, and I also came across the diaries of Kate Mangen, an extraordinary Anglo-Irish woman who happened to be in the Republican Press Office having gone to Spain in search of her German lover who had joined the International Brigades. Her diary was full of amazing stuff with walk-on parts for Stephen Spender and W.H. Auden as well as the great journalists of the day. Part of the fascination of the work was the fact that she used pseudonyms and I had to work out who everyone was and once I'd done that, then I could find their papers. Again, that's a book that is largely based on diaries and letters but is rather strangely structured. Basically the book is half about what it was like to be a war correspondent in each of the war zones, and all of the problems, and the political reaction to correspondents and how people treated them, whether they were controlled and so on. The second half was a collection of biographies of my favourites – Jay Allen, Louis Fischer, George Steer who broke the story of Guernica, the great *Pravda* correspondent Mikhail Koltsov and two short lives, of Herbert Southworth and of Henry Buckley.

After finishing *We Saw Spain Die*, I went back to *The Spanish Holocaust*, and finished it. Then I had another bizarre or serendipitous experience which led to me writing a biography of Santiago Carrillo who, for many years, was secretary general of the Spanish Communist Party. Not long after *The Spanish Holocaust* came out, Carrillo died aged ninety-seven. In *The Spanish Holocaust*, by dealing with the violence in both sides, I'd gone into great detail about Carrillo's role in the violence in Madrid in the autumn of 1936. He had always denied knowing anything about it. Since my book established his role in organizing the operation in which around 2,500 right-wing army officers were murdered at Paracuellos, just outside Madrid, he was bombarded with questions by the media, 'You've been lying about it, saying for years that you had nothing to do with it, you knew nothing about it, so how do you respond to Paul Preston's book?' Carrillo replied, with the absolute genius that he had for manipulation, 'I'm deeply grateful to my friend Paul Preston, for telling me so many things about that period that I didn't know'. Anyway, Carrillo died, and I had written ages ago an obituary for *The Guardian*, which came out, and someone then suggested to me that it would be a brilliant life to have as a biography in English. I initially dismissed the idea but then I had a think about it and it reminded me that in the 1970s I'd got to know him and other senior figures on the left. I had had a very, very minor and peripheral role in the anti-Franco opposition, and in the course of it, I had acted as the English interpreter for the anti-Franco front, the Junta Democrática. One of my plans which in a sense had been knocked askew by taking on the Franco biography, had been to write a history of the anti-Franco opposition. And I'd always had this idea that I'd write a trilogy which would be: first, *The Destruction of Democracy* (which is the Spanish translation of my *The Coming of the Spanish Civil War*); then, my book on the transition, *The Triumph of Democracy*; and in the middle there was going to be *The Struggle for Democracy*. In the event, I had to accept that the way the transition took place, as a transaction between progressive Francoists and the moderate left, meant that the anti-Franco resistance had relatively little to do with the eventual return of democracy. In the meanwhile, I had acquired virtually a garage full of material for the planned book for which I'd done a lot of research. So I began to think about this Carrillo proposal: I knew him pretty well, had very cordial relations with him. I had just done all the research on his role in the atrocities during the civil war; I've got vast amounts of material, some including speeches with marginal annotations by Carrillo himself, for example 'don't include this bit', 'this isn't to go in', and so on. So I thought about it and then I said to my Spanish editor, 'would you be interested in a biography of Carrillo?' and she said, 'when can we have it?!' So I got back to the English publisher, and said 'OK, I'll have a go, see what you think'. So I wrote it, and did it pretty quickly, and it was a very shocking experience – because here was this man whom I'd always liked, always had a cordial relationship with; I could, in the course of many of my books, phone him up, get through all the filters immediately – 'Oh, it's Paul on the phone', got through immediately. He was always cordial, though in retrospect I realise I no doubt got my share of bullshit too – you know, I'd ask, 'so why did so-and-so submit to being tortured and humiliated by party comrades?', and he'd answer, 'Oh well, we were like medieval knights, we had a code of honour'.

When I started the book, I assumed that Carrillo's role in the wartime violence would be the worst part of a life devoted to overthrowing the dictatorship. I had been shocked by the way that he lied about it instead of acknowledging the nature of the siege of Madrid and the pressures to stop these army officers joining Franco. Instead, over many years, he'd denied everything in the course of many different interviews and accounts in his numerous books of memoirs. In fact, you could actually piece together his real role just by collating the inconsistencies and contradictions of his many denials. But the thing that was most shocking was of course his appalling role in the elimination of comrades, people who were in his way in his own scramble for power. So I ended up with the conclusion that, while the Communist Party was the most effective resistance against Franco, Carrillo's Stalinist behaviour had severely weakened it. So it was quite surprising to see how my views on him changed dramatically in the course of the writing. With the Franco biography, of course I was writing about someone deeply unsympathetic, and in other things I had people I'd written about, where I obviously felt the opposite. But in the case of Carrillo it was an odd one – it was writing about someone I had known, and then discovered that the person wasn't the person I believed I'd known.

The next book which will be out next year, *The Last Days of the Spanish Republic*, is not ostensibly a biography but it is the story of the humanitarian tragedy that came out of the clash between the principal protagonists – and so it's two, well really three, biographies. It's about Casado, Besteiro and Negrín [Segismundo Casado, the commander of the Republic's army of the centre, and Julián Besteiro, the veteran socialist leader, together headed the rebellion against Republican prime minister, Juan Negrín, which brought about the end of Republican military resistance in March 1939]. The book is based on a lot of private documentation: through Carmen Negrín (his granddaughter) I was given a free run of Negrín's private archive, but I also found a lot of Casado's private correspondence, as well as using Besteiro's published correspondence, so much of the book is biographical.

**HG**: And what about the big biography of Franco? What are the issues in terms of situating him for a popular audience, whether English or Spanish?

**PP**: The problems are magnified massively for a Spanish audience. In a sense, when I started, my reluctance was partly to do with the fact that from the start you have to deal with a series of myths: the myth that Franco is the genius who won the Spanish civil war by military prowess and sheer strategic genius; the myth that Franco heroically saved Spain from the Second World War and from falling into the clutches of Hitler; the myth that Franco masterminded the economic recovery of the late 1950s and early 1960s. Then there are all kinds of subsidiary myths: that he saved Spain from an alleged international siege during the Cold War or that, in his later years, he masterminded the subsequent transition to democracy. It was a daunting challenge. It took me ten years to research and write. At the time there was very little access to materials in Spain – there were important published memoirs and I was able to interview a lot of his collaborators, particularly Ramón Serrano Suñer, his brother-in-law and closest collaborator up to the early 1940s, and several later ministers, such as Manuel Fraga, Laureano López Rodó and José Utrera Molina. I think the most useful documentary sources, apart from Franco's own voluminous writings, were actually the diplomatic materials – German, Italian, Portuguese, French and British. There was a lot of perceptive insight from diplomats who are trained observers.

Of course once I got into it, the myths gradually crumbled. However, the efforts of Franco himself and his propaganda machinery to rewrite the history of his rise to power and how he stayed in power required quite a lot of dismantling. That, plus the sheer length of the life of a man who dealt with Hitler, Mussolini and Pétain as well as with Churchill, Eisenhower and Nixon meant a very long book. So in terms of the audience, there's the problem of making digestible a book that's a thousand pages long. But you're also faced with the first problem of a biographer which is, it seems to me, that in order to write an effective biography you have to create the illusion that you know the character to be able to transmit to the reader the illusion that, after they've read the book, they've also known the character. Both problems, the readability and the illusion of acquaintance were helped by the fact of Franco being such a mediocrity at one level and immensely cunning at another. A lot of what he did and said was quite amusing, because it was stupid: for example, he believed in alchemists and that he could solve the energy deficit with a kind of Nescafé of petrol, a powder to be added to water. He often fell for confidence tricksters.

**HG**: Strange, given that he was one of the greatest confidence tricksters of all!

**PP**: Yes! But anyway, a big issue in terms of the reception of the biography was that because of the power of these myths, there were going to be two potential audiences in the Anglo-Saxon world – the very pro-Franco audience, which was really considerable in the US and to a lesser extent here in the UK. Many in the West saw Franco in a very positive light – the 'Sentinel of the West', a guaranteed bulwark against communism, the reasons why, unlike his Axis cronies, he wasn't overthrown in 1945. So he enjoyed a favourable press on the one hand, and on the other, of course, there was the left-wing view that he was a loathsome collaborator of Hitler. Of course I was writing from an anti-Franco point of view, but I tried to be fair. So there were things in the book which I know people on the left didn't like – the fact that I wrote a sympathetic view of his childhood and a relatively sympathetic account of his death agony, but the nine hundred pages in between were highly critical. In Spain, the same was true of these two audiences, but more so. The book, obviously, infuriated the extreme right and I got some amazing abuse, but, you know, the book was a massive success. The first print run was 10,000 copies and it sold out by mid-morning on the first day. The publishers hadn't expected anything like that and they had no paper to do a reprint. But it had some mind-boggling press – I remember having about two weeks of interviews, just one after another, eight to ten per day, day after day after day. Since, it has been regarded as the standard biography. Obviously new detailed research on specific areas has come out subsequently. For instance, Angel Viñas' next book is about the corruption of Franco personally and of his regime, which is really interesting. One has always known the broad picture of an essentially corrupt regime based on theft. Where Angel has refined the picture is the actual detail. It's astounding how much of a paper trail was left and Angel has got chapter and verse. But I don't think that the overall picture has changed much since my Franco biography – a slight detail here and there, but overall it's the same picture.

Actually I've just been working on a revised Spanish edition – this year is the fortieth anniversary of Franco's death, there's a minor publishing frenzy in Spain, quite a lot being published or republished about Franco. And there's now the new Franco biography by Stanley Payne and Jesús Palacios. Its critical apparatus is weak with no original research although the English edition is quite agreeably written. A reader who has no prior view of the subject might like the studiously moderate tone. For a well-informed reader, there are some outrageous things, such as the virtual excision of anything on Franco's repression. One of the things that I find extraordinary about the English edition of the Payne/Palacios biography is that there are references to how handsome Franco was, how muscular, how gallant – and stuff that's really obsequious.

As for my own Franco biography, I've been doing the new Spanish edition over the last few months. In the interim since it came out in 1993, I have kept up with what has been published and, as far as I see that, I can't find an awful lot that's changed since my biography came out. For example, my broad view of Franco and the Second World War remains absolutely as it was, and in a sense it could be strengthened now by the fact the work of Manuel Ros Agudo has turned up even more about Franco's collaboration with the Nazis. I have noted and filled a real gap in my book. Although I had a certain amount about Franco's antisemitism, I just didn't go into the regime's treatment of the Jews – and so I have added a little appendix. It is an area where there has been some very interesting new research which I've acknowledged obviously.

The need to go on combatting the myths is as great as ever. And now with the revisionists on the scene and as part of this anniversary frenzy, one of the new Franco books is by the king of the revisionists, Pío Moa. In his book, there are some striking statements, such as the assertion that the Division Azul [the Spanish military units which fought with the German army on the Eastern Front in the Second World War] was 'the most humanitarian military unit on either side in the whole of the Second World War'!

**HG**: Yes, the problem of revisionism ... which brings up the whole thorny question of the transition to democracy. Looking back on it, do you think anything could have been done to have embedded a better base for a post-transition democratic culture?

**PP**: Well, as you and I know, it was the best transition possible in the circumstances – at the point at which Franco died, everything was weighted against democracy. You have an army trained and educated in the academies which Franco created, whose job was to protect Spain from internal enemies, defined as democrats, leftists, etc. There was the Civil Guard, whose job was the same; the armed police, whose job was the same; and there were 200,000 members of the Falange who had licences to carry guns. So, you know, clearly it's touch and go. And I remember, I was around at the time, there was an atmosphere of very considerable fear, so people were prepared to go along with anything that would (a) avoid another civil war, and (b) avoid another dictatorship. So that explains why there was a limited transition that was a transaction, a transaction between the more moderate elements of the left, and the more progressive elements of Francoism, looking out to protect as much as they can.

So, what went wrong? Well. There are probably two big things: first, one of the major problems not addressed was the memory issue. As you know, there are people, a large chunk of the population who have been appallingly treated in one way or the other – ranging from family members murdered, families left without breadwinners and condemned to appalling poverty, women forced into prostitution, people simply not able to speak freely for fear of arrest. Despite, or perhaps because of that background, there emerged the so-called 'pact of silence' [*pacto del olvido*]. At the beginning there was a widespread civic reaction, which included people who were treated badly by the regime, of 'let's not rock the boat', the important thing is to move on from the dictatorship. But how long was this pact supposed to stay valid? Its only legal basis was the amnesty of October 1977 which eliminated the possibility of the executioners, torturers and gaolers being prosecuted. However, that left the issue of why nothing was done about other things, recognition of the crimes of the past. For three decades after Franco's death nothing was done by politicians, particularly the politicians of the left during that long period that the Socialists were in power from 1982 until 1996. What was done was done by a small army of local historians acting on their own initiative.

In a curious way, the reaction to what little *has* been done helps explain why so little was done. I'm referring, just at an anecdotal level, to the stories in the book *Shoot the Messenger?* (2013), by Francisco Espinosa, one of the most important of those local historians. That book looks at the legal challenges posed to journalists, historians and others who have attempted to open up the story of Francoist repression, especially by identifying actual perpetrators. His new work, *Lucha de historias; lucha de memorias. España 2002–2015*, is even more illuminating. The second big disappointment about the transition is corruption, the scale of which wasn't anticipated. Clearly, the Franco regime was an utterly corrupt regime, and I think that one of the things that has led to massive disillusionment with the transition is the fact that corruption is just as bad if not worse. It certainly seems worse, although that might be at least partly to do with the transparency that comes with a free press. Laws have been changed in a way that has opened the floodgates to corruption, for instance the *Ley de ordenamiento territorial* which has facilitated illegal land speculation and the great building boom. But I also think that there were two consequences of the endemic corruption of the Franco regime. On the one hand, local politicians of the right saw no reason to change their ways and, on the other, when the Socialists got into power at all levels, local and national, they thought, 'right, it's our turn now'.

One of the themes of my new book [see below] is the perception that participation in public service is for private benefit, as against being for public good. That's so ingrained although you could say the same about Greece, or about Italy. In consequence, a problem for me with this next book is that somehow it's going to come out as anti-Spanish which is absolutely not the intention, rather its intention is to show how the Spanish people have been betrayed by their political class. Anyway, going back to the criticisms of the transition to democracy in Spain, there are now two principal arguments against the transition circulating (well there are umpteen). On the one hand, there is the perfectly valid point that the transition did nothing about justice for the oppressed and the repressed. That is not an entirely clear-cut argument because the failures were also about the enduring power of the Francoist institutions – the armed forces, Civil Guard, police, judiciary – long after Franco died. So, a judgement hinges on what was possible and when it might have become possible. Secondly, there's the resentment about corruption. Of course, there are also utopian notions that the problem with the transition is that it wasn't a revolution . . . which is crass.

**HG**: Well, the problem with corruption is a very large part of the bigger problem, that there was an almost total continuity of political culture across the transition.

**PP**: Well how could there not have been? As you've pointed out – from the PSOE's accession to power in 1982, apart from the patrimonial notions of the left that go back a long way, the party was swamped by new members brought up with Francoist concepts of clientelism. In a lot of interviews and stuff I've written, I make the very obvious point that because Franco wasn't overthrown in 1945 by external forces, there was no denazification process such as took place in Germany, Japan, Italy and elsewhere. Inevitably, the new (PSOE) members were largely people who'd been brought up in the environment created by decades of the Francoist monopoly of the media and the education system, with the total support of the Church. During the transition, there was rightly no counter-brainwashing. After all, it would have been impossible in a democracy with freedom of speech for there to have been a countervailing governmental campaign. How do you find an antidote to forty years of Francoism? It would be difficult under any circumstances, but something should and could have been done, such as the government not financing the Fundación Nacional Francisco Franco, an outfit dedicated to protecting the memory of the dictator.

**HG**: Well you'd have thought they'd have been more careful – senior legal figures and such like, why didn't the PSOE ensure more renovation of the high judiciary?

**PP**: Yes, the judiciary was the least changed. Going back to the corruption issue, one of the things that helps is that '*prescripción*' [the statute of limitations] of certain crimes (probably that excludes murder) for fiscal issues in Spain is five years. The judiciary works so slowly that they never catch up. In theory the clock stops at the point when the judiciary starts to investigate, but in practice the law rarely seems to catch up. And of course so many people (not everyone, but many), even within the judiciary, are on the take, that it's hard to solve the problem. This is a delicate point. In order not to appear as a foreigner coming from outside and pronouncing on all this, it is necessary to keep stressing that there is corruption elsewhere, in Britain, even in Germany, it's everywhere.

**HG**: So what's the next project?

**PP**: What's under contract next is a book called *Spain: A People Betrayed*. It's a history of Spain from the late nineteenth century to the present day. The reason for that title is that it tries to illuminate the political developments through the prisms of the incompetence and corruption of successive ruling classes. It will also obviously look at issues like the militarism and violence that has infused Spanish society over the last two hundred years. The chronological limits are vague because there is no starting date for *caciquismo* [clientelist networks] or for militarism. How it will work out, who knows. It'll keep me off the streets for a bit.

# CHAPTER 13
## PhDs SUPERVISED BY PAUL PRESTON

This list includes, in date order, all the PhD theses on Spanish history which Paul Preston has supervised (and thus excludes other doctoral theses supervised by him on Italian, British, Greek and French history).

### (1) Theses successfully submitted and published, with the title of the resulting book

(Items marked * have also been published in Spanish translation.)

Heine, Hartmut, *La Oposición política al franquismo* (Barcelona: Crítica, 1983)

Ellwood, Sheelagh, *Spanish Fascism in the Franco Era* (London: Macmillan, 1987)*

Shaw, Duncan, *Fútbol y franquismo* (Madrid: Alianza Editorial, 1987)

Shubert, Adrian, *The Road to Revolution in Spain: The Coal Miners of Asturias 1860–1934* (Urbana and Chicago: University of Illinois Press, 1987)*

Sullivan, John, *ETA and Basque Nationalism: The Fight for Euskadi 1890–1986* (London: Routledge, 1988)*

Balfour, Sebastian, *Dictatorship, Workers and the City: Labour in Greater Barcelona since 1939* (Oxford: Clarendon Press, 1989)*

Heywood, Paul, *Marxism and the Failure of Organised Socialism in Spain 1879–1936* (Cambridge: Cambridge University Press, 1990)*

Bin Ahmad, Qasim, *Britain, Franco Spain and the Cold War, 1945–1950* (New York: Garland Publishing, 1992)

Durgan, Andrew, *BOC 1930–1936: el Bloque Obrero y Campesino* (Barcelona: Laertes, 1996)

Brassloff, Audrey, *Religion and Politics in Spain: The Spanish Church in Transition, 1962–96* (London: Macmillan Press, 1998)

Herman, John, *The Paris Embassy of Sir Eric Phipps: Anglo-French Relations and the Foreign Office, 1937–1939* (Brighton: Sussex Academic Press, 1998)

Liedtke, Boris N., *Embracing a Dictatorship: US Relations with Spain, 1945–53* (Basingstoke: Macmillan Press, 1998)

Richards, Michael, *A Time of Silence: Civil War and the Culture of Repression in Franco's Spain, 1936–1945* (Cambridge: Cambridge University Press, 1998)*

Romero Salvadó, Francisco J., *Spain, 1914–1918: Between War and Revolution* (London: Routledge/Cañada Blanch, 1999)*

Townson, Nigel, *The Crisis of Democracy in Spain: Centrist Politics under the Second Republic 1931–1936* (Brighton: Sussex Academic Press, 2000)*

Baxell, Richard, *British Volunteers in the Spanish Civil War: The British Battalion in the International Brigades, 1936–1939* (London: Routledge/Cañada Blanch, 2004)

Ealham, Chris, *Class, Culture and Conflict in Barcelona* (London: Routledge/Cañada Blanch Studies, 2004)*

Ojeda Revah, Mario, *México y la guerra civil española* (Madrid: Turner, 2004)

Interrogating Francoism

Palomares, Cristina, *The Quest for Survival after Franco: Moderate Francoism and the Slow Journey to the Polls, 1964–1977* (Brighton: Sussex Academic Press, 2004)*
Güell, Casilda, *The Failure of Catalanist Opposition to Franco (1939–1950)* (Madrid: Consejo Superior de Investigaciones Científicas, 2006)
Rohr, Isabelle, *The Spanish Right and the Jews, 1898–1945: Antisemitism and Opportunism* (Brighton: Sussex Academic Press, 2007)
Smith, Angel, *Anarchism, Revolution and Reaction: Catalan Labour and the Crisis of the Spanish State, 1898–1923* (New York: Berghahn Books, 2007)

## (2)  Theses successfully submitted and as yet unpublished

Montero, Enrique, 'The Forging of the Second Spanish Republic: New Liberalism, the Republican Movement and the Quest for Modernization, 1868–1931' (1989)
Anson, Beatriz, 'The Spanish Communist Party and the Intellectuals, 1954–1968' (2002)
Pliego, Iván, 'Optimism Betrayed: The Golden Age of Mexican–Spanish Relations, 1931–1939' (2006)
Blaney, Gerald, 'The Civil Guard and the Second Republic, 1931–6' (2008)
Volodarsky, Boris, 'Soviet Intelligence Services in the Spanish Civil War, 1936–1939' (2010)
Serém, Rúben, 'Seville in the Spanish Civil War' (2011)

# INDEX

23-F 8

# Index

# Index

# Index

# Index